A Paradise Lost

YOUNG-TSU WONG

A Paradise Lost

THE IMPERIAL GARDEN YUANMING YUAN

 University of Hawai'i Press | *Honolulu*

For Hua-hua (Walter) and Wei-wei (Virgil)

©2001 University of Hawai'i Press
All rights reserved
Printed in the United States of America
06 05 04 03 02 01   5 4 3 2 1

LIBRARY OF CONGRESS CATALOGING-IN-PUBLICATION DATA
Wong, Young-tsu.
    A paradise lost : the imperial garden Yuanming Yuan / Young-tsu Wong.
        p. cm.
    Includes bibliographical references (p.).
    ISBN 0–8248–2226–9 (cloth : alk. paper) — ISBN 0–8248–2328–1 (pbk. : alk. paper)
    1. Yüan Ming Yüan (Beijing, China) — History. 2. Historic gardens — China — Beijing.
3. Gardens, Chinese — China — Beijing — History. 4. Landscape architecture — China —
Beijing — History. I. Title

SB466.C53 Y838 2001
712'.6'0951156 — dc21   00–036879

University of Hawai'i Press books are printed on acid-free
paper and meet the guidelines for permanence and
durability of the Council on Library Resources.

Designed by Diane Gleba Hall
Printed by The Maple-Vail Book Manufacturing Group

CONTENTS

ILLUSTRATIONS

All maps and plans are oriented with north at the top of the page.

ACKNOWLEDGMENTS

MY INTEREST IN THE IMPERIAL GARDEN Yuanming Yuan began in the summer of 1981, when I first visited its ruins site near Peking University. During the subsequent years, I read and collected books and articles on the Yuanming Yuan. In 1986, Virginia Polytechnic Institute and State University allowed me to teach an honors course on the Yuanming Yuan with Professor Joseph C. Wang of the school of Architecture. I learned a great deal more about the garden from Jo and students in the class. In the summer of the same year, I was able to visit the Yuanming Yuan again and read some very interesting archival sources at the Chinese First Historical Archive in Beijing. Professor Yang Tianshi of the Institute of Modern History, Chinese Academy of Social Sciences, kindly made the arrangement to copy hundreds of pages of documents from the archives for me, for which I am very grateful.

The growing interest in making an inquiry into the imperial garden inspired me to write a book about the subject. During the years of preparation, Jo Wang again offered his assistance. Especially, under his guidance, Mr. Sam Xinbai Yue offered to draw many lively illustrations of the garden scenes for the book. I must express my deep gratitude to both Jo and Sam.

During the 1980s, I had the privilege of seeing Professor Qian Zhongshu (1910–1998), arguably the greatest man of letters in modern China, four times at his home in Beijing. Each time, I had the enormous pleasure of hearing his humorous and erudite remarks about Qing rulers and the imperial gardens, among many other subjects. I shall always cherish the memory of this highly admirable scholar.

I would like to thank Professor Peter Zarrow of the School of History, University of New South Wales, Australia, who spent his precious time in 1997 reading my first draft in its entirety. He kindly gave me many valuable suggestions and much needed encouragement. I wish to express my gratitude to two anonymous reviewers of the manuscript for their comments and suggestions. During the final stage of revision, Professor Susan Naquin of

Princeton University, whom I still have not met, kindly answered my e-mail enquiry from Tianjin, People's Republic of China, and made it possible for me to reach Regine Thiriez in Paris. From Dr. Thiriez I obtained her new book entitled *Barbarian Lens* for reference. In 1998, Dr. Sun Ruoyi of Chung-Hsing (Zhongxing) University generously sent me a copy of her recently completed doctoral dissertation on the European section of the Yuanming Yuan, which in time provided me with useful information for updating my manuscript.

In the spring of 1998, thanks to the invitation of Dr. Hsiung Ping-chen (Xiong Bingzhen), I was able to present my work on the Yuanming Yuan to her colleagues and scholars from other towns in northern Taiwan at the Institute of Modern History, Academia Sinica (Taipei). I benefited greatly from an hour-long discussion. My talk was subsequently published as an essay in a book coedited by Dr. Hsiung (Xiong Bingzhen and Lü Miaofen 1999, 285–293, 353–354).

My thanks also go to Patricia Crosby, the executive editor of the University of Hawai'i Press, for her interest in my work. Masako Ikeda, the managing editor, and Robyn Sweesy, my copy editor, have rendered me excellent assistance. Their professionalism, in managing and editing, make me feel that I am fortunate to have had the opportunity to work with them. Finally, I am indebted to my wife, Shanyi (Sylvia) Lu, for her time and artistic skills in helping with the illustrations and maps included in this book.

INTRODUCTION

THE RISE AND FALL of the palatial imperial garden Yuanming Yuan is the history of the Sinic Qing Empire in miniature. Its rise paralleled the beginning of the *Pax Sinica* at the time of the great Kangxi emperor (r. 1662–1722). It took one and a half centuries of endless constructions to become arguably the greatest imperial garden China had ever built, a shining pearl of the great empire. This vast pleasance was indeed "a paradise on earth" in the eyes of the visiting French priest Attiret.

"Yuanming" literally means "round and brilliant," implying perfection and excellence; however, the name actually alludes to Buddhist wisdom. The distinguished Tang dynasty monk Xuan Zhuang (600–664) was quoted as saying that the birth of the prince caused so much joy because he would become a buddha and make "all wisdom round and brilliant" *(yuanming yiqie zhi)* (Xuan Zhuang 1977, 132). There is no secret that both Kangxi and Yongzheng were extremely fond of Buddhism. While Kangxi had been honored as the "Buddha-Hearted Son of Heaven" *(foxing tianzi),* the Yongzheng emperor addressed himself as a "secular Buddhist of Yuanming" *(yuamming jushi).* Hence, that Kangxi chose this name with a clear-cut Buddhist allusion for the garden was not accidental at all. Also not accidental is that the Yuanming Yuan and the Qing Empire shared the same fate of glory and shame and that the Yuanming Yuan's fall corresponded with the decline of the empire. It was precisely the empire's folly in the nineteenth century that rendered the imperial garden unprotected.

This "brilliant" imperial garden, with or without the blessing of the Buddha, fell from the sky like a shining star and suddenly vanished from the planet. But the historical memory of the lost garden has persisted. Post-Qing modern Chinese continued to view the tragedy with deep emotion, a mixture of nostalgia and sadness. Its destruction by foreign forces was especially painful in the context of the century-long sharp memory of Chinese humiliation.

Figure 1. The Yuanming Yuan and environs. The Changchun Yuan in the front was the Kangxi emperor's Joyful Spring Garden distinguished from the Eternal Spring Garden, part of the Yuanming Yuan. Plan by Sylvia Lu Wong.

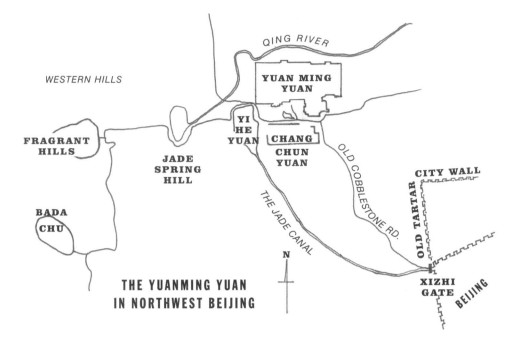

There have been repeated but unsuccessful efforts to redress the humiliation by reviving the glory of the Yuanming Yuan. The heroic ambition of rebuilding the lost garden has never materialized not only because of the enormous cost but also due to the loss of knowledge in the horticultural arts. It has seemed utterly impossible to revive the grandeur, which had been brought into being by the century-long effort of a rising empire. If the Yuanming Yuan were the pride of a mighty empire, the fall of the empire would render the restoration of the great garden as impossible as that of the empire. Only after the conclusion of the Chinese revolution did it become possible to make sense of historical preservation. A few new structures rebuilt on the ruined site for tourism demonstrated defects in design and workmanship that exacerbate worries about a losing art. The dexterous craftsmanship that created the magnificent garden may have been forever lost.

Since the prospect of reviving the "lost paradise" is slim, perhaps we can only appreciate the magnificence and glory in memory. But even the memory is fading fast. Especially in the English-language literature on the subject, no serious new research has been done since the publication of Caroll Malone's *History of the Peking Summer Palaces Under the Ch'ing Dynasty* (1934) and Hope Danby's *The Garden of Perfect Brightness* (1950), both of which lack rigorous scholarship. Not surprisingly, many recent sinologists were unable to identify this great imperial garden properly. Maurice Adam links "Yuen Ming Yuen" (Yuanming Yuan) with "*L'Oeuvre Architecturale des Anciens Jesuites au XVIII Siecle*" (The Architectural Works of the Old Jesuits in the Eighteenth Century) (1936). So does a recent French study, which refers to "Le Yuanmingyuan" (the Yuanming Yuan) in the European section (Perazzoli-t'Serstevens 1988). A noted historian recently wrote that "Qianlong employed

Jesuit architects and designers to work on a magnificent European-style summer palace, the Yuanming Yuan, erected in a lake-side park just outside Peking" (Spence 1990, 100). As a matter of fact, the European palaces designed by the Jesuits only represented a small and peripheral section of the Yuanming Yuan. Nor is it appropriate to term the Yuanming Yuan a "summer palace," since the Qing emperors from Yongzheng (r. 1722–1735) on had never considered the garden their summer home. It was, in fact, a principal imperial residence of five Manchu monarchs, namely, Yongzheng, Qianlong (r. 1736–1795), Jiaqing (r. 1796–1820), Daoguang (r. 1821–1850), and Xianfeng (r. 1851–1861). They spent their summers instead at the "Chengde Summer Mountain Retreat" (Chengde bishu shanzhuang) in Rehe, or Jehol (cf. Zhang Dongpan 1984).

The Yuanming Yuan is better known in contemporary China due to persistent public interest, even fascination, in the burning of the magnificent royal garden by foreign troops. Modern Chinese authors were thus eager to tell the story in order to attract readers. Anecdotes of various sorts have appeared ceaselessly in magazines and literary supplements of newspapers. The Hong Kong-based director Li Hanxiang made a film called *Huoshao yuanming yuan* (Burning of the Yuanming Yuan), which has been ranked as one of the best historical movies in the Chinese-speaking world. Scholarly works on the garden in Chi-

Figure 2. Bird's-eye view of the Yuanming Yuan in its heyday, facing south. Source: Yuanming Yuan Guanli chu (The Administrative Office of the Yuanming Yuan), Yuanming Yuan yuanshi jieshao (An introduction to the history of the Yuanming Yuan), an informal pamphlet for public distribution, p. 21.

nese have also appeared in an increasing number since 1980, following the opening of the Yuanming Yuan Ruins Park to the public. Authors from different disciplines produced various microstudies of a technical nature. The Yuanming Yuan Study Society *(Yuanmingyuan xuehui)* founded on December 1, 1984, has promoted the preservation of the garden through source collection, research, and publication. But, to this day, a comprehensive in-depth study of this magnificent garden still awaits its author.[1]

My own interest in the subject originated in 1981 during my first visit to the ruins in the east Haidian district of west Beijing. The wilderness that was all I could see inspired my historical imagination. Nowhere could I find any indication of the vast garden composed of more than 150 scenic units skillfully designed between hills and lakes, not to mention the countless buildings, chambers, and pavilions. I have since tried to locate literature on the Yuanming Yuan. A series of books compiled by Qing scholars, such as Yu Mingzhong's *Rixia jiuwen kao* (The histories of the imperial capital) (1774), and Cheng Yansheng's *Yuanming yuan kao* (A critical study of the Yuanming Yuan) (1928), together with poems and maps of the garden's famous Forty Views, are very informative. There are also valuable Western sources, such as the eyewitness account of Father Jean Attiret, who attended the Qianlong court for many years, and the written testimonies made by British and French army officers who had plundered and burned the garden. Not until 1985, however, did I learn of the existence of a large quantity of documents pertinent to the Yuanming Yuan in the possession of the Chinese First Historical Archive in Beijing. I copied some interesting pieces from the archive during my 1986 visit, but they represented only a drop in the bucket. In 1991, a large selection of the archival documents was published in two thick volumes, which have significantly supplemented the documentary sources available since the 1930s. These two volumes not only offer the researcher a sampling of the sorts of documents available in the archives but also comprise the documents most pertinent to the Yuanming Yuan's history, construction, management, major political activities, royal life, looting, destruction, repairs, and deterioration (*YMYA* 1991, 1:5). The collection, however selective, serves my purpose very well. With these hitherto unused materials in hand, plus the old literary sources, I felt confident enough to begin an in-depth inquiry into the subject. My main purpose was to reconstruct the lost garden on paper as fully as possible and to answer two questions: first, what did it look like and how did its appearance evolve, and second, what happened in it and to it?

This study covers three aspects of the garden. First, I present the Yuanming Yuan's physical appearance and its architectural elements, such as buildings, courtyards, bridges, and landscaping, discussing in some cases where elements came from, how they gradually evolved, and what meanings the aesthetical designs and arrangements possessed. The Yuanming Yuan's original section was completed in 1744; the Changchun Yuan (Eternal Spring Garden) was incorporated on its completion in 1749, and the Qichun Yuan (Variegated Spring Garden), which was composed of a number of small gardens, was annexed in 1772. Thus the garden we know in effect consisted of "three connected imperial gardens" *(yuanming sanyuan)* during its heyday.

The site, according to a recent survey, occupied 3.4 square kilometers, or 5,100 Chinese *mou* (775.5 acres), and measured 10 kilometers in perimeter with a rectangular shape, approximately 2,415 meters from east to west and 1,890 meters from north to south. On this immense space once stood 160,000 square meters of man-made structures (Bai Rixin 1982, 79; Yuanming yuan guanliju 1981, 24). Many of the structures represented the cream of traditional Chinese architecture and fit well in the specific environment. Meticulous care and immense creativity were evident everywhere, including the distinct European section, where Western-style buildings and gardens were skillfully integrated. To recreate the physical look of the Yuanming Yuan, it is useful for us to consult the still well-preserved Yihe Yuan, originally one of the subsidiary gardens of the Yuanming Yuan; the Chengde Summer Mountain Retreat in Rehe; and a few other surviving Ming-Qing gardens throughout China. Mindful of the uniqueness of each garden, they provide us with a visual sense of Chinese imperial gardens and a foundation to the literary sources. Last but not the least, three large maps of the whole garden and some original models of individual buildings offer valuable guidance as well. The description of the garden's landscaping and the man-made structures comprises the first part of this book.

Second, I examine the rise and fall of the Yuanming Yuan. This is a historical recounting of the glory representing the culture, intellect, and esprit of the great Qing Empire and the tragedy of invasion, plundering, and burning that foretold the downfall of the empire and the decline of the culture. I shall also look into the aftermath of the damaged garden. Not fully aware of the depth of its problems, the Qing dynasty entertained the idea of rebuilding the burned garden. Some construction yielded results, but in the end it was left incomplete. Then the Boxer catastrophe delivered another blow to the damaged garden, and the hapless Qing dynasty let the damaged garden estate slowly deteriorate under the relentless onslaughts of both man-made and natural disasters. This story of the sublime and the shameful will be told in the second part of this book.

Third, I explore some aspects of human activity in the Yuanming Yuan, where five Qing emperors made their home. Together with their consorts, high- and low-ranking officials, eunuchs, soldiers, monks, and members of the so-called Garden Household, the emperors led real lives in the garden, including sight-seeing, receiving guests, managing state affairs, and writing essays and poems. More important, since the Qing emperors lived for so long in the Yuanming Yuan, they made the imperial garden the de facto hub of the empire.

The Yongzheng emperor first built inside the garden a replica of the principal imperial court, identical to the one in the Forbidden City. It is understandable that the Sons of Heaven preferred the pleasant garden environment to the more solemn palace grounds in the Forbidden City. Making the Yuanming Yuan their permanent home, the Qing rulers naturally attached the greatest importance to it. As time went on, the garden collected an extraordinary number of treasures, including jewelry, cultural relics, and books. One of the seven complete editions of *Siku Quanshu* (Four treasures), comprising virtually all available Chinese books, was housed here. Besides books and artifacts, luxurious furniture and expensive decoration could be found in the hundreds of buildings and chambers. Beyond doubt, had the garden survived to this day, it would be one of the greatest and richest museums in the world. With the destruction of the garden, however, much of the bygone political and cultural life of the Yuanming Yuan, like the pattern of last year's wind, moved beyond recapture. Nonetheless, thanks to the recently available archival sources, I was able to obtain some evidence to reconstruct a limited aspect of bygone human life in the garden, including the Qing emperors' daily activities, administrative structure and functions, as well as crime and punishment.

PART ONE

Architecture

❦

CHAPTER I

PROVENANCE

BEFORE DISCUSSING THE RISE of the Yuanming Yuan, the greatest garden the Chinese have ever built, let us first summarize traditional Chinese garden art. Garden design and construction constitute a vital part of the Chinese cultural tradition. Living in a beautiful and diverse natural environment with a unique landscape, the Chinese have developed a distinct garden aesthetic over the span of three thousand years. Generally speaking, Chinese artists, whether poets, painters, or garden designers, have emulated nature and appreciated the feeling of a genuine harmony between man and nature.

It is well known that in China poetry and painting have a close kinship. Modern scholars have often quoted Su Shi's (1036–1101) celebrated comment on the works of the Tang artist-poet Wang Wei (699–759), "whereas a poem conceives a painting, a painting suggests a poem" *(shizhong youhua huazhong youshi)* (quoted in Zhao Lingchi n.d., *ce 22*, 8:9a). To be sure, each genre has its own standard and style, but both share the popular theme of underlining the beauty of the landscape and implying intangible sentiments. A close kinship also exists between poetry and garden. "Ideal gardens," as an eminent scholar of Chinese gardens has put it, "are like superb lines of verse" (Chen Congzhou 1994, 5).

The same kinship can be found between landscape painting and garden design (cf. Fu Baoshi 1973, 33–48). Both Chinese painters and garden designers share, for example, the fundamental principle of suggestiveness: showing no base of distant mountains, no roots in distant forests, and no hulls of distant ships. Not rare at all in the history of Chinese gardens were designs built on the basis of a famous landscape painting. As a recent writer has rightly pointed out, Chinese painting in effect sets the tone for Chinese garden making (Peng Yigang 1988, 7).

Indeed, profoundly inspired by the vast stretches of the countryside, Chinese landscapers were heavily influenced by the ink-wash landscape paintings and the poems reflecting the natural beauty. It can be said with certainty that both painting and poetry have rendered an especially refined sensibility in the conceptualization of the traditional Chinese garden art. Like poems and paintings, gardens are integrated works of art, lyricism, and picturesqueness. Many designers, who were also competent painters and poets, quite naturally gave the garden environment a compositional form, which spontaneously yielded an atmosphere of pictorial and poetic feeling. This is why a standard traditional Chinese garden can often be considered the physical expression of the slow unfolding of a painted scroll (Wu Shichang 1934, 80–114). For all its artificiality, the overall outlook of a Chinese garden should appear to be formed as naturally as in nature. Since the harmony of garden architecture with the surrounding landscape is essential for Chinese garden design, superimposing man-made structures on landscape requires integrating the artificial with the natural into a symphonic unity.

In contrast to the geometric formality of Renaissance gardens, Chinese garden art appreciates untrammeled beauty with an emphasis on free form, continuous flow, and unexpected twists and turns. The ambiance of being in real nature, however, is artificially created. The vastness of nature has to be shrunk into a landscape mode, requiring only "a foot to create whole nature," or squeezing "the world in a pot." Miniature mountains with peaks, precipices, gorges, valleys, streams, and cataracts are common in Chinese gardens. This "symbolic representationism" differs from the European tradition of realism, although English gardens of the eighteenth-century had become pastoral.

The traditional Chinese gardens generally can be classified into four different categories, namely, the scenic park for the general public, the monastic gardens of religious institutions, residential gardens owned by literati, and the oldest and most spectacular royal demesne *(huangjia yuanlin),* or imperial garden.

A quick survey of royal demesnes in Chinese history readily yields three common characteristics. First, they are colossa, with a huge enclosure of the best scenic parkland and numerous structures, in order to convey the awe-inspiring might and prestige of the Son of Heaven, the ruler of the universal empire. Dignified grandiosity is an essential artistic feature of the royal demesne. Second, the garden structures are destined to be luxurious, sublime, and palatial-looking so as to give an image of architectonic sumptuousness. Third, they recreate settings of fairy tales, such as a jeweled palace in Elfland's hills, to express the delight and fantasy of the immortal world.[1] The Yuanming Yuan was the greatest royal demesne ever created in the history of Chinese landscape design.

The Rise of Imperial Gardens

Royal demesnes began very early in Chinese history. The Chinese rulers, like their counterparts all over the world, had a passion for pleasure, and with ample resources at their disposal they constructed magnificent parklands and palatial gardens in and out of their formal palaces. The earliest Chinese royal demesne appeared almost simultaneously with the beginning of the Chinese state. It is said that King Jie of the semilegendary Xia dynasty

(2033?–1562? b.c.) once built a lavish Jade Terrace *(yutai)* for his personal pleasure.[2] The oracle-bone inscriptions, excavated from the ruins of the subsequent Shang dynasty (1562–1066? b.c.), made no doubt about the existence of hunting grounds for the pleasure of the king. The king owned various pleasure grounds sitting near or within the imperial ramparts. Between the Shang and the rise of the Qin Empire in 221 b.c. the Chinese sovereigns often found access to attractive open settings, far away from the royal palace, in which to marvel at the beauty of the landscape and to build menageries *(you)* for resting and lodging.[3] Most of these menageries featured watchtowers, flower beds, fish ponds, bird cages, animal pits, and comfortable lodging. Many of the facilities were gradually transformed into country houses called the "suburban pleasure palaces." Other names for pleasure grounds, such as "divine terrace" *(lingtai),* "divine pound" *(lingzhao),* and "divine menagerie" (lingyou), which appear in the Book of Poetry *(Shijing),* refer to the royal demesnes of the Zhou kings.[4]

The "first emperor," the Qin Shi Huangdi (r. 221–210 b.c.) constructed lavish palaces on the model of the six great states he defeated during his conquest of China. In the end, he assembled no less than three hundred palaces along the River Wei, of which the most magnificent megapreserve was the Upper Woods (Shanglin) situated on the southern bank of the river. Five miles outside the imperial capital Xianyang and facing the River Wei, the Upper Woods featured terraces, ponds, menageries, forests, and the legendary A-pang Palace (A'fang Gong).[5] This palace, according to a Qing scholar, was actually a gigantic compound of palaces looking much like a "city" (Xu Angfa 1985, 71–72; Wang Shixin 1981, 46–47). This remarkable Upper Woods royal demesne was further expanded by the subsequent Han dynasty.

By the time of the Han, menageries were transformed into "gardens" *(yuan),* which comprised enclosures, palaces, temples, ponds, and lakes. In 104 b.c., Emperor Wu (r. 140–87 b.c.) built twelve more palatial gardens for his pleasure. The most magnificent one was the Jianzhang Palace standing at the southern end of the Lake Taiye, together with artificial hills surrounded by water to make a "heavenly paradise" *(Gujin tushu jicheng* n.d. 97:546–547, 523). Beautiful scenery surrounding man-made structures thereafter became an essential element in the construction of royal demesnes. The imperial gardens of the Han, though long since vanished, provided a model for the magnificence of royal demesne for many generations to come.[6]

The Han dynasty also witnessed the rise of private gardens owned by royalty and high-ranking officials. Obviously, the rich and powerful had become resourceful enough to tread in the emperor's steps to build their own pleasure gardens, even though they were normally far less spectacular.[7] Between the decline and fall of the Han in the second century and the rejuvenation of the Chinese Empire in the sixth century, the political center moved from Changan to Luoyang, where new imperial and private gardens flourished. Of the royal demesnes, the most renowned was the Fragrant Wood Garden (Fanglin Yuan) created by Emperor Ming of the Wei (r. 227–239). The emperor was so passionate about the project that he employed thousands of workers, with the support of officials and scholars, to build the garden at the northeast section of Luoyang. He dug a huge lake called the Blue Dragon Meer (Canglong Hai) and erected the Jingyang artificial hill with rocks transported directly from the distant Taihang mountain in Shandong (Chen Shou 1959, 3:712).

The Emperor Wu of the Jin dynasty (r. 265–290) substantially refurbished this imperial garden. Because of the simultaneous existence of several dynasties during this long period of China's disunity, imperial gardens could be found in Pingcheng (near present-day Datong), Longcheng (in the present-day Liaoning), and Jiankang (the present-day Nanjing). And with the rise of wealthy aristocratic families in both north and south China at the time, private gardens flourished everywhere. Some of these gardens were magnificent enough to rival imperial ones.[8] This era also featured literati gardens of various sorts in the wealthy Yangzi delta. Though not as spectacular, these gardens aimed at elegance in the expression of the literati's appreciation of the tranquil and rustic country style of life—a common spiritual response to the tumultuous world of the time. A combination of escapism and naturalism inspired the rise of the so-called landscape gardens, corresponding to time-honored landscape painting and poetry. This type of naturalistic "landscape garden," or parklike garden, featured streams, lakes, gorges, rock formations, valleys, trees, and miniature hills, together with chambers and pavilions. Integrating artificial creations with the natural surroundings became an essential element in the construction of imperial gardens as well (Ren Xiaohong 1995, 45–46).[9]

When the Sui dynasty (605–618) built a new imperial city—the Daxing Cheng—south of the River Wei after its reunification of China in the early seventh century, the entire northern section of the city was designated as royal demesne. Emperor Yang of the Sui, known to history as a playboy ruler, soon added the magnificent West Garden (Xi Yuan or Huitong Yuan) in Luoyang, already a city renowned for gardens and flowers. The West Garden comprised three man-made islands created on the basis of fairy tales. On each of the islands stood numerous pavilions and temples spreading into sixteen courtyards without losing any sense of a harmonious unity with the natural landscape. The principal lake of the garden was more than ten *li* (approximately three miles) in diameter. The huge size of the garden reportedly allowed the emperor to bring with him an entourage, including as many as one thousand singsong girls. The same emperor later built more royal demesnes in southern China. Later historians wrote that Emperor Yang was so "fickle in affection" that he was never content regardless how many pleasurances he already possessed (Sima Guang 1978, 8:5639). His relentless pursuit of pleasure was blamed for the quick fall of the Sui dynasty.

The great Tang dynasty (618–907) consolidated the rejuvenated empire. Its tremendous wealth and power elevated landscape painting and garden design to an even higher level of aesthetic standard. The Great Shining Palace (Daming Gong) was the most impressive of all royal palatial gardens the Tang built. Completed in 634, it consisted of more than thirty structures and featured elegant architecture, exquisite decorations, and large lakes and woods. A recent excavation has brought to life the foundations of the Hanyuan Court, one of the palace's many structures, which stood 75.9 meters from east to west and 41.3

meters from north to south. One can imagine the magnificence of the entire palace (cf. Meng Ya'nan 1993, 56–57).

The Maturity of the Garden Arts

Along with the gigantic imperial gardens, literati gardens also flourished during the Tang. Liu Zongyuan (773–819), for example, transformed wildness into a pleasant garden comprising lakes, hills, chambers, and a pavilion (Liu Zongyuan 1979, 3:774). The garden villa at Wangchuan owned by the great Tang poet Wang Wei (699–759) featured rock hills, a winding lake, bamboo pavilions, a willow forest, flower beds, and a dock, where the poet enjoyed composing poems and entertaining his friends (*Xin Tangshu* 1975, 18:5765). Bo Juyi, another poet of great fame, built in the spring of 817 his Thatched Hall *(caotang)* at Kuanglu in Jiangxi, where he was overwhelmed by the scenic beauty (Bo Juyi 1955, 7: 2a). Enjoying scenic beauty aside, these private gardens also served as retreats for literati who suffered career setbacks or other disappointments. They found their feelings in landscapes and used landscaping to express their feelings. In any event, Tang poet-scholars of renown were eager to construct their gardens in natural settings based on their own artistic ingenuity during this golden age of Chinese poetry. They often styled their gardens, halls, and pavilions with poetic names in fine calligraphy to enhance the atmosphere of urbanity and elegance. Later designers of imperial gardens adopted the literati sensibility. In addition, the Tang's extensive cultural contacts with Central and Southwest Asia gave the Tang gardens a distinct foreign influence, such as the apparatus for circulating cold water, the Greek-style columns, and possibly the use of the arc in architecture and the stone *pailou* (Tung 1938, 413–414).

Landscape gardens reached an aesthetic peak during the Song (960–1279), absorbing the influence of Chan (Zen) Buddhism. The natural beauty of hills, streams, trees, and flowers provided Chan adepts with the inspiration to attain "enlightenment" *(chanwu)* as well as the means to suggest the metaphysical Chan world. It was not surprising to find Chan temples in the midst of beautiful scenery; indeed, Chan temples were de facto landscape gardens. Inevitably, Chan aesthetics, meaning, and delight were injected into the garden arts. Chan Buddhism, as a recent writer maintains, was instrumental in the increase of private gardens and affected the characteristics of Chinese gardens (Ren Xiaohong 1995, 44). Not only was an element of refined sensibility added but also, thanks to technological advances, architectural construction reached high maturity. The general wealth of upper-class people, advanced techniques, and artistic taste facilitated a boom in garden construction. The entire elite population developed a passion for building their own gardens in which to enjoy the beauty of hills, ponds, streams, trees, and flowers of artificial creation and where invited guests could enjoy good wine, beautiful music, and poetry. These traditional functions of private gardens continued into the Ming-Qing prior to the dawn of the modern era.

Against this background, no one should be surprised at the magnitude and level of luxury of the imperial garden. In 962, the founding emperor constructed at the northeast section of Kaifeng a palatial garden city on the model of the Luoyang palaces and gardens (*Songshi* 1977 7: 2097). In addition to refurbishing two old gardens, namely the Suitable-Spring Garden (Yichun Yuan) and the Jade Ford Garden (Yujing Yuan), the royal family built two brand new imperial gardens, the Jade Forest Garden (Qionglin Yuan) and the Golden-Shining Pond (Jinming Ci) in 966 and 980, successively. They came of age by the early twelfth century. Every spring the Song emperor proudly led his entourage to open these two magnificent gardens in person. The gardens closed when the emperor left in winter (Ye Mengde 1984, 4; Meng Yuanlao 1961, 189–190).

Perhaps the greatest imperial garden the Song built was the famous Gengyu completed by Emperor Huizong (r. 1101–1125) in 1117. It covered a mountainous site four miles in diameter with a huge lake. Though a mediocre ruler, the emperor was a gifted artist who specialized in calligraphy and painting. He inevitably gave his own artistic touch to the numerous chambers, pavilions, terraces, galleries, as well as precious trees, flowers, and bamboo forests in the garden. To make the garden still greater, he requested a large quantity of the expansive "flowery rocks" *(huagang shi),* or really the Taihu rocks (rocks from Lake Tai) to be transported from South China. The price for obtaining the rocks was extremely high. It not only required tremendous manpower to carry the heavy rocks all the way to Kaifeng, but also down the road along the Grand Canal, numerous bridges and irrigation systems were either damaged or destroyed to make way for the rocks (*Songshi* 1977, 7:7101–7102; cf. *Gujin tushu jicheng* n.d., 97:525–526 and Hargett 1988–1989, 1–6). Many historians believe that the hateful rock transport contributed to the downfall of the Northern Song. The Gengyu and its great artistic creation, however, fundamentally set a brilliant example for the construction of the Yuanming Yuan centuries later, evident especially in the arrangements of hills, lakes, rocks, trees, flowers, and man-made structures. The only noticeable difference was that the Yuanming Yuan did not have the Gengyu's sizable zoo.

The Qidan (Khitan) Liao and the Ruzhen (Jurchen) Jin dynasties, generally parallel to the Song, had ruled North China for centuries. Both Qidan and Ruchen leaders constructed elegant country homes in the present-day Beijing area. Then the Mongols founded the Yuan dynasty and made Beijing their Great Capital (Dadu). Although the Mongol rulers and princes were no great garden builders, landscape painting during their time had reached arguably the most glorious period of all, and it undoubtedly had a positive impact on later garden design and construction. Distinguished artists such as Zhao Menghu (1254–1322) won their reputation by transforming their painting skills into garden design (Meng Ya'nan 1993, 139). Almost all the imperial gardens were built around the neighborhood of Beijing, where the Mongols set up the central government of China. The subsequent Ming emperors, in particular the Yongluo emperor (r. 1403–1424), refurbished and expanded the imperial compound, later known as the Forbidden City (Zijin Cheng), in Beijing, including the completion of the Rear Garden (Houhua Yuan), which still exists. It was during the Ming that an increasing number of gardens appeared in the northwestern suburb of Beijing, where the Yuanming Yuan was eventually built.

While the elegant gardens of rulers and princes were being built in northwestern

Beijing during the Ming-Qing period from the fourteenth to eighteenth century, the making of private gardens, especially in south China, also improved greatly. Splendid garden villas in large numbers were found in such prominent cities as Suzhou, Hangzhou, Nanjing, and Yangzhou. Even though these privately owned gardens were generally small in comparison to royal demesnes, exceptions existed, such as the Sui Garden owned by Yuan Mei, the great eighteenth-century Chinese scholar and poet. His Nanjing garden featured thirty-eight man-made structures, including his main library and studio and twenty-four separate pavilions (Yuan Mei 1892, 39:7a–8b).

More importantly, the southern gardens of the Ming-Qing period were more skillfully landscaped. They demonstrated a more sophisticated aesthetic taste in general and a gracefulness and elegance of individual structures in particular. In particular, the wealthy gentry-scholars of Suzhou during this period created the best models of classical Chinese gardens, which in the opinion of an eminent modern scholar-architect were the "representative specimens of privately owned gardens in southern China" (Liu Dunzhen 1993, 3). As we shall see later in this study, the cream of the southern gardens was highly appreciated by the Qianlong emperor, who borrowed many of the southern scenes and architecture when he expanded the Yuanming Yuan, and when he constructed the Rehe retreat, in the eighteenth century.

We should at least mention two traditional Chinese designers, Li Cheng and Ji Cheng, who were highly influential in the long history of garden making. Both deserve our attention because their ideas undoubtedly contributed to the design and construction of the Yuanming Yuan. Li Cheng was an architect of Song China and the author of the monumental *Yingzao fashi* (The construction manual) published in 1103. The book, which richly illustrates and substantially details the methods of design and construction, deals with how to build "arch bridge" (*gongqiao*) and to beautify a garden with water, in addition to standardizing the use of "glazed roofs" (*liuli wa*) which came to characterize the palaces, halls, chambers, pavilions, kiosks, terrace houses, and corridors. The *liuli* (glazed tile), a term originated in the Sanskrit *vaidurya,* was first introduced into China through Southwest Asia and took five hundred years to be used as an essential building material. It is certain that He Zhou, who began manufacturing glazed tiles in the color of green, and thereafter Tang craftsmen furthered the technique to produce the world-renowned *liuli* in three bright colors, usually yellow, blue, and purple.[10]

Ji Cheng was a seventeenth-century scholar from Wujiang in Jiangsu province, and he authored the celebrated *Yuanye* (The craft of gardens). The first part of this landmark book includes an introduction and chapters on site selection, foundation setting, and the construction methods of roof making. Part Two is devoted to balustrades, while Part Three discusses such topics as how to make doors, windows, and walls, select rock, and construct artificial hills. This ten-thousand-word text was accompanied by two hundred plates defining the standard Chinese-style gardens, in particular the landscape garden with its meticulous attention to the composition of individual scenes. It emphasized the importance of creating a "main scene" to distinguish one garden from another and adapting man-made structures to harmonize with the natural surroundings (Ji Cheng 1983, 1–39; Alison Hardie 1988).[11] There is general consensus that the works of Li and Ji helped to elevate the standard of Chinese garden art by harmonizing the making of hillocks, lakes, buildings, and courtyards as well as the planting of trees and flowers in late Ming and early Qing China.

A Great Synthesis of the Garden Arts

Just as the Ming-Qing gardens synthesized traditional Chinese garden art, so the Yuanming Yuan synthesized the Ming-Qing gardens. Indeed, it was constructed at a time when Chinese garden art had long since reached maturity. Besides the availability of specific skills, this was the Qing's most affluent period, making it possible to create an imperial garden unrivaled in style as well as grandeur. In general, the Yuanming Yuan was constructed on level land, and it was an amalgam of palaces and pavilions, scenic enclosures, landscaping, artificial hills, and numerous clusters of chambers to serve various functions, such as courts, temples, schools, and libraries. All of the man-made structures were organized on a north-south axis in the classical style of courtyard compounds together with secondary axes linking lesser structures. Thus, whitewashed walls, black-grey tile roofs, chestnut-brown pillars, railings, overhanging ornaments, hillocks, lakes, flowers, and trees composed the majestic garden scenery of the Yuanming Yuan. There were hundreds of beautiful scenes in the garden, of which the Qianlong emperor designated forty best views. After having carefully selected the well-defined scenes, His Majesty gave each of them an elegant name and an illustrative poem. Moreover, the emperor instructed court artists to create the images of the Forty Views in an album. These paintings survived the Yuanming Yuan and have become world renown.

Given its size, variety, and complexity, the Yuanming Yuan possessed virtually every form of structure appropriate for a garden. The principal ones are summarized as follows (cf. Ji Cheng 1983, 74–82, 84; Ji Cheng 1988, 66–71; Zhou Wuzhong 1991, 74–85):

1. Halls *(tang),* the principal edifices in garden architecture or the main buildings adjacent to a particular scenic object, usually face south—the imperial direction—with a large empty space in the front. A Chinese hall is normally built of round timber, standing tall, spacious, and open to observe the surrounding views. Prominent halls in the Yuanming Yuan were numerous, such as the Cool Summer Hall (Qingxia Tang) in the Variegated Spring Garden (Qichun Yuan) and the Calm Sea Hall (Haiyan Tang), a large European building in the Eternal Spring Garden (Changchun Yuan). The most distinguished hall in the royal garden was surely the Main Audience Hall, a replica of the principal Imperial Court inside the Forbidden City.

2. Pavilions *(ting),* the basic meaning of which is "to make a stopover," are designed for rest and enjoyment of scenery during garden tours. As Ji Cheng noted, "there is no fixed design for pavilions" (Ji Cheng 1983, 81; Ji Cheng 1988, 69). However, no matter what the form of design (square, round, hexagonal, oblong, octagonal, fan-shaped, or plum-flower

shaped), a pavilion is open on all sides to maximize views. Hence, it is not accidental that pavilions are often located in places with better views, in particular on the tops of hills, amid groves, or at the water's edge, while their size and shape are adapted to the surroundings. Given the number of scenic spots in the Yuanming Yuan, pavilions of various shapes and designs in the garden were too numerous to count. One of the most unusual, for instance, was the Five-Bamboo Pavilion (Wuzhu Ting).

3. Terraces *(tai)* are high, raised, roofless platforms made either from piles of rocks or of flat planks. They are constructed in highly selective locations in order to allow travelers to admire both distant and nearby views. Normally, a terrace is situated either on high ground or beside a lake. The Peony Terrace on one of the Nine Isles in the neighborhood of the royal living quarters of the Yuanming Yuan was the best known, for it had once hosted the well publicized gatherings of the three generations of the royal family, namely, grandfather (Kangxi), father (Yongzheng), and son (Qianlong).

4. Chambers *(lou)*, normally two stories and cuboid in shape, are built between hill and lake to catch natural beauty through open windows. Chambers were very common in the Yuanming Yuan; however, the Yongzheng emperor especially enjoyed the Catching Evening Sunlight Chamber (Ranxia Lou) at one of the famous Forty Views.

5. Belvederes *(ge)* can be identified as "storied houses," with open windows on all four sides. Not surprisingly, many library buildings were named belvederes, including the main library in the Yuanming Yuan, the Wenyuan Ge (Library of Literary Sources).

6. Gazebos *(xie)* are constructed at scenic spots, either beside water or among flower beds, in an attempt to "borrow" the views. Since most are found at the water's edge, gazebos are often referred to as "water gazebos" *(shuixie)*. They appeared in large number at the scenic views surrounding the largest lake, called Fuhai; for instance, the Clear Void Gazebo (Chengxu Xie) at the southern end of the lake.

7. Garden porches *(yuanlang)* are long and winding walkways and corridors that serve as the arteries and veins between scenic views regardless of weather conditions. Corridors in particular have many types and are classified either by shape, such as straight, wavelike, and winding, or by function, such as the open, two-story, hill ascending, and waterside corridors. The double corridor—two corridors in one separated by a wall with tracery windows, giving a sense of depth and surprise—is generally rare but found often in the Yuanming Yuan.

8. Galleries *(xuan)* take after the model of the ancient Chinese carriages, which look spacious and lofty, so they are also known as "carriage galleries" *(juxuan)*. They are built in high open space to capture the best views. A distinctly unique gallery was the Chunhua Gallery in the Eternal Spring Garden, where the Qianlong Emperor exhibited his huge collection of famous inscribed stone tablets.

9. Chapels *(zhai)* are secluded retreats for self-reflection or meditation in a quiet surrounding, in a sense similar to European chapels, where one seeks spiritual comfort and tranquility. Small studies or libraries can also be called "book chapels" *(shuzhai)*, where the owner of the garden can read and write in solitude. Moreover, *zhai* in Chinese tradition

was the place where one abstained from meat, wine, and sex before offering sacrifices to gods or ancestors. It was not uncommon for Qing emperors to use one of the chapels, or *zhai,* in the Yuanming Yuan for private moments of self-reflection and worshipping.

10. Lodgings or cottages *(fang)* are private quarters including living rooms and bedrooms. Some of "mountain lodgings" *(shanfang)* in the Yuanming Yuan were very large, such as the Beauty-Covered Mountain Cottage (Xiujie Shanfang), included in one of the famous Forty Views.

11. Landboats *(fang)* were constructed for enjoying scenic views and merrymaking. The best known landboat is the Marble Boat *(Shifang),* which was first built at the Kunming Lake in the Qingyi Yuan and is now a favorite spot for tourists in the Yihe Yuan.

12. Studios *(guan)* are alternative dwellings, usually for the purposes of reading and creating artistic works. In the Eternal Spring Garden, the Qianlong Emperor created the interesting and playful Exquisite Jade Studio (Yulinglong Guan) sitting on an island connected by a winding bridge.

Structures of various styles in the Yuanming Yuan were by no means isolated units; combinations of pavilions and terraces or chambers and belvederes or a group of different buildings and courtyards with great complexity and irregularity suggested a majestic piece of the integral whole. Virtually every one of the Forty Views was a compound of various style structures.

In addition, three common Chinese-style structures were found in large number in the Yuanming Yuan. First, bridges *(qiao),* which separate as well as integrate one scenic space with another, were essential in a garden connected by large bodies of water and complicated networks of canals such as the Yuanming Yuan. They augmented the scenery with a variety of exquisite styles, ranging from a zigzag stone bridge across a narrow channel to a high-rise marble round arch bridge vaulted over passing barges. Winding bridges are usually built on the same level as the surface of the watery area to allow viewers to appreciate the swimming fish and the floating lilies. Quite clearly, a bridge can also serve as foil to discover a nearby scene. It is quite common that lakestone was used as railings on stone-slab bridges which can be piled up with yellow stones. Wooden bridges, while rarely seen in a small private garden, were numerous in the Yuanming Yuan.

Second, walls *(qiang),* which surround virtually every Chinese garden, extended many miles in the gigantic Yuanming Yuan. There are also walls within a garden, built either of stone or brick, designed in many different ways, and decorated with artistic carvings of flowers, birds, or fairies. The largest wall inside the Yuanming Yuan was the Wall of Sarvatis, a secluded compound, standing prominently at the northeast corner of the original Yuanming Yuan.

Third, pagodas *(ta),* the Buddhist structures, are almost indispensable elements to magnify any sizable garden, including the Yuanming Yuan, and add religious meaning and aesthetic value. Also, the Yuanming Yuan possessed many stone boats and archways, which are extremely rare in ordinary gardens.

The overall design of the Yuanming Yuan creatively syncretized the Chinese views of nature and life, artistic craftsmanship, aesthetic taste, and garden techniques. Devices, such as contrast, foil, effect, relative dimension, sequence in depth, and scenery in contraposition, were all employed in the planning of this great garden. Every piece of the structure was skillfully and flexibly matched to the topography and terrain in western Beijing. Even roads, streams, and lakes were embellished with flowers, trees, animals, and rocks. Arrangements of scenic objects were often highly complex in order to increase the feeling of depth and to make it impossible to take in all the views at one glance.

In general, the construction of the Yuanming Yuan employed three key technical elements for creative integration, namely, adapting *(yin),* borrowing *(jie),* and coping *(dui).* Adapting is to adapt the garden creatively to its natural setting—land form and physical features—to make it an integral whole. A fitting adaptation facilitates borrowing of both nearby and distant surrounding views. The idea of borrowing also reflects the distinct Chinese aesthetic taste and worldview. That is, a garden is an integral unit of the whole universe, while the natural beauty surrounding the garden is part of its views. A line of the Tang poet Du Fu illustrates this idea very well: "My window contains the ageless snow on top of the West Hills, while my door faces the countless boats anchoring at the Suzhou wharf" (1972, 12:5a). The West Hills snow and the Suzhou wharf boats become the "borrowed views" of the poet's villa. The Yuanming Yuan sitting in the beautiful landscape of northwest Beijing and surrounded by three elegant hills had much view to borrow from. In terms of borrowing, the Yuanming Yuan also fully used the skills in "spreading views" *(fenjing),* or entertaining different views from all sides, and in "dividing views" *(gejing),* creating smaller gardens within a garden, as we shall discuss below.

As for the technique of "copying," this matches one structure with another in order to accentuate symmetry. All these elements involve the skills of arranging, organizing, creating, and even widening space, thus requiring that careful attention be paid to "general layout" *(buju),* "tidying up water" *(lishui),* "piling up hills" *(dieshan),* "putting up structures" *(jianzu),* and "planting trees and flowers" *(huamu).*[12] Even if there are guidelines, there is no formula. Chinese garden designers, including Ji Cheng, emphasized the importance of inventive applications of the rules.

The traditional skills and techniques plus imagination helped to produce in the Yuanming Yuan more than one hundred different scenes by "copying" famous legends, great paintings, imaginary palaces, historic temples, and unique libraries. The quantity and variety of flowers and trees in this enormous imperial garden certainly made it a marvelous botanical garden as well. Tree selection and flower arrangement are part of the overall design that set off beautiful effects in the scenic environment. As early as 1725, the Yongzheng emperor asked the Imperial Household to give the tributary plants from Burma to the Yuanming Yuan for cultivation *(YMYA* 1991, 1:10–11).

Designers of the Yuanming Yuan clearly had in mind the overall views of the garden and its surroundings before they created a landscape of hillocks, rills, lakes, and countless structures. They were determined to give a fresh and more elegant look when adapting some admirable features of famous southern gardens. Even the Qianlong emperor's visibly distinctive European-style buildings and gardens were skillfully integrated with the other scenes, thus causing no sense of overall disharmony. Furthermore, the entire outlook of the garden was to show both the gracefulness of country life as well as the grandeur of imperial power to endorse and underline the Chinese political culture of the unified one world.

Water, which suggests calmness and quietude, is an indispensable element for any type of Chinese garden. Dainty ponds, which are seldom geometric, establish a contemplative aura to delight garden-dwellers. The Yuanming Yuan especially can be characterized as a "water garden" *(shuijing yuan),* covered by lakes, large and small, connected by a network of canals and winding watercourses. As maps of the garden show, all structures appeared to be situated on islets or spits of land surrounded by artificial hills, terraces, hollow rocks, and flowering trees and shrubs. According to the tradition of Chinese garden design, designed water areas are given the shapes and characteristics of lakes, brooks, ravines, and waterfalls in the natural world, as to imitate nature is the fundamental principle in the theory of garden making.

Water areas, in whatever forms, provide attractive scenes contrasting with adjacent hillocks, groves, and halls. Needless to say, the ample water resources in the area supplied the Yuanming Yuan with the necessary drinking water, in addition to moderating temperatures and irrigating the plants. The Yuanming Yuan's lakes branch out into numerous streams and canals connecting one section to another, which served the convenient routes to transport people and goods.

The great imperial garden Yuanming Yuan was a gigantic architectural creation of man-made hills, landscapes, ponds, and canals, together with palaces, halls, chambers, pavilions, and basilicas, embodying hundreds of smaller gardens and scenic points. And one scenic spot and another in this vast space are artistically integrated by winding roads and streams. The specifically designated scenes actually consist of an independent and yet cohesive garden complex. The huge size, grand architecture, exquisite interior designs, and numerous priceless antiques as well as cultural relics made the garden truly unmatched.

The Yuanming Yuan finally came of age during the Qianlong reign (1736–1795), when it comprised five gardens, namely, the original Yuanming Yuan; Changchun Yuan (Eternal Spring Garden, which is different from Kangxi's Changchun Yuan, which means "joyful spring"); Qichun Yuan (Variegated Spring Garden); Xichun Yuan (Loving Spring Garden), also called Qinghua Yuan (Pure Flowery Garden); and Jinchun Yuan (Spring-Coming Garden). This pealed northwest Beijing's fame for the "Three Hills and Five Gardens" *(sanshan wuyuan).* The last two gardens, however, were given to princes in the nineteenth century and were later turned into the campuses of Tsing Hua and Peking Universities (cf. *Gujin tushu jicheng* n.d., 97:1100).

The most important designers of the Yuanming Yuan were members of the Lei family. For several generations, the Leis maintained an office inside the garden to carry on the endless repairs and new construction work. Lei Fada, who first won wide recognition in his profession at the beginning of the Qing dynasty, earned official rank after having helped the Kangxi emperor rebuild the Grand Harmonious Court (Taihe Dian) inside the Forbidden City. His son Lei Jinyu showed comparable family talent in designing and constructing Kangxi's Joyful Spring Garden, for which he earned a Rank Seven and a permanent job in the Yuanming Yuan as an employee of the Office of the Imperial Household (Neiwu Fu). The emperor, who was very fond of him, honored his seventieth birthday in person.

The descendants of Lei Jinyu continued to serve as the principal architects and builders of the garden. Three Lei brothers, Jiawei, Jiarui, and Jiaxi, accompanied the Qianlong emperor's South China tours to study and copy southern gardens to be rebuilt in the Yuanming Yuan. The Leis thus earned the nickname "Model Lei" (Yangshi Lei) from their ability to produce excellent architectural models. Hundreds of the models displaying judicious designs and fine craftsmanship, still available today, provide us with an extremely useful guide to the once glorious garden (Zhu Qiqian 1984, 102–104; Shan Shiyuan 1984, 95–101).

The Leis were constantly at His Majesty's disposal. Normally, the emperor's wishes to add a ceiling here or a veranda there were transmitted to the Leis through the garden's general manager *(zongguan);* occasionally they were communicated through eunuchs. On March 8, 1859, for instance, General Manager Wang delivered a decree to paint all of the newly built terraces and eaves in bamboo green (*YMYA* 1991, 2:1066; cf. 1063–1070).

The Leis were so dexterous in garden making that they impressed the Qing court generation after generation. Their skills, rooted in traditional Chinese culture, used familiar symbols to underline the grand imperial ideology and to display the unitary concept of the world as a concrete aesthetic entity. That is, the harmonious unity of Heaven, Earth, and Man reflected a cohesive impression of natural components and artificial creation. They no doubt took into consideration the Confucian interpretation of the human world. Many palace buildings, including their interior decoration, indeed followed the Confucian views of appropriation contained in the *Book of Rites (Zhouli),* which stresses solemnity and dignity. At the same time, since the purpose of the garden was for pleasure, Confucian conformity was emphasized less in the garden design. In the Yuanming Yuan, except for the ostentatious Main Audience Hall displaying Confucian solemnity, many other structures, in particular those located in the Eternal Spring Garden, showed an explicit Daoist influence of cheerfulness and relaxation. The Mind-Opening Isle (Haiyue Kaijin) in the Eternal Spring Garden appeared extraordinarily unconventional and lively. The Daoist universe, however, weaves a network of the man-nature relationship no less, if not more, harmonious than the Confucian universe. In fact, the artistic formations of the Daoist sense of untrammeled natural beauty combined with man-made structures emulating celestial phenomena, or recreating the world of fairy tales, equally signify a harmonious dimension of the universal empire. The Yuanming Yuan also included a Muslim mosque and Baroque building, and yet none of the alien influence seemed to have affected the harmony of the imperial garden as a whole.

The designers of the Yuanming Yuan also took the popular Chinese practice of *fengshui* (geomancy) into consideration. *Fengshui* had affected Chinese social life in virtually all aspects for millennia. Even the well-educated literati often regulated their domestic affairs, in particular the construction of a grave or house, in accordance with the cannons of *fengshui*. They believed that selecting a spot for construction condemned or approved by the *fengshui* experts would impose dire calamities or lasting fortune on all those who lived there and their offspring. Fearful of calamities and longing for fortune made geomancers valuable experts. Since a good siting for living space that fully fit the principles of geomancy would favor the inhabitants' wealth, health, and happiness, the Chinese have taken for granted to select a "lucky site" for construction, in whatever manner, as an assurance of peace and security for millenarian. Although imperial Chinese governments with whatever ethnic background never acknowledged the orthodoxy of *fengshui,* they actually sanctioned the practice. Modern Chinese to this day still try to adapt their residences to cooperate with the basic principles of *fengshui*.[13]

Despite its superstitious nature, *fengshui,* which emphasizes a delicate balance of *yin* and *yang* currents in the earth's surface, is fully in agreement with the idea of harmonizing men and nature cherished by the Chinese tradition. Usually places approved by geomancers appeared to be tranquil burial grounds or delightful and beautiful home settings. Interestingly, the noted historian of sciences Joseph Needham also finds that *fengshui* embodied "a marked aesthetic component." Needham sensed "a feeling of desolation" when revisiting the gardens and park of Versailles, which he had "greatly admired" in his youth. This was so, because his experience with Chinese gardens, such as the I Ho Yuan (Yihe Yuan), convinced him that the geometrical garden as Versailles represents "imprisoning and constraining Nature rather than flowing along with it" (Needham 1956, 2:361).

As a synthesis of Chinese art of garden construction, the Yuanming Yuan could not possibly ignore the crucial element of geomancy. Indeed, Manchu rulers took geomancy seriously for the sake of good luck. For instance, in 1724, the Imperial Household summoned a highly acclaimed geomancer, a certain Magistrate Zhang from Deping of Shandong province. He inspected the construction sites of the Yuanming Yuan, in particular analyzing the garden terrain in both physical and psychic senses, in order to diagnose their features (*YMYA* 1991, 1:6–7).

The Haidian area in northwest Beijing had been chosen as a nice siting for garden construction long before the founding of the Qing dynasty. In aerial photographs, its natural configuration is smooth in form and outline, with virtually no difficult terrain that would be in discordance with Nature. To the west of this flat area, however, there are dozens of mountain chains and streams, generally known as the Western Mountains (Xi Shan). Slightly north of the Western Mountains stand the Jade Spring Hills (Yuquan Shan), where the Yuanming Yuan drew their fresh water. Also nearby is the Fragrant Hill (Xiang Shan). Its ridges were described by Ming scholars as the "skins of an Azure Dragon" *(qinglongpi)* (Liu Tong and Yu Yizheng 1980, 296; cf. Gu Zuyu 1956, 2:476). And the mountain Weng stands about five *li,* or 1.5 miles, west of Haidian, particulary its graceful curve like a "water jar" *(weng)* for which its name is derived (Jiang Yikui 1980, 73). The interaction of these two mountain ranges is like the convergence of the male and female energies in harmony. It is clearly an auspicious model of *fengshui* topography.

The Yuanming Yuan occupied one of the best lots in the area. The arrangement of its general layout was in distinctive harmony. The numerous artificial hills in the imperial garden could be deliberately made in accordance to geomatic theories. The color pictures of the Forty Views clearly show respectively man-made structures in a secluded spot, where a loft mountain range called "Azure Dragon" and a lower ridge called "White Tiger" converge. Each of the scenes, in a sense, represents an auspicious model in geomantic terms.

The imperial garden's *fengshui* seems too good to be found fault with. Hence even in the wake of its calamity, the eventual burning down, no one seemed to have taken the advantage of hindsight and blamed the bad geomancy for its ultimate fate. There is, however, an interesting minor charge. According to a Qing scholar, in 1839, the Daoguang emperor tore down an arch-shape bridge outside the Inner Gate of the original Yuanming Yuan for his convenience to watch target shooting. The scholar cited a geomancer as saying that a river needs its bridge just like a bow its target, and by removing the bridge it symbolized the targetless bow, a bad omen for the decline of the military. China's defeat in the Opium War in the years that followed made the scholar feel that the geomancer's predestination seemed to have come true (Yao Yuanzhi 1982, 5).

Chapter 2

DISPOSITION

 The Yuanming Yuan imperial garden consisted of the most magnificent architectural works the Qing Empire ever created. It represents a glory in the Chinese cultural tradition and the pinnacle of Chinese garden arts.

The site on which the Yuanming Yuan was built is a plain rich in fresh water at the foot of the Jade Spring Hills near present-day Haidian, northwest of Beijing. The water from the Jade Spring has been described as cool and clear, to be admired as "pearls under moonlight" *(mingyue yeying qingguang yuan)* (Liu Tong and Yu Yizheng 1980, 297). The plentiful spring accounts for the abundant groundwater in Haidian and its neighborhood. In fact, *"dian"* means the place where water runs together (Jing Yikui 1980, 69). Moreover, the terrain allowed a gigantic garden to achieve its maximum aesthetic effects. As the great modern Chinese architect Liang Sicheng summarizes, the Yuanming Yuan was essentially a design of hillocks and lakes with buildings, courts, chambers, pavilions, arbors, and other structures in between. Even though symmetry and balance were stressed, Liang goes on, greater emphasis was placed on variations and liveliness in accordance with topography to the extent of being unconventional. Although the garden, for Liang's critical eyes, perhaps contained too many man-made structures, which jeopardized the beauty of the landscape, he has no doubt about its lively creativity (1985, 3:225, 231).

A more recent scholar has called the Yuanming Yuan the "the garden of ten-thousand gardens" *(wanyuan zhi yuan)* in reference to its ingenious and judicious disposition on a large lake and near the tall West Hills in the neighborhood (Chen Congzhou 1994, 5). Indeed, due to the excellent location, pleasant country homes appeared here as early as the Yuan dynasty in the thirteenth century. By the sixteenth century, natural beauty made this region so attractive that the Marquis Li Wei of the Ming was inspired to construct the well-known Clear Flowery Garden (Qinghua Yuan), which had claims to be "the leading garden in the region" *(jingguo diyiyuan)*. Shortly afterward, the distinguished calligrapher Mi Wanzhong built the equally famous Ladle Garden (Shao Yuan) in this area. Both celebrated gardens, according to the Peking University scholar Hou Renzhi, deteriorated during the transition from the Ming to the Qing (1991, 99).

The Qing rulers constructed gardens in the Haidian region all over again. As the three available maps show, the Yuanming Yuan contained vast lakes connected by a network of canals and winding waterways. From a bird's eye view, all of the structures in the garden appear to have been situated on islets or spits of land surrounded by artificial hills, terraces, hollow rocks, and blooming trees and shrubs. The specially named "scenes" *(jing)* comprised a series of independent and yet cohesive smaller gardens. And this huge park, as a Briton observed, "contained a vast variety of elegant little buildings" (Holmes 1798, 134).

In 1737, the second year of his reign, Qianlong instructed the distinguished court artists Castiglione, Tang Dai, Sun You, Shen Yuan, Zhang Wanbang, and Ding Guanpeng to draw a silk map of the Yuanming Yuan. Once completed, it was hung on the north wall of the Clear Sunshine Belvedere (Qinghui Ge). The belvedere was situated on the west side of the royal living room at the center of the Nine Continents. Its structure, a simple rectangle with elaborate motifs and decorations carved on the posts and beams by carpenters, fit beautifully in the landscape and among other surrounding structures. Noticeably, it had a large overhang to protect the inhabitants from foul weather and was carefully painted to protect it from decay. The right angles and axial symmetry reflected the sublime order. This was the place where the emperor and his companions enjoyed the quiet pleasures of composing poems, drawing pictures, and admiring the landscape (cf. Yu Mingzhong 1985, 2:1333–1334).

The famous Forty (Best) Views *(sishi jing)* of the Yuanming Yuan were completed and designated in 1744, of which twelve views, or scenes, were constructed after Qianlong became emperor in 1736. Even though Yongzheng had completed so many of the forty views, Qianlong continued to refurbish all the views extensively. The urbane Qianlong gave every one of the Forty Views a cultured name with an explanatory poem (*Yuanming Yuan sishijing tuyong* 1985). The emperor's practice was quite in line with what a refined scholar did for his private garden, that is to use an elegant name and poetic theme to make manifest a pictorial image of the uniquely created scene. Moreover, the proud Qianlong commissioned the court artists Shen Yuan and Tang Dai and the calligrapher Wang Youdun to produce a two-volume silk atlas, 2.6 feet high and 2.35 feet wide, to convey impressionistic images of all forty scenes. This set of pictures and poems was taken away by the French during the war of 1860, and it subsequently found a home in the Bibliotheque Nationale in Paris. The French gave the Chinese a duplicate color set of the atlas in 1983 (*Yuanming cangsang* 1991, 16; cf. Cai Shengzhi n.d., 135). The woodcut version of the same atlas signed by Sun Hu and Shen Yuan was published in the 1920s (Cheng Yansheng 1928, 1).

Different parts of the garden were reached by various roads that deliberately made "various turnings and windings" (Attiret 1982, 9). There was perhaps a geomantic element in it. Perhaps the evil spirits, which would travel in a straight line, would be diverted by a winding course. But turnings and windings also were essential for creating surprises. A narrow, tortuous, and dark mountain road would seem to guide viewers into a dead end, but before long a broad space would open to them. Suddenly they would be surprised by a view of elegant trees, blue sky, white cloud, flying birds, beautiful flowers, and a stream of water escaping down from higher ground into a pool. At that moment, they might even enjoy the clean and soft winds blowing from distant hills. Roads thus facilitated visitors' pleasure of admiring successively unfolding views from spot to spot. The element of surprise endorsed the art of mixing concealment *(cang)* and revelation *(lu)*. The European buildings at the northern end of the Eternal Spring Garden would seem to be hidden from the Chinese architectural structures by walls and hills, with only tall roofs visible from distance. But concealment was not used simply to communicate that "nothing Western could mar the harmony of the main garden" (Thiriez 1998, 51); it was used to create surprises as well.

Unlike the technique of concealment used to completely hide elements in prose or in a poem, concealment in the garden means to bring forth a reserved and implicit expression, thus unfolding scenes that cannot be viewed in a single glance.[1] The British took note of the effect of intricacy and concealment when they visited the Yuanming Yuan at the end of the eighteenth century. "At Yuen-min-yuen (Yuanming Yuan)," it is said, "a flight wall was made to convey the idea of a magnificent building, when seen at a certain distance through the branches of a thicket " (Staunton 1799, 2:114).

In addition to roads, a network of canals linked to almost every corner of the garden served the same purpose of circulation. Numerous barges and boats traveled in the garden. The successive Qing emperors all preferred smooth boat traveling. To facilitate this service, the Yuanming Yuan employed an increasing number of sailors, boathouse keepers, and boat repairmen. Since all these people lived and worked in the garden, they formed the garden's "boat household" *(chuanhu),* one of many households in the service of the emperor and the royal family.[2]

Scenic Structures in the Original Yuanming Yuan

The original configuration of the imperial garden before the completion of the Sea of Blessing (Fuhai) was square in shape. It consisted of three principal groups of man-made structures, namely, the administrative buildings, the royal residence compound, and a complex of rural scenes spreading along the central axis from south to north, in addition to numerous composite smaller enclosures scattered throughout the huge garden.

The main entrance, facing south, was named the Grand Palace Gate (Da'gongmen); it was one of the garden's eighteen major gates. On top of the gate hung a wooden tablet with three large Chinese characters, *yuan ming yuan,* in the style of Kangxi's calligraphy. Centered in front of the Grand Palace Gate was a five-column wide section of rooms used as office space for representatives from virtually all major government agencies, including the Grand Secretariat *(neige),* the six boards, Hanlin Academy, and the Bureau of the Clansmen (zongren fu). Beyond the main gate was the Inner Palace Gate, or the Gentlemen's Entrance (Churu Xianliang Men), guarded by a pair of gilt dragons across an arch bridge over a moat. On both sides of the entrance there were rooms for visitors to wait.

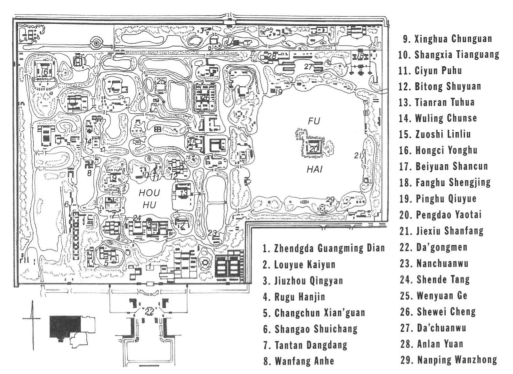

9. Xinghua Chunguan
10. Shangxia Tianguang
11. Ciyun Puhu
12. Bitong Shuyuan
13. Tianran Tuhua
14. Wuling Chunse
15. Zuoshi Linliu
16. Hongci Yonghu
17. Beiyuan Shancun
18. Fanghu Shengjing
19. Pinghu Qiuyue
20. Pengdao Yaotai
21. Jiexiu Shanfang

1. Zhendgda Guangming Dian
2. Louyue Kaiyun
3. Jiuzhou Qingyan
4. Rugu Hanjin
5. Changchun Xian'guan
6. Shangao Shuichang
7. Tantan Dangdang
8. Wanfang Anhe

22. Da'gongmen
23. Nanchuanwu
24. Shende Tang
25. Wenyuan Ge
26. Shewei Cheng
27. Da'chuanwu
28. Anlan Yuan
29. Nanping Wanzhong

Figure 3. Overview of the original Yuanming Yuan showing twenty-nine man-made structures or scenes mentioned in the book. Plan by Sylvia Lu Wong with reference to the map in YMYJ *1 between pp. 122–123 and to He Chongyi, Zeng Zhaofen's work in* YMYJ *1:81–92.*

This was the place where the emperor reviewed the annual archery contest of his troops (Yu Mingzhong 1985, 2:1325).

The grand Main Audience Hall (Zhengda Guangming Dian), the name of which means open-mindedness and magnanimousness appropriate to a great ruler, stood at a central position inside the Inner Palace Gate. This piece of architecture was a replica of the imperial audience hall called Great Harmony Hall (Taihe Dian) in the Forbidden City. It was "well adorned exteriorly with paint and gilding, and netted with iron wire under the fretted eaves to keep the birds off" (Yu Mingzhong 1985, 2:1326). The hall had seven columns made of solid wood, 129 feet long and 63 feet wide, sitting on a 4–foot-high terrace of round stone pedestals, each 2 feet 9 inches in diameter. Inside, an "antithetical couplet" *(duilian)* written by Emperor Yongzheng himself was displayed on a pair of scrolls hanging on each side of the hall in symmetrical fashion. The building's floors were paved with *dalishi* (slabs of a white marble veined in black) 2 feet square and about 3 inches thick on a brick-lime foundation ascended by three sets of stone steps. In the front there was an open courtyard with two side halls *(piandian)* on each side, and in the back a rock hill resembling a gigantic jade bamboo shoot in upright form. This hall was the place where the emperor met with his officials and foreign dignitaries as well as served banquets, in particular the grand banquets for such special occasions as the emperor's birthday, and the metropolitan examinations. In general, this administrative section, with the Main Audience Hall as its principal structure, is a large enclosure surrounded by walls. Looking out from inside one

could catch the pleasant views of dark-foliaged trees and flowers mixed red with purple. With the rise of the imperial garden's political stature, this audience hall soon acquired two wings. The east wing provided office space for the grand councilors *(junji),* who made policy decisions on a daily basis, while the west wing was used as waiting rooms (Yu Mingzhong 1985, 2:1326; Swinhoe 1861, 294; cf. Malone 1934, 75–76). The Qianlong emperor designated this place the first of his Forty Views.

To the east of the Main Audience Hall was the Diligent Court, or the Royal Office Room (Qinzheng Dian). It contained a large compound of halls, with the Baohe and Taihe Courts in the middle sandwiched by the Flush Spring Chamber (Fuchun Lou) in the back and the Fragrant Azure Grove (Fangbi Cong) in the front. This court was the place in which the Qing emperors summoned officials, read memorials, or ate simple meals; comparable with the Qianqing Palace in the Forbidden City. A large screen behind the throne in the main office room showed two big Chinese characters, *wu yi,* meaning not to indulge in pleasure (Yu Mingzhong 1985, 2:1330–1331; *Yuanming Yuan sishijing tuyong* 1985, 9; cf. Zhu Jiajin and Li Yeqin, comps. 1983, 2:55). This place provided the Qing emperors from Yongzheng onward with the administrative space to conduct state affairs. Qianlong designated it as the scene of the "Diligent and Talented Government" *(qinzheng qingxian).*

Behind this administrative section across the Front Lake (Qianhu) was the royal residential area called Nine Continents, consisting of nine islets, connected by bridges and encircling the 200–square foot Rear Lake (Houhu).[3] The so-called Nine Continents, ostensibly from the Confucian *Book of History*, refer to the known world in ancient China (*Shujing* 1911, 2:1). The Yongzheng emperor, who named this area, wanted to signify his universal empire surrounded by the seas and to symbolize "all under heaven" *(tianxia)* under peace and prosperity. I contest that neither Yongzheng nor Qianlong ever considered the miniature Nine Continents to be an example of the "last radiance of the setting sun" *(huiguang fanzhao)* in the history of the imperial garden construction. I think that it is a misunderstanding for Wang Yi to assert that creating the immense universe in miniature unknowingly displayed the loss of a broad intellectual vista and a sign of the decline of the imperial grandeur (1990, 177–181). It is a remarkable art to "create a world in a pot." Rather than losing a broad intellectual vista, such a design implies exactly the majestic worldview the imperial ruler entertained. It is in effect a vital aesthetic element in the Chinese garden art, which allows a small man-made structure to symbolize the immense nature, not just a part of the earth but also a part of the universe. As a matter of fact, most classical Chinese gardens are enclosed within a limited area but with the clear intention of creating a sense of infinite space. The creation of spaciousness is the essence of garden art. Condensation that produces the effect of making the small look like the spacious is no doubt a refined technique. And the Nine Continents in the Yuanming Yuan are precisely the grand center of this magnificent imperial garden symbolizing the universal Chinese world. It is surely through symbolism that the feeling of grandness rather than smallness communicated.

The islet on the north-south axis in the Nine Continents accommodated three architectural units in a row from north to south, namely, the seven-column-wide Nine Continents in Peace Hall (Jiuzhou Qingyan), the Honoring Three Selflessnesses Court (Feng

Figure 5. Jiuzhou Qingyan (Nine Continents in Peace), the royal living quarters. Sketch by Joseph C. Wang and Xingbai Yue.

Sanwusi Dian), and the five column-wide Yuanming Yuan court facing the Front Lake. The row of three courts laid on the central axis with the Grand Palace Gate. On the east side of these courts stood Family of Spring Between Heaven and Earth (Tiandi Yijiachun) and the Benevolence Receiving Hall (Cheng'en Tang). The latter hall housed apartments for imperial ladies to live. On the west side of these three courts was the eminent Clear Sunshine Belvedere (Qinghui Ge) in which, on its northern wall, the map of the Yuanming Yuan was hung between 1737 and 1860. Sandwiched between two small lakes, the emperor's own bedroom was also located in this vast compound, which Qianlong designated as the Nine Continents in Peace (Yu Mingzhong 1985, 2:1331–1332; Wang Wei 1992, 21). This designation seems to suggest that the emperor wished to survey "all under heaven" in microcosm.

The imperial bedroom and seraglio in the Nine Continents were forbidden ground, and yet the European visitor Father Attiret was able to see them. He found there "all the most beautiful things that can be imagined as to furniture, ornaments, and paintings. . . . [There are] the most valuable sorts of wood; varnished works, of China and Japan; ancient vases of porcelain; silks, and cloth of gold and silver. They have there brought together, all that. Art and good taste could add to the riches of nature" (Attiret 1982, 23). In 1860, when the European invaders seized the garden, a British officer saw the royal living quarters where "a large niche in the wall, curtained over and covered with silk mattresses, served for the bed; and a sloping platform enabled his majesty to mount into it." Under a pillow, the Briton noticed "a small silk handkerchief with sundry writings in the vermillion pencil about the barbarians." Near the bed on a table there were "pipes and other Chinese luxuries" (Swinhoe 1861, 298). This description at least reflects the setup of His Majesty's bedroom during the Xianfeng emperor's time.

Figure 6. *Jiuzhou Qingyan showing Feng Sanwusi Dian (Honoring Three Selflessnesses Court) in the lower center. Plan by Joseph C. Wang and Xingbai Yue.*

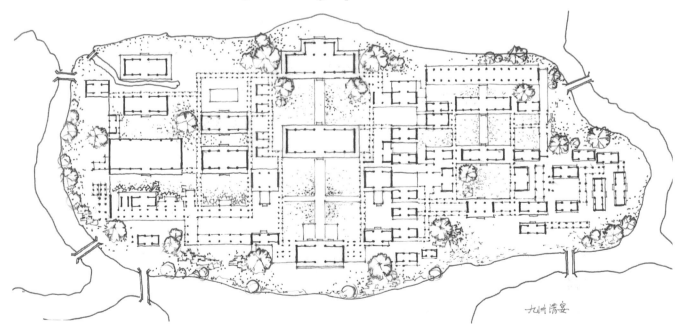

九州清宴

Figure 7. *Louyue Kaiyun (Engraved Moon and Unfolding Clouds) showing Ji'en Tang (the Memorial Hall) in the background. Plan by Joseph C. Wang and Xingbai Yue.*

On the second islet of the Nine Continents sat the famous Peony Terrace (Mudan Tai), which Qianlong eventually designated the scene of the Engraved Moon and Unfolding Clouds (Louyue Kaiyun). Its main hall in the front was built using precious nanmu *(Phoebe nanmu)* timber with tiles in splendid green and gold, yielding a look of resplendence. The elegant-looking gallery behind the main hall was named the Imperial Orchid Fragrance (Yulanfen). Further back was an expansive complex of structures consisting of the Memorial Hall (Ji'en Tang) in the middle, the Nourishing Simplicity Study (Yangsu Shuwu) to the west, and the Resting Cloud Chamber (Qiyun Lou) to the east (Yu Mingzhong 1985, 2:1336; *Yuanming Yuan sishijing tuyong* 1985: 13). The central theme of this scene was the peony. The great Song philosopher Zhou Dunyi (1017–1073) had designated this particular flower to symbolize riches and honor, and Kangxi identified ninety different kinds of peony in his imperial garden (Wu Zhenyu 1983, 278). Every blossom season, normally late spring, when hundreds of peonies came into bloom, the Qing emperors arrived at the terrace to observe the magnificent "embroidery view" against the background of enormous green pines. It is not at all surprising that Qianlong found the Peony Terrace his favorite place to compose poems.[4]

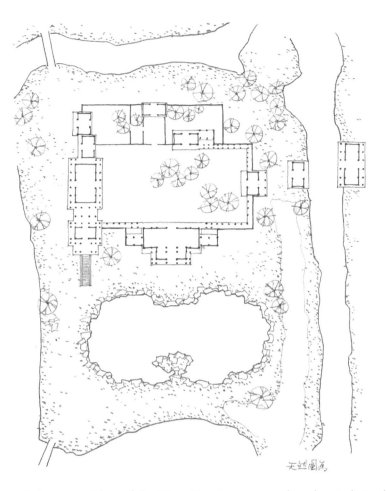

The remaining seven islets of the Nine Continents complete the circle in the following order. At the northeast corner of Rear Lake was the Natural Scenery (Tianran Tuhua), which is also the name of its principal structure standing in the middle with two wings. Its west side included a pavilion and a chamber, and its east side included the Five-Fortunes Hall (Wufu Tang). In front of this scenery extended a large courtyard featuring numerous phoenix trees in the midst of a bamboo grove. Crossing a stream over a flat bridge from the site of the Five-Fortunes Hall, one arrived at the Blue Phoenix-Tree Academy (Bitong Shuyuan). Its main structure, facing south, included a three-column front house, a five-column main court, and a five-column rear court. Tidy Wutong trees grew on each side of the courtyards to provide long shade over the houses, which appeared to be hidden. Qianlong is said to have loved coming here to hear the sounds of rain, which inspired him to write poems. Westward from the academy was the Gentle Clouds Cover All (Ciyun Puhu). With the unique Bell Tower (Zhong Lou) at its back and slightly to the west, the three column-wide main front court named the Happy Buddhist Ground (Huanxi Fochang) faced the Rear Lake to the south. To the north of the court, beside a Daoist shrine, was a three-story chamber in which Avalokitesvara and Guan Gong, the legendary military hero, were worshipped. To the east of the main court stood the Court for the God of Rain (Longwang Dian) for worshipping the Yuanming Yuan's Dragon King named Zhaofu. The name *Gentle Clouds Cover All* obviously refers to the merciful protection over all souls (Yu Mingzhong 1985, 2:1337–1340).

One left this religious land over a stone bridge westward to the Sky in Reflections (Shangxia Tianguang). Its main structure, a two-story chamber overlooking the Rear Lake, was a replica of the famous Yueyang Chamber (Yueyang Lou) at the Tongting Lake in the central Yangzi valley. On both sides of the chamber extended two narrow banks like rainbows, and at the middle of them stood a hexagonal arbor. Behind the chamber was a compound of smaller structures called the Silent Courtyard (Ping'an Yuan), where the Nine Continents made a southwest turn to the islet named the Apricot-Flower Villa (Xinghua Chunguan). The villa was composed of the Apricot Grove (Xinghua Cun), the Spring Rain Gallery (Chunyu Xuan), the Green Shady Hall (Cuiwei Tang), the Restrained Chapel (Yi Zhai), and the Water Reflection Chapel (Jingshui Zhai). Yongzheng had created this scene, while Qianlong embellished it and designated it as one of the Forty Views. Qianlong liked to come here in late spring when flowers blossomed, and he described the view as splendid as the "rosy rays of light" (Yu Mingzhong 1985, 3:1341).

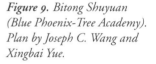

Figure 9. Bitong Shuyuan (Blue Phoenix-Tree Academy). Plan by Joseph C. Wang and Xingbai Yue.

Figure 10. Principal building on Shangxia Tianguang (Sky in Reflections). Sketch by Joseph C. Wang and Xingbai Yue.

The islet on which stood the Apricot-Flower Villa was connected to the Magnanimous World (Tantan Dangdang) by the Blue Wave Bridge (Bilan Qiao). Its front structure had three sections: the Pure Heart Hall (Suxin Tang) in the middle, the Knowing-Fish Arbor (Zhiyu Ting) to the northeast, and the Double Beauty Chapel (Shuangjia Zhai) to the northwest. Behind the front structure was the Splendid Wind and Moon (Guangfeng Jiyue). The unique feature of this scene was the square fish pond, which was very much to the pleasure of Qianlong who cited in a poem the saying of the great Daoist philosopher Zhuangzi: "See how the minnows are darting about! Such is the pleasure that fish enjoy" (Wang Xianqian 1972, 108). South of this scene, the islet named the Harmony of the Past with the Present (Rugu Hanjin) sat at the southwest corner of the Rear Lake and connected by bridges to the main living quarters and to the Eternal Spring Fairy Hall

Figure 11. Tantan Dangdang (Magnanimous World). Sketch by Joseph C. Wang and Xingbai Yue.

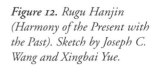

Figure 12. Rugu Hanjin (Harmony of the Present with the Past). Sketch by Joseph C. Wang and Xingbai Yue.

(Changchun Xian'guan). All galleries, chapels, and studios here were built in a large square lot connected by delightful winding corridors. In designating this scene, Qianlong quoted the great Tang poet Du Fu: "While I hold my contemporaries with no contempt, I have my affection for the ancients" (Yu Mingzhong 1985, 3:1341–1343; cf. *Yuanming Yuan sishijing tuyong* 1985, 10–27). The scenes on the nine islets arguably constituted the best of the Forty Views.

Across the Nine Continents to the west was the Swastika House. Qianlong designated it as the Universal Peace (Wanfang Anhe), with houses constructed in a swastika shape on a lake.[5] Cool in summer and warm in winter, the houses were built on a solid brick foundation surrounded by water. Here the Qianlong emperor was especially fascinated by the inverted golden reflections of the swastika formation in the lake under the autumn moon. The golden reflections recalled the brilliant light of the Buddha (*Yuanming sishijing tuyong* 1985, 31). Other scenic sites with ostensible religious significance included the better-known Cloud-Living on the Moon Land (Yuedi Yunju), a secluded enclosure surrounded by short red walls and green pines and sitting at the northern end of the Drill Field. Its main building faced a stream in the front and was backed by a small hill. This was a favorite place for members of the royal family to perform their Buddhist worship (Yu Mingzhong 1985, 3:1347; *Yuanming yuan sishijing tuyong* 1985, 37).

Just north of the Swastika House was the Peach-Blossom Cove (Taohua Wu). This scene recalls the famous legend invented by the third-century poet Tao Qian (372–427), also known as Tao Yuanming. In the legend, a fisherman loses his way and discovers a hidden paradise called the Peach-Blossom Cove in which people live happily without knowing the outside world. The fisherman returns home and tells the story, but he cannot find the cove again. The lost cove has since inspired Chinese literati into utopian thoughts of

Figure 13. Rugu Hanjin showing the principal building in the front. Plan by Joseph C. Wang and Xingbai Yue.

Figure 14. *Wanfang Anhe (Universal Peace) showing the Swastika House. Sketch by Joseph C. Wang and Xingbai Yue.*

Figure 15. *Wanfang Anhe showing Ping'an Yuan adjacent to the Swastika House. Plan by Joseph C. Wang and Xingbai Yue.*

a legendary happy land. The Peach-Blossom Cove contained a series of halls and galleries. The hall named Deep Source of Peach Blossom (Taoyuan Shenchu) at the northeast end (*Yuanming yuan sishijing tuyong* 1985, 33) was created by Yongzheng, who was very pleased with the ingenious design and inscribed with his own calligraphy names for each chamber on the horizontal board.[6] Qianlong designated this cove Spring Beauty at Wuling (Wuling Chunse) and selected it as one of the Forty Views (Yu Mingzhong 1985, 3:1347–1348).

The Drill Field was located at the southwest corner of the original Yuanming Yuan. It featured a review stand and a large flat field for military exercises. Qianlong designated it as the High-Reaching Mountain and Outstretched River (Shangao Shuichang) (*Yuanming yuan sishijing tuyong* 1985, 35). Across the Cloud-Living on the Moon Land and in the northwest corner, Qianlong spent 600,000 taels to complete the Ancestral Shrine in 1742. The main structure, called Blessing Palace (Anyou Gong), was set all the way back in the middle facing south (*Yuanming yuan sishijing tuyong* 1985, 39).

Unlike most other structures in the garden, the construction materials of the Ancestral Shrine were mainly stone and marble. In the distance from the entrance, one could observe two pairs of "ornamental columns" (*huabiao*)[7] in front of the Memorial Archways (*paifang*), which was crowned with light yellow glazed tiles and eaves. The columns, each standing twenty feet high and about a hundred feet apart, were surrounded by four marble pillars carved with dragons, clouds, and flames alongside a marble balustrade and a stone animal. Five parallel marble bridges crossed a moat with three screen-shaped memorial archways that led to the palatial gates. Each bridge was guarded by two stone Chinese unicorns, or *kylin (qilin),* approximately 174 centimeters tall on 98–centimeter-high stone platforms (cf. *YMYJ* 1983, 3:133). The gates led the way to the shrine's tall, reddish outer wall, which was crowned with a yellow glazed tile roof. The inner wall was also red and covered by a yellow glazed tile roof. Inside the courtyard were the waiting rooms. The main gate stood

***Figure 16.** Ping'an Yuan (Silent Court) in Wanfang Anhe. Sketch by Joseph C. Wang and Xingbai Yue.*

on top of a splendid marble terrace ascended by marble stairs and balustrade, and a pair of bridges stretched across a moat. On both sides of a vast courtyard were guestrooms, two large incense burners, and a pair of pavilions with double roofs. The main shrine palace stood on a large marble terrace ascended by five stairways escorted by bronze animal figures. The central stairway, which was richly decorated with carved dragons, was reserved for the emperor's use only. Qianlong designated it the Most Kindness and Eternal Blessing (Hongci Yonghu). Inside the shrine, Qianlong placed the portraits and name tablets of Yongzheng and Kangxi to show his affection for his deceased forefathers. After Qianlong died, his own portrait and memorial tablet were placed here for remembrance and

***Figure 17.** The principal structure of Wuling Chunse (Spring Beauty at Wuling). Sketch by Joseph C. Wang and Xingbai Yue.*

Figure 18. The Ancestral Shrine
showing the Anyou Palace (top).
Plan by Joseph C. Wang and
Xingbai Yue.

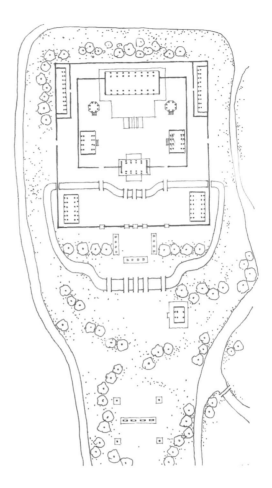

worshipping by his successor. The shrine, to which the Manchu royal family always attached great importance, would have been considered a truly exceptional structure in any type of garden (Yu Mingzhong 1985, 3:1351–1353; Zhao Lian 1980, 391).

To the east of the Ancestral Shrine was the Faculty Club (Huifang Shuyuan). It consisted of such structures as the Expressing Excellence Gallery (Shuzao Xuan) in the front, the Conceiving Distance Chapel (Hanyuan Zhai) in the rear, the Relaxation Room (Sui'an Shi) to the west, and the Lofty Clouds Chamber (Zhuoyun Lou) to the east. Further east from the Faculty Club was the Half-Moon Gallery (Meiyue Xuan). South of the gallery between an arbor and a chamber stood an open-air structure, about three column-wide, facing the uniquely designed scene called Traces of Snow on a Broken Bridge (Duanqiao Canxue) (cf. Yu Mingzhong 1985, 3:1354; *Yuanming yuan sishijing tuyong* 1985, 41). The bridge was made of broken rocks in dozens of different shapes, some of which are still visible at the present-day ruin site.

Below the Faculty Club was a religious complex that emulated the famous Lamaist temple known as Yonghe Gong in Beijing. It had three sections: two rows of seven-column chambers connected by two hallways to the west; three rows of seven-column chambers in the middle; and the Good Omen Palace (Ruiying Gong) comprising three Buddhist-style courts to the east. Qianlong designated this Buddhist compound the Dazzling Eaves under Heaven (Ritian Linyu) (cf. Yu Mingzhong 1985, 3:1355; *Yuanming yuan sishijing tuyong* 1985: 43).

East of the religious complex was the largest scenic point, approximately twelve acres, with several magnificent pieces of architecture, including the nine-column principal structure surrounded by hills and brooks. One of the unique features of this scene was the great number of lotuses floating in shallow water. It is well known to Chinese literati that the great Song philosopher Zhou Dunyi (Zhou Lianxi, 1017–1073) authored the celebrated essay "Passion for Lotus" (Ailian shuo) to compare the lotus to gentlemen. Qianlong appreciated the essay and thus dubbed this scene the Scholar's Wonderland (Lianxi Lechu) to indicate that he would be content to be surrounded by well-bred gentlemen.

Walking further to the east in a bookish journey, we observe the Sounds of Wood and Water (Shuimo Mingse) with a Western-style water wheel pumping water into a room. The sounds of water, *sese, lingling,* echoing the rustling woods, helped the emperor attain a lofty realm which combines kindness with wisdom (cf. Yu Mingzhong 1985, 3:1362; *Yuanming yuan sishijing tuyong*: 1985:49, 51).

Several rural scenes appeared around the northern end of the original Yuanming Yuan. The Yongzheng emperor first created a farm in the garden to remind himself of the daily basis of rural China, where millions of subjects lived (Yu Mingzhong 1985, 3:1356).[8] His Majesty could observe from a pavilion how farm work was performed. Later he added to this rice field a silkworm farm and a brocade and dye mill. Ever since the Wei-Jin period, between the third and fourth centuries, the Chinese literati continuously tried to find their own distinct character in the expression of garden design in general and flower arrangement and rock formation in particular. While some wanted to show their unique ambition, others wanted to demonstrate their stainless, magnanimous, or aloof personalities. Character and

Figure 19. The main structure of Lianxi Lechu (Scholar's Wonderland). Sketch by Joseph C. Wang and Xingbai Yue.

taste have long since been considered the "soul" of a garden and of its owner. Clearly mindful of his responsibility to diligently attend to government affairs and the people's welfare, Yongzheng purposefully created a farm scene inside his beloved imperial garden to show his concern about the people as well as to underline his benevolent rule. It seems quite clear that the emperor used this theme to make a political claim to be a conscientious ruler of the majority farming population as well as to rehearse the self-serving Confucian moral ideology.

Qianlong designated five rural scenes. The one at the southeast neighborhood of the Sounds of Wood and Water (Shuimu Mingse) was dominated by a house in the shape of a gigantic Chinese ideogram, *tian,* meaning "rice field," which the emperor dubbed Simple Life in Quietude (Danpo Ningjing), with the Rising Sunshine Chamber (Shuguang Lou) at its side. There were four other rural scenes. The Bountiful Farms (Duojia Ruyun) was a large rice field with a few small houses. The Orchid Fragrance over the Water (Yingshui Lanxiang) consisted of rice fields, weaving mills, and fishing ponds. The Fish-Leaping and Bird-Flying (Yuyue Yuanfei) contained numerous village huts surrounded by a stream. And the Northernmost Mountain Village (Beiyuan Shancun), originally known as Teaching

Figure 20. Maimaijie (Shopping Street) at Zuoshi Linliu (Sitting Rocks and the Winding Stream). Sketch by Joseph C. Wang and Xingbai Yue.

ZUOSHI LINLIU

1. **SHEWEI CHENG**
   (Wall of Sravasti)

2. **LAN TING** *(Orchid Pavilion)*

3. **MAIMAIJIE**
   (Shopping Street)

4. **DA'XITAI** *(Theatre)*

5. **QINGYIN GE**
   (The Clear-Sound Pavilion)

6. **TONGLE YUAN**
   (All-Happy Garden)

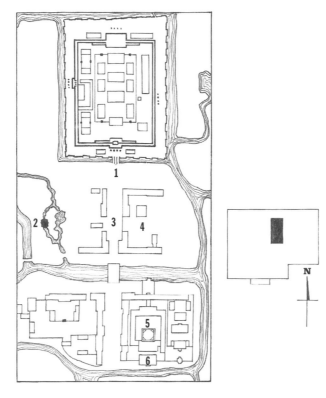

Figure 21. Shewei Cheng (Wall of Sravasti), Maimaijie (Shopping Street), and Tongle Yuan (All-Happy Garden) in Zhuoshi Linliu. Plan by Sylvia Lu Wong.

Farming Gallery (Kenong Xuan), contained rows of small yet elegant chambers and villas on both sides of a narrow river (cf. Yu Mingzhong 1985, 3:1341–1375; *Yuanming yuan sishijing tuyong* 1985:45, 47, 53, 55, 57).

On the east side of the Northernmost Mountain Village arose the Sitting Rocks and the Winding Stream (Zuoshi Linliu), which included a replica of the celebrated Orchid Pavilion (Lan Ting) located at Shaoxing in Zhejiang province. The Orchid Pavilion was the garden estate of the great East Jin calligrapher Wang Xizhi (321–379), who spent time there in the company of scholarly friends drinking wine, practicing calligraphy, and composing poems. When reciting poems outdoors, they sat on rocks and set their drinking cups in the nearby stream to see which cup would float downstream.[9] Qianlong, a poet in his own right, delighted in recreating Wang's pleasure. Other structures to enrich the scene included the Clear Sound Pavilion (Qingyin Ge) and the All-Happy Garden (Tongle Yuan), where Qianlong dined frequently. Directly adjacent to this pavilion and garden was the Curving Courtyard and Lotus Pond (Quyuan Fenghe), modeled after the famed lotus view from Hangzhou's West Lake. A nine-hole bridge *(jiukong qiao)* bisected the large rectangular pond. The three-mile-long left bank was also a replica of the famous Su Dongpu Bank in the West Lake (cf. *Yuanming yuan sishijing tuyong* 1885, 80–83; Yu Mingzhong 1985, 3:1376). These are the scenes that Qianlong brought back to the Yuanming Yuan from his southern tours.

Figure 22. Shewei Cheng (Wall of Sravatis) as depicted in the Forty Views *by the eighteenth-century court artist Tang Dai.*

The Majestic Sunset-Tinted Peaks of the West Hills (Xifeng Xiuse) was located at the northeast corner of the original Yuanming Yuan. It featured a sumptuous chamber designed especially for the Yongzheng emperor to admire the sunset. The design was to bring the magnificent mountain view of sunsets into the broad and bright windows on the west side of the chamber, a good example of the "view borrowing" technique. In fact, as Yongzheng's poem indicates, this design borrowed from the sunset view at the famed Mountain Lu (Lushan) in Jiangxi province (Yu Mingzhong 1985, 3:1365; cf. commentaries in *Yuanming yuan tuyong* 1987). East of this viewing chamber was a larger structure named the Hanyuan Zhai surrounded by magnolia trees, which fill the air with fragrance when they blossom. Northeast of the chapel was the delightful Admiring Fish at the Flourish Haven (Huagang Guanyu), built to observe countless gold fish in a stream. At the foot of a nearby hill was the Cave of the Three Fairies (Sanxian Dong), which was large enough to accommodate two hundred persons (Yu Mingzhong 1985, 3:1365–1366; *Yuanming yuan sishijing tuyong* 1985, 59). Qianlong gladly included this in his Forty Views.

Let us now turn our gaze to the southeastern edge of the garden entrance to find a small garden designated as the secluded Deep Vault of Heaven (Dongtian Shenchu). It was the campus of the royal school and comprised rows of elegant classrooms and dormitories concealed in a bamboo grove, orchids, and pine trees. Both Yongzheng and Qianlong attended school here when they were princes (cf. Qianlong's 1744 poems in Yu Mingzhong 1985, 3:1378).[10] On the other side of the entrance stood the Eternal Spring Fairy Hall (Changchun Xian'guan), where Qianlong resided as crown prince for many years. It consisted of a three-column-wide front structure, a five-column-wide main building dubbed the Green Shade Gallery (Lüyin Xuan) in the rear, and a compound of galleries, studios, chapels, halls, and rooms to the west. After Prince Hongli had become Emperor Qianlong, he invited his beloved mother to live here (cf. Qianlong's poem in *Yuanming yuan tuyong* 1987; *Qingshigao* 1976, 14:3862–3863, Chong Xian 1984, 240–262; Yu Mingzhong 1985, 3:1349–1350).

Scenes Surrounding the Lake

The second phase of construction in the Yuanming Yuan extended eastward to surround the largest lake of the garden, known as the Sea of Blessing (Fuhai). The square lake was about 700 meters on each side, which yielded the impression of a broad, extensive surface as well as a feeling of openness. The lake's shore, which was supported by stone precipices, projected crumbling cliffs. There were steps leading to a half-moon shaped terrace, which in turn led to a tree-lined boulevard embellished with colorful flowers. The open space around the lake was ideal for watching fireworks after sunset. When fireworks lit up the dark sky, lanterns of different colors and various shapes were normally hung on top of numerous buildings. Qianlong enjoyed sitting at the lakeside under the full moon. Attiret, who often accompanied the emperor on his boating trips, calculated the lake to be "very near five miles round" and considered it "one of the most beautiful parts in the whole pleasure ground" (Attiret 1982, 16). The calculation was obviously the priest's impression rather than an accurate measurement. It is no doubt an artistic success to yield such a sense of extensiveness. The Yongzheng emperor first called it a "sea" (hai), with the deliberate intention of exaggerating.

At the center of the lake was the Fairy's Islet (Penglai Zhou), designed on the basis of a fairy tale drawn by the great Tang artist Li Sixun (651–716). Together with Wu Daozi, Li

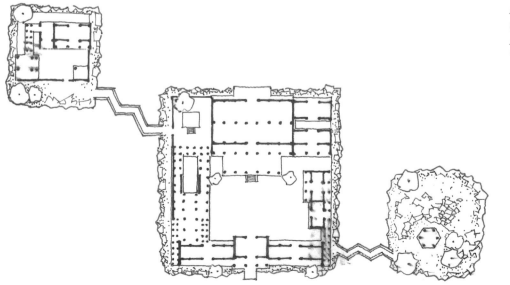

Figure 23. Pengdao Yaotai (Immortal Abode on the Fairy Islet). Sketch by Joseph C. Wang and Xingbai Yue.

was one of the most accomplished painters in the tradition of Chinese landscape painting established since the Six Dynasties period.[11] This technique gives landscape painting a three-dimensional prospect. The designer of the Fairy's Islet evidently had in mind the surrounding topography and views, so that the whole landscape and architecture were dynamically adapted into the scenic environment. When designating his Forty Views, Qianlong called the Fairy's Islet the Immortal Abode on the Fairy Terrace (Pengdao Yaotai).

The Fairy's Islet, rising six feet above the surface of the water, actually comprised three islets with the large one at the center named the Fairy Terrace. Exactly square in shape, this terrace accommodated a dozen splendid chambers, principally the Reflection Pavilion (Jingzhong Ge) to the north, the Mind-Opening Chamber (Changjin Lou) to the east, and the World of Paradise (Jile Shijie), for the performance of either Buddhist or Daoist rites, to the west. The small islet to the southeast was called the Fairy Hill at the Sea (Yinghai Xianshan), while the Jade House on North Isle (Beidao Yuyu) was located to the northwest. The Fairy Terrace compound, which had four facades, each overlooking the large lake with "shining reflections of the colorful chambers," gave rise to a magnificent overall view (Yu Mingzhong 1985, 3:1371). Every man-made structure was half hidden in the midst of

Figure 24. The principal structure of Pengdao Yaotai. Sketch by Joseph C. Wang and Xingbai Yue.

misty hills to project the image of a fairy tale. Fully charmed by this scene, which he referred to as the Big Rock, Father Attiret described it as having "inexpressible beauty and taste":

> From it you have a view of all the palaces, scattered at proper distances round the shores of this sea; all the hills, that terminate about it; all the rivulets, which tend thither, either to discharge their waters into it, or to receive them from it; all the bridges, either at the mouths or ends of these rivulets; all the pavilions, and triumphal arches, that adorn any of these bridges; and all the groves, that are planted to separate and screen the different palaces, and to prevent the Inhabitants of them from being overlooked by one another.[12]

Figure 25. Pengdao Yaotai (Immortal Abode on the Fairy Terrace) as depicted in the Forty Views *by the eighteenth-century court artist Shen Yun.*

The Fairy Islet could only be reached by boat. Yongzheng regularly sailed on the lake with his favorite relatives and officials. His dragon barge was lavishly built. Normally a fleet of thirty boats followed the emperor's lead. Qianlong seemed to have enjoyed boating even more. He started the popular dragon boat race here to celebrate the Mid-May Festival Day (Duanwu Jie) annually (Zhao Lian 1980, 378). Attiret also had the privilege to observe this particular festival with the emperor on the scene. He noted that numerous boats on the lake, either gilt or varnished, served different purposes: "sometimes, for taking the air; sometimes, for fishing; and sometimes, for jousts, and combats, and other diversions" (Attiret 1982, 20–21). In the summer of 1860, the Xianfeng emperor had the pleasure of boating on the lake for the last time. Only four months later, the foreign invasion destroyed the garden (*Yuanming cangsang* 1991, 11).

The most impressive structure surrounding the Sea of Blessing was the so-called A Wonderland in the Square Pot (Fanghu Shengjing), which the Qianlong emperor completed in 1740. Situated at the northeast corner of the lake, with the Welcoming Warm Wind Arbor (Yingxun Ting) in front, was Wonderland's principal structure, a pair of chambers with gold glazed tiles. The Fine-Brocaded Chamber (Jinqi Lou) to the east and the Green Pyroxene Chamber (Feicui Lou) to the west stretched forward like two arms. Behind the two chambers rose a large enclosure surrounded by decorated gates and courtyards replete with pines, magnolias, common trees, and incense ornaments. In the front section of the enclosure, a colorful court was sandwiched by the Purple Cloud Chamber (Zixia Lou) to the east and the Blue Cloud Chamber (Biyun Lou) to the west.

Surrounding the enclosure were the Flowery Chamber (Qionghua Lou) sandwiched by the Ample Luck Court (Qianxiang Dian) and the Abundant Fortune Pavilion (Wanfu Ge). To the east of the enclosure was the Pistillate Pearl Palace (Ruizhu Gong), and south of the palace was a shipyard and the Temple of the Dragon King (Longwang Miao). The pillars and beams of the numerous structures in the Wonderland were painted in deep red with ornaments in green, white, and blue, which sharply distinguished the white marble from the blue water.

On the west side of the Wonderland was a scene borrowed from the West Lake of Hangzhou known as the Three Pools Reflecting the Moon (Santan Yinyue), which yielded the impression of three moons on the water surface. The overall design of this scenery

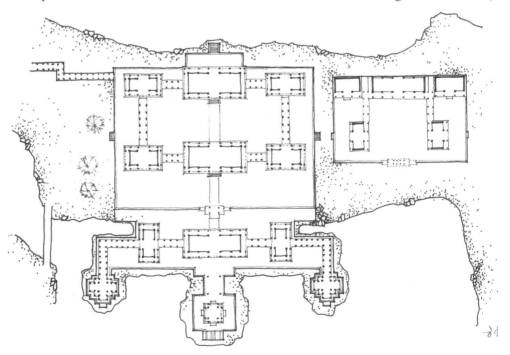

Figure 26. Fanghu Shengjing (Wonderland in the Square Pot). Plan by Joseph C. Wang and Xingbai Yue.

Figure 27. Yingxun Ting (Welcoming Warm-wind Arbor) in front of the principal structure of Fanghu Shengjing. Sketch by Joseph C. Wang and Xingbai Yue.

clearly bore the elements of Daoist mystery. In fact, as Qianlong's own statement shows, the intention was to create a fairyland on earth so that finding a paradise overseas, as Qin Shi Huangdi had tried in vain to do, was absolutely unnecessary (Yu Mingzhong 1985, 3:1368–69; cf. *YMYJ* 1983, 2:50).

To the west of the Wonderland laid the Calm Lake under Autumn Moon (Pinghu Qiuyue), one more replica from the West Lake of Hangzhou. Qianlong, who created the replica, enjoyed the bright and golden reflections on the lake on a clear mid-August full-moon night. If the emperor left here and walked westward, he would enter the Boundless

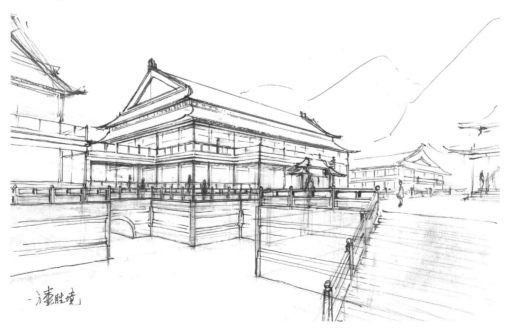

Figure 28. The principal structure of Fanghu Shengjing. Sketch by Joseph C. Wang and Xingbai Yue.

Figure 29. The principal structure of Pinghu Qiuyue (Calm Lake under Autumn Moon). Sketch by Joseph C. Wang and Xingbai Yue.

Impartiality (Kuoran Dagong) at the northwest corner of the lake. This scenery consisted of a seven-column main structure also called the Boundless Impartiality; the All-Round Pretty Cottage (Huanxiu Shanfang); the Double Cranes Chapel (Shuanghe Zhai); the Lakeside Chamber (Linhu Lou), and a large pond. At the southern end of the lake's west shore stood the Bath in Virtue (Zaoshen Yongde), which features the three-column Clear Void Gazebo (Chengyuan Xie) facing east with two smaller structures on its sides, namely, the Conceiving Pure Light (Han Qinghui) and the Conceiving Wonderful View (Han Miaoshi). North of the gazebo was first the Lookout Stand (Wangying Zhou) overlooking the lake then the Thick Willows Cover the Study (Shenliu Dushu Tang) (cf. Yu Mingzhong 1985, 3:1370–1371; *Yuanming yuan sishijing tuyong* 1985, 64).

On the south shore of the lake was a large scene designated the Double Reflections and the Roaring Waterfall (Jiajing Mingqin), which Qianlong derived from Li Qinglian's poem to suggest two adjacent lakes as a pair of mirrors (Yu Mingzhong 1985, 3:1373). Indeed, between the large lake on the one side and a small inner lake on the other, a long narrow bank separated this artificially created scenery. Its main structure was a colorful pavilion standing on a long straight bank connecting two islets, one at each end, thus enclosing a space of water behind the bank. Reflections of the pavilion on both water surfaces produced a terrific view. South of the pavilion across a strip of water stood the Chamber of Distance (Juyuan Lou). On its south side, a straight bank seemed to have been hooked by a U-shaped bank.

The islet to the east side of the bank had an artificial hill with a waterfall. The roaring sounds of the falls could be heard from the nearby Nourishing Palace (Guangyu Gong), which was accompanied by the Luck-Gathering Court (Ningxiang Dian) to the south. East of the palace on a hill was the site of the famous bell duplicated from Mt. Nanping near the West Lake in Hangzhou, known as the Evening Bell at Nanping (Nanping Wanzhong). The duplicated bell was the exact shape and size of the original (Yu Mingzhong 1985, 3:1372; *Yuanming yuan sishijing tuyong* 1985, 74). According to a legendary story, when the bell was first placed here, its sounds were not so loud as they should have been. An ingenious young craftsman in the Yuanming Yuan dug a deep well beside the bell, and the setup accelerated the vibration of the sounds. Then Qianlong heard the bell loud and clear from his living quarters on the Nine Continents (Peng Zheyu and Zhang Baozhang, 1985, 134–136).

At the southeast corner of the lake was the scene designated as the Other Paradise (Bieyou Dongtian). Its main structure, about five columns wide and surrounded by a group of spotless villas, included the better-known Green Gathering Chamber (Nacui Lou) as well as the Pretty Water and Wood Chamber (Shuimu Qinghua) and the Appreciating Chapel (Shishang Zhai) (Yu Mingzhong 1985, 3:1372; *Yuanming yuan sishijing tuyong* 1985, 72). On the east shore of the lake were the cottages designated by Qianlong as the Belle Villa (Jiexiu Shanfang). The principal structure, approximately three columns wide, was accompanied by the Green-View Arbor (Lancui Ting) below, the Cloud-Searching Chamber (Xunyun Lou) above, and the Smooth-as-Silk Chamber (Chenglian Lou) and the Pleasant Study (Yiran Shuwu) in the rear. With hills to its back, the Belle Villa was fully open to the lake, and this was where Qianlong was most pleased with the fog floating at sunrise and with the shady west hills at the sunset (Yu Mingzhong 1985, 3:1371–1372; *Yuanming yuan sishijing tuyong* 1985, 70).

At the northern end of the east shore, a group of lakeside houses were designated Contemplation at the Lakeside (Hanxu Langjing). This elegant name, which was also the name for its principal structures, as in most of other designated names, alluded to a Tang poem that compared the clear lake to a penetrating mirror reflecting one's mind. The scenery contained a gallery called Sunset at the Thunder Hill (Leifeng Xizhao), in which the name board of "Hanxu Langjing" was hung. At its side, to the northwest, stood a square-shaped structure named the Springlike Kindness (Hui Ruchun), and the Cloud-Searching Gazebo (Xunyun Xie) together with the Orchid Courtyard (Yilan Ting) were to the northeast (Yu Mingzhong 1985, 3:1372, 1373; *Yuanming yuan sishijing tuyong* 1985, 77).

All the scenic points around the large Sea of Blessing lake gave rise to a charming poetic atmosphere in which reality and fantasy were mixed. Reality *(shi)* refers to the accentuation of the structural substance, while fantasy *(xu)* derives from the mind, which creates the reality. Fantasy in Chinese garden art, however, is not completely abstract; rather, it is the intangible, implicit, and reserved elements in garden-making. If reality is form, fantasy is the content absent of transparent intelligibility. Thus, the interplay of reality and fantasy in the search for fantastic views is an epistemological prerequisite of any Chinese designer. In this sense, the specially designated Forty Views in the Yuanming Yuan provide an excellent model of such interplay.

Father Attiret came to see the Yuanming Yuan only a year before the designation of the Forty (Best) Views was complete. He saw "numerous pleasure houses" on "a vast compass of ground," and the "raised hills from 20 to 60 foot high," which formed many "little valleys." The "valleys" in Attiret's writing could well be the designated scenes. He also took note of many "clear streams" running into large or small lakes and a magnificent boat "78 foot long and 24 foot broad with a very handsome house raised" on one of the canals. He was impressed by the "different courts, open and closed porticos, parterres, gardens, and cascades, which when view'd all together, have an admirable effect upon the eyes." The more than two hundred buildings, which constitute the Forty Views, convinced Attiret that he had never seen such pleasure grounds in Europe. He considered the Yuanming Yuan simply "a veritable paradise on earth" (Attiret 1982, 7–8).

CHAPTER 3

EXPANSION

THE QIANLONG EMPEROR considered his garden project complete when he designated in 1744 the Forty (Best) views, a kaleidoscopic series of selected scenic spots in the Yuanming Yuan. But, actually, the emperor's extraordinary passion for building more gardens had just begun. In addition to the summer retreat at Chengde and the Skinny West Lake (Shuo Xihu) in Yangzhou, he expanded the Yuanming Yuan so much that it eventually consisted of many more dozens of smaller gardens and distinct scenic units. Each unit had its own style and theme, but without losing a general sense of integrity. One scenic area overlapped another, with adjacent areas half-closed from and half-open to each other, thus resulting in the simultaneous impression of sequence and cohesion. Clearly, when the emperor was unable to restrain himself from endless garden constructions, no one dared to stop him. Perhaps more important, the empire of Qianlong's time was still rich enough to satisfy, or justify, his passion for gardens (cf. Sugimura 1961, 218–223).

The Eternal Spring Garden

The year 1749 marked the beginning of the great expansion of the Yuanming Yuan. It set the stage for including 1,059 acres of land to the east soon to be called the Eternal Spring Garden (Changchun Yuan), named after Qianlong's boyhood residence, the Eternal Spring Fairy Hall (Changchun Xian'guan).

This huge annex was designed and built from blueprint as the most comprehensive and costly single project in the garden's history. The justification was Qianlong's need to have a retirement home, as he promised to abdicate at the age of eighty-five, having completed sixty years of his reign (Yu Mingzhong 1985, 3:1380). His retirement, however, was still more than forty years away when the Eternal Spring Garden was completed in 1751, and in the years up to Qianlong's retirement, it would become an integral part of the Yuan-

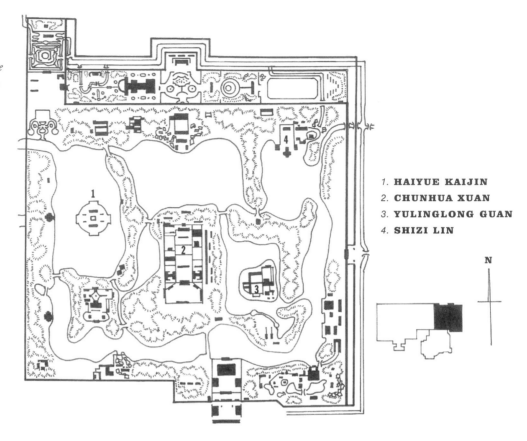

Figure 30. *Overview of Changchun Yuan (Eternal Spring Garden) showing the four best-known scenes and the European section in the north. Plan by Sylvia Lu Wong with reference to the map in* YMYJ *1987, 1.*

1. **HAIYUE KAIJIN**
2. **CHUNHUA XUAN**
3. **YULINGLONG GUAN**
4. **SHIZI LIN**

N

ming Yuan. Because this particular garden was constructed for the emperor's retirement, the entire design stressed pleasure. Delightful structures of various sorts featured the fascinating Daoist aesthetic Administrative buildings, which were abundant in the original Yuanming Yuan, were absent from the Eternal Spring Garden.

If the Yuanming Yuan proper can justifiably be called a water garden, the Eternal Spring Garden appears even more deserving of such a name. The design was based on a lively large water space divided into irregular shapes by numerous isles and sandbars connected by bridges and banks. Construction began with the Classics Hall (Hanjing Tang) and the Homely Memorial Hall (Danhuai Tang) on a large open field east of the Shuimo Village, which was located adjacent to the Yuanming Yuan's east gate, known as the Bright Spring Gate (Mingchun Men). To make the Eternal Spring Garden look like an imperial garden, a palatial front gate about five columns wide was constructed, together with a pair of kylin standing on white jade stands. Like the front gate of the original Yuanming Yuan, it also has two wings of offices outside the gate (Yu Mingzhong 1985, 3:1379–1380; Cheng Yansheng 1928, 30a). But this palatial gate was rarely used because it was more convenient for the emperor and his entourage to pass through the Bright Spring Gate, which directly linked the two sections of the imperial garden.

Striding through the front gate into the precincts, immediately visible was the nine-column Broad-Minded Hall with two side halls and the South Long River (Nan Changhe) at its back. To the west side of the hall, was a ten-hole stone bridge, approximately forty meters long, known as the Eternal Spring Bridge (Changchun Qiao), crossing the river. Over the bridge was the central islet, the largest in the Eternal Spring Garden, on which stood a large compound of buildings comparable in size to the Nine Continents, or approximately 10 percent of the entire Eternal Spring Garden. In the compound was a pair of two main buildings, the Classics Hall (Hanjing Tang) to the south and the Truthful Chapel (Yunzhen Zhai) to the north. This group of architecture surrounded by green hills and beautiful flowers created a tranquil environment in which colorful *pailou,* or decorated archways, each sandwiched by short walls stand in three directions: south, east, and west. The Classics Hall was a vast complex of 480 structures, large and small, including kitchens, warehouses, apartments, and verandas. It was apparently His Majesty's living quarters in the Eternal Spring Garden, and Qianlong found it his favorite place to relax, read, or recite Buddhist scripts for moments of tranquility and meditation after a busy day's work (Qianlong's poem in Yu Mingzhong 1985, 3:1381–1382; Jiao Xiong 1984, 14).

The Truthful Chapel was guarded by a pair of lion sculptures made of white marble and flanked by a row of apartment houses on each side. Here in 1773 Qianlong placed a set of the "Little Four Treasures" *(Siku quanshu huiyao),* a condensed version of the monumental Four Treasures, and thus the chapel was also known as the Rich-Taste Library (Weiyu Shuwu). This splendid little library was lost forever in 1860, together with the set of the Four Treasures kept at the Yuanming Yuan's Literary Source Library.[1]

The Classics Hall and Truthful Chapel were separated by a large courtyard, in which Qianlong built the unique Chunhua Gallery (Chunhua Xuan) to house the best inscribed stone tablets, many of which were exhibited on the walls of a long corridor connecting the two main buildings. This remarkable collection of the inscribed stone tablets, which elegant styles from the best hands always serve as model calligraphy, was clearly to please the Qianlong emperor, who was an accomplished calligrapher in his own right.[2]

Two smaller islets flanked this larger central islet. On the islet to the west stood the Eternal Thoughtful Chapel (Siyong Zhai), the name for a vast compound of structures of various sort that connected the Little Haven to its east. Its main structure, also called the Eternal Thoughtful Chapel, was five columns wide and had two wings of corridors facing an open lake and leading to a three-column hall with various sitting rooms displaying numerous priceless bronze antiques. The north side of the hall faced the Distant Wind Chamber (Yuanfeng Lou). Further north was the octagon veranda with exquisitely carved white balustrade leading the way to a courtyard containing an octagonal pond with goldfish (Zhao Guanghua 1984, 2). Demonstrating a well thought-out symmetry, on the east side of the central islet was the parallel structure named the Exquisite Jade Studio (Yulinglong Guan). The floor plan of the Exquisite Jade Studio shows two contrasting sections linked by corridors: a naturalistic design to the east and a rectilinear design to the west. The lodging to the east contained a huge curve-shaped marble bathtub, specially built for Qianlong's use. Standing southeast of this complex was the unique Clear Reflection Chapel (Ying-qing Zhai), surrounded by hills. Its several structures were also connected by long, winding verandas (Jiao Xiong 1984, 16–17, 18–19).

The three principal structures on the central islet, namely the Classics Hall, the Chun-hua Gallery, and the Truthful Chapel, formed a south-north axis extending across the lake to an impressive high-rising islet. On this islet was another architectural group consisting of the Green-Crossed Gallery (Cuijiao Xuan) to the south and the Mountain-Loving Chamber (Aishan Lou) and the Watering Orchid Hall (Zelan Tang) to the north. To the west side of the latter hall stood a number of interesting temples, in particular the Fahui Temple, which possessed a 73.5–foot-tall pagoda made of colorful *liuli* (colored glaze) tiles with a grand tower sitting on a large white jade terrace. Between halls and chambers were courtyards and corridors to connect them (Yu Mingzhong 1985, 3:1386). Extra effort was made to make the artificially created background look absolutely natural. Stone bridges, caves, chairs, and even man-made waterfalls could be found under fully planted pine trees in the surrounding rising ground.[3] This was the place, because of its higher position, that yielded a bird's-eye view of the entire garden.

The most spectacular piece of architecture in the Eternal Spring Garden was the Mind-Opening Isle (Haiyue Kaijin) sitting on a round islet in a rectangular lake west of the central islet and looking splendid in green and gold. The whole architectural complex sat on a two-level round terrace. The lower level, about 80 meters in diameter and surrounded by white marble balustrades, was easily accessible to the waterfront in all directions. On the upper level, about seventy meters in diameter, stood a quadrilateral pavilion covered by yellow *liuli* tiles on top of a three-storied structure. Its appearance was similar to the Temple of Heaven (Tiantai) in the Forbidden City, and yet in this particular environment it yielded the image of a resplendent structure sitting on a giant jade bowl. Here many elegant structures appeared hidden among pomegranate trees of various sorts. They looked like a mirage from a distance and like a fairyland in close range (Zhao Guanghua 1984, 3). The flowers, when blossoming in May, made a charming view of red-white embroidery. On the east side of the pavilion was a large pond surrounded by weeping willows and covered with fully-grown lotus in summer (Yu Mingzhong 1985, 3:1385).[4]

To the east of the Mind-Opening Isle across a narrow strip of water was the Long Island Fairy Terrace (Changshandao Xianrentai), a square brick structure approximately 350 meters long and 20 meters wide. Rising almost two stories high, steps with carved jade railings ascended to the fairy terrace. Crepe myrtle, sweet-scented oleander, pomegranate, Rose of Sharon, and palm and pine trees were abundant, particularly the densely planted white-skinned pines (popisong), which cast long shadows over the terrace. On top of the terrace stood a cross-shaped arbor with gold copper roofs and yellow glazed *liuli* tiles in which a huge female Buddha statue was accompanied by a dozen statuettes. Around the arbor, elevated flower beds full of large peonies on both sides of the hill, north and south, offered a terrific view in spring.

To the west side of the Mind-Opening Isle across the water was the beautiful Pomegranate Fragrant Islet (Liuxiang Zhu), which featured a golden-pillar, double-eave, four-cornered arbor standing on a white marble terrace surrounded by a carved balustrade. Outside the arbor were planted numerous pomegranates; at the time of blossom in May, the colors of white and red created the look of embroidery. The lake at the east side of the arbor was filled with seemingly boundless lotus (Yu Mingzhong 1985, 3:1386; Zhao Guanghua 1984, 2–3). The whole setting on the islet gave rise to a vivid sense of a Daoist fairyland (see Qianlong's poem in Yu Mingzhong 1985, 3:1385). Noticeably, this Pomegranate Fragrant Islet together with the Mind-Opening Isle and the Long Island Fairy Terrace formed a west-east axis, which, in the opinion of a recent garden architect, represents the most ingenious design of all in the royal demesnes (Zhao Guanghua 1984, 3). The maps of the Yuanming Yuan that are available to us suggest the traveling route of the emperor and his entourage. They may have proceeded on the winding road from the east shore of the Sea of Blessing through the Bright Spring Gate, which separated the Eternal Spring Garden from the original Yuanming Yuan, and immediately observed this spectacular view.

Most of the rest of the architectural units that were built in the Eternal Spring Garden were reproductions from the attractive gardens and scenic spots that Qianlong studied in South China on his many southern tours. He visited as many famous southern gardens as he possibly could, and in fact he brought with him craftsmen and artists, who dutifully copied whatever garden structures in which the emperor showed interest and intended to recreate in the Eternal Spring Garden under construction. It was not uncommon that he instructed designers to copy an entire southern garden. Eventually, no less than five complete southern-style gardens were transposed to the Eternal Spring Garden (see Chapter 4).

The Garden of Compliance (Ru Yuan), situated at the southeast corner of the Eternal Spring Garden, was built on the model of Zhan Yuan in Nanjing, which specialized in artificial hills and rockery, yet it is much larger than the original. Its best scene was located to the east, where a large pond separated a hall in the north from a chamber in the south. To the east side of the pond rose a 7–meter-high man-made hill. There were pavilions on both sides of the foot of the hill, and on top of a terrace one could see the Eternal Spring Garden in one direction and the rural scene outside the southern walls in the other. Below the terrace were hundreds of precious peonies of different colors. To the west side of the pond was a rockwork hill with caves. On top of this hill stood the Pure Jasper Gazebo (Qingyao Xie) facing the Blue-Conceiving Chamber (Hanbi Lou). To the south of a hexagonal arbor was the Green Gallery (Weilu Xuan). On the north side of the gazebo the Lengthening Purity Arbor (Yanqing Ting), seven columns wide. West of the arbor is the Green-Conceiving Gallery (Hancui Xuan). From the decks of this hall looking northward, one could view lakes and hills as far as six hundred meters away; thus, the isolation of this smaller garden inside a large enclosure (Yu Mingzhong 1985, 3:1390; Jiao Xiong 1984, 14–16) was ameliorated using the technique of "view borrowing."

The Alizarin-Red Garden (Qian Yuan), to the side of the Broad-Minded Hall, consisted of the Bright Glossy Chapel (Langrun Zhai), the Exquisite View Chamber (Zhanjing Lou), and the Fragrant Water Chestnut Flat (Lingxiang Pian) (Yu Mingzhong 1985, 3:1382).

The design exquisitely utilized southern skills of arranging space, water, banks, and architecture on the 1.2–acre lot, approximately 100 meters long and 50 meters wide. A small river to the east was crossed by three elegant bridges—an arch bridge, a winding bridge, and a three-hole stone bridge. The riverbank, composed of skillfully constructed rock formations, supported a city-gatelike structure, and, together with plants of various sorts in the water, gave rise to a pleasant feeling of wildness. The garden also featured flower arrangements, miniature trees, and a large pond, in which thousands of golden carp swam.

Inside a courtyard on the west side of the Bright Glossy Chapel a very precious piece of delicate green lake rock was erected. Qianlong took it from the desolated Southern Song palace in Hangzhou in 1752, named it the Green Lotus (Qinglian Duo), and designated it as one of the eight views in this particular garden (Wu Zhenyu 1983, 272).[5] The emperor was so fond of the lake rock that he composed at least four poems praising it. One reads:

> A lotus was carved out of stone, so beautiful
> It strikes me, like a Chan Buddhist, a sudden enlightenment
> The rock, it appears, has flown here from nowhere
> I deserve to have it not,
> But it pleased me so immensely.[6]

The Little Haven (Xiaoyoutian), on the northeast side of the Eternal Thoughtful Chapel, was duplicated from Wang Zhier's villa at Nanping in Hongzhou, a famous rock garden Qianlong had visited in 1751 (Liang Zhangju 1981, 234). It is a compact garden full of flowers, hills, caves, and man-made falls. The Lion's Cove (Shizi Lin), in the northeast corner of the Eternal Spring Garden, was a copy of the most celebrated rockery garden, Suzhou's She Yuan, reportedly designed by Abbot Weize in 1342 and where Qianlong paid a visit in 1762. The distinguished Yuan dynasty artist Ni Zhan (1301–1374) added to its fame by producing an excellent portrait of the garden (Yu Mingzhong 1985, 3:1387; Wu Zhenyu 1983, 198; Liu Dunzheng 1993, 105; cf. Zhao Guanghua 1984, 3:5; Tung 1936, 235; Liang Zhangju 1981, 220).

Long before the rise of Suzhou's She Yuan, the Song dynasty scholar Ye Mengde (1077–1148) had built the famous Rock Groove (Shilin) at his native Huzhou in Zhejiang province. Since the Rock Groove had long since perished, however, She Yuan was surely the best surviving model for Qianlong. The Lion's Cove was constructed on a 2.2–acre plot featuring houses mostly on the west side and rock formations mostly on the east side. The man-made structures included the Bring-Up Moon Arbor (Yangyue Ting), the Fast-Growing Flower Studio (Huazhou Guan) in the rear, and the Horizontal Blue Gallery (Hengbi Xuan) leading into the rock section to the east. Rockery formation, as Qianlong himself noted, was the principal theme of the cove. His Majesty personally instructed the best craftsmen from Suzhou to pile the rocks to form a forest of hillocks exactly like the Lion's Cove in Suzhou. The mission was obviously accomplished, as the emperor noted that the site instantly reminded him of his southern tours (Yu Mingzhong 1985, 3:1387, 1388–1389).

The Viewing Garden (Jian Yuan) was a small secluded garden surrounded by water north of the Garden of Compliance (Wu Zhenyu 1983, 199). This was a skillfully designed compact enclosure. It comprised many large man-made structures. A main hall of two dozen rooms extended on both sides of the corridors. A two-story library called the Ten-Thousand Source Belvedere (Wanyuan Ge) was the home of precious books, paintings, and calligraphy. A three-column study named Library under the Shade of the Phoenix Trees (Tongyin Shuwu) had a fishpond surrounded by a white marble balustrade. A winding veranda at the north side of the pond led the way to a complex of architectural units, such as the Longevity Gallery (Yishou Xuan), the Ancient Moon Gallery (Guyue Xuan), and the Self-Reflection Chapel (Zixing Zhai), all bearing the influence of southern-style Chinese gardens. Reflections of some of the galleries could be seen in the Long River. Qianlong liked to come here for reading, thinking, and meditation. He wished to spend a considerable amount of time here in retirement.

Across the Long River from the Viewing Garden, a hilly road led to the Pure Reflection Chapel (Yingqing Zhai), connected with several chambers by corridors. Directly behind the Viewing Garden was a dockyard to service the numerous garden boats, each of which had an elegant name, such as Moon-Carrying Showboat (Zaiyue Fang) and the Flying-Cloud Tall Ship (Feiyun Louchuan), recorded in *Daqing Huidian (The comprehensive canon of the Great Qing)*. Surrounded by hills, the whole setting offered a sense of privacy and tranquility. At the chapel's northwest end across a winding bridge stood the Exquisite Jade Studio (Yulinglong Guan) on a large island in a lake surrounded by hills (Yu Mingzhong 1985, 3:1389; Zhao Guanghua 1984, 4–5; Jiao Xiong 1984, 14; Cai Shengzhi n.d., 134).

Rockery is best in South China, and Qianlong was determined to get the best of it. As a form of art, rockery and hillocks have been made since the beginning of Chinese garden-making. Unlike stones and rocks in a Western or a Japanese garden, Chinese rockeries are usually fanciful recreations of a painting, a poetic theme, or a scene from the wild world of nature. They are famous for steepness and precipitousness and composed of fantastically shaped limestone through the action of water. The best available materials are from Lake Tai, known as the "lake rocks from Taihu" *(taihu shi)*. The rocks, usually white, blue, and light green, appear porous, spare, and grotesque after centuries of washing and scouring at the bottom of a lake. The rocks with the best shapes come from the very bottom of the lake. Diving into the lake and pulling them out with heavy ropes was the only available means to obtain them in the premodern China. Lake rocks aside, there are at least fifteen other sorts of rocks, usually named after the place where they were first found (Ji Cheng 1987, 218–238).

We may also observe that the art of rockery arrangement emphasized proper foils to show off shapes and contours in contrast to the surrounding structures and natural scenery. The craze for elegant rocks was such that garden owners were most proud of their rockeries. Some strived for magnitude, while others liked exquisiteness, but all appreciated the rocky solidarity and were accustomed to endowing their rocks with personality, carrying over the life impulse of nature into the cold artificiality of human creation. It was not unusual for

Chinese garden lovers to treat their favorite piece of rockery as a delightful companion or even an admired hero. Indeed, it was not unusual for them to instill sentiments into their favorite rocks.

Zhang Dai, a Ming writer, once saw a white rock on the ground, 10 feet tall and 20 feet wide, and found it "crazy," wonderfully crazy; he also saw a black rock, 8 feet wide and 15 feet tall, looking skinny and wonderfully skinny (1982, 59). Likewise, a Qing scholar by the name of Liang Zhangju found three outstanding characteristics for rocks, namely, transparency *(tou),* wrinkles *(zhou),* and skinny *(shou)* (1981, 21–22). The Song emperor Huizong so indulged in the rocks that he risked the people's anger by crowding the Grand Canal with barges loaded with much treasured rocks from the south for his gardens in Kaifeng (*Songshi* 1977, 39:13684).

Piling rocks to form successful hillocks requires constructing a near-exact resemblance to a wild hill. That is why Chen Congzhou said: "it is difficult to achieve weightiness and unsophisticatedness in rockery formation, still more so in laying a hill of primitive simplicity" (1994, 16). Simplicity means conforming to nature: "No traces of artificial tricks or unnatural devices are visible," the rockery-piler Li Yu insisted, "and a hillock should really look like a real one from a distance" (Liu Dunzheng 1993, 34).

The major components of hillocks include peaks and hilly ridges, gorges and gullies, terraces and footpaths, bridges and waterfalls, all of which stress infinite variety, clear contours, and a three-dimensional presence (cf. Liu Dunzheng 1993, 36). Because the Eternal Spring Garden occupied a huge flat land, hillocks were particularly significant to the overall garden layout. The massive dredging of the lakes yielded a large quantity of mud and loose earth with which to create as many as fifty man-made hills in the garden. Although the hilly ridges were not very high, ranging from 10 to 15 meters, efforts were made to avoid any trace of artificiality by planting plenty of trees and by integrating the hillocks with lakes (Zhang Jiaji 1986, 167).

Rockery and hillocks are no doubt indispensable elements of Chinese gardens. Following his repeated trips to South China, Qianlong brought back the essence of the art and created a large number of rockeries and hillocks in the Eternal Spring Garden. In the process of duplicating southern-style gardens in the Eternal Spring Garden, however, designers strived for creativity. Much ingenuity was exercised to transform or upgrade the original designs and their meanings. For instance, the original theme of the Fish-in-the-Stream, a scene copied from a Hongzhou temple, was a mere expression of the Buddhist compassion of setting fish free in the stream; the replica in the Eternal Spring Garden, however, magnifies it by incorporating the spirit of imperial benevolence. More often, the replicas distinctly superseded the original design. Qianlong was so satisfied with the results in his garden that he asked himself rhetorically: "Why should I miss South China any more" *(hebi gengxian wujiang)?* Not any more, because he "magically transplanted much of the beautiful southern scenes into his royal demesne" (quoted in Wang Kaiyun's poem in *YMYZ* 1984, 328; cf. Yu Mingzhong, 1985, 3:1387). Indeed, compared with the old sections of the Yuanming Yuan, the Eternal Spring Garden looks far more playful. The layout of the entire garden was well planned to suit the best personal taste of the Qianlong emperor for His Majesty's pleasure only.

The Chinese Versailles

The section of European palaces and gardens, known as the Western-Style Buildings (Xiyang Lou), *les palais europeens du Yuen-ming-yuen,* or simply the Chinese Versailles, spreads across the northern end of the Eternal Spring Garden. This was the most extraordinary garden project taken on by Qianlong. To be sure, China had adopted foreign architecture long before this time. It was no later than the Tang dynasty that central Asia made its impact on Chinese architecture. Under the Eurasian empire created by the Mongols, Christian influence appeared in the Yuan capital of Dadu, or present-day Beijing. And Western-style commercial buildings and private homes were built in Canton following the opening of the Canton system of trade in the seventeenth century, not to mention the presence of Portuguese architecture in Macau since the sixteenth century. But, beyond a doubt, Qianlong was the first Chinese ruler to accommodate any substantial European architecture in an imperial garden.

The European section, with many of its buildings based on Baroque models, was constructed on a 65–acre strip of land, 750 meters long and 70 meters wide (Jin Yufeng 1984, 22). A recent survey shows that Maurice Adam's figures, 300 meters long and 100 meters wide (1936, 15, cf. 16–36), were inaccurate. The design followed European models closely. European materials, such as huge columns, marble balustrades, and glass windows were used extensively. But an oriental touch to the occidental architecture was also unmistakable, as seen in the red-tinted brick walls, colorful *liuli* tiles, Chinese-style ornamentation and decoration, Taihu rocks, and bamboo pavilions (Jin Yufeng 1984, 21).

Qianlong's interest in constructing this Western-style palatial garden was first inspired by his fascination with exotic European fountains that appeared in pictures presumably

Figure 31. Overview of the European section. By Sylvia Lu Wong with reference to Jin Yufeng, "Yuanming Yuan xiyanglou pingxi" [An analysis of the European buildings in the Yuanming Yuan], YMYJ 1987, 3:22–23 .

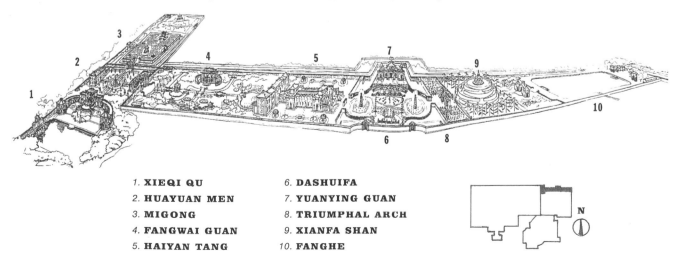

1. **XIEQI QU**
2. **HUAYUAN MEN**
3. **MIGONG**
4. **FANGWAI GUAN**
5. **HAIYAN TANG**
6. **DASHUIFA**
7. **YUANYING GUAN**
8. **TRIUMPHAL ARCH**
9. **XIANFA SHAN**
10. **FANGHE**

N

presented by one of the Jesuits. Fountains are an ancient Western pleasure that became exceedingly popular in seventeenth-century France and Italy. To be sure, there were already a few fountains in the original Yuanming Yuan, such as the Sounds of Wood and Water, but none had great magnitude.

It is possible that the Italian and French Jesuit fathers at the Qianlong court tried to impress the emperor with great Western fountains. The emperor asked Father Giuseppe Castiglione (1688–1766, Lang Shining in Chinese), a Milano-born Jesuit artist who arrived in China in 1715 at the age of twenty-seven, to draw pictures of Italian and French palaces and fountains to be built in the Eternal Spring Garden. Castiglione submitted to Qianlong designs of a "fascinating kind of Baroque, reminiscent of the style of Borromini" (Beurdeley 1971, 5, 11, 45, 59, 66–67). He then solicited assistance from Father Michel Benoît (1715–1774, Jiang Youren in Chinese), who had been in China since 1744. Thanks to his knowledge of mathematics and hydraulics, Benoît was able to present a model fountain to the Qing emperor. The delighted Qianlong quickly authorized the Jesuits to begin.

To accommodate fountains, however, required gigantic Baroque-style palace buildings. Neither Castiglione nor Benoît was a professional architect; nevertheless, they successfully transformed some models into a series of European palatial structures in the Eternal Spring Garden. A number of European experts were consulted in the process: Father Jean-Denis Attiret (1702–1768), Ignatius Sickelpart (1708–1780), and the architect Ferdinando Moggi (?). In addition, the botanist Pierre d'Incarville (1706–1757) helped draw the garden setting, and Father Gilles Thebault (1703–1766) manufactured the steel railing designed by Castiglione. For completing the project, these foreign missionaries were given freedom of travel inside the garden. They worked diligently regardless of "the heat, the rain, the wind and the blazing sun of the dog days" (Beurdeley 1971, 68). As for information, they mainly relied on engravings in some of the books they brought from Europe or borrowed from three Christian institutes in Beijing.

In the process, a large number of Chinese architects, engineers, and masons, though unfamiliar with foreign architecture, also contributed to the successful completion of the project under the guidance of two Jesuit fathers. It is truly remarkable that a handful of European amateurs did their job and satisfied the Chinese emperor's new interest.[7] Modern Western experts may not fully approve or appreciate the results, but it seems quite extraordinary that the European architecture was well adapted in the Chinese imperial garden. Indeed, the Le Notre palace, in an attempt to mix Europe with China, appears to have no negative effect on the unity of the Yuanming Yuan as a whole. The price tag for this enormous construction project was surely high, but money posed no problem when Qianlong's purses, both privy and public, were quite full (Cai Shengzhi n.d., 123–127; Jin Yufeng 1984, 24; Goto Sueo 1942, 117–132).

According to Benoît, when the first Western-style buildings facing a lake were in shape in 1747, "the emperor was very happy with the work" *(L'Empereur parut très satisfait)*.[8] The two-story Chamber for Gathering Water (Xushui Lou) was in a paved courtyard. The central building soon acquired a pair of glazed pavilions on both sides joined by a long curved

corridor. Qianlong was particularly pleased with the dynamic and pulsating look of the Baroque-style architecture. He could watch the large and colorful fountain with fourteen sprinklers in front of the main building from either side of the two pavilions. Inside the pavilion, he could enjoy the performance of exotic music from Mongolia and Chinese Turkestan, "the overture of the music of the Western Section." This first phase of the European section was officially completed in 1751, and the emperor named this first enclosure of Western structures the Symmetric and Amazing Pleasure (Xieqi Qu) (Jin Yufeng 1984, 21; cf. Beurdeley 1971, 70, and Sun Ruoyi 1998, 17).

Westward from here stood the Peacock Cage (Yangque Long), or the aviary for peacocks and exotic birds. Besides the wrought iron door with a jigsaw pattern, the cage's walls were covered with paintings of boats and pheasants. To the east of the Peacock Cage rose a highly decorated gate in the center of a half-moon wall enclosing a carved white marble fountain. Further north toward the end of the courtyard was the Entrance of the Flower Garden (Huayuan Men), which led into a large Maze (Migong).

The maze was a European concept. One of the earliest mazes was near Lake Moeris in Egypt. It was the tomb designed by King Amenenhat III in the twenty-third century B.C. Mazes appeared as garden ornaments in late fifteenth century A.D., when they became a regular element in the villa gardens in Renaissance Italy. By the sixteenth and the seventeenth centuries, few large European gardens lacked a maze.

Figure 32. South facade of Xieqi Qu (Symmetric and Amazing Pleasure). From a copperplate engraving by the eighteenth-century Jesuit designers. Source: YMYJ 1984, 3:99.

The maze in the Eternal Spring Garden was symmetrical on a central north-south axis. Nearly perfectly rectangular, it was surrounded by five-foot high walls made of carved gray bricks, which were surrounded by slender pines. The pines, it seems, were planted before the construction of the walls around them. A moat surrounding the walls was crossed by bridges, one on each of the four sides, leading to the maze's four entrances. The principal structure was a central, south-facing octagonal kiosk, rising from a platform with circular stairs to dominate the courtyard. A secondary structure to the north was a white marble chamber, which overlooked the maze and housed mechanical singing birds, or a large music box, which had been brought to China by a certain European to amuse the Qing emperor. Both structures bear explicit European characteristics in design and carving. Outside the walls, a small wayside pavilion sat on a hill further to the north.

Within the maze, there were nine perfect circles of various sizes, representing the "six-sided world"—top, bottom, four sides, plus past, present, and future. A planter was placed at each corner of a square—the Chinese symbol for the earth—in the central portion of the maze. The north and south gates were aligned on the north-south axis, which bisected the main structures and the courtyard. In general, the maze from the front entrance to the back door had three layers: the flower garden gate, a bridge over a stream, and the interior entrance to the maze.[9]

Figure 33. Migong (Maze), known also as Wanhuazhen (Ten-Thousand Flower Formation). From a copperplate engraving of by the eighteenth-century Jesuit designers. Source: YMYJ 1984, 3:103.

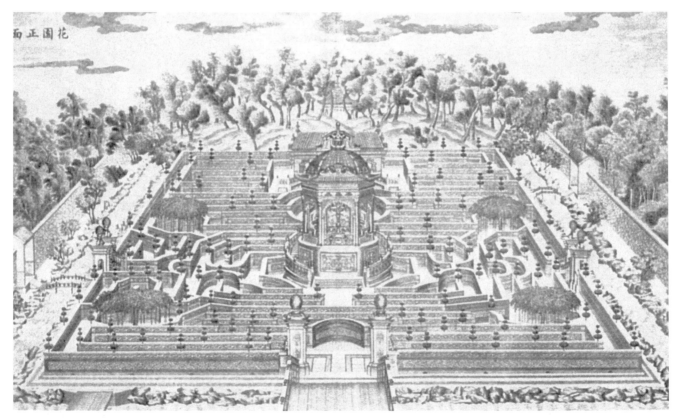

It was a memorable event for Qianlong to celebrate the colorful Moon Festival, the fifteenth day of the eighth month in the lunar calendar, in the maze, where he witnessed ten-thousand lanterns, known as the "yellow flower lanterns" (huanghua deng), displayed in different formations. Court maids in rows carried the lanterns, flitting like countless fireflies. Then the imperial consorts and distinguished guests entered the maze and struggled through the dead ends, detours, and intersecting multiple routes in order to reach the emperor, who sat on his throne at the center of the maze. When they triumphantly arrived, the emperor delightfully showered them with candies and fruits and laughed loudly. After sunset, yellow flower lanterns lit the dark sky and flashed like countless gold stars (*YMYZ* 1984, 63; Adam 1936, 27–28).

It took another eight years to finish the second phase of the European section in time to celebrate Qianlong's fiftieth birthday. In 1759, a new crescent-shaped palatial building with marble balustrudes enclosed by a moat and standing east from the Peacock Cage was completed and named the Square Outlook (Fangwai Guan), or the Belvedere. The bronze outdoor stairways stretched downward from the second floor of the building. Two 4–foot-tall stone tablets with Arabic inscriptions were placed in its main hall. Although both tablets are lost, rubbings of them still exist. In April 1760, when General Zhaohui returned from the successful Turkestan campaign, he brought back a beautiful Aksu woman, better known as the Fragrant Lady (Xiangfei), for His Majesty. The lady took residence here and renamed the palace in which she lived the Muslim Mosque (Qingzhen Si). She and her fellow religionists routinely worshipped here every Friday.[10] The mosque's front door faced a marble bridge with ostentatious balustrades, which crossed a moat and led to a pleasant little garden called Bamboo Pavilion (Zhu Ting). This 1770 pavilion was connected to another pavilion by covered walks and decorated with colorful glass and shells (Adam 1936, 29–30; Tong 1981, 71–80).

Moving eastward, beyond a curtain of trees rose a large palatial building fronted by a fountain. Known as the Calm Sea Hall (Haiyan Tang), this enclosure was officially designated no later than the spring of 1781 (*YMYA* 1991, 2: 1560). Despite its Baroque details, the architectural layout of the main hall was instantly reminiscent of the Court of Honor at Versailles (Beurdeley 1971, 68). It housed a vast reservoir with goldfish under a large glass ceiling, 180 square millimeters, and was named the Sea of Tin (Xihai). Wire netting filled with grape vines surrounded the reservoir, and a large room on each side of the reservoir kept the hydraulic machines that pumped water for the fountains and cascades.

From the main facade of this gigantic structure, as the floor plan shows, stretched two broad, symmetrically winding staircases on each side of the main building, thus giving rise to a palatial impression. A pair of dolphin figure fountains on the second floor between the two staircases released water, which leaped down from one large carved marble block of the balustrade to another until it filled a basin below. Outside the staircases, a fountain sprang from the mouths of two stone lions leaping down to two stone basins. Each of the three stone basins had a fountain with fifty-four sprinkler heads. A large fountain spouted in the central pool, accompanied by a Chinese-style water clock *(louhu)* and surrounded by twelve bronze animal heads, namely, rat, bull, tiger, hare, dragon, snake, horse, goat, monkey, rooster, dog, and boar. These twelve animal heads with human bodies, six on each side of the pool, symbolized the twelve-year cycle of birth and represented every two-hour period in which the Chinese divide their day and night. Hence, each animal figure spouted a stream of water to the pool one after the other every two hours. At high noon, all the animals' mouths spouted.[11] Not surprisingly, Qianlong was most proud of this group of fountains (Adam 1936, 30–33; Jin Yufeng 1984, 22).

Further east of the Calm Sea Hall stood the awe-inspiring Great Fountains (Dashuifa), composed of pyramids, formal pools, fountain statues, and rock and shell ornamentation. The fountain in the main pool was in the shape of eleven animal figures: one deer and ten hounds. When streams of water spouted from all eleven animals at the same time, they created the impression that the deer was being chased by the hounds. An imperial throne standing on top of marble paving and below a beautiful canopy occupied the best possible position to capture the views of these fountains. Behind the throne, stood a large brick screen on which were mounted five marble panels with carvings of European weapons and from which two gateways extended from each side. The wall behind the screen separated the European section from the rest of the Eternal Spring Garden. The Great Fountains readily reminded the visiting Jesuits of the *"buffets d'eaux"* at Versailles and St. Cloud. The emperor was so proud of these great fountains that he commissioned two copper plate engravings of the fountains and presented them to the court, one in 1784 and the other in 1785 (*YMYA* 1991 2:1565).

North of the Great Fountain was the Great View of the Distant Seas (Yuanying Guan), completed no later than 1781 (*YMYA* 1991, 2:1567), sitting on a large, high terrace so as to avoid blocking views. This large brick building was decorated with carved marble around the doors and windows. A pair of elaborately carved marble pillars stood on either side of the main entrance. The Qianlong emperor often used this building as a royal vacation home or resting place, where once were displayed the six Beauvais tapestries sent as gifts by Louis XVI of France in 1767. It once was the home of the Muslim concubine Xiangfei (Tong 1991, 128). This marks the high point of the European section.

A triple gateway together with three triumphal arches resembling the Triumphal Arch in Paris stood at the center of the Western-Style Buildings or east of the Great View of the Distant Sea. The gateway led the way eastward to the tree-covered Perspective Hill (Xiangfa Shan). The hill appeared to have different layers and steps when observed from a distance. The Qianlong emperor reportedly enjoyed riding horses to the octagonal kiosk on the hill-top to admire the different views. The Lake Square (Fanghe), actually rectangular in shape, was further down the hill to the east. Across the 167–meter-long lake to the east was an open-air art gallery, a totally different setting, named the Perspective Pictures (Xiangfa Tu), or the Perspective Wall (Xiangfa Qiang), in which pictures of central Asian towns and sceneries were hung, five on each side. Obviously, the European perspective method was borrowed to help create an illusion of distance, a new pleasure for Chinese eyes (cf. Adam 1936, 33–36; Malone 1934, 158; Tong 1981, 78–80).

Overall, the European section of the Eternal Spring Garden exhibited the features of Western architecture and design of various sorts with the exception of the roofs, which were covered with Chinese yellow, blue, or green tiles. The Symmetric and Amazing Pleasure, the Square Outlook, and the Calm Sea Hall represent three short vertical axes and divide the long horizontal axis into sections. Glass windows, plank floors, handrails, lawns, flower terraces, the short glazed brick walls, clocks, hanging lamps, oil paintings and numerous decorative accessories all manifested the Western characteristics, so much so that the borrowed *"xiyang polang"* (Western plan) entered into the "Construction Proposal of the Yuanming Yuan" (Yuanming yuan gongcheng zuofa) to become a technical term (Tong 1991, 129; Sun 1998, 31–33).

These European buildings naturally required compatible interior designs, such as a profusion of superfluous ornaments and decoration with European furnitures, clocks, pictures, and mechanic toys. Notably, the set of Gobelins tapestries, with full-length portraits of French beauties, and the magnificent pierglass, which were gifts from Louis XV in 1767 were placed here (Sullivan 1973, 67–68). Nevertheless, a compromise with the Chinese taste in interior design was still inevitable. For instance, the large nude figures, which commonly accompany fountains in Europe, were culturally impermissable. Besides, Qing emperors generally were not accustomed to stay or rest in a totally strange setting.

The limitation of Qianlong's borrowed taste for Western architecture and garden arts did not end here. The emperor's cultural background also did not allow him to understand the importance of the mechanization of the universe with mathematic precision as demonstrated in Baroque architecture. His Majesty had no way of knowing that the analytical geometry setting industrialization in motion would eventually make it possible for European armies to invade China and leave the Yuanming Yuan in ruins. In the end, the European section served no more than as another pleasant environment in which he could stroll, rest, entertain, and assemble treasures of European arts. It became an appropriate casket for the emperor's *"cabinet de curiosites"* (Perazzoli-t'Serstevens 1988, 10).

Thus construction, whether of such enormous units as the European section or for improving old structures in various parts of the Yuanming Yuan, continued relentlessly after the designation of the Forty Views.

More New Additions

Following the completion of the Eternal Spring Garden, Qianlong added more structures in the original Yuanming Yuan. Two principal projects deserve close attention. First, in 1762, taking the opportunity to remodel the All-Season Library (Siyi Shuwu) sitting at the north shore of the Sea of Blessing, the emperor deliberately recreated in his imperial garden the Yu Yuan owned by Chen family at Haining in Zhejiang province (Wu Zhenyu 1983, 326).

Qianlong had visited the Yu Yuan repeatedly during his well-publicized southern tours and brought back its blueprint. When the remodeling was complete, the scene was renamed the Wave-Pacifying Garden (Anlan Yuan) by the emperor, a reminder of the severe flooding problem he had witnessed on the Zhejiang coast (see Qianlong's notes in Yu Mingzhong 1985, 3:1376). The name, though devoid of artistic elegance, was a good way for the ruler to express his sincere concern about the flooding. Moreover, Qianlong argued that the remodeling saved money, like "killing two birds with one stone" (*yiju liangde),* because he believed he had transformed something old, which was due for repair, into a new garden that could also remind him of the plight on the coast (Yu Mingzhong 1985, 3:1366). But, in fact, Qianlong did not save any money. He insisted on following exactly the model of the Yu Yuan, which required expensive structural changes. In addition, he requested new additions to accommodate an architectural group, which included the Catching Evening Sunlight Chamber (Ranxia Lou) behind the main hall, the Quick Glance Pavilion (Feidi Ting) on a man-made hill, and the Classics-Worshipping Studio (Zuojing Guan) behind the hill. In the end, the Wave-Pacifying Garden was composed of no fewer than ten integrated sections of scenic structures (Yu Mingzhong 1985, 3:1367–1368).

The fantastic rumor that Qianlong was actually born as a Chen boy was not accidental. The emperor showed unusual interest in the Yu Yuan. He paid frequent visits to the Chen family. On the record, he even remarked, "I often confuse the All-Season Library in the imperial garden with the Yu Yuan in Haining" (Yu Mingzhong 1985, 3:1367). The rumor at last galvanized an unverifed popular story that the Grand Secretariat Chen Bangzhi's wife and Yongzheng's empress each gave birth to a child on the same day, and the empress secretly exchanged her baby girl for Chen's baby boy. Eventually aware of his roots, the emperor not only showed kindness to the family but also brought the family garden back to the Yuanming Yuan to make himself feel close to home (see Peng Zheyu and Zhang Baozhang 1985, 131–132). This popular story, however, is groundless.

Qianlong also set out to build the largest library in the Yuanming Yuan beginning in 1774. The Library of Literary Sources (Wenyuan Ge) on the north side of the Sounds of Water and Wood was constructed to accommodate a set of the Complete Collection of the Four Treasures (Siku quanshu huiyao). Initiated by the emperor in 1772, this monumental collection involved editing, appraising, and reproducing all of the finest Chinese books in four principal catagories: Confucian classics (*jing),* history (*shi),* philosophy (*zi),* and literature (*ji).* Many "undesirable books," from the Qing point of view, were not included. Perhaps the most ambitious literary project of Qing China, it took more than twenty-two years and thousands of literary workers, including 3 editors-in-chief, 160 assistant editors, 368 staff members, and 2,000 calligraphers, to produce seven manuscript collections in elegant calligraphy of 3,747 titles in 6,752 cases, accompanied by an annotated catalog of nearly ten thousand titles. The third manuscript copy, completed in 1775, was placed in the Library of Literary Sources under specific instructions by the Qianlong Emperor (Guy 1987). This library should not be confused with the Wenyuan Ge library in the Forbidden City, which housed the chief set of the Siku books.

Given his strong interest in literary works and in patronizing literature and the arts, it is not surprising that Qianlong kept a complete set of the Four Treasures in his most precious imperial garden. He personally wrote as many horizontal tablets and vertical parallel phrases for the great library as he possibly could. Tablets and couplets, which could be found in various other places of the garden, were considered indispensable parts of the garden arts (cf. *YMYJ* 1991, 1:47–53). In 1784, upon the completion of the library, the emperor inscribed an essay on a marble monument. It was placed in a kiosk east of the main library building for permanent display (cited in Yu Mingzhong 1985, 3:1360–1361; Anonymous 1981, 95; see also Qianlong's notes in Yu Mingzhong 1985, 3:1301; cf. Liu Jiaju 1987, 1–30).

The architecture of the Library of Literary Sources followed the model of the 210-year-old Single Heaven Library (Tianyi Ge) of the distinguished Fan family at Ningbo in the province of Zhejiang (Luo Zhaoping 1993, 1–14). Fan Qin first built the library in 1561 in a walled family garden. The library hall's "column grid," according to an on-site measurement conducted in October 1989, "measures about 23.0 m. wide by 11.0 m. deep on center" (Liu 1997, 135). Gardens and libraries had served as symbols of wealth and prestige ever since Ming China.

Once the model of private library was chosen, it was inevitably made more suited to palatial decorum. Qianlong chose the model, as he himself put it, because Fan's library was the greatest of all libraries (Yu Mingzhong 1985, 3:1360). Although the facade and details were identical to Fan's, Qianlong's library was twice as large and was taller, with three decks. The central area of the lowest deck housed the Confucian classics, together with the annotated catalog and the huge set of the *General Collection of Books* (Tushu jicheng); the middle deck comprised the history section; and the upper deck was reserved for philosophical works and literary anthologies. Four distinct colors—green, red, white, and black—marked the different sections of books for easy identification. On the ground floor, the front corridors with balustrades faced a wide open space for entry. Inside the entrance, a stairway led to the upstairs collections. The library was, after all, tailor-made to accommodate bookcases and yield sufficient open space.

The environment around the library was also meticulously managed. A viewing terrace in front of the main building overlooked a rectangular pool 50 meters long and 23 meters wide containing numerous goldfish. At the center of the pool stood a 10-meter-tall rock sculpture named the Splendid Summit (Lingfeng), pierced with many holes (Cai Shengzhi n.d., 134). The pool was designed not only to contrast with the library building and nearby rockery but also to serve as a water reservoir in case of fire. No trees were planted anywhere near the main building in order to keep insects and ants away (cf. *YMYZ* 1984, 189–196).

As early as 1774, Qianlong integrated into the Yuanming Yuan the Variegated Spring Garden (Qichun Yuan), which was originally the Grand Secretary Fu Heng's garden residence (Wu Zhenyu 1983, 197). The emperor also annexed two smaller neighboring gardens, namely, the Spring Pleasure Garden (Chunxi Yuan) and the Loving Spring Garden (Xichun Yuan). Hence, at one time, Qianlong's Yuanming Yuan consisted of five gardens in the neighborhood of three hills, namely, the Longevity Hills (Wanshou Shan), the Jade Spring Hills (Yuquan Shan), and the Fragrant Hills (Xiang Shan).

In 1750, in honor of his mother's sixtieth birthday, Qianlong built a birthday temple

Figure 34. Qichun Yuan (Variegated Spring Garden) showing four best-known scenes. Tiandi Yijiachun (Family of Spring Between Heaven and the Earth) was the favorite residence of the Empress Dowager Cixi. Plan by Sylvia Lu Wong with reference to the map in YMYJ 1987, 1.

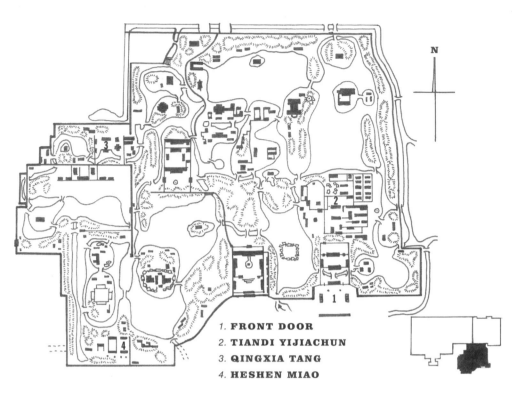

1. **FRONT DOOR**
2. **TIANDI YIJIACHUN**
3. **QINGXIA TANG**
4. **HESHEN MIAO**

(shousi) at Mt. Weng, which he renamed the Longevity Hills. He also redirected water from the Jade Spring Hill to fill the West Lake (which had been renamed the Kunming Lake) to create a subsidiary garden called the Pure Ripple Garden (Qingyi Yuan) (Cai Shengzhi n.d., 127; cf. *YMYJ* 1981, 1:21).

The continuous growth of the Yuanming Yuan did not end with the death of Qianlong in 1799. His immediate successor, the Jiaqing emperor, continued the endless repairs and remodeling of the Yuanming Yuan. Most noticeably, Jiaqing renovated the Grand Palace Gate, the Main Audience Hall, the Wave-Pacifying Garden, the Wall of Sravasti, the All-Happy Garden, and the Eternal Sunshine Hall (Yangri Tang). He also added some new structures, such as the Smoky Rain Chamber (Yanyu Lou), the Spreading Spring Hall (Fuchun Tang), and a new rice field at the northern end of the Yuanming Yuan, which he named the Economized-Ploughing Villa (Xinggeng Bieshu) (Wu Zhenyu 1983, 190, 197).

The Variegated Spring Garden

The Jiaqing emperor gave the highest priority to the Variegated Spring Garden (Qichun Yuan), which originally was a collection of many small gardens. Officially integrated into the Yuanming Yuan administration in 1772, it was further expanded by Jiaqing to draw water from the Wanquan River. Eventually, Jiaqing designated Thirty (Best) Views in the Variegated Spring Garden. This construction, as usual, required a great deal of money; for example, the construction in the single year of 1809 of 173 units of halls, rooms, and chambers; 260 corridors; 6 pavilions; and 2 decorated archways cost 328,775.331 taels of silver.[12]

The landscape design of the Variegated Spring Garden generally falls into two major sections, east and west, each containing bridges and lakes, large and small, and scenic islets. The east section, with the Grand Palace Gate (Da'gongmen) and the Inner Palace Gate (Er'gongmen) to the rear, faced northward toward the largest compound of the garden, approximately 300 meters deep. It consisted of several structures. The Sunshine Court (Yinghui Dian) was the principal hall. The Hall of Harmony (Zhonghe Tang) connected with the Sunshine Court by way of two corridors to yield a large courtyard. The Spreading Spring Hall (Fuchun Tang) contained the composite living quarters of the dowager empresses and imperial concubines. The Rear Court (Houdian) and the Admiring Moon Chamber (Langyue Lou) were situated at the end of the compound. It seems that a major purpose for Jiaqing's incorporation of the Variegated Spring Garden into the Imperial Garden was to find new accommodations for the imperial ladies, as Kangxi's Changchun Yuan had deteriorated with time. (Today, the only remnant of Changchun Yuan is a small boundary tablet near Peking University.) Indeed, upon the completion of the Variegated Spring Garden, Jiaqing welcomed his mother, the Empress Dowager Xiaohe, and his younger brother, Prince Chun, to live there (Huang Jun 1979, 2:433).

Looking north from the Variegated Spring Garden, one could observe a magnificent lake view, with the Phoenix Isle (Fenglin Zhou) in the middle and a uniquely designed Fairy Terrace (Xianren Chenglu Tai) on the west of another isle. To the west of this major section, in the midst of an open lake, stood an isolated, neat, square islet on which the Blue Shadow Kiosk (Jianbi Ting) was located (Wu Zhenyu 1983, 197–198).

The geometric center of the Variegated Spring Garden was composed of three principal structures, the Spring Watery Chapel (Chunze Zhai), the Winter Room (Shengdong Shi), and the Sleeping Cloud Gallery (Woyun Xuan). They were constructed on a south-north axis without any sense of monotony because they are separated artistically by two water spaces, different in size and shape, together with the elegant All-Season Library to the west. Looking southward from the Winter Room, the Sleeping Cloud Gallery could be seen sitting on a tiny isle and creating a dramatic view. Further south from the gallery was a large plot of hilly land, about fifteen acres. On top of any one of the 5-to-6-meter-high hills, lake views could be enjoyed on both sides. South of this hilly land stood the secluded rectangular compound of a Lama Buddhist temple called the Temple of Enlightenment (Zhengjue Si), which occupied a lot 150 by 80 square meters. It was composed of three main layers of court for worshiping Buddha with a separate front door opening to the south.[13]

On the west side of the Variegated Spring Garden was the Cool Summer Hall (Qingxia Tang), together with a pavilion and corridors, built on the 6.6-acre Phoenix Isle and surrounded by walls. The main hall faced a terrace with a small lake to the south. South of the lake were low rock hills. This complex, which included various pleasant elements, such as a lake, hill, pavilion, house, and corridors, made an ideal summer home. Looking southward from here, one could see the Pure Mind Hall (Chengxin Tang) sitting on an islet surrounded by a lake and the All-Green Gallery (Manlu Xuan) and the Joyous Hall (Changhe Tang) built on two connected isles in another, rectangular, lake. A long narrow bank split the rectangular lake into two sections, and on the southern end of the bank stood the high-rising Streaking Void Kiosk (Lingxu Ting), echoing the Fairy Terrace to the north. This southwest section of the garden yielded several small islets dotting wide open water space to underline the natural beauty and man-made structures.[14]

With the completion of the Variegated Spring Garden, the greater Yuanming Yuan came of age. The Yuanming Yuan became known as the "Three Gardens of the Yuanming Yuan," namely, the original Yuanming Yuan, the Eternal Spring Garden, and the Variegated Spring Garden, or the Ten-Thousand Spring Garden.

PART TWO

History

CHAPTER 4

RISE

THE HISTORY OF THE YUANMING YUAN began with Kangxi, the emperor
of China from 1662 to 1722. He was the Son of Heaven and the ruler of the Celestial Empire, with Beijing as his imperial capital—the center of his imperial
world. When he fully secured his immense power in the final decades of the seventeenth
century, he had already refurbished many desolated gardens and parklands left behind by
Khitan (Qidan), Jurchen (Ruzhen), and Ming princes at the foot of the Western Hills in
the northwest suburbs of Beijing. His first principal garden was the Joyful Spring Garden
(Changchun Yuan), which in his own words was built on the basis of the desolated Pure
Flowery Garden (Qinghua Yuan) originally owned by Marquis Li Wei of the Ming (Yu
Mingzhong 1985, 2:1268–1269). It was a very modest imperial garden, as the Koreans
observed, in comparison to the Yuanming Yuan (*Yanxinglu xuanji* 1961, 201). In 1720, the
Russian ambassador had the opportunity to see the garden at the invitation of Kangxi. The
Russians called it "Tzan-shu-yang." They found an elegant court, rows of forest trees, the
Hall of Audience, and many handsome royal apartments (Bell 1788, 6 7; cf. Sugimura Yūzō
1961, 217–218; Maurice Adam 1936, 1–2; Yu Mingzhong 1985, 2:1268–1285; *Yanxinglu xuanji*
1961, 201, 320). In 1722, Kangxi passed away at the age of sixty-nine in this particular garden
(Feng Erkang 1995, 58–59).

In 1709, taking *fengshui* into consideration, Kangxi selected a site on which to build
a brand new garden, soon to be named the Yuanming Yuan, approximately 500 to 600
meters north of his Joyful Spring Garden.[1] When the first phase of the Yuanming Yuan
was completed, Kangxi graciously awarded it to his fourth son, Prince Yinzhen (Yu
Mingzhong 1985, 2:1321). The prince was the legitimate successor regardless of endless
rumors to the contrary (Feng Erkang 1995, 64). He eventually succeeded his father to be
the Yongzheng emperor, and he made the Yuanming Yuan his principal imperial garden,
leaving the Joyful Spring Garden to the Imperial Mother and her royal consorts. Yongzheng's successors continued to use the Yuanming Yuan as the imperial garden, and it

inevitably superseded Kangxi's Joyful Spring Garden. But the Joyful Spring Garden as the home of dowager empresses remained for a long time to come a significant royal garden with impressive palatial gates, courts, halls, chambers, galleries, libraries, docks, and even a make-believe "shopping street" *(maimaijie)*. The Qianlong emperor visited his mother here very often. In 1778 he built inside the garden the Mother's Memorial Temple (Enmu Si) in her honor, parallel to the Enyou Temple that Yongzheng had built in honor of his father, Kangxi (Yu Mingzhong 1985, 2:1274–1279). Not until the Jiaqing emperor, who made the Variegated Spring Garden the home of the royal mothers, did the Joyful Spring Garden gradually fall into oblivion.

From a Prince Garden to the Imperial Garden

When Prince Yinzhen occupied the Yuanming Yuan soon after its completion in 1709, the garden was still modest in size. It was, however, not a renovation of a desolate Ming garden; rather, it was a new garden *par excellence*. According to the estimation of Zhou Weiquan, the Yuanming Yuan at its inception already covered the area between the Front Lake and the Rear Lake, about 91 acres. But Zhang Enying has disputed this estimate by citing some poems composed by Prince Yinzhen that suggest that the garden had already extended beyond the Rear Lake, covering an area no less than 180 acres (Zhou Weiquan 1981, 31; Zhang Enying 1986, 24). Whoever is right, the Yuanming Yuan upon its completion was less than one-third of its full size. In any event, in 1722, the Yuanming Yuan had become magnificent enough for Prince Yinzhen to invite his aged father, Kangxi, and his youthful son, the future Qianlong emperor, to the Peony Terrace to appreciate the flower blossoms (Yu Mingzhong 1985, 2:1335; cf. *Yuanming yuan sishijing tuyong* 1985, 13).

After the prince became emperor in early 1724, construction to expand the Yuanming Yuan began. The official designation of the Yuanming Yuan as the prime imperial pleasance of the new emperor, however, was postponed due to the sudden death of the imperial mother. As a filial son, he had to observe a period of mourning. He thus suspended moving into the garden for pleasure living (*YMYA* 1991, 1:8). Not until August 27, 1725, did Yongzheng decide to end his mourning at the repeated petitions from high-ranking officials. On the lunar New Year's Day in 1726, the emperor formally occupied the Yuanming Yuan. He rode on a gilded wagon with an entourage of eleven carriages and proceeded from Beijing to his imperial garden. To celebrate this occasion, the princes and grand officials presented three thousand lanterns to the throne (*YMYA* 1991, 1:15, 16; Wu Zhenyu 1983, 293).

Although Yongzheng returned to the Forbidden City after having spent only two days in the garden, he had already decided to make the garden not only his pleasure ground but also a workplace. He formally instructed the Boards of Personnel and War that "there is no difference to me whether to conduct routine state affairs in Beijing or in the Yuanming Yuan" (*YMYA* 1991, 1:17, 19, 32, 35). He reiterated the remark by adding a decree that from 1725 daily affairs would be conducted in the garden in the same manner as in the Forbidden

City. Clearly, he wanted to make sure that his garden living would not hamper the routine business of the state. This shows the emperor's sensitivity to possible criticism of his neglect of duty; indeed, he was somewhat defensive about his garden life. Not incidentally, he named his royal office in the Yuanming Yuan the Diligent Court.

The emperor meant what he said; however, at least in the outset, no official seemed to take serious matters seriously in the garden atmosphere. On January 20, 1726, when Yongzheng sat on his throne in the Diligent Court ready to hear reports, no one came forward. Visibly displeased, the emperor protested that garden living was not at all to neglect duty; on the contrary, so far as he was concerned, a better job could be done in such a comfortable and pleasant environment as the Yuanming Yuan. He warned with a threat that if they should continue to take things casually in the garden, he would consider it an objection of his presence in the Yuanming Yuan (*YMYA* 1991, 1: 22).

Before long, both the emperor and his officials were accustomed to performing official duties in the imperial garden. Obviously lured by the attractiveness of the surroundings and natural setting, Yongzheng spent more and more time in the Yuanming Yuan. Returning to the Forbidden City from time to time as he had to, he became increasingly reluctant to leave the garden. He thereby started the tradition of regular garden living for Qing emperors (Cheng Yansheng 1928, 1a–3a).

After having decided to conduct official business in the garden, the Yongzheng emperor completed an elegant stone-paved road lined with pretty willow trees between the Yuanming Yuan and Beijing, about six miles long in George Macartney's estimation (Crammer-Byng 1962, 84; Mageerni 1916, 1:36). The stone road left the Forbidden City through the West Straight Gate (Xizhimen), crossed the moat over the Gaoliang Bridge, and finally turned northwest to Haidian before arriving at the gates of the Yuanming Yuan.[2] The road facilitated the emperor's frequent travels between the two places. Whenever the emperor arrived at the front gate of the Yuanming Yuan, Manchu princes, senior officials, scholar-attendants of the South Studio (Nan Shufang), and several rows of soldiers were supposed to line up to welcome and show respect.

Needless to say, the road also served numerous people, from officials to workmen, who were summoned to the garden from time to time. Normally, one had to begin at midnight in order to reach the imperial garden from the Forbidden City in time (Wu Zhenyu 1983, 245). Hence, regular travel between the two places was painful, especially for the senior officials of advanced age. Yongzheng was kind and gracious enough to exempt them from attending early morning meetings in the Yuanming Yuan. In winter, especially when the harsh cold wind was blowing down from Siberia, the emperor would excuse most officials, barring emergency, from coming to the Yuanming Yuan (cf. *YMYA* 1991, 1:19). By the twentieth year of Jiaqing, or 1815, the emperor permitted deputies to deliver memorials and high-ranking officials to report to the garden later in the day (Wu Zhenyu 1983, 245).

Historians generally consider Yongzheng to have been a frugal ruler; in regard to enlarging and beautifying the Yuanming Yuan, however, he was a big spender. As early as the beginning of 1724, his second year on the throne, he approved the plan to add more structures to the garden and authorized the purchase of wood materials (*YMYJ* 1981, 1:4, 6; Wang Wei 1992, 81). The construction initially met the desperate need to accommodate administrative functions, including the enormous Main Audience Hall and its annexes for attendants and guests. Accordingly, unlike ordinary Chinese gardens, which represented a retreat from the political world, the Yuanming Yuan emerged as the center of the political world. Prior to the completion of these administrative buildings, Yongzheng had set up his temporary royal office inside the royal living quarters on the Nine Continents, nine artificial islets forming a semicircle around the Front Lake and the Rear Lake. This indicates that no later than 1726, the fourth year of the Yongzheng reign, the structures on the Nine Continents were substantially completed (cf. Xu Enyin 1991, 137).

In 1727, Yongzheng still found it necessary to justify his prolonged garden living, as he was sensitive to the moral concerns derived from the Confucian codes of conduct. He stated in a decree that he really needed a pleasant setting, referring to the Yuanming Yuan, to fulfill his duty as the ruler of the vast empire. Seemingly trying to prove that he meant what he said, the emperor not only required his officials to work harder in the garden but also redoubled his own effort to be as diligent as he possibly could (*YMYA* 1991, 1:22). Keeping himself alert, he hung inside the Main Audience Hall a large antithetical distich *(duilian),* which read:

> Taking Heaven's heart as my own heart,
> I care about my people all the time;
> Taking people's happiness as my own happiness,
> I should always be kind and cheerful.[3]

That was not all. On a screen behind his desk, two large Chinese characters were prominently displayed: *"wu yi"* (Don't indulge in pleasure). He also inscribed on the walls of his garden office an essay, showing how serious was his responsibility to maintain peace and prosperity, how determined he was to uphold the empire, and how he knew that his responsibility to maintain the empire was no easier than his forefathers' great enterprise of empire building (Yu Mingzhong 1985, 2:1327–1331).

His reassurance was not empty words. Yongzheng spent long hours in his office reading government papers and talking to close advisors. Since there were so many issues waiting for his decision, as he himself noted, he could afford wasting no time while living in the garden even during the hot summer days. In fact, regardless of the season, the emperor rarely missed his office hours in the garden. On one occasion, so far as we know, he stayed in his office in the evening concentrating so hard that he was unaware of how late it had become. To record this experience, he composed a poem wishing the shining moon in the dark sky to witness of his vigilance (Zhu Jiajin and Li Yeqin, comps. 1983, 55).

Rather than for amusement, but actually to show his conscientiousness in a different way, Yongzheng created a large rice field at the northern end one of the Yuanming Yuan's scenes to be named Bountiful Farms, or "Crops as Plentiful as Clouds" (Duojia Ruyun).

Thus, Yongzheng expressed his moral concern about the well-being of the vast peasant population by his daily observation of how the land was ploughed, the seeds were sowed, and the crops were harvested (Yu Mingzhong 1985, 3:1356). In August 1729, he added a silk-worm farm, which a head eunuch was appointed to supervise. Consequently, those who worked on the farm comprised the Silkworm Household *(chanhu),* new members of the growing Garden Household *(yuanhu),* the men and women working in the garden. The silk production eventually led to the founding of a brocade and dye mill, situated at the foot of the Longevity Hills, where the workers could gain easy access to the chrysalises and minerals for the mill (*YMYA* 1991, 2:1018–1019).

Once the Yongzheng emperor made the Yuanming Yuan his regular residence, security of the royal demesne had to be reinforced. In 1724, following Yongzhgeng's ascendancy, the original 620–man Green Battalion *(lüying),* which included 180 cavalrymen and 440 infantrymen, was immediately increased to 1,000, which included 200 cavalrymen and 800 infantrymen (*YMYA* 1991, 1:18; 2:1643). In the spring of the following year, a practice ground for the troops was completed (Zhang Enyin 1991a, 136). Every soldier received 20 taels of silver as a bonus for taking up the prestigious duty to defend the imperial garden (*YMYA* 1991, 1:18).

As the Yuanming Yuan became more and more important, the security force known as the Yuanming Yuan Eight Banners eventually commanded 3,232 troops. All officers and soldiers in this force without exception were ethnic Manchus. They were carefully selected from trusted clans proficient in military skills. Before long, the standard size of this security force amounted to 3,456, with 136 officers and 3,120 men, under the command of two Manchu princes. For generations to come, these guardsmen were positioned around the Yuanming Yuan. Their responsibilities were mainly twofold: to secure the Yuanming Yuan in general and to assist the Imperial Body Guards to facilitate the smooth passage of the emperor and his entourage to and from the garden in particular. A normal day's training included horseback riding and archery practice. Occasionally, the emperor participated in the drills. The huge Drill Field, together with a tall review stand, situated at southwest side of the garden precisely for this purpose. A 1747 record shows that 2,328 additional barracks units were completed to accommodate more troops (*YMYA* 1991, 1:60–61; *Qingshigao* 1976, 14:3862–3863; *YMYZ* 1984, 240–262; Yu Mingzhong 1985, 3:1349–1350).

Working hard in the Yuanming Yuan though he was, Yongzheng would surely not refrain from the pleasure of the magnificent garden. Particularly fond of boating on the Sea of Blessing, the largest lake in the garden, His Majesty often invited his guests, normally high-ranking officials and favorite consorts, to sail around the smooth lake visiting sites. His own dragon barge *(longzhou)* usually led a fleet of some thirty boats. After cruising, in the evening, an exciting fanfare always followed, particularly on festival days. His successor, the Qianlong emperor, who grew up in this environment, liked lake cruising even more. Having the privilege of being on the emperor's guest list, Father Attiret once shared this pleasure of boating. He described an occasion where numerous boats on the lake, gilt and varnished, served different purposes: "sometimes, for taking the air; sometimes, for fishing; and sometimes, for jousts, and combats, and other diversions" (Attiret 1982, 20–21). It seems that the emperor and his entourage, while boating, simultaneously enjoyed many different activities on the lake.

The celebration of the spring Duanwu Festival, on the lunar calendar's middle of the fifth month, was the greatest annual event on the lake. The festival is in honor of the ancient patriotic poet Qu Yuan (340–278 B.C.) who drowned himself in a river in order to awaken the conscience of his prince, the Duke of Chu. The dragon boat race, honored no later than the sixth century A.D., was understood to be searching for the drowning patriot (cf. Schneider 1980, 142–157). The Manchu monarch clearly observed the major activity of the Chinese festival day in the imperial garden. Boat racing on the Sea of Blessing was rarely missed, except on a bad rainy day. Normally, on this specific day, when both the emperor and his guests arrived at the Sea of Blessing, several colorful dragonhead boats started racing on the lake in the midst of loud drums and flying flags, much like the ordinary Chinese folk festivities throughout the country. When the excitement was over, both the host and his guests landed at the granite bank of the lake before ascending the steps to the half-moon terrace and heading home on a tree-lined boulevard embellished with colorful flowers (Zhao Lian 1980, 378).

The lakeside was an excellent place to watch fireworks after sunset. Lighting up the dark sky, the fireworks shone on the colorful lanterns hung in various patterns on the tops of numerous buildings. Qianlong was also fond of admiring the full moon beside the lake. A popular anecdote has it that on one midsummer night, when the emperor and his entourage were enjoying opera under the bright moonlight at Immortal Abode on the Fairy Terrace, sudden bursts of a loud noisy sound of frogs caused a great embarrassment. The clever minister Liu Yong (1714–1779), half-jokingly, begged the emperor to silence the frogs by decree. His Majesty agreed and let a eunuch proclaim his words by the lake. Miraculously, the frogs were instantly silent. Liu Yong quickly congratulated the emperor's awesome power and rushed to offer flattery. Before long, however, the frogs resumed their noisy sounds. The panicky officials and eunuchs desperately threw stones into the lake in the hope of scaring the frogs away (Peng Zeyu and Zhang Baozhang 1985, 158).

It is said that Yongzheng particularly enjoyed watching the sunset-tinted peaks of the West Hills from his sumptuous chamber north of the Sea of Blessing (the scene was completed in July 1728). The surroundings reportedly made him feel open-minded and completely free from worry. Behind the chamber, the Hanyun Studio was lined by magnolia tree. The blossoms, as the court official Yu Mingzhong (1714–1779) recorded, filled the air with fragrance (1985, 3:1366; cf. Wang Wei 1992, 83). After sunset on one of the Weaver days, the seventh day of the seventh month, Yongzheng came here and had a banquet with a group of royalty and court ladies, while observing the reunion of the Cowboy and the Weaver in the Milky Way (Yu Mingzhong 1985, 3:1365–1366).

The Yongzheng emperor also had a sentimental attachment to the Deep Vault of Heaven, a secluded area near the southeastern edge of the Yuanming Yuan, where he had spent much of his boyhood. He thus erected there an inscribed tablet to make it a monument. Later, a royal school with rows of classrooms and dormitories found a home at this scenic site. Qianlong, when he was still Prince Hongli, attended this school with other princes and remembered well that the quiet daytime and beautiful nights made him forget the time (Yu Mingzhong 1985, 3:1378).

A strong earthquake suddenly hit the tranquil imperial pleasance in the autumn of 1730 (*Qingshigao* 1976, 3:329). The beautiful garden, according to the testimony of a Jesuit father, was instantly "reduced to a piteous condition." When the ground was shaking on September 20, the Yongzheng emperor fled to a dragon barge for safety, and he remained on his boat throughout the night. Fearful of aftershocks, he and his family lived in a large tent for a lengthy period of time. As late as October 5, His Majesty still received European priests in his tent (Malone 1934, 58). He was obviously humbled by the quake; like other Sons of Heaven before him, he considered it a serious warning from Heaven. Hence, he issued a decree seeking Heaven's pardon and forgiveness. Repairing the damaged Yuanming Yuan was not so difficult, as the royal treasury remained immensely rich.

Yongzheng spent most of his remaining years in the Yuanming Yuan. He rarely left the garden. Overall, he had a wonderful time. His enjoyment and delight were expressed in one of his many poems:

> My royal garden is always delightful
> In rain or under sunshine.
> When the Spring comes to my chamber
> The gill fungus look so clean.
> A few petals of the falling flowers
> Awoke me from a noontime snooze.
> The sound of fishermen, I hear.
> Relaxed, I feel.
> Sitting under a pine tree, I enjoy
> The music of birds from the bamboo forest.
> Alas! The gentle east wind which reads my mind
> Bows green grass into gentle waves.[4]

His pleasures in the garden were myriad. He enjoyed watching sunrise and sunset around the beautiful surroundings, reading and writing in his elegant chambers, conversing with officials and relatives in halls or in studios, and entertaining guests in flower-blossom-filled courtyards (cited in Yu Mingzhong 1985, 2:1322). He died at the age of fifty-eight in the Yuanming Yuan on the third day of his illness in the autumn of 1735 (*Qingshigao* 1976, 3:340; Wu Zhenyu 1983, 297). Yongzheng's secretive court life and sudden death inevitably caused rumors. It has been suggested that the emperor was assassinated by Lü Siniang, the daughter of the prominent Ming loyalist Lü Liuliang (1629–1683) (for example, see Peng Zeyu and Zhang Baozhang 1985, 115–120), but more serious scholars find this fascinating story groundless. His sudden death was more likely caused by the misuse of drugs. It was no secret that Yongzheng had many Daoist alchemists, such as Zhang Taixu and Wang Dingqian, in the garden to manufacture drugs to cure his sickness (Feng Erkang 1995, 545, 548, 549).

The Golden Years

The crown prince Hongli's succession was never in dispute. The Yongzheng emperor left behind in the Yuanming Yuan a copy of a concealed decree, which designated Hongli as his legitimate successor. After the posthumous decree had been announced, the prince ascended to the throne in the garden and then escorted the casket to the Forbidden City (Feng Erkang 1995, 553–554). As the Qianlong emperor, he formally occupied the Yuanming Yuan in 1738 after having fulfilled the three-year mourning period (*Qingshigao* 1976, 3:356). The young emperor had been born and raised in the Yuanming Yuan, where he was given the Eternal Spring Fairy Hall as his residence. When he was only six years old, he attended the memorable flower blossom party at the Peony Terrace on the Nine Continents together with his grandfather Kangxi and father Yongzheng. Years later, in 1722, the young prince again joined his grandfather and father to celebrate the lovely peony season in their beloved garden. These two gatherings of three generations of Manchu monarchs at the Yuanming Yuan's Peony Terrace were proudly recorded in the imperial annals. The Qianlong emperor later erected on the spot a stone tablet inscribing the events with affection and gratitude to his forefathers, as well as a reminder that his was a great responsibility inherited from them (Yu Mingzhong 1985, 2:1335–1337).

Qianlong continued to make the Yuanming Yuan the principal imperial garden and was most eager to expand it during his long reign (Yu Mingzhong 1985, 2:1323–1324). No place in the garden meant more to him than the Eternal Spring Fairy Hall, where he spent his childhood. The hall was a huge compound consisting of a three-column-wide front building and a five-column-wide main building. Qianlong remembered when he sat in his study under the shadow of the tall evergreen trees with great pleasure. He spent many happy hours in his well-insulated warm room in winter and in an open-air pavilion near the hall during summer nights (cf. Qianlong's poems as cited in *Yuanming yuan sishijing tuyong* 1985, 28). Once he became the reigning emperor, he let his beloved mother use this hall for the rest of her life.

Like his father, Qianlong also attached deep sentiment to the Deep Vault of Heaven, where he spent his school years. As he vividly remembered, the moonlight threw the bamboo shadows on the whitewashed walls in the midst of the elegant school buildings. The surrounding wood was filled with orchids and pine trees. He enjoyed reading books in the midst of the magic sounds of the bamboo music (cited in Yu Mingzhong 1985, 3:1378). Another memorable place for Qianlong was the Swastika House. It was built in 1727 on a solid brick foundation surrounded by water, cool in summer and warm in winter (*YMYA* 1991, 2:1182). Qianlong was fascinated especially by the golden reflections of the Swastika on the lake under an autumn moon, reminding him of the Buddha's brilliance; he later renamed this scene the Universal Peace in honor of the Buddha's blessing. Slightly north of here was situated the Peach-Blossom Cove, a pleasant hideout for quiet moments.

In 1736, barely a month after he had ascended to the throne, Qianlong commissioned the court artists Castiglione, Tang Dai, and Shen Yuan, to draw a large atlas of the Yuan-ming Yuan. The collaborative drawing was completed in 1738 and hung on the northern wall of the Clear Sunshine Pavilion to the west side of the royal living quarters at the center of the Nine Continents (*YMYA* 1991, 2:1245).[5]

Drawing a picture of the entire Yuanming Yuan, however, did not mean that the garden was complete. Qianlong seemed to have made up his mind to expand the garden ever more grandly very early on, but he was also sensitive to criticism for too much pleasure seeking. He ended all construction in 1740 in the aftermath of serious floods in west China at the request of the censor Liu Zao (*Qingshigao* 1976, 3:366). As late as 1742, he still pledged not to undertake any additional garden projects (Yu Mingzhong 1985, 2:1323). But by this time, the new and gigantic Ancestral Shrine, which cost more than 600,000 taels of silver, had already been completed.[6] Perhaps he could justify this particular project for filial reasons. Indeed, after its completion, to show his filial devotion, he paid frequent visits to the shrine. On the Qingming Festival, every fifth day of the fourth month of the lunar calendar, he personally performed the ceremony of ancestral worship in front of the memorial tablets of his forefathers. The other members of the royal family followed his lead. The event was well-described in his poem entitled "Paying a Visit to the Ancestral Shrine on the Memorial Day" (Qingming ri baiyi Anyou gong):

> Together with members of my family
> I pay tribute to the Shrine.
> Shadows of moving persons
> Confuse which is real and which is fantasy.
> I enjoy the mist in the air
> Which contains green willows near the bank.
> I feel no pity for the phoenix
> Who envies red peaches near the castle.
> I look in the distance from east to west
> At the tombs of my father and my grandfather.
> My soul and thoughts go with them
> I know how they feel.[7]

The completion of designating the Forty (Best) Views and their 200 structures in 1744 was a high mark in the history of the Yuanming Yuan. The delighted Qianlong ventured to write a poem for each of the impressionistic views drawn by the court artists Tang Dai and Shen Yuan. Indeed, the emperor expressed much of his satisfaction in living in his "paradise" in the form of poetry. He composed no less than 42,000 poems during his long life, of which many were written in the Yuanming Yuan.

The poetic visualized images may help us capture his sentiments derived from the changing seasons he observed in the garden. He liked to feel the fresh morning, following an overnight rain, at the front door of his hall in late spring. He sensed the spirit of the garden refreshed by the season's blossoming trees and flowers. The morning breeze carried with it the delicate fragrance and scent of wildflowers. He was immensely fond of spring-time. When the early summer arrived, he was aware that the long green shades had covered the courtyards and created countless artful shadows on the different floors. The summer heat with soft winds made him sleepy at noon. The returning swallows busily rebuilding their once abandoned homes reminded him that the summer was fading. This was the time to hear the sounds of cicadas coming from the willow trees, even though the noisy sounds were not particularly to his liking. He watched the autumn winds gradually turning the leaves in the woods and the hills into red or yellow to create an embroidery effect. The autumn was as agreeable as spring. He welcomed the warm sunshine by lifting the curtains of his south-side studio. Walking in the courtyard, he saw the pearly dew on the trees and the half-hiding fish in the ponds. The evening showers, quick and cool as he always sensed, made the Wutong trees wet and sparse. He admired the wonderful chrysanthemum bravely weathering frost in mid-September. He sometimes kept chrysanthemums and plums in a small greenhouse for a longer time. He fully confined himself to indoor activities during the deep winter. He often sat by the glass windows to watch the half-frozen waterways, a boundless blank view before him (Qianlong's poems in *YMYJ* 1983, 2:57).

Just before completing the designation of the Forty Views, the Qianlong emperor, who was sensitive to the Confucian ideal of frugal life, had pledged that he would not start any new garden projects. Actually, however, he soon started seemingly endless construction inside the imperial garden. Besides the emperor's personal passion for garden beauty, two main reasons contributed to letting his passion prevail over his moral concerns. The first was that the empire during his reign had reached its peak and the imperial treasury was full enough to finance his indulgence (Sugimura 1961, 218–223). Second, his repeated southern tours exposed to him the most attractive gardens and scenery in the lower Yangzi valley, thus tempting him to recreate in his own imperial garden the gentle southern scenes he liked the most.

Officially, the southern tours were to inspect his domain and the well-being of the people; however, he missed no opportunity for sight-seeing. His first trip, stretching from February to May 1751, had ninety-two stops en route. He repeated similar tours in 1757, 1762, 1765, 1780, and 1784 to show his continuous fascination with the unique natural environment of the south and with the refined southern-style architecture, in particular the elegant Suzhou gardens. He had draftsmen and artists accompany him to copy southern wonders that he wanted to recreate in the Eternal Spring Garden. It was not uncommon that he brought back the blueprint of a complete garden and rebuilt it to scale at a particular site in his imperial pleasance.[8] Numerous gardens, structures, and scenes borrowed from the south were recreated in the Eternal Spring Garden, which was an integral part of the Yuanming Yuan. When Qianlong celebrated his eightieth grand birthday in 1790, the garden had fully grown into a glory of which the aged emperor was immensely proud.[9]

When Qianlong enjoyed his grand birthday gala in his imperial garden, the outside world had changed dramatically. The rising British commercial empire wanted to extend its trade to the "immobile" Celestial Empire. Cultural exclusiveness and lack of communication and understanding at last brought "two worlds in collision" (cf. Peyrefitte 1992).

The Macartney Mission

In 1792, London sent the senior diplomat Lord Macartney (1737–1806) to China for the expansion of trade in the name of honoring the Qianlong Emperor's eightieth birthday. Regional officials in Guangdong, however, reported to the court that the king of England sent his envoy with "precious tribute" *(guizhong gongwu)* for the emperor's birthday celebration (Gugong bowuyuan 1990, 612–614). The mission was clearly taken by the Qing side as a tributary mission. Qianlong appointed the Salt Administrator Zhengrui, who began his career as an Imperial Household man in the Yuanming Yuan, to take care of the guests from afar (Gugong bowuyuan 1990, 674, 692).

Macartney and his suite "prosecuted their journey towards the capital of China without fatigue and inconvenience." The ambassador reached Beijing on August 21, 1793, and the arrival "was announced by the firing of guns; and refreshments were made ready for all the gentlemen, at a resting place within the gate." Then the ambassador proceeded on a granite pavement to arrive at the town of Haidian on August 23. The Britons were assigned to a twelve-acre villa containing "a garden laid out in serpentine walks," and the "buildings in this place consisted of several separate pavilions, erected round small courts." The ambassador's lodging was obviously the Grand Elegant Garden (Hongya Yuan), or "Hoong-ya-yuen" in Staunton's account (Staunton 1799, 2:2, 19, 24, 29; Crammer-Byng 1962, 92), a distinguished guesthouse in the neighborhood of the Yuanming Yuan.

In the morning on August 24, the Imperial Household man Jin Jian arranged a tour for the guests to see the Main Audience Hall in the Yuanming Yuan. Samuel Holmes, a soldier of Macartney's guard, caught sight of the imperial garden, which "contained a vast variety of elegant little buildings" (Holmes 1798, 134). To show his interest in the mission, Qianlong also asked his favorite official Heshen (Ho-shen, 1714–1799), already a rising star in the imperial officialdom (Hummel 1975, 288–290), to look after the foreigners. According to Jin Jian and Yi Ling'a's report to the court, the lodging for the British had been thoroughly cleaned, sufficiently supplied with provisions, and fully secured by troops. The foreigners, they said, were content with the large and comfortable accommodations and plentiful food supply (*YMYA* 1991, 1:342–343, 350).

George Staunton also recounted Ambassador Macartney and the condition of his suite. The "apartments were handsome, and not ill-contrived," as Staunton put it, and "several of them were adorned with landscapes, painted in water-colours." The regret was that the guesthouse "wanted repairs for being empty for sometime" (1799, 2:24). Also, the presence of the security guardsmen made the Britons feel that they were denied the liberty of passing beyond the walls of the palatial garden, and they even took it as an insult and felt "in a state of honorable imprisonment" (Anderson 1795, 112). While the food was delicious, especially the northern Chinese-style noodles, the Britons complained about being placed in the "charming and delightful" woods farther from the heart of the Chinese capital (Peyrefitte 1992, 130; Mageerni 1916, 1:43–44). The ambassador and his advisors seemed unaware of the importance of the Yuanming Yuan as the center of Chinese political activity.

While Lord Macartney's lodging appeared handsome and comfortable, John Barrow, together with Dr. Dinwiddie and two mechanics, found their accommodations shabby, filthy, miserable, and more fitting "for hogs than for human creatures." In fact, they lived inside the Yuanming Yuan, "scarcely two hundred yards from the great hall of audience" (1805, 73). Apparently, they lived near the Audience Hall for the convenience of installing the presents that the ambassador had brought to the Qing emperor. It was entirely possible that the Chinese took them as less prestigious people and actually allotted them the servants' apartment at the Inner Palace Gate. Each of the seventy-four English craftsmen and servants working in the Yuanming Yuan, however, was awarded ten taels of silver by the Imperial Household (Zhongguo diyi lishi dang'anguan 1996, 570).

On August 26, the embassy was transferred to Beijing as Macartney requested; however, John Barrow, the ambassador's personal secretary, together with the astronomer, James Dinwiddie, were left behind in the Yuanming Yuan in order to help in the slow process of assembling the gifts to the emperor. It was Qianlong's wishes to display eight major pieces of the British tributes inside the Yuanming Yuan, and he would personally view them upon returning from Rehe (Gugong bowuyuan 1990, 671; Zhongguo diyi lishi dang'anguan 1996, 139, 564, 568, 569). Macartney was also eager to show the British gifts in order to impress the Qing emperor and to facilitate the process of negotiation.

John Barrow thus lived in the Yuanming Yuan longer than any other Britons, but he found the imperial garden not really impressive. For him, the general appearance was being "broken into hill and dale, and diversified with wood and lawn." The abundant canals, rivers, and large sheets of water "are neither trimmed, nor shorn, nor sloped like the glacis of a fortification, but have been thrown up with immense labour in an irregular and, as it were, fortuitous manner, so as to represent the free hand of nature." In short, in his opinion, the Yuanming Yuan fell "very short of the fanciful and extravagant descriptions that Sir William Chambers has given of Chinese gardening." Nevertheless, he still admired the "bold rocky promontories jutting into a lake, the pleasure-houses erected in particular spots, and the trees being placed according to their magnitudes" (Barrow 1805, 83)."

Barrow also admitted that he had only made "little excursions" into the garden "by stealth," because his pride made him extremely unwilling to be stopped by a eunuch or an inferior officer. His miserable living condition plus anxiety over being "watched" might very well have affected his opinion that the Chinese "are as deficient in proportion as their construction is void of every rule and principle which we are apt to consider as essential to architecture" (Barrow 1805, 84). Obviously, his opinion ran counter to the ambassador's observation. Macartney found "some buildings at Yuan-ming Yuan which, as pieces of brickwork, are superior both in point of materials and workmanship to Tyrconnel House in the south-west corner of Hanover Square, which is boasted of as the most perfect thing of the sort in England" (Crammer-Byng 1962, 264). In fact, Barrow himself was conscious of his subjectivity. He cited in great length Lord Macartney's favorable observation of Chinese architecture and gardening (Barrow 1805, 86–92).

Macartney saw the Chengde summer resort quite extensively, but he also had the opportunity to tour a part of the Yuanming Yuan on August 23. He was impressed by the artistic creativity and by the magnificent landscape dotted with numerous pavilions linked "by passages earnestly cut through stupendous rocks, or by fairyland galeries" (Robbins 1908, 275; Mageerni 1916, 1:48). The ambassador was deeply impressed by the 150–foot-long and 60–foot-wide Main Audience Hall. In it, he admired the splendid room, showed respect to the throne, and offered a Latin translation to the hall: *"Verus, Magnus, Gloriosus, Splendidus, Felix"* (Upright, Great, Glorious, Famous, Fortunate) (YMYA 1991, 1:345; Staunton 1799, 2:25; Crammer-Byng 1962, 95; Peyrefitte 1992, 136; Mageerni 1916, 1:49).

Eight pieces of the gifts, or articles of tribute for the Qing emperor, the Britons brought with them were unloaded in the Yuanming Yuan to be assembled for His Majesty's inspection (Gugong bowuyuan 1990, 671, 698, 700). The terrestrial and the celestial globes were placed on both sides of the throne in the Audience Hall. The "lustres" were hung from the ceiling. The planetarium, which took about eighteen days to assemble, was put at one end of the hall. The Vulliamy clocks, the barometer, the Wedgwood porcelain, and Fraser's orrery were settled at the other end (Mageerni 1916, 1:51; cf. Fang Yujin 1984, 93, 95). More noticeably, the model of a warship and six small field guns were displayed inside the Main Audience Hall and the Homely Memorial Hall (Danhuai Tang) respectively. "It looked like a preview of the British pavilion," as Peyrefitte puts it, "at an international exhibition" (*YMYA* 1991, 1:331, 342; Peyrefitte 1992, 138–139; Staunton 1799, 2:25–29). Indeed, Manchu princes, Tartar generals, and Chinese mandarins arrived in large numbers to see the "exhibition" (Mageerni 1916, 1:54–55).

Qianlong took note in his official correspondence of these impressive "strange tributary goods" from a distant country, and he instructed the Chinese workers and craftsmen to learn from the British how to install and dismantle foreign equipment. He was distressed to hear that the large astrological piece could not be dismantled once it was installed and insisted in his instructions to the responsible officials on knowing the tricks. But he seemed unaware of the scientific implications of this equipment, except for his concern that Chinese workmen might not know how to handle them well after the departure of the foreigners (cf. YMYA 1991, 1:344, 348–354; Gugong bowuyuan 1990, 695–696; Fang Yujin 1984, 96).

It was on September 2 that the Macartney party of seventy, leaving twenty-one men behind either in Beijing or the Yuanming Yuan, set out for Chengde to meet with the Qianlong emperor. The Britons passed the Great Wall and altogether took six days to arrive at Qianlong's summer palace (Staunton 1799, 2:45–60; Mageerni 1916, 2:1). Due to the controversy over protocol, Qianlong did not grant the Britons an audience until September 14. The historical encounter took place in a vast yurt, and a ritual banquet followed the ritual presentations. On the next day, Macartney followed the Qianlong emperor to visit a Buddhist temple and toured the imperial parks known as the Chengde Summer Mountain Retreat in Rehe, in which the British took great delight (Staunton 1805, 2:80–84; cf. Peyrefitte 1992, 223–235, 249–251; Mageerni 1916, 2:10–23).

September 17, 1993 was the Qianlong emperor's eighty-third birthday. His Majesty received well-wishers, including the Mongolian princes and Burmese envoys, at the Danpo Ningjing (Simple Life in Quietude) Court in the mountain retreat. Macartney and his deputy Staunton, according to Grand Council archival sources, "were present in front of the throne," and performed the full kowtow, "kneeling three times, each time bowing their head to the ground thrice" (Zhongguo diyi lishi dang'anguan 1996: 147; cf. Qin Guojing 1996, 50). Beyond doubt, the British resisted performing the kowtow, but Qianlong and his officials persisted in stating that the universal rule of the Celestial Empire made no exception for the British. The foreigners from afar were earnestly warned about the importance of being acquainted with the ritual. At one point, Qianlong made himself clear in a decree that he was accommodating anything so long as it upheld the Tizhi (the well-established polity), which required the kowtow in imperial audience. The emperor even reiterated that even the king himself should perform the ritual at his court (Zhongguo diyi lishi dang'anguan 1996, 9, 174; cf. 10, 13, 148, 172, 173; Gugong bowuyuan 1990, 715–716).

The kowtow in modern Western discourse is an insulting and degrading act. Especially in Britain, kneeling had always been associated with subjugation. But the Qing Empire representing the Confucian world order took it for granted that the ritual was simply a time-honored gesture of showing respect to the sovereign, in no way humiliating the performer (cf. Hevia 1995, 225–248). Qianlong could not possibly allow Macartney to bend one knee only, thus violating the integrity of the long-standing imperial audience. Nor was it necessary for Qianlong to make such concession under the circumstances. In fact, the Grand Council specifically instructed Zhengrui on August 18 that the Englishmen "must be verse in the kowtow before they could be present to an imperial audience" (Gugong bowuyuan 1990, 692). Moreover, it was extremely unlikely that should the British refuse to perform kowtow, the Qing emperor would invite the British ambassador and his suites to attend a banquet and watch fireworks at the Wanshu Yuan (Ten-Thousand Tree Garden) in the evening on September 18 (Staunton 1799, 2:68, 73–79). Very possibly, the British at last reluctantly abided by the ritual in hopes of achieving the objectives of the mission. In any event, Macartney was the British diplomat who performed the kowtow. After all, the archival documents have confirmed the Chinese assertion and the Russian interpreter Vladykin's testimony that "the British ambassador did perform three kneelings and nine head-knockings" (Rockhill 1905, 31).

The British mission left Chengde on September 21 and was back in Beijing on September 26.[10] Upon the British departure, Qianlong learned about the requests of a permanent British presence in Beijing and expansion of trade on the coast. These requests, if granted, would inevitably alter the Chinese Tizhi, as Qianglong noted in his message to the British king. Upset, His Majesty instructed that "they are definitely unpermitted" (*duan buke xing).* He even would have cancelled the big banquet in honor of the British at the Main Audience Hall in the Yuanming Yuan had it not been promised. This was quite a change in attitude toward the British. Initially, on August 14, the emperor enthusiastically instructed Jin Jian through the Grand Council that the foreign guests should be fully entertained. His Majesty even specifically suggested a dragon boat show in the Yuanming Yuan (Zhongguo diyi lishi dang'anguan 1996, 14, 154, 172; Gugong bowuyuan 1990, 677, 738). But the British intention of chanllenging the Tizhi turned his stomach.

Hoping to speak to the emperor again, regardless of being hobbled by rheumatism, Macartney moved to Haidian on Sunday, September 29, in order to meet the returning emperor on the road. But the emperor was eager to end the mission, since all the British "tributes" had been laid out for exhibition in the Yuanming Yuan. Still showing his generosity to the people from afar, however reluctantly, the returning Qianlong instructed Jin Jian, the director of the Imperial Household, through the Grand Council that the leaving foreign guests should be properly housed, fed, and entertained, including a tour of the imperial garden and the nearby Longevity Hills. In addition, they could also attend the ceremony to welcome His Majesty's return to be held at the Grand East Gate of the Yuanming Yuan (*YMYA* 1991, 1:330–331, 335–338).

On September 30, the Britons got up at four o'clock in the morning and arrived at their ground about six to join the crowd of several thousand at a place north of the Yuanming Yuan. The emperor rode on a palanquin carried by eight men, followed by a chariot. With troops in holiday dress standing at intervals of fifty yards from each other and with a blowing trumpet, the imperial procession moved slowly on a newly paved road, which had been watered to lessen the dust. "The approach of the emperor," as Barrow observed, "was announced by a blast of the trumpet, followed by softer music, and at that time, when all the people heard the sound of the cornet, flutes, harp, sackbut, psaltery, and all kind of music." The emperor passed the mounted Briton, who saluted the procession, but Macartney obtained no opportunity to speak to Qianlong. He had a brief meeting with the powerful minister Heshen inside the Yuanming Yuan on October 2 and returned to Beijing in exhaustion (Barrow 1805, 80; cf. Crammer-Byng 1962, 144–145; Mageerni 1916, 2:51–52, 54). The scheduled banquet in honor of the British guests in the Yuanming Yuan was relocated inside the Forbidden City as a farewell dinner (*YMYA* 1991, 1: 357–358).

The emperor set October 7 (the fifth day of the ninth month by the Chinese calendar), or five days after the final ceremony, as the deadline for the departure of the British because the mission, judged as a regular tributary mission by the Chinese, was accomplished. Since the tributary goods were fully delivered and the gifts from the Celestial Empire were also given, there was no reason for the British to remain in China (cf. Fang Yujin 1984, 96; Peyrefitte 1992, 272–273).

The archive contains a poem composed by Qianlong about the Macartney mission at the time of the audience. The contents of the poem, if accurately scrutinized, give no doubt to the fact that the emperor was determined to put the British under the control of the Sinocentric world order:

The Portuguese had once come to pay tributes,
Now the English have arrived to render allegiance.
Neither Shu Hai nor Heng Zhang were such wide ranging travelers
The Virtue of my ancestors had extended across the distant ocean.
(So the coming of these men from afar).
Though unsurprised, I am truly heartened.
I treasure not so much the exquisite gifts from alien lands,
But I am concerned about how to control men from afar
 through mollification.
I must show them generosity and magnanimity,
So to maintain prosperity and peace (of the world).[11]

To Qianlong, he was not adopting a closed-door policy. Rather, he was defending the integrity of a world order that was vitally important to the security and peace of his vast empire. In his mind, stationing a permanent British ambassador in Beijing, or imposing the alien system of nation-states on China, was utterly out of the question. Yet, he was concerned when the Grand Council reported that the Englishmen showed displeasure when they were requested to leave. His Majesty instructed the governors-general in the coastal region to be attentive and on guard for fear that the resentful British might disrupt coastal peace (Gugong bowuyuan 1990, 746, 749).

The Titsingh Mission

In 1795, less than two years after the departure of Lord Macartney, there came the Dutch mission headed by Isaac Titsingh (1745–1811) and Andreas Everardus van Braam Houckgeest (1739–1801). The latter had been in charge of the Dutch factory in Guangzhou (Canton) since 1790. He had an ardent interest in China and wished to represent the Dutch in Beijing. He seized the opportunity of Qianlong's jubilee celebrations in 1795–1796 to recommend to his superiors at Batavia to send a congratulatory mission. The Dutch commissioners-general at Batavia accepted the recommendation, but he appointed Isaac Titsingh, once head of the Dutch factory at Deshima in the harbor of Nagasaki, Japan, as ambassador. Van Braam was made Titsingh's deputy (Duyvendak 1938–1939, 4, 11; Boxer 1939, 9–12).

Titsingh sailed from Batavia on August 15, 1794, and met van Braam on board his ship two days later. The Dutch then traveled from Guangzhou to Beijing during the severest winter season, and they suffered from appalling lodging and food on the road. For them the journey "more resembled a forced march" (Boxer 1939, 16). Their plight caught the attention of the Qing court, and the Qianlong emperor specifically decreed on December 22, 1794, that on their return trip, the Dutch "should be given the same courtesy as given to the British" (Duyvendak 1938–1939, 43; the decree is cited on p. 88).

The Dutch arrived at the imperial capital on January 9, 1795, and the first imperial audience took place on January 12. They took carriages to the Forbidden City at 5:00 A.M. They all performed the kowtow when the Qianlong emperor arrived. They found the aged emperor "had a good and kind appearance, and was dressed in black fur" (Boxer 1939, 21). Perhaps because they were more accommodating of the Chinese court-etiquette, the Dutch received greater attention than the British, including a trip with the emperor to the Temple of Heaven on January 27. No doubt they managed to see a lot more of Beijing and its environs than their British predecessors (Duyvendak 1938–1939, 53–54, 63).

On January 30, the Dutch followed the Qianlong emperor to the Yuanming Yuan imperial garden. They took lodging at Haidian. Early the next morning, the Dutch ambassador served his duty at the garden court as he had inside the Forbidden City. Shortly after sunrise, the octogenarian Qianlong sat in an armchair inside a dome-shaped tent in the Drill Field to receive both the Dutch and the Korean visitors. The Koreans came specifically to commemorate the sixtieth anniversary of the Qianlong reign. The emperor then invited his Korean and Dutch guests to have breakfast with him at the Drill Field, a great open space in a wood." Each table served fifty dishes with wine, plus the usual entertainment of acrobatics and dancing. The aged emperor spoke kindly to his guests and offered Chinese music and skits to entertain them. Van Braam, however, disliked the Chinese entertainment, which he found confusing and his mind was soon fatigued, thus banishing "every idea of amusement." Afterward, most extraodinarily, they were taken to see the royal living quarters on the Nine Continents. Titsingh left behind his observation as follows:

> Never did I see a more enchanting spot either in reality or in picture. From here we were pulled across the ice to the other side in sledges with yellow ropes; there we visited five temples in beauty equalling those of Peking but far surpassing them with respect to their site, being constructed in terraces on the hillside, as well as by their natural and artificial rockeries and the free view across the water. The beautiful buildings on the other bank and the entire region furnished a picture whose beauty cannot be adequately described. From the highest temple we had a wide view on the city of Peking and this enchanting place. . . . All the picturesqueness so much admired in Chinese paintings was relished here in the highest degree. One was completely transported by the beauty.[12]

The Dutch, in time, were to observe the lively Lantern Festival with their Chinese hosts. They saw theatricals and watched fireworks on the Drill Field in the evening on February 3. The next morning, they ate breakfast with Qianlong in the Main Audience Hall in the garden. On February 5, they watched "good" fireworks again, as well as enjoyed "a dance performed by two dragons pursuing the moon." The Dutch left the garden for Beijing on the following day (cf. Duyvendak 1938–1939, 68–70).

It seems that the Dutch toured the Yuanming Yuan quite extensively largely due to the hospitality of the emperor's favorite minister Heshen, to whom the Dutch referred as the "Voo-tchong-tang," He Zhongtang (The Honorable He) in correct transliteration.

Heshen patiently showed the Dutch how to see goldfish of various sorts, to travel on the frozen canals, and even to inspect the emperor's living quarters. Van Braam described the royal room as "neatly furnished in the Chinese taste, containing a few books and some very valuable curiosities" (cited in Danby 1950, 155).

Also, the Dutch visited the "magnificently beautiful" new palace garden at the foot of the Longevity Hills, presumably the Pure Ripple Garden (later renamed the Yihe Yuan in the late nineteenth century). The Dutch watched the emperor skating in his sleigh on a frozen lake, most likely the Kunming Lake. Van Braam only regretted that he missed the European section in the Eternal Spring Garden. We have no way of knowing why Heshen was not eager to show the Europeans their own style of buildings. However, on behalf of the emperor, Heshen presented to the Dutch very valuable gifts and entertained them with wrestling, tumbling, music, fireworks, and a lavish banquet in the presence of Qianlong. Van Braam also saw the Main Audience Hall, which he found "paved with white marble and hung with lanterns." Most likely, no other European at the time had seen much more of the Yuanming Yuan than van Braam (cf. Danby 1950, 156–158).

That the Dutch, unlike the British, gave no challenge to the host country's Tizhi certainly minimized bad blood, and the fact their arrival corresponded incidentally with the Koreans in honor of Qianlong's grand anniversary might also have given the proud old man a good impression. Evidently, the Dutch made no complaints about being in the company of the Koreans to pay tribute to the Celestial Empire.

The Dutch returned from Beijing to the Yuanming Yuan on February 8, 1795, to attend more entertainment on the Drill Field. On this occasion, both Titsingh and van Braam were very impressed by Qianlong's presence. They noticed "how straight Ch'ien Lung (Qianlong) held himself and how he walked without any support, his stature being higher than the average" (Duyvendak 1938–1939, 70–71; Boxer 1939, 24–25). On February 10, the Dutch received another audience inside the Forbidden City. Qianlong, besides bestowing presents, likewise wrote a letter to the king of Holland, then already in exile in England, to underline his magnamity and unwaving stand on the established Chinese system. The Dutch left Beijing on February 15. On their way southward, after a side trip to Hangzhou, they returned to Guangzhou on May 9, 1795. Clearly, the mission was far more ceremonial than substantial (Duyvendak 1938–1939, 72–74, 76–77, 85, 90, 92; cf. Peyrefitte 1992, 498).

The Amherst Mission

Since the Qianlong emperor assigned the same tribute-bearers to the British and the Dutch as he had to the Koreans, he missed the historic significance of the presence of the Europeans in China. He showed no detectable anxiety and uneasiness even after Lord Macartney tried deliberately to impress him with the open display of modern field guns inside the Yuanming Yuan. Nor were any of his numerous officials immediately aware of the potential menace of the impressive guns. Two mountain howitzers were still sitting quietly among countless jade stones, jars, enamels, bronzes, clocks, and watches in a building near the

Main Audience Hall when the Anglo-French allied forces captured the Yuanming Yuan in 1860 (General Grant's account cited in Malone 1934, 182). The guns were stored in the same manner as the jade and jars. Apparently, Qianlong considered the guns merely newfangled gadgets.

The guns as well as the three elegant and comfortable carriages made by John Hatchett of Long Acre and taken by Lord Macartney to the Qianlong Emperor were never used but were kept in one of the buildings as tributary trophies. The Dutch van Braam saw the coach still "exquisitely painted, perfectly well varnished, and the whole of the carriage covered with gilding." More than half a century later, after the Anglo-French force occupied the Yuanming Yuan, Elgin's interpreter Robert Swinhoe discovered in the garden two of the three carriages Macartney presented to Qianlong still "intact and in good order" (cf. Crammer-Byng 1962, 366–367; Barrow 1805, 76–77, 145). The question about why the Qianlong emperor stuck by his clumsy chariot and never used the elegant easy carriages the British had brought to him is quite revealing. Apparantly the Hatchett-designed carriage did not take into consideration Chinese etiquette, so the driver would have sat on the elevated box higher than the seat of the emperor and with his back turned to His Majesty. Here Qianlong unequivocally sacrificed modern convenience for the pride of the throne.

Many years after the Macartney mission, in 1816, London requested to send another mission to China so as to remove the "grievances of the Canton trade." Evidently, having virtually no idea of how mighty was Britain's power, the Jiaqing emperor, like his father Qianlong, took it to be just another tributary mission from a foreign country. Following the precedents of the 1793 visit, Jiaqing would grant an imperial audience, offer a grand banquet, and entertain the visitors in the Yuanming Yuan (Zhongguo diyi lishi dang'an-guan 1996, 208). A seven-day agenda was set. Give a reception in the Yuanming Yuan on the first day. Present the guests formally in the Main Audience Hall on the second day, after hearing an opera at the All-Happy Garden. Offer a grand banquet in the Main Audience Hall on the third day. Show the English visitors around the Longevity Hills on the fourth day. Bid farewell in the Yuanming Yuan on the fifth day. Give the official farewell banquet at the Board of Rites, together with a ceremony to bestow rewards on the Britons in the Forbidden City, on the sixth day. Finally, on the seventh day, bid farewell to the visitors departing from Beijing (*YMYA* 1991, 1: 448). This agenda indicates that Jiaqing's understanding of the mission was no different from Qianlong's, that it was ceremonial, customary, and recreative as a normal tributary mission, in clear contrast to the British intention of expanding trade.

Earl William Pitt Amherst (1773–1857) headed the second British mission. Despite the more than two decades since Macartney's visit, no improvement in understanding between China and Britain had come about. Moreover, with its increased strength, London was less willing to compromise, in particular on the question of the kowtow.

After Amherst arrived in Tianjin, he expressed gratitude to the throne by only removing his hat thrice and nodding his head nine times. The mandarins rebuffed Amherst by pointing out that Macartney had performed the kowtow in 1793. They even solicited the testimony from the young Staunton in the Amherst party, who had been with the Macartney mission as a little boy. The mandarins were furious when Staunton replied that he did not recall what had happened twenty years ago. But they were firm that the set rule of the Celestial Empire required all officials, high and low, and envoys from many dozens of vessel states, such as Korea and Vietnam, to perform the kowtow in imperial audiences. "Should you refuse to abide by the Chinese ritual," they insisted, "an imperial audience would definitely not be granted to you." Inevitably, Amherst was repeatedly pressured by his Chinese hosts along the way to follow the ritual (Zhongguo diyi lishi dang'anguan 1996, 210, 212). The controversy plagued and deepened the ill feeling on both sides.

When Amherst definitely refused to comply, the procession was stalled at Tongzhou, ten miles from Beijing. Ten days of tense negotiation did not really settle the problem. In ambiguity, the Amherst party of seventy-five moved on toward the Yuanming Yuan. They took lodging at Haidian in a hot summer night. Apparently unaware of how exhausted his guests were, the Jiaqing emperor wanted to see them early next morning at the Main Audience Hall in the Yuanming Yuan as scheduled. Reluctant to be presented in any undignified manner, however, Amherst pled for more resting time. Nevertheless, the mandarins, who dared not alter the imperial agenda, rudely tried to force his hand. The furious Amherst thus abruptly shook off the twisting arm and instantly antagonized the mandarins, who reported to the court the viciousness and arrogance of the British. Badly disturbed, Jiaqing abruptly ended the mission. This was a real expulsion, and consequently the British turned back home without even seeing the Yuanming Yuan, which was within walking distance. In his letter to the king of England, Jiaqing complained specifically of Amherst's refusal to abide by the ritual Macartney had performed in 1793. The emperor laid the blame squarely on the British envoy (Zhongguo diyi lishi dang'anguan 1996, 213, 214; *YMYA* 1991, 1:448–450; Malone 1934, 173–174; Danby 1950, 170–175; Hsu 1983, 163–166).

The Twilight Years

Qianlong abdicated in 1795, not because he was ready to yield power but because he had once promised to Heaven that with the grace of longevity he would not occupy the throne more than sixty years, which represents a complete cycle in the Chinese tradition of dating. He thus summoned his sons to the Diligent Court, or the royal office room, in the Yuanming Yuan on the Chinese New Year's Day of 1796 (February 9, 1796) to designate his successor. The fourteenth son, Yunguan, or Prince Jia, was chosen to become the Jaiqing emperor. But the change of the throne turned out to be a mere formality. Qianlong continued to make decisions behind the scene in the name of the "Super-emperor" *(taishang huang)* (*Qingshigao* 1976, 3:563; Kahn 1971, 191–199).

Moreover, afraid of losing power, Qianlong actually placed Jiaqing under surveillance. His trusted henchman Heshen reported to him details as trivial as what route or gate the emperor took to go to the Yuanming Yuan and what clothes he put on during the hundred-day mourning period for the imperial mother (cited in Yao Yuanzhi 1982, 14–15). Under the circumstances, the Jiaqing emperor had to keep a low profile and do his best to be a filial son. Once he tried to please his father by inviting the most senior scholar-officials, some of them over ninety, to a banquet in his father's honor. He gladly announced at the banquet that the combined age of the hosts and the guests was exactly one thousand, implying that he wished his father good health and a long life (*Qingshigao* 1976, 3:567). When Qianlong finally passed away on February 7, 1799, however, Jiaqing lost no time in seizing power. The corrupt Heshen was quickly put on trial and executed. Incidentally, Qianlong, the greatest patron of the Yuanming Yuan, died suddenly in the Forbidden City instead of the imperial garden as he had planned.

The Jiaqing emperor did not occupy the Yuanming Yuan until after his father died. Like his father, he continued spending generously on garden projects. He expended an astronomical sum to finish the incomplete projects in the Variegated Spring Garden, which had been recently integrated into the imperial garden.[13] In 1812, for instance, he gave the Grand Palace Gate and the Main Audience Hall a new look. In the short span of six months, he spent 40,000 taels of silver for garden works. Then he renovated the Wave-Pacifying Garden, the Wall of Sravasti, the All-Happy Garden, and the Eternal Sunshine Hall, successively. In the end, he added many significant new scenes to the Yuanming Yuan, including the Smoky Rain Chamber, the Spreading Spring Hall, the Economized-Ploughing Villa, and a new rice field (Wu Zhenyu 1983, 197).

Despite the continuation of construction in the Yuanming Yuan, the finances to sustain such enormous expenditures up to this time were still sound. Importantly, Jiaqing had a helping hand from the highly profitable Salt Administration, an official organ, which monopolized the lucrative salt business. Early in 1800, for example, he had 100,000 taels delivered from the Yuanming Yuan to the Salt Administration for earning interest (*YMYA* 1991, 2:1003). Another government agency, the Department of Storage (Guangchu Si), had once given 50,000 taels to the Yuanming Yuan as a reserve (Yang Naiji 1986, 37).

In fact, the imperial garden received from elsewhere not only large sums of cash but expensive gifts. Upon completion of the Bamboo Pavilion in 1814, the Huai Salt Agency donated more than two hundred pieces of valuable purple sandalwood furniture. Their quality and design were in the tradition of the Zhu family craftsmanship from Yangzhou, the best since the Ming period. The sandalwood furniture of various different designs was considered a precious gift to wish people pomegranates and eternity. A few years later, prior to the completion of the Beauty-Covered Mountain Cottage (Xiujie Shanfang) in 1817, the same agency offered two hundred more sandalwood window frames and lattices. These were not isolated instances. Whenever a new garden structure was completed, agencies or persons always rushed to offer valuable gifts, usually artistic and useful pieces to decorate the newly complete structures (Wu Zhenyu 1983, 207).

Jiaqing definitely showed greater concern over security. With the increasing unrest throughout the empire since the turn of the century, the court had upgraded the security of all imperial gardens. No sooner had he assumed power in 1799 than he enlisted five more companies of troops from the reorganized Manchu Banner Battalions for the defense of the Yuanming Yuan (*Qingshigao* 1976, 14:3853; Yao Yuanzhi 1982, 22). As a result, the total number of garden guards rose to 6,408 (*Qingshigao* 1976, 14:3886).

Threats to security, nonetheless, occurred. First in 1803, when the Jiaqing emperor traveled from the Yuanming Yuan to the Forbidden City, a Manchu bannerman tried to attack him. It was a scare, even though the assassin was quickly apprehended (Feng Erkang 1995, 546). Then, on an autumn day in 1813, a party of rebels led by Chen Shuang sneaked into the grounds of the Forbidden City. Although no rebels escaped alive, the emperor and his mandarins were shaken, as never before had rebels of any sort come so close to the emperor (*Qingshigao* 1976, 3:603). Such alarm naturally called for tighter security. Indeed, the Imperial Household quickly appropriated 169,907,374 taels of silver in 1815 to build 1,096 more units of barracks in the vicinity of the Yuanming Yuan in order to accommodate more troops (*YMYA* 1991, 1:442–444).

Threats, however, were not confined to the hinterland. Menace along the coast also loomed large. Even though the tranquility of the Canton system of trade was generally maintained, rising British maritime power and the discontented European traders inevitably threatened the status quo. The British seized Macau in 1802 and 1808, attacked the Chinese tributary of Nepal, and took custody of an American steamer off Canton in 1814. Great Britain got away with all these incidents by forcing her way, with no regard to the Chinese protests.

The Amherst mission of 1816, as discussed earlier, was disastrous. Jiaqing seems to have regretted it for a while but obviously did not take it very seriously. Nor did he take any significant action to meet the potential British challenge. He continued spending more money on garden projects than on maritime defense. He had already spent 40,000 taels of silver for projects in the Yuanming Yuan within six months after Amherst's departure. When the emperor was sixty years old in 1819, the royal treasury could still afford a lavish celebratory fanfare, with colorful decorations extending all the way from Beijing to the gates of the Yuanming Yuan, compatible with Qianlong's grand birthday (Wu Zhenyu 1983, 132). There was no noticeable sense of crisis.

Suddenly in 1820 Jiaqing died during his annual hunting trip to Rehe. The suggestion that he was stricken by "lightning" (Danby 1950, 174) cannot be verified. Jiaqing's successor was Daoguang, his second son, who escorted the coffin in a procession of one hundred twenty-seven men, plus a company of imperial guardsmen, back to Beijing (Yao Yuanzhi 1982, 16). The newly ascended emperor did not occupy the Yuanming Yuan until he fulfilled the mourning period in 1823. He made some significant new arrangements in the imperial gardens. He moved the dowager and concubines from the Joyful Spring Garden, Kangxi's original imperial garden, to the Variegated Spring Garden (Huang Jun 1979, 2:433; Cai Shengzhi n.d., 128). The absence of the imperial consorts and much of the staff inevitably led the Joyful Spring Garden to sink into oblivion. Also, he generously gave the Xichun Yuan to his brother Prince Chun. This cessation together with that of Chunxi Yuan to Princess Gulun by Jiaqing in 1802 at last defined the principal components of the Yuanming Yuan as three (*YMYA* 1991, 2:1671, 1674).

A poem written by Daoguang reveals his feeling when he rode a horse entering into the gates of the Yuanming Yuan for the first time as emperor. The familiar garden struck him as beautiful as ever. The sleek snow, he noticed, still covered the creeks and hills in the distance. No sooner had he walked into his royal office, known as the Diligent Court, than he sensed the great responsibility he had newly assumed. The garden environment made him nostalgic about the happy bygone days, and he was most grateful to his forefathers for leaving behind such a marvelous palatial garden. Gratitude made him take a vow that he would forever follow the good examples set by his predecessors to be a benevolent ruler with a prudent policy (cited in Sun Xiong 1971, 21).

Daoguang is known as a prudent, kind, and thrifty ruler (*Qingshigao* 1976, 4:709). But he cannot be considered frugal so far as spending on the Yuanming Yuan is concerned. In fact, he was as eager as his predecessors to make the imperial garden appear greater and better. Moreover, the financial condition of the Yuanming Yuan upon his ascendancy was still solvent. The 1824 review of the Yuanming Yuan treasury showed significant surplus. The 1818 garden account recorded 92,343.925 taels of silver in surplus, and in five years the garden had collected 1,486,757 more taels plus cash (*YMYA* 1991, 1:494). Besides interest and land rents, much of the revenue drew from rich agencies. The Department of Storage continued delivering cash to the Yuanming Yuan as a reserve (*YMYA* 1991, 1: 507–508).

Ample available money allowed Daoguang to construct the Luxurious Prudent Virtue Hall (Shende Tang), new royal living quarters, on the Nine Continents in 1830. The hall featured three connected waving roofs on a square-shaped structure. The waving roofs with their light wings and pointed corners express in a lively manner the unique character of Chinese garden art and stand out among the most commonly used roof forms, such as the "full-gable roof" *(yingshan),* the "gable-and-hip roof" *(xieshan),* and the "pyramidal roof" *(tiaoshan).* The new hall did not look as splendid as ordinary Chinese palaces, as it showed a distinct character—a greater degree of freedom—in arrangement and design, markedly departing from the more rigid Confucian-inspired architecture. When it was completed in 1831, the price tag was 252,000 taels, 121,700 more than the initial estimation (Huang Jiangtai 1986, 4:18–22; Shu Mu 1984, 373). A fire on October 4, 1836 consumed three sections of this newly built hall, but all the vitally important residential sections for His Majesty were quickly rebuilt, regardless of financial conditions (Cai Shengzhi n.d., 128; Zhang Enying 1991b, 148).

Because of Daoguang's unusual passion for the performing arts, theaters became His Majesty's favorite form of architecture and many more were built in the Yuanming Yuan. As he could no longer be content with the new stage near the Chunhua Gallery in the Eternal Spring Garden built by Jiaqing in 1814, he constructed a gigantic theater chamber in the All-Happy Garden situated south of the Wall of Sravasti. This new theater had two wings, one two-story wing to the north and one three-story wing to the south. Also, he added seven units of performing rooms to the Spreading Spring Hall in the Variegated Spring Garden in addition to one more large stage in a three-story building, which reportedly allowed hundreds of actors and actresses to perform at one time.

Some evidence shows that Daoguang rarely missed special occasions, such as the Chinese lunar New Year's Day, his own birthday, and the birthday of his imperial mother, to stage entertaining programs for several days. According to one anecdote, during a performance on stage to celebrate his mother's birthday in a certain year, the emperor was so carried away that he mixed with the actors and actresses. His Majesty even put on a costume and make-up to play with them. Ever more remarkably, the Son of Heaven suddenly decided to change the scripts, which caused instant confusion and chaos. The show thus became a comedy and ended in a clap of thunder and laughter (Peng Zheyu and Zhang Baozhang 1985, 171–173). Daoguang not only built more theaters in the Yuanming Yuan than his predecessor but also started the tradition of opera entertainment inside the imperial garden.

During the Daoguang era, the great poet Gong Zizhen (1792–1841) visited the Yuanming Yuan in late spring of 1823 and left behind his impression of the imperial garden.[14] His sensitive poetic eyes captured a number of the most beautiful scenes in the garden. He was deeply impressed by the southern-style gardens, which made him nostalgic for his native Zhejiang province. He found the palatial garden a truly tranquil place for the emperor to meditate, rest, and enjoy as well as to please his royal mother. In addition, as he observed, the emperor often served lavish banquets in the garden to honor distinguished guests, including foreign visitors. He also noted that the Yuanming Yuan had grown immensely large since its inception at the beginning of the Yongzheng reign, not to mention that pines and willows in the garden were fully grown. Overall, for Gong, the buildings with their interior furnishing and the landscapes were all in excellent shape (Gong Zizhen 1975, 468).

Gong was not the only scholar to tell what he had seen. Another man of letters saw not only the scenic garden setting but also the lavish interior decorations inside many of the buildings and observed the following:

> Countless precious things make me wonder and dazzled. Take jade; for example, its square-shape vase in milk white stands fourteen to fifteen inches high. The large pieces of jade carved in human figures are so delicate that they make me wonder if they are truly man-made. There is a jade dish, about two feet in diameter, on which stands a jade pine tree, vividly real, with white roots and green leaves. There are also some coral trees as tall as a grown man and as thick as a boy's arm, and their red color with dazzling brilliance cannot be watched intently. Even more attractive is a blue jade melon with its base and leaves, and on top of it stands a grasshopper with a green head and blue wings, tottering as if it is about to fall. Besides, there are numerous rare agate bowls, crystal kettles, amber cups, etc.[15]

This observation offers a rare glimpse of the treasures that the magnificent royal garden possessed. Jades aside, there were other numerous artifacts, precious furniture, priceless paintings, rare books, exquisite silks, and antiques of various sorts kept in various places throughout the garden.

In the winter of 1842, a few months after the conclusion of the disastrous Opium War, Daoguang reviewed his troops on the Drill Field in the Yuanming Yuan. This was perhaps a routine exercise. Even though the emperor became a bit more concerned about security in the wake of military defeat, he did not fully capture the meaning of the historical event. He made no special effort to reinforce maritime defense, let alone to propose significant changes to meet the unprecedented challenge. Finally, he passed away quietly in his favorite Luxurious Prudent Virtue Hall in early 1850, on the eve of the rising empire-wide turmoil (*Qingshigao* 1976 4, 588).

The nineteen-year-old crown prince became the Xianfeng emperor in this unfortunate time, in which he had to face the dire consequences of dynastic decline. He was blamed for all the troubles of the empire. Personal attacks on him were truly vicious; for instance, he was denounced as a man of debauchery, being "occupied in orgies of unspeakable debauch in the lowest haunts of Peking (Beijing), the Flower Streets and Willow Lanes where the prostitutes lived, and also at the Yuanming Yuan" (Danby 1950, 184). But it was impossible for the emperor to visit "the Flower Streets and Willow Lanes," and it was inconceivable that prostitutes would be allowed in the Yuanming Yuan. To be sure, like his predecessors, Xianfeng had many concubines and sought pleasure in his beloved garden. But none of this was illegitimate or extraordinary. After all, the Yuanming Yuan was built for the pleasure of the Qing emperors. He was condemned for seeking pleasure in the garden mainly because he presided over a troubled empire. In a sad time, even the pleasure of the emperor appears inappropriate and, indeed, deplorable.

Nevertheless, the crises that Xianfeng had to face were truly serious. Not only was he confronted with the formidable menace from the West on the coast but also the rise of the most disruptive Taiping Rebellion in southwest China. Xianfeng did take several positive steps, such as to rehabilitate the able minister Lin Zexu (1785–1850), whom Daoguang had unjustly dismissed, and to entrust regional leaders, such as Zeng Guofan (1811–1872), Yuan Jiasan (1806–1863), and Shengbao (1798–1863), to deal with the rebellious situation (*Qingshigao* 1976, 4:711–736). He was no doubt weary from many late nights in his Yuanming Yuan office. On one occasion, on the eve of a scheduled trip to the Temple of Heaven for worshipping, he cried out aloud, as witnessed by the attendants at the court (cited in *YMYZ* 1984, 322, 330).

Xianfeng's melancholy was well conveyed by a poem composed by the gifted late Qing scholar Yang Yunshi:

> Violent killings in Nanjing and in the Yangzi delta.
> Gates, hills, and rivers are bloody red;
> Apes and cranes cow the dark moon;
> Fishermen and woodcutters weep in chilly autumn.
> Nothing but bad news piles up on His Majesty's desk.
> Fill up the mellow wine cup.[16]

Under the circumstances, the growth of the Yuanming Yuan had to come to an end. The rapidly increasing military expenses in the midst of the collapsing traditional economy rendered any spending on the garden not just morally wrong but financially out of the question. The fact that the Yuanming Yuan obtained a small sum of 1,212 taels from Shandong in February 1858, desperately borrowed money from the Department of Storage in April of the same year, and eagerly requested to expedite transference of cash indicates its financial stringency (*YMYA* 1991, 1:548–550). The imperial garden was difficult to maintain let alone to expand.

Like his predecessors, the Xianfeng emperor used the Yuanming Yuan to conduct state affairs. But he was the last Qing emperor to do so. For example, the eminent scholar-diplomat Guo Songtao (1818–1890) was granted an audience in the garden after he had accepted an assignment to go to Tianjin to assist the Mongol prince Sengge Linqin (d. 1865) to reinforce maritime defense.[17] Guo first arrived at the garden's front gate on February 18, 1859. By noon he saw that the emperor, wearing a fur coat, had arrived in a large palanquin with scores of royal princes. They were followed by the grand secretaries, the imperial tutors, and ministers of the Imperial Household, respectively, into the Inner Palace Gate of the Yuanming Yuan (Guo 1981, 1:213). It does not appear that Guo had an audience with the emperor this time.

He returned to the imperial garden eight days later. He reported to the guards at the Grand Palace Gate at two o'clock in the morning before going to nearby lodging for some rest. He came back to the gate at six o'clock that morning. The eunuch announced seven names to be granted an audience by His Majesty on the day, and Guo was the fourth. Finally, his name "was called" *(jiaoqi)* at nine o'clock, and an eunuch showed him the way into the East Warm Belvedere (Dong Nuange) inside the Diligent Court, a favorite audience place since the Qianlong emperor. The court was divided by screens into front and rear sections, as Guo observed, and the warm study was connected to a modest-size room on the north. The emperor walked into the room from behind a screen and sat on his chair facing south. In this room, according to the Qing scholar Yao Yuanzhi (1776–1852), in addition to a porch in front of the southern entrance and a heating stove placed on the left side of the throne, there was a large glass window behind the throne since 1837 (Yao Yuanzhi 1982, 4). Guo entered the room from a southern door and immediately went down on his knees facing the emperor sitting on his dragon chair.

Conversation in the study indicated that the Xianfeng emperor was well prepared. He first told Guo the purpose of the trip to Tianjin. In response, Guo pointed out the importance of building Western-style vessels as a means to strengthen maritime defense. When the emperor considered it too ambitious to pursue at the time, clearly due to the lack of funding, Guo acquiesced but insisted that since the Westerners came from the sea, China had to meet the challenge on the sea. When the emperor solicited straightforward advice with regard to domestic problems, Guo stressed the importance of knowing the exact condition of the people and the state, because most officials in the government, in his opinion, knew too little to tackle problems. He wished the emperor to set a personal example of concern so as to raise a new spirit against abusive and corrupt practices, for only by doing so could talented civil and military servants be recruited to run the government. The emperor nodded his head before starting small talk, such as how many members of Guo's family would go to Tianjin with him and whether Guo took lodging at the Mansion for the Hanlin Compilers in the Yuanming Yuan, as the emperor knew that Guo had been to the Hanlin. Guo actually had stayed at a friend's residence because the mansion had no vacancy. Finally, the emperor raised himself slightly from his chair, a gesture to indicate that the audience was over. Guo rose quickly, took a few steps backward, went to his knees again, and left the room slowly with a shout: "I, Guo Songtao, wish Your Majesty excellent health!" (Guo 1981, 1:214–215).

The Yuanming Yuan fell victim to the invading foreign force less than two years after this conversation between Xianfeng and Guo inside the imperial garden. The failure of maritime defense, however, was not Guo's fault. In fact, Guo complained in writing that despite the emperor's confidence in him, he could not make Prince Sengge Linqin listen to his advice. The prince turned a deaf ear to his opposition to provoking military confrontation with Britain when problems could still be resolved by diplomacy. Moreover, the hawkish prince denounced Guo as cowardly and unpatriotic. In the end, Guo had to leave his post in Tianjin not long after his arrival. Hence, he did not personally see the disaster provoked by the prince at the Dagu Fort, which resulted in the sack of Beijing and the burning of the Yuanming Yuan.

When Guo returned to Beijing from Tianjin to seek retirement in 1860, he made a pleasant tour to the Pure Ripple Garden, a subsidiary garden of the Yuanming Yuan, in the company of several friends on an April day. The group, as Guo depicted in his diary, walked through a left-side door of the garden first to see the Diligent Court before going around the rock hill behind the court to reach the Jade Wave Hall (Yulan Tang). Guo and friends saw the dragon throne in the hall.

Walking behind the Jade Wave Hall, they arrived at the Warm East Room (Dong Nuanshi) to admire a large Buddha statue. When they ascended the Good Evening Chamber (Xijia Lou), they overlooked the Kunming Lake and saw the amazing reflections of the hill and the chamber. Then they took a boat ride to the Gratitude and Longevity Temple (Da'baoen Yanshou Si) with the Longevity Hills in the background. From there they climbed steps to arrive at the unique Copper Court (Tong Dian) made from nothing but copper, before reaching a pavilion on top of the hill to see a bird's eye view of the entire garden. At the other side of the hill, they discovered a magnificent temple and the interesting Shopping Street. The artificial market consisted of streets and shops as well as streams, bridges, and pavilions, reminding them of a typical South China scene.

Next, they rode their boat again near the Fish-Algae Veranda (Yuzao Ting) and to the back side of the Diligent Court, where they found two imported bicycles. They had their lunch at the East Room (Dong Chaofang) near the court. In the afternoon, they dropped by the three-story Literary Pavilion, in which Guo found a Western clock on the second floor. They then visited the Inspiring Rain Temple (Lingyu Si) with the Cloud Fragrance

Pavilion (Yunxiang Ge) on the left and the Moon Wave Chamber (Yuebo Lou) on the right, where they could admire the chambers and pavilions on the hillside in the midst of pine trees. A sudden severe wind, however, cut short their tour by almost half. After a brief rest, they were on their way out from the garden. Guo was deeply impressed by the "most exquisitely beautiful scenery" he had ever seen (Guo 1981, 1:307, 330–331; cf. Wang Rongzu 1993, 84–85; Yu Mingzhong 1985, 3:1391–1411).

This Pure Ripple Garden was severely damaged together with the Yuanming Yuan during the Anglo-French invasion; however, it was rebuilt and renamed the Yihe Yuan (Cheerful Harmony Garden) by the Empress Dowager Cixi. The Yihe Yuan remains the only well-preserved imperial garden in the suburbs of Beijing. Guo's diary entry of his April tour in 1860, only half a year prior to the invasion, left behind a glimpse of the garden before its destruction and restoration. Guo would regret he had not taken another close look at the magnificence of the Yuanming Yuan before leaving for home. He was shocked and shaken when he heard in his native Hunan province the news of the fall of the Yuanming Yuan and the death of the emperor late in the year (cf. Wang Rongzu 1993, 90–91).

CHAPTER 5

STRUCTURE AND FUNCTION

WE HAVE THUS FAR recounted the physical appearance as well as the historical evolution of the Yuanming Yuan. In this chapter, we shall look into the inner
operation of the garden. How was the garden administered? Who ran the daily
matters? How was security maintained? What was the punishment when rules were violated
or crimes committed? From recently available archival sources, the human dimension of
the garden can be at least partially reconstructed. Let us delve into the sources to look at
how the Yuanming Yuan functioned during a period of one hundred fifty years.

The Garden Administration and Its Services

Administratively, the Yuanming Yuan was directly under the supervision of the Imperial
Household (Neiwu Fu).[1] The Qing's Imperial Household had its roots in the Manchu
banner tradition. Once the Manchus secured power in China, this particular office was
reorganized into the Qing emperor's personal treasury, and by the time of Qianlong it "had
already reached its final, definitive form," as Chang Te-ch'ang has pointed out (1972, 50).

At the end of the Qianlong reign in 1796, the Imperial Household employed as many
as 1,623 men. Their prime duty was solely "to manage the emperor's private life" (Torbert
1977, 29, 39). The final form of the Imperial Household featured three divisions, namely,
the Palace Stud, the Imperial Armory, and the Imperial Gardens and Hunting Parks, to
which the Yuanming Yuan belonged.

Presiding over the Imperial Household was the general director *(zongguan dachen),* who
was selected by the emperor from a pool of high-ranking Manchu officials. Apparently, as
it turned out, more than one general director could be appointed. The general director
appointed by the Qianlong Emperor in 1749 was given the prestigious second rank. Normally, two deputies, responsible for personnel and communication, respectively, assisted
the general director; and they were each assisted by thirty-six secretaryships *(bitieshi),* half
of whom could be Chinese. The secretaryship, which was an established Manchu system,

dated from as early as 1631 (Fuge 1984, 22). Under its supervision, a group of assistants performed various services, such as logistical supply management, accounting, security, legal services, construction and maintenance, managing the pasturage of cows and sheep for sacrificial and worship purposes, embroidery manufacturing, ceremonial scheduling, and general management of His Majesty's personal matters, including daily court services (*Qingshigao* 1976, 12:3421–3424).

The Imperial Household drew its revenues from the royal domains, such as rents collected from the land in the neighborhood of the Yuanming Yuan. It received contributions from the provinces, including the best sorts of local food and products, and tributary goods from the vassal states. It also obtained profits from monopolized trade, in particular ginseng and furs, quota surplus from customs, and took fines and confiscated goods from various sources. It also played a major role in the Salt and Tax Administrations. Its various lucrative activies, as Torbert points out, "guaranteed a steady flow of funds in to the emperor's personal coffer" (1977, 43; cf. 103, 106, 108, 113, 120). In short, the Imperial Household's financial reservoir appeared huge and ample until the mid-nineteenth century when the finances of the empire as a whole faltered.

Under the division of imperial gardens and hunting parks of the Imperial Household, the Yuanming Yuan had its own structure of management. Early in 1723, upon the ascendancy of the Yongzheng emperor, who officially made the Yuanming Yuan the principal imperial garden, the office of general supervisor was created. In the following year, with its growth, the garden administration had six managers *(zongling)* and twelve deputy managers *(fu zongling)*. In 1730, the managers enjoyed the prestige of the sixth rank, and the deputy managers the seventh or eighth rank. The number of managers and deputy managers was sharply on the rise following the vast expansion of the Yuanming Yuan during the Qianlong reign. In 1741, the sixth year of the Qianlong era, two new acting deputy managers *(weishu fuzongling)* were added. There were as many as seven a decade later, and by 1767 the number rose to sixteen (*Qingshigao* 1976, 12:3429; cf. *YMYA* 1991, 2:992).

The appointments of key garden administrators were always made by special imperial decree *(tezhi)*, which underlined the importance of the Yuanming Yuan to the Qing emperors. Once appointed, they could recommend their own deputies; however, the nominees needed the approval of the throne. The relatively low-ranking secretaries were commonly chosen from the regular staff of the Imperial Household by lot. Personnel matters, such as promotions and demotions in the Yuanming Yuan, were the responsibility of the Imperial Household with the consent of the throne. Everyone who worked within the precinct of the garden had to do his best to satisfy the emperor on a daily basis, and job performances were regularly and rigorously checked. Evaluation reports were made available routinely, and anyone deemed unsatisfactory would be expelled from the garden at once (cf. *YMYA* 1991, 2:992–997).

The Garden Treasury (Yinku) was set up in 1749. The Qianlong emperor appointed a chief treasurer *(kuzhang)*, comparable to garden manager in status, an acting chief treasurer *(weishu kuzhang),* and six treasury keepers *(kushou),* whose principal duties were to make payments of various sorts and to make available daily supplies. All these appointments were made on a highly selective basis; for example, none but those who had a good education and affluent family background were eligible. Obviously, Qianlong wanted to have the rich garden treasury in reliable and honest hands (*YMYA* 1991, 2:993; *Qingshigao* 1976, 12:3429).

A new office named the Warehouse of Imperial Utensils (Qiminku) was created in 1750 as an extension of the Garden Treasury. The appointees of this new office were likewise selected from a pool of officials with good reputations; however, their terms were limited to three years as a safeguard against potential abuses. From 1763 on, additional measures were taken to prevent dishonesty, including a policy that the treasury keepers serve the night shift by turn and that ten guards be assigned to the company of the keepers. Furthermore, to make the Yuanming Yuan treasury sound, the Qianlong emperor required that accounts had to be clearly squared annually and that the treasury should be thoroughly reviewed every five years. The inspectors should carefully look into the procedures for submitting accounts, applying for reimbursements, turning in unused materials, and handling cancellations. Failure to clear up accounts within a set period of time could result in severe punishment (cf. *YMYA* 1991, 2:1001, 1002, 1003).

With the expansion of the Yuanming Yuan, the administrative staffs of various ranks steadily increased in number. Whenever a hall, a temple, or a chamber was completed, a new set of workers and supervisors was needed to maintain and secure the new place. The growth of the administrative body in the garden, sooner or later, required more high-ranking administrators. By the summer of 1742, the Imperial Household appointed new deputies and assistant secretaries, two each, to the Yuanming Yuan. Two years later, upon the completion of the Forty Views, Qianlong created additional positions: sixth-rank director *(zhushi),* a new deputy manager of the seventh rank, and a new assistant manager of the eighth rank.

In 1749, the Imperial Household with the approval of the emperor further introduced a new head of treasury *(kuzhang)* of the sixth rank specifically to oversee the large collections of silver, silk, and utensils in the imperial garden. The new head of the treasury chose a deputy from the secretaries and appointed six treasury keepers to assist him. When the Eternal Spring Garden was finished in 1751, another set of administrative staff, including a manager of the sixth rank, two deputy managers of the seventh rank, and two assistant managers of the eighth rank were appointed. In 1759, the manager and deputy manager were renamed garden official *(yuancheng)* and deputy garden official *(yuanfu),* respectively. The integration of the Variegated Spring Garden into the Yuanming Yuan in 1774 called for a new garden official of the sixth rank, a deputy garden official of the seventh rank, a deputy garden official of the eighth rank, and a secretary (*YMYA* 1991, 2:985, 986, 987).

Upon the ascendancy of the Daoguang emperor to the throne in 1821, the administrative hierarchy of the Yuanming Yuan was at last finalized. It consisted of 2 ministers *(langzhong),* 1 councilor *(yuanwailang),* 1 director *(zhushi),* 1 deputy director *(weishu zhushi),* 1 head of treasury of the sixth rank, 8 garden officials of the sixth rank, 1 head of treasury of the seventh rank, 1 garden official of the seventh rank, 8 deputy garden officials of the eighth rank, 15 acting deputy garden officials, 14 secretaries, 18 treasury keepers, 2 student secretaries *(xuexi bitieshi)*, 6 helpers *(xiaoli botangao)*, 35 foremen of the Garden Households, 615 Garden Households, 53 associates to the Garden Households, 148 garden workers, 54 water gate guards, and 3 head sailors *(shuishou manzi)* *(YMYA* 1991, 2:992). The numbers indicate that the Yuanming Yuan personnel had grown threefold in size since its inception at the beginning of the eighteenth century.

The total number of eunuchs in the Yuanming Yuan reached 502 by the end of the Qianlong reign. They were recruited, assigned to positions, and rewarded and punished by the Imperial Household. They composed one of the largest groups in the garden and continued growing. In 1805, their number rose to 620, of whom 88 were eunuch supervisors and 532 were common eunuchs *(YMYA* 1991 2:1039–1040).

The eunuchs were His Majesty's loyal servants, performing indispensable chores such as cleaning rooms, waiting tables, guarding gates, and planting trees and flowers. Many of them had to be on call to respond to the emperor's wishes. By performing their humble yet demanding duties, they received relatively low monthly salaries; for instance, their monthly payment in the year of 1754 ranged from 0.66 to 1.30 taels of silver, according to seniority. The average was 1 tael, approximately equivalent to U.S. $1.5 at that time. Exceptions could only be found among a few of the most senior eunuchs who had the emperor's extraordinary trust. The monthly pay scale of a head eunuch of the fifth rank working in the Mind-Nourishing Study (Yangxin Dian), the emperor's study, could be as high as 7 taels of silver plus 7 piculs of rice *(YMYA* 1991, 2:1039). If we assume 1,000 copper cash to 1 tael, 7 taels could buy fourteen gooses or seventy fowls at the price of the late Qianlong era. An ordinary eunuch's pay, however, was about what a Chinese peasant earned (cf. Crammer-Byng 1962, 244).

Also, there were numerous Buddhist monks and Daoist priests living and working in the Yuanming Yuan, and their numbers also rose with constant additions of temples and shrines to the imperial garden. Many of the monks and priests appeared to be very young. For instance, in 1753, Qianlong incidentally found twenty boy priests in a Daoist temple. The unexpected discovery made the emperor feel that the number of monks and priests in the garden was perhaps excessive and thus recommended a significant cut *(YMYA* 1991, 1:71–72). Nevertheless, given the multitude of religious structures and functions in the garden, especially in the new Eternal Spring Garden, the newly constructed temples and shrines needed to enlist the services of monks and priests. In the end, their numbers instead of being cut, continued to rise.

It was the Yongzheng emperor who in 1729 first introduced the Garden Households (Yuanhu) into the Yuanming Yuan. All members of the households belonged to one of the Manchu Banners. They were trustworthy workers providing service of various sorts. Some of them, for example, raised silkworms *(canhu)* near the Northernmost Mountain Village. In 1762, they developed a working relationship with the Bureau of Brocade Mill and Dye Work (Zhiranju) situated at the foot of the Longevity Hills.

The Han Chinese workers in the garden were identified as the "garden laborers" *(jianyi);* specifically, they were gardeners *(huanerjiang),* repairmen *(gongjiang),* carpenters *(mugong),* boatmen *(shuishou manzi),* bricklayers *(wajiang),* decoration workers *(dacaijiang),* monks and priests *(shengdao),* and porters and guards *(pingding).* As time went on, the number of both Manchu and Chinese workers operating in the Yuanming Yuan was also on the rise. For example, upon the completion of many large fountains in the Eternal Spring Garden in 1760, no less than thirty new gardeners and repairmen were instantly employed. In 1770, the Garden Households numbered as many as six hundred; seventeen years later, in 1787, sixty-seven more households made their homes in the garden. The households were under the supervision of garden foremen *(yuanhu toumu),* whose numbers also rose from eighteen to twenty during the same period of time. Not too long afterward, the garden appointed fifteen more foremen due to the rapid increase in the number of Garden Households *(YMYA* 1991, 2:987).

The daily maintenance of the Yuanming Yuan was as demanding as it was complex. Theoretically the garden depended on the Imperial Household for support; however, in real practice, the garden had to have its own independent sources of revenue in order to meet the growing expenses. One source was from the rents collected on the neighboring lands owned by the Yuanming Yuan (cf. *YMYA* 1991, 2:1000–1001). Reportedly, these rents could pay for repairs in the garden at least during the eighteenth century, when the finances of the Yuanming Yuan were sound. The Yuanming Yuan administration also received cash donations from the rich, such as the wealthy salt merchants in Lianghuai; for instance, the merchant Huang Yuande "humbly presented" one million taels to the garden in 1757 *(YMYA* 1991, 1:88). Some of the cash was apparently the interest that the garden received from the lucrative business of "salt merchants" *(yanshang) (YMYA* 1991, 1:255).

By the time of Qianlong's death at the very end of the century, there were still no signs of financial stringency. As a matter of fact, in February 1799, the newly ascended Jiaqing emperor found 693,290 taels of surplus silver in the Yuanming Yuan's accounts, not including cash in copper coins. One tael of silver at the time equalled 1.388 U.S. dollars, so that the surplus amounted to U.S. $962,287. This was impressive, given the fact that Qianlong had spent an enormous sum of money on the garden; for example, from 1794 to 1799, he had overdrawn his allowance for garden expenses by 448,582 taels of silver, approximately U.S. $622,732 (cf. Yang Naiji 1986, 36). Had he lived still longer, he could have depleted the surplus.

Jiaqing took a precautious measure by transferring 100,000 taels to the profitable Lianghuai Salt Administration to earn interest. In the end, the rich Salt Administration provided him not only with handsome interest but also with valuable materials to beautify the garden, such as window frames. Most of the windows in the garden were made of paper or bamboo with latticework in summer and fur screens in winter (Wu Zhenyu 1983, 207). The Jiaqing emperor was not a big spender like his father, but he still needed a huge sum of money not just to keep the garden functioning but also to retain its grandeur. Moreover, Jiaqing expended large sums on the Variegated Spring Garden, which, though integrated into the Yuanming Yuan in 1772, had not been heavily constructed. The year 1809 marked the peak of construction, during which as many as 173 rooms, 260 corridors, 6 pavilions, and 2 decorated archways had been built. The total cost was 328,775.331 taels of silver (cited in Yang Naiji 1986, 36). Jiaqing in the end designated Thirty (Best) Views for the Variegated Spring Garden.

The Yuanming Yuan did not appear to have financial troubles throughout the Jiaqing reign. During the first six months of 1815, following the disastrous Amherst mission, the emperor spent 40,000 taels for construction in the garden. No new building was behind schedule because of money, and whenever a new hall or chamber was finished, there was no lack of lavish gifts, usually expensive sandalwood materials for decorative purposes, from enthusiastic officials.[2] In 1819, the year of Jiaqing's sixtieth birthday, the Yuanming Yuan administration could still afford a big fanfare as spectacular as his predecessor's birthday celebration (Wu Zhenyu 1983, 132).

The Daoguang emperor, who succeeded Jiaqing, had a prudent, kind, and thrifty reputation (*Qingshigao* 1976, 4:709); but, so far as the Yuanming Yuan was concerned, he retained a big budget. He found in 1824, shortly after his ascendancy to the throne, a surplus in the garden's finances. But the surplus was more apparent than real, because shortfalls had been covered by various government agencies. The Department of Storage (Guangchu Si), for example, had delivered 50,000 taels to the Yuanming Yuan as reserve on one occasion (Yang Naiji 1986, 37). Clearly, the Imperial Household alone could no longer sufficiently finance the imperial garden. Nonetheless, Daoguang had no intention of suspending construction. Most noticeably, he spent a great sum in 1830 to complete the famous Luxurious Prudent Virtue Hall, new living quarters on the Nine Continents. A fire on October 4, 1836, consumed three structures of the hall, but it took less than a year to repair all the damage (Zhang Enyin 1991b, 148).

The Yuanming Yuan administration handled routine matters no more efficiently than any of the major government agencies. Its overriding concern was to make the emperor and the royalty feel comfortable while living in the garden. Its daily matters were tediously numerous. Besides the management of finance and supervision of construction, the administrators were responsible for the designation of names to newly completed structures and the maintenance of garden facilities. It was also their duty to enforce garden security, to investigate any incident, and to file documents of various sorts. As well, they were obligated to perform rituals, such as the expression of gratitude to His Majesty from officials in and out of the Yuanming Yuan. After the imperial garden had incorporated the Variegated Spring Garden and the Eternal Spring Garden, the immediate problem was the insufficient supply of fresh water from the Ten-Thousand Spring River (Wanquan He). To resolve the problem, the administrators undertook the project of constructing a new canal to draw water from Kunming Lake, the largest reservoir at the foot of the Jade Spring Hills (See He Chongyi and Zeng Zhaofen 1981, 1:43).

Of all the administrative responsibilities, the supervision of construction was particularly demanding, given the fact that construction never really ceased. Indeed, many garden administrators shouldered this burden. They oversaw financial transactions, supervised workers, and checked items before acceptance, each of which was a tedious and precarious process. The importance of garden construction eventually called for the creation of a special agency named the Office for Supervising and Speeding Up Fulfillment of Assigned Tasks (Ducui So), which monitored the processing of all the documents for the garden and the delivery of squared accounts on time. The set rule was that any account over one thousand taels be squared within a month, over ten thousand within two months, and even larger amounts within three months. The agency required all applications, statements, and accounts to be registered in its office in the first place so as to ensure that deadlines were met in the end (*YMYA* 1991, 2:1023, 1028, 1030).

The Yuanming Yuan administration also had its Department of the Cashier (Xiaoshuan Fang) to estimate expenses. Taking a construction project, for example, this department had the obligation to determine estimated costs, both in terms of monies and materials, within ten days and send the results to the Office for Supervising and Speeding Up Fulfillment of Assigned Tasks for recording (*YMYA* 1991, 2:1028–1029). Given the intensity of construction, the workload of the office became increasingly unbearable, so that an effort of simplifying the process was made in 1777. Consequently, only one proposal to the office through the Archival Office (Dangfang) was required, which meant that it was no longer necessary to register at the Office for Supervising and Speeding Up the Fulfillment of the Assigned Task before concluding a specific matter. In case of urgency, the applicant could proceed with a plan using his own signature while simultaneously fulfilling bureaucratic procedures (*YMYA* 1991, 2:1034, 1035).

The Stockpile Agency in the Yuanming Yuan administration kept open the garden's supply line. It stored a huge supply of such small items as paper, brooms, candles, lanterns, and gunpowder and made them available for usage on a daily basis. Applications for supplies, regardless of quantity or quality, were to be submitted ahead of time for approval; however, disapproval was exceptional. In the year of 1752, for example, the Archival Office obtained from the Stockpile Agency as many as 6,300 sheets of paper, 60 brush pens, and 16 ounces of ink. The Grand Palace Gate received in the same year 270 brooms of different sizes, 27 winnowing baskets, and 13 feather dusters, large and small. The Library of Literary Sources, upon its completion, acquired 62 brooms, 25 dusters, 42 winnowing baskets, and 50 yards of cloth. The Anyou Palace at the Ancestral Shrine daily consumed 6.5 pounds of charcoal and 13 pounds of firewood in order to keep all the teapots warm (*YMYA* 1991, 2: 1029). These few examples revealed the elephantine nature of the function of the supply-consumption activities in the Yuanming Yuan, which consisted of hundreds of structures and units. The excessive or even wasteful consumption of the daily supplies eventually caught the attention of the Qianlong emperor, who in 1757 instructed that "the allocation of coal and wood to the various places in the Yuanming Yuan should take an appropriate cut" (*YMYA* 1991, 2:1005).

Unquestionably, the Yuanming Yuan administration took security measures in the garden most seriously. Fire prevention, for one thing, was high on the agenda, as so many structures were made of wood. The Eternal Spring Garden alone was equipped with seventy-five gigantic water baskets *(jitong)* for the purpose of fire fighting. Meticulous fire drills were required twice a year, in spring and autumn (*YMYA* 1991, 2:1019). Regardless of the tight safety measures, however, fire incidents still took place from time to time (cf. *YMYA* 1991, 1:74–78, 508–510).

Keeping unauthorized persons out of the Yuanming Yuan was also indispensable for the safety of the imperial garden, for which the entire garden population was placed under tight control. The garden's "chief eunuch" *(zongguan taijian),* with the authorization of the Imperial Household, kept in his office a comprehensive record of personnel files, including physical descriptions of everyone living and working in the Yuanming Yuan. This was clearly to prevent strangers or unauthorized persons from sneaking into the garden. When the tributary goods from provinces reached the garden, it was the duty of the chief eunuch to make a thorough inspection before granting permission to transport them through the canals to their assigned place for display.[3]

On a normal day in 1749 Qianlong, while disembarking from his barge, came across a judicial official in the company of his family, who as rule should not be present on the forbidden grounds. This security slip caught the emperor's personal attention, to the security officers' great embarrassment. On the following day, the garden administration promptly ruled that with the exception of a few highly prestigious princes and senior mandarins, who were allowed to have two escorts, no one else should have the privilege. Commoners, such as peasants, workers, or physicians, whom the garden administration had summoned to perform duties, had to submit their names beforehand for meticulous checkups. Before they entered the garden, they had to present themselves at the gate for a roll call (*YMYA* 1991, 2:1045–1050).

In 1752, the Imperial Household strengthened the garden's security by implementing two additional measures. First, thorough checkups had to be made on a regular basis even during the absence of the emperor; and second, a housecleaning program was introduced to sort out unauthorized persons who assumed the names of others living in one of the Garden Households. As a result, illegal residents and those who the Imperial Household considered senile, idle, dubious, or tricky were all expelled from the garden without delay (*YMYA* 1991, 1:67–68).

To improve garden security further, all residents from 1757 onward were required to carry a "branded waist plate," comparable to a present-day identification card. Whether entering or leaving the garden, everyone was subject to a thorough inspection, conducted usually by eunuchs. Restrictions on visitors were also tightened, such that any visitor had to come in and go out from the garden through the exact same gate so their whereabouts could be accurately reported. Living and working in the garden by assuming an authorized person's name or taking his place was strictly forbidden, and deception was subject to severe punishment (*YMYA* 1991, 1:68).

The administrative structure of the Yuanming Yuan seems comparable to a minisociety. Even though theoretically the garden was serving just one man, the son of Heaven, the highest magnitude of the best possible service was made available on a daily basis. The social functions of the imperial garden were carried out in meticulous detail by thousands of people in many different roles.

Crime and Punishment

As an exclusive royal demesne giving the highest priority to security, the Yuanming Yuan tolerated no crimes, and any form of crime, however trivial, was subject to severe punishment. Prosecution and punishment were in the hands of a committee of an unspecified number of senior officials whom the Imperial Household had appointed. They wished to prevent anything unpleasant from happening in the garden; however, if rules were violated or consequential mistakes made, they would act aggressively to pursue the case and to impose strict punishment so as to keep the imperial garden absolutely safe. The available evidence shows no violent crimes, such as murder and robbery, ever occurring inside the Yuanming Yuan during its one hundred fifty years of history.

As a matter of fact, anyone in the garden who violated any set of rules, whether intentionally or unintentionally, or even behaved so presumptuously as entering or leaving the garden without authorization would be considered a "criminal" subject to punishment.

In 1574, for instance, a patrolman caught a teenage Manchu boy by the name of Erge, who had been working in the European section of the Eternal Spring Garden, climbing a garden wall. The testimony of both sides was recorded. The boy testified that he wanted to escape from the garden because his supervisor had given him a harsh caning for being late on returning from a leave and threatened him again with the same terrible punishment. The chief eunuch of the Eternal Spring Garden who supervised the boy's supervisors found out that the boy got himself in trouble because he was "unruly and lazy." He broke a rule by leaving without permission in the first place, for which he deserved to receive flogging thirty times; yet, only two days after the punishment, he sneaked out of the garden again. His immediate supervisor, Chen Jinzhong, went all the way to Beijing trying to find him before he returned to the garden. The boy, apparently fearing an even harsher punishment for the repeated offense, tried in vain to climb the wall to flee.

The investigation, after being concluded by the responsible officials at the Imperial Household, was reported to the Qianlong emperor. The recommendation for punishment was based on the penal codes of the Great Qing, which stipulated that climbing the imperial walls was a serious crime. No clemency was given in consideration of the offender's tender age, even though the earlier arbitrary caning for being late had been recognized, obviously because the emperor and his Imperial Household refused to exchange tight security for leniency. The Manchu boy thus received an incredible punishment of one hundred strokes before being banished a thousand miles away. Due to his Manchu ethnic background, however, he could substitute the banishment with two months in the cangue. This punishment was carried out with the final approval of the throne (*YMYA* 1991, 1:72–74). The case may reveal that an offense such as absconding was a serious crime subject to very severe punishment. Cruel punishments were no doubt practiced behind the beautiful facade of the garden, and a high human price was paid for the strict security.

There were numerous punishments to be imposed on unintentional negligence. In 1744, Qianlong saw the eunuch Liu Yu sitting on a handrail, which the emperor considered "extremely having no manners" and sent him to his supervisor for forty strokes with a plank. On the same day, a eunuch who fell asleep while on duty also received the same punishment (Eertai [Ortai], Zhang Tingyu et al. 1987, 50). In the summer of 1770, the garden official Changgui went to the Imperial Household to answer the charge that the water level in the fountains at the Symmetric and Amazing Pleasure was 1.5 to 2.0 inches lower than it should have been. In 1773, the garden officials Mingde and Qingde were held responsible for the missing remnants and railings from the Grand Palace Gate. Both men lost six months' salary for their carelessness in patrolling. In the summer of 1779, a number of garden officials took the blame for the lotus on the ponds being few and sparse. They were found guilty of cultivating the lotus inappropriately and of wasting money. Each of them was given a fine from three to six months' stipend. In 1787, Fu Chang'an and Jin Jian, two servants working in the garden, were severely reprimanded for igniting the lanterns behind schedule during the display of fireworks at the Drill Field. And in 1796, because the aged Qianlong emperor complained that the fireworks were soft and mellow, those who had purchased the fireworks had to pay back the cost of all the fireworks plus pay fines ranging from three to twelve months of salary (*YMYA* 1991, 1:132, 162–163, 207–208, 264–265, 366–367).

The tenants working on the farms of the Yuanming Yuan were not for window dressing. They were expected to work as hard as the rest of the peasantry in the country. Hence, when the wheat seedlings on the farms appeared disorderly and weak in the spring of 1787, obviously due to insufficient care, the Imperial Household quickly blamed the supervisors for being too lazy to inspect the fields and inspire the tenants. Consequently, the supervisor Changfu and his deputies each paid a year's salary for their negligence; and their boss by the name of Xiangrui also was charged a fine of six months' salary. The poor wheat harvest in the Yuanming Yuan in the autumn of 1797 also caught the attention of garden authorities, who immediately investigated the matter. When it was determined that idleness rather than weather caused the poor harvest, each of the three supervisors in the wheat farms paid a fine of three months' salary. Ding Yong, who headed the village of the wheat farms, got the severest punishment of all. He was beaten with a flogging board thirty strokes (*YMYA* 1991, 1:266–267, 290).

Even unintentional mistakes, when they occurred in the Yuanming Yuan, could result in punishment of considerable severity. A case in point took place on April 19, 1790. On that day, according to Heshen's report, a group of princes and princesses were badly shaken by a storm and waves when they were crossing the Sea of Blessing on their way to worship at the Guangyu Temple. Heshen blamed the chief eunuchs Liu Bingzhong and Xiao Yunpeng, who had accompanied the royalty, for failing to prevent the hazardous crossing in stormy weather, thus involuntarily risking their safety. Even more inexcusable, for Heshen, the eunuchs who had the responsibility for the safety of the royalty did not even think of choosing the alternative land route.

The Imperial Household acknowledged that no one drowned or was hurt in the incident. Nevertheless, on the basis of Heshen's report, it still imposed on the eunuchs Liu, Xiao and Chen Sheng, together with the captain and sailors of the barge, a large fine equivalent to two annual stipends. The punishment was carried out with the approval of the throne. Most surprisingly, the worst punishment was reserved for the three eunuchs who had piloted the barge. They each received painful floggings, regardless of whether they were following orders or making their own decisions. No one asked whether the royalty themselves held any responsibility. The punishment made manifest the nature of justice under the imperial system; however, showing his mercy and kindness, the emperor reduced the recommended punishment for all by half (*YMYA* 1991, 1:289–290).

Petty crimes, such as stealing, were committed from time to time within the precincts of the imperial garden. In 1757, for instance, the garden administration received the report that a man named Feng Si had sneaked into the Diligent Court to steal a number of jade vessels (*YMYA* 1991, 1:79). The case, however innocuous it seemed, sounded the alarm of security loopholes on the forbidden ground, thus reminding the Imperial Household of the importance of reinforcing the rules with regard to all security measures. Consequently, everyone who lived in the garden was required not only to register his age and portrait with the authorities but also to carry an identification card at all times.

Moreover, in the wake of the stealing incident, the authorities launched another round of Garden Household checkups and found, to their great surprise, that there was still a significant number of "hidden" members of households. Ji Qing, the head of the special investigation team, estimated that eight out of ten men working in the Majestic Sunset-Tinted Peaks of the West Hills had assumed other workers' places. Altogether, 144 unauthorized workers out of 1,314 listed as members of the Garden Households in the Yuanming Yuan and its subsidiary gardens were identified. This finding of approximately 1 percent illegal dwellers on the forbidden grounds surely embarrassed those who bore the direct responsibility of security. The remedial measures included the immediate banishment of all unauthorized persons without a moment's delay and floggings of one hundred strokes for each of those who had violated the rules by allowing the unauthorized people to live in the garden for whatever reasons. As well, a number of eunuchs were subject to punishment of different sorts for this matter because they had not checked the households as carefully as they should have (*YMYA* 1991, 1:79–80; 82–83).

Not surprisingly, thieves in the Yuanming Yuan were mostly the insiders entrusted with particular responsibilities. On the Dragon Boat Festival Day in 1764—the fifth day of the fifth lunar month—the houses at the Honoring Three Selflessnesses Court caught fire. After the fire was extinguished, the eunuch Wang Jinfu from the Purple-Blue Mountain Cottage, who had assisted in fighting the fire, dug into the ashes to find approximately 113 taels of silver. His colleague, the eunuch Cui Wengui, reported him for stealing, and the authorities took the matter very seriously. What troubled the Imperial Household most was that the eunuch, who had no accomplice, was so wicked to take advantage of such a tragic moment. Largely for this, not just for stealing, the eunuch suffered an unusual punishment for the crime: he was banished to the remote Heilongjiang (Amur River) region as a slave (*YMYA* 1991 1:98–100).

When the general condition of the Qing Empire gradually deteriorated in the nineteenth century, stealing in the Yuanming Yuan also became bolder. During the Daoguang reign, as the 1832 Imperial Household record shows, a eunuch by the name of Wang Deshun working at the Wave-Pacifying Garden broke into a warehouse, stole fourteen different items of yarn, and pawned them in downtown Beijing. Even more serious, his superior Zhang Jingui covered up the theft. Once found out, both eunuchs were taken to the Imperial Household for questioning. The theft and cover-up suggest the laxity of discipline for the large number of eunuchs working in the imperial garden. Laxity was further confirmed by the 1837 report that five eunuchs, who had assignments at the Yuanming Yuan's Construction Department, were found fishing covertly in a stream. In the following year, Guo Yao, a sixty-four-year-old eunuch from the island of Taiwan, dared to spread omens and predictions inside the garden, which were absolutely forbidden for fear of causing disturbances (*YMYA* 1991, 1:511–513, 536–537, 541–542).

All these cases deeply concerned the garden authorities, as the eunuchs, who lived in large number in the garden and had access to the emperor and his royal family on a daily basis, no longer seemed to be observing the rules strictly. Given the fact that the eunuch offenders had always suffered harsher punishments than others and that they often received such severe punishments as caning, imprisonment, and banishment to the Manchurian frontiers as slaves, their loafing on the job, negligence of duty, and even stealing were particularly ominous. The decline of alertness and diligence in the garden inevitably raised questions about the security and effective operation of the Yuanming Yuan on the eve of its downfall.

One of the more common types of "crimes" committed in the Yuanming Yuan was construction-related offenses, of which the most common was falling behind schedule. For example, in 1764, two builders by the names of Sen Yuwen and Xi Yang'a failed to meet the schedule at a certain location of the garden. They excused themselves by arguing that the delay was caused by having to complete higher priority work in the Honoring Three Selflessnesses Court. The Imperial Household director Sanhe, however, rejected their explanation, which the director took as mere pretext for negligence. Under pressure, the builders rushed to complete the work perfunctorily. This resulted in the demand from Sanhe to do their job all over again at their own expense. The supervising officials Chaertai and Wushisi and the secretary Shu Tong were each fined their annual salary. Even Sanhe himself admitted to the Qianlong emperor his own guilt of insufficient supervision. The emperor forgave Sanhe but punished the rest as Sanhe had recommended (*YMYA* 1991, 1:101).

In cases of poor quality construction work, blame was often laid on the shoulders of the project supervisors. In 1771, the supervising official Zhengrui together with his deputy

Aerbang'a were responsible for a construction flaw found at the Sky in Reflections, where some bridge banisters connecting a hexagonal pavilion were not perpendicular. They each received forty strokes and paid a fine of six months' salary. The strokes were part of the punishment presumably because the flaw could cause safety problems. The punishment for their supervisor, Deputy Commander Heerjinge, was a fine of three months' salary. Later in the year, the paint on the column of a chamber inside the Wall of Sravasti, which had been applied in 1760, over a decade earlier, was peeling and cracking. Among the five who had been responsible for the painting, three were deceased and two others had left the garden sometime before. Since there was no person available to be punished, the blame was thus laid at the door of the Imperial Household director Sanhe. He and his deputy Wufu each received a fine of three months' stipend for negligence (*YMYA* 1991 1:144–145, 146–147).

In 1770, the glazed color drawings at A Wonderland in the Square Pot, which cost 12,418 taels of silver to complete about a decade earlier, were deteriorating at an alarming rate. The officials, Lu Jin and Aerbang'a, took the blame for supervising this specific project. They each paid a fine equivalent to half of their annual salary. Their supervisor, director Sanhe was also implicated in this matter. For his share of the mishandling of an expensive project, the director took a fine equivalent to three months of his annual salary (*YMYA* 1991, 1:129–130). Sanhe lost three months' salary again in 1771 for his carelessness in substituting cypress for pine as the building material at the Double Cranes Chapel (*YMYA* 1991, 1:139). Then in 1776, when the walls at the front gate of the Library of Literary Sources showed cracks due to bad workmanship and poor quality materials, Heerjing'e, the general supervisor of the library project, was demoted with three other high-ranking garden administrators, including Zhengrui (*YMYA* 1991, 1:182–184).

It was a more serious crime for garden administrators to abuse their power by purposefully inflating the price of construction materials and embezzling public funds (cf. *YMYA* 1991, 1:124–126, 127–132, 138, 139–148). In 1769, for instance, the garden administrator Ji Rong was found guilty of inflating the estimated price of the painting work at the Fish-Leaping and Bird-Flying by approximately 10 percent, or about 136 taels of silver. When found guilty, Ji received a flogging of fifty strokes and lost his job (*YMYA* 1991, 1:127–128). In the spring of 1770, the ministerial councillor Wu Bao and his team were found guilty of peculating 1,330 feet of precious *nanmu* lumber while undertaking construction projects at no less than ten sites in the garden. Wu was deprived of his prestigious title and put on trial as a criminal (*YMYA* 1991, 1:130–131).

A distinctively unique punishment was the self-punishment of the Xianfeng emperor, who ascended the throne in a very troubled time. In 1852, he punished himself by cancelling his regular residence in the imperial garden, as he felt too ashamed to seek pleasure in the aftermath of the tumultuous Taiping Rebellion. This self-imposed punishment, however, did not last long. The emperor wished to return to the garden to admire the flower blossoms in the spring of 1854. First, his financial minister Wang Maoyin offended him by opposing the decision. The minister, though showing his courage, ended up punishing himself by losing the throne's favor. But the consequence of Wang's unpleasant advice did not deter other officials from speaking straightforwardly. The censor Xue Minggao reminded the throne that the return of His Majesty to the Yuanming Yuan for regular living would require substantial renovations, costing an unbearable sum of money in this time of great difficulty. Displeased as he was, Xianfeng argued that he had no intention of seeking personal pleasure in the garden. Instead, the pleasant garden environment would be helpful for his conduct of state affair in the time of crisis. Moreover, none of his predecessors had been absent from the imperial garden so long as he had been. Hence, he wished for both the mandarins and the people to understand his devotion to the active military campaigns against the rebels and to see that his performance should not be judged by where he was to live. Having justified his return to the Yuanming Yuan, the emperor rejected the censor's implication of his self-indulgence. False accusation of the throne could be a serious offense. The censor was later accused of fishing for fame and recognition by having committed an injustice to His Majesty. He was thus subject to a "proper investigation and punishment," even though retaining his office. (*YMYA* 1991, 1:544–545).

Whoever caused a fire, however unintentionally, was thoroughly investigated for responsibility. Deliberate arson, though rarely occurring in the Yuanming Yuan, was considered one of the most serious crimes. Even those who appeared less ingenious in preventing or fighting fires were subject to punishment. A number of eunuchs were disciplined in February 1756 because fire accidentally broke out at the Comfort Inn under Spring Roof twice within a few days while they were on duty. When the investigation determined that the eunuch Yang Ming had been smoking while sweeping the second floor of the summer chamber and presumably caused the fires, the eunuch was banished into servitude in the remote Manchurian frontier near the Amur River. Cao Yushan, the eunuch who had accompanied Yang on the second floor, was also banished, though to a less harsh place, for failing to stop his fellow worker from smoking while on duty. Both eunuchs' supervisor, Yang Jinchao, was guilty of negligence and was sentenced to two months in the cangue, one hundred strokes, and an assignment of hard labor. The eunuchs of still higher ranks, Li Yu and Chen Jinzhong, each paid a fine of an annual stipend for their share of the responsibility for the fire incidents. Two on-site workers who had taken temporary assignments elsewhere during the nights of the fires were spared for their absence (*YMYA* 1991, 1:76–78). The actual existence of group responsibility in these cases underlined the seriousness of fire.

After having carefully guarded against fire hazards for more than a century, the Yuanming Yuan was finally burned to the ground in 1860. The imperial garden subdued under the wrath of aggression and defeat. The perpetrators were the victorious enemies, and both the imperial capital and the imperial garden were at their mercy. The high-ranking officials who were responsible for securing the imperial garden, including Prince Zai Huan, dutifully requested punishment in the aftermath of the inferno. But the Xianfeng emperor spared them all. The emperor knew at the bottom of his heart that no one but he himself should be blamed. In the end, he chose a face-saving way out of the embarrassment by stripping a number of officials of honorable titles, while asking them to remain in office (*YMYA* 1991, 1:554, 586). In short, no one was punished for the burning of the Yuanming Yuan.

Though still under careful supervision, the severely burned Yuanming Yuan became ever more difficult to secure. The Immortal Abode on the Fairy Terrace in the middle of the lake, which had escaped the 1860 inferno, suddenly caught fire on August 21, 1870. Although the watchmen noticed the flames late at night and quickly reported to the head eunuch in the garden, the rescue efforts were handicapped by the lack of equipment to cross the lake and fight the fire. Consequently, the palaces on the abode, which had survived the earlier inferno, were consumed by fire a decade later. The Imperial Houschold, though suspecting arson, could never determine the actual cause of fire. The blame was laid on the head eunuch and watchmen for having failed to take enough precautions against fire in the first place and then showing insufficient effort in fighting the fire. They were either stripped of titles or caned or both. Dong Fu, then the general supervisor of the Yuanming Yuan, paid a fine equivalent to his three-month revenue allowance for this particular fire incident (*YMYA* 1991, 1:621–623).

As time went on, an increasing number of points of illegal access were open to the quickly deteriorating Yuanming Yuan. How to keep intruders out became more and more difficult. Countless thieves easily broke into the crumbling walls. One of them, named Mi Laoer, was caught on June 13, 1861, when he sneaked into the European section to steal bronzes, vessels, and stoves (*YMYA* 1991, 1:598, 600).

On January 24, 1862, under the Tongzhi reign, the newly founded Zongli Yamen (the bureau for managing the general affairs concerning the west) reported to the court that a certain foreigner had stealthily climbed the Fuyuan Gate to enter into the Yuanming Yuan without permission. He was discovered by the on-duty eunuchs when he was looking over some books in a room. The foreigner was detained and identified as Zhang Mianxing, presumably Ernst Ohlmer's Chinese name. Serving as a clerk in the Chinese Customs Office in Tianjin, Ohlmer presumed innocence for not knowing the rules, not to mention that he could be protected by extraterritoriality. The Qing authorities at the Zongli Yamen duly pardoned the foreigner on the grounds that he did not actually steal anything, conveniently leaving out the offense of intrusion. On the other hand, the eunuchs who guarded the garden, for fear of punishment, painstakingly explained to the Imperial Household how strenuously they had tried in vain to stop the intruder. The incident further confirmed the difficulty of securing a crippled garden. Besides trying to deter local intruders by promising harsh punishment, the Qing authorities also notified through the Zongli Yamen the four foreign legations in Beijing that the imperial garden was still off-limits to any visitor (*YMYA* 1991, 1:603–605). Regardless, theft and intrusion never ceased in the decade from 1861 to 1871, as numerous memorials reported, and the situation turned from bad to worse thereafter.

The trickiest problem, it turned out, was theft by those whom the Imperial Household entrusted to take care of the garden. In May 1861, for instance, the eunuchs Yue Chenggao and Han Deshou smuggled some brassware out of the garden for profit. Not just eunuchs but also Manchu Bannermen and former members of the Garden Household knew their way in the Yuanming Yuan well enough to steal and get away with it most of the time. Occasionally, they were caught; for example, two former members of a Garden Household of Manchu origin by the names of Guan San and He Anrui stole dozens of jade objects from the Purple-Blue Mountain Cottage in June 1863. They admitted sneaking into the mountain retreat, with which they were familiar, to steal the valuable jade wares to sell in an antique shop in the neighborhood. Their poverty was no excuse; they were convicted and thrown into prison, where they died of illness before long. Their alleged accomplices, however, got away for lack of evidence (*YMYA* 1991, 1:607–610).

Many of the poverty-stricken Manchu bannermen had once lived and worked inside the Yuanming Yuan and thus knew well where valuable things could be found. One record shows that the craftsman Lu Yuzi, together with a dozen others, broke through the northern walls of the Variegated Spring Garden under the cover of darkness on January 25, 1866. They entered into the River Goddess' Temple (Heshen Miao) through a sewer, stole nineteen bronze Buddha statues, large and small, and smashed all of them to sell as brass scrap in a Haidian shop (*YMYA* 1991, 1:611).

About half a year later, on the night of July 20, 1866, Li Sansheng, a former member of a Garden Household, returned to the Yuanming Yuan through a sluice gate with two helpers, Rui Guizi and Li Xiao'er. They took four planks from a bridge and sold them in a market for cash at the Desheng Gate in northern Beijing. When they came back again on the evening of July 21, however, Li was caught red-handed by the eunuch supervisor Dong Fu, though his two accomplices escaped (*YMYA* 1991, 1:613).

In the same year, on November 16, three thieves from Wanping, namely, Liu Yu'er, Zhao Ying, and Zhao San, climbed through the fallen walls into the European section. They cut more than 640 ounces of bronze pipe with a saw from a fountain and sold it on the following day to the tin shop owner Zhao Yuncheng for sixty strings of cash. The success encouraged them to try it again at night on November 21. They slipped through a water gate into the Eternal Spring Garden to steal about 500 ounces of scrap brass and sold it to the same person for fifty-five strings of cash. While taking the familiar route into the Eternal Spring Garden in darkness for their third attempt on November 30, they ran across the patrolling eunuchs at the Symmetric and Amazing Pleasure. Zhao Ying was immediately caught. His two accomplices were eventually captured by the patrolmen. All three thieves were thrown into prison (*YMYA* 1991, 1:614–615).

But captured thieves, it seems, represented only a small percentage of all thieves. The thief Wang Jiushi and his gang, for instance, testified in 1868 that they were caught after five successful attempts. Each time they stole hundreds of ounces of scrap brass, iron, tin, and small bronze Buddha statues for numerous strings of cash. The thieves were interested in scrap brass and iron pieces obviously due to their availability and good price. Reportedly, not surprisingly, the local markets were filled with illegal items taken from the Yuanming Yuan. Local residents also testified that it was easy for them to buy a few things that had belonged to the imperial garden. The Imperial Household just had too many lost things to be accounted for. The promise of amnesty for returning garden objects did not inspire many to surrender what they had obtained voluntarily (cf. *YMYA* 1991, 1:616–618).

According to the penal code of the Qing dynasty, stealing royal property was punishable by death. But executions due to stealing Yuanming Yuan properties seemed rare, presumably because there were simply too many small cases to be prosecuted or pursued. Moreover, a large percentage of the thieves seemed to be Manchus, the royal family's own people who had been victimized by poverty, and they were generally exempt from capital punishment. A report by the Imperial Household on October 3, 1868, is revealing. A certain Manchu person of the White Banner by the name of Zhangba, also known as Lin San, who had worked in the Yuanming Yuan, stole the tail of the famous Bronze Buffalo at the Kunming Lake in 1862. He was found guilty; however, instead of being put to death, he was expelled from the Clan Registration, branded as a thief by tattooing his face, beaten with one hundred strokes, and sent into exile at a distance of 2,000 *li* (about 666 miles). Remarkably, when he was pardoned and returned from exile some years later, he dared to sneak into the garden and steal scrap brass again (*YMYA* 1991, 1:619–620). No record shows his eventual fate.

The Boxer Rebellion of 1900 marked another major turn for the worse, so far as keeping thieves out from the Yuanming Yuan was concerned. The new blow to the garden rendered it totally defenseless. The garden in effect became ruins. Then, with the downfall of the Manchu dynasty in 1912, the abdicated emperor and his Imperial Household lost their legitimacy and power to protect the site. Nor was the feeble Republican government able to secure the historical relics. Under the circumstances, thieves and robbers were rampant. Control over the Yuanming Yuan was not established until after the conclusion of the Cultural Revolution in 1976.

CHAPTER 6

ROYAL DAILY LIFE

THE EMPEROR OF CHINA, or Son of Heaven, was entitled to the maximum pleasure. In imperial China, it was taken for granted that the country and people are both "to consecrate one person" *(gongfeng yiren)*. Only the ruler's own conscience could restrain his passion and desire. In this sense, the magnificent Yuanming Yuan only matched the paramount status of the Qing emperors who conquered a vast empire. The garden came of age in 1723 upon the ascendancy of the Yongzheng emperor, who added courts and office buildings to the pleasure environment and set the precedent for running state affairs from the Yuanming Yuan. Indeed, from Yongzheng to Xianfeng, five Qing emperors thoroughly enjoyed the more than 500–acre scenic land, with hundreds of halls and pavilions, and the extremely luxurious living. They inevitably transformed it into a regular residence, or even their principal residence, and spent increasing amounts of time each year in the garden. Britain's Lord Elgin, who saw both the Forbidden City and the imperial garden, quickly remarked that "I don't wonder that the Emperor preferred Yuen-ming Yuan" (Walrond 1872, 369).

What was royal life like in the imperial garden? It has been a mystery until the availability of archival sources in recent years. These sources, regardless of their limitations, at least allow us to dig into the dust of history to scan some aspects of the life of the Qing emperors in the Yuanming Yuan and even to capture a glimpse of their activities behind the walls of the magnificent, palatial garden.

Of the five Qing emperors, it was Qianlong who spent the longest time in and the most money on the Yuanming Yuan. He chose to stay in his beloved palace garden as long as he possibly could. He returned to his palace in the Forbidden City often only out of absolute necessity, such as to perform rituals and celebrations at the beginning of every lunar New Year and to take customary hunting trips to Rehe, usually in the midst of summer. Take the year 1775: altogether Qianlong spent 168 days, or 43.86 percent of the year, in the garden. In the remainder of the time he spent 105 days in the Forbidden City, 66 days (from August to October) in the Chengde summer retreat in Rehe, and 44 days (from February to March) in Confucius' hometown at Qufu (cf. *YMYA* 1991, 2:827–911; Yu Mingzhong 1985, 1:178–179). This was not significantly different from the year of 1752, during which Qianlong spent 175 days in the garden (Wan Yi, Wang Shuqing, Liu Lu 1990, 296).

Qianlong became homesick even during a short absence from the Yuanming Yuan. He revealed this feeling upon his return from the annual hunting trip in 1752 in one of his numerous poems:

> Returning to my royal demesne from the frontiers,
> I appreciate more the sprouting scenes of this fairyland.
> Now I admire the picturesque hills,
> Now I enjoy boating on lakes,
> Maples trees are still in red,
> They inspire me to write poems.
> Look, chrysanthemum flowers are in brilliant yellow,
> Seemingly slowing down the passing autumn.[1]

One Day of Qianlong's Life

The year 1756 marked twenty years of the Qianlong reign. As usual, the emperor spent the lunar New Year's Day inside the Forbidden City, where he performed various ceremonial duties. About a week later, he departed for the Yuanming Yuan. He rose early in the morning on the day of departure. He wore a sable skin headgear, a fox fur-lined robe with a silk dust coat in dark reddish brown, heavy cotton-padded trousers with leather girdles, several strings of beads around his neck, and a pair of white cotton socks in green satin-covered sheepskin boots. This illustrates the ornamentation and color of dress to be worn by the emperor on a normal day.

After fully dressing with assistance from his attendants, the emperor walked into a four-man sedan chair to be carried to the Qianqing Palace, his study, through the Fortunate Gate. Inside the palace, he met with representatives of the Dalai Lama from Tibet. After the meeting, he ate his breakfast at the West Warm Room (Xi Nuange) before going on to perform the kowtow to deities at the Doutan Altar of the Qin'an Dian. When these duties were completed, he left for the Yuanming Yuan (*YMYA* 1991, 2:827).[2]

It took an eight-man heated palanquin to transport the emperor from the Forbidden City to the Yuanming Yuan. Upon arrival, Qianlong and his entourage went through the Inner Palace Gate and stopped at the Honoring Three Selflessnesses Court to pray briefly. Then he proceeded to his living quarters on the Nine Continents for a short rest. The next activity of the day was to take a boat ride to pay homage in the Buddhist temple at the Gentle Clouds Cover All and to worship at the Anyou Palace of the Ancestral Shrine. On his way back, he stopped at the Eternal Spring Fairy Hall to see his mother. He returned to the Nine Continents for resting before having his dinner at the All-Happy Garden, situated south of the Wall of Sravasti. After the dinner, he stopped at the Xiuqing Village and the Pleasant Studio before retiring to his bedroom on the Nine Continents (*YMYA* 1991, 2:827; cf. Yu Mingzhong 1985, 1:178–179).

The following day, the ninth day of the lunar New Year, was the birthday of the Jade Emperor (Yuhuang Dadi, the supreme deity of Daoism). Qianlong got up early to perform the kowtow to the Jade Emperor in the Nine Continents in Peace, where food had been prepared for His Majesty's sacrifices. After eating his breakfast, the emperor rode on a dragon barge to the Cross Pavilion (Shizi Ting) to board a four-man palanquin carrying him to a large yurt, where he met with an awaiting Mongolian prince. When the meeting was over, Qianlong toured Longevity Hills, paid a tribute at a Buddhist temple, and finally ate supper at the All-Happy Garden. He took an after-meal nap before proceeding to the waterfront to wait for his mother's arrival. The son accompanied the mother to observe the colorful lantern performance in the Drill Field. After the party was over, the emperor escorted the dowager in person to the waterfront to see her off before retiring to his bedroom on the Nine Continents (*YMYA* 1991, 2:828).

Qianlong was present in the Forbidden City on the tenth day of the year for unknown obligations. But he stayed there for just two short days. Upon returning to the Yuanming Yuan in the evening, he had his meal again at the All-Happy Garden. When he was full, he went to the Drill Field to watch wrestling and fireworks and to entertain with princes and high-ranking officials. Afterward, a four-man palanquin took him to the Cross Pavilion for a boat ride to the All-Happy Garden, where he had his last refreshments of the day before going to bed (*YMYA* 1991, 2:829).

Qianlong's activities in the Yuanming Yuan reveal that his mother was in his company regularly. Indeed, he had the reputation for being extraordinarily kind to his mother, known in history as Empress Xiaosheng (1693–1777). He had placed her at his favorite Eternal Spring Fairy Hall upon his ascendancy to the throne. He seemed not merely to fulfill the Confucian moral obligation as a filial son but also to show his genuine love and respect to the imperial mother. He was his mother's only child, and they were indeed very close to each other. Whenever he had spare time, he was eager to accompany her to tour the garden. On every Duanwu Festival Day, he rarely missed the opportunity to accompany his mother to watch at the Fairy Terrace nine dragon boats racing (Wu Zhenyu 1983, 155). He dined with her very often as well. The January 1775 record shows that the emperor and the dowager ate together in the dinning hall of the All-Happy Garden almost on a daily basis (*YMYA* 1991, 2:831, 832, 833, 834, 835, 836, 837, 838).

Qianlong's love and kindness to his mother never faded. On March 2, 1777, the dowager suddenly fell ill while observing a lantern show in the Drill Field. She was taken to her bedroom in the Eternal Spring Fairy Hall but died shortly afterward at the age of eighty-five. Grieving deeply, Qianlong not only gave her a lavish funeral but also erected a temple, named the Mother's Memorial Temple, in her memory. It was built inside the Ancestral Shrine, known as the Boundless Kindness and Eternal Blessing, in the same style of architecture as the temple that the Yongzheng emperor had built for the deceased Kangxi emperor (cf. Kahn 1971, 88). This temple remained standing in the ruins of the Yuanming Yuan as late as the 1930s.

The Royal Gourmets

Feeding the emperor and his royal family was a massive task. The Imperial Butlery (Yu Shanfang) had the responsibility of "feeding His Majesty, managing imperial foodstuffs, and preparing banquets on special occasions" (Zhang Naiwei 1988, 355).

It seems that the Qing emperors ate two principal meals a day, breakfast and dinner, even though food of various sorts was made available to them continuously throughout the day. Each meal was lavishly, carefully, and timely prepared by a huge staff of cooks employed by the Imperial Butlery. The royal food service demanded not only good quality food but also superabundance and variety. From the famous recipe book left behind by the eminent scholar-poet Yuan Mei (1716–1798) of the Qianlong era, we know how Yuan and Yuan's wealthy contemporaries prepared their meals. Citing Confucius' *Golden Mean (Zhongyong),* "everyone eats his (or her) meal, but a few enjoy the tastes of food," Yuan advocated the pleasure of eating. No sooner had he enjoyed a tasty dish at a friend's house than he sent his cook to learn it (Yuan Mei 1892, 1a–1b). His recipe book became in effect a synthesis of the culinary arts. It details how to execute cookery exquisitely, from understanding the natural properties of a given food, choosing the condiments, determining the correct heat, and using the appropriate types of utensils to determining the overall strategy of a meal (cf. Yuan Mei 1892, 1a–29a). The gourmet in the imperial garden could not be less sophisticated or extravagant than Yuan Mei in his Sui Garden, not to mention that the scale of culinary operations had to be much greater.

The royal feasts sanctioned by the Confucian codes of conduct consist of twenty-six dishes chosen out of one hundred and twenty different entries in the standard royal menu. Evidently for security reasons, every dish that was served to the emperor had to be recorded beforehand by officials from the Imperial Household along with the name of the chef (Zhang Naiwei 1988, 355). The normal size of a royal main meal in the Yuanming Yuan was about two dozen dishes, comparable to that served in the Forbidden City. No one had the appetite to consume so much food in one meal. Hence, the Qing emperors, in particular Qianlong, customarily offered some of the dishes to a specifically named person, or persons, to show his favor or appreciation. Also, different royal kitchens served the empress, dowager, and other consorts. The Imperial Butlery was ready for any sort of requests, including banquets of whatever size, at short notice. Feeding the court was a luxury, which represented not simply vanity but more importantly the dignity of the throne. Real luxury and sophistication were always a part of the eating habits of China's rulers. Table luxury included crockery, silver, and golden utensils. Because of their huge quantity, specially appointed men took care of them (Zhang Naiwei 1988, 355, 356). The suggestion that "many of the Ch'ing (Qing) emperors had in fact quite simple tastes" (Chang 1977, 281) is contrary to the archival evidence. A series of recorded royal menus (*YMYA* 1991, 2:924–958), indeed, sounds flamboyant.

Some spectacular banquets were given inside the Forbidden City. For instance, Kangxi once held there a thousand-man banquet. Qianlong also hosted a grand banquet of ninety-nine guests, including Manchu noblemen, grand secretaries (Da Xueshi), and high-ranking mandarins at the Qianqing Palace in 1740. Twenty years later, the same emperor offered an extremely lavish banquet at the Fragrant Hill in honor of his mother's seventieth birthday. In 1782, upon the completion of the first set of the Four Treasuries, the emperor invited all those who were involved in editing the project to a lavish banquet and gave presents after the banquet (Wu Zhenyu 1983, 165, 167).

The kitchens inside the Yuanming Yuan also prepared celebrated banquets. For example, it took eight full days for the fifth-rank chief eunuch Liu Jingzhong to prepare a banquet in the garden on January 19, 1727. He had to propose a menu, schedule entertainment (usually fireworks and wrestling), and finalize the guest list, which included Princes Yi, Zhuang, Kang, Gou, and Xin (*YMYA* 1991, 1:23–24).

A lavish banquet was given at the hall of the All-Happy Garden to celebrate the lunar New Year of 1757. Guests included the royal clansmen, meritorious officials, and distinguished visitors from Mongolia and Tibet. This banquet, like numerous others, was followed by entertainment, such as dramatic theater performances or the recitation and composition of poems. In 1790, envoys from Korea, Ryūkyū, and Annam (Vietnam) joined others to come to Beijing to celebrate Qianlong's eightieth birthday. The emperor offered a grand banquet in their honor at the Yuanming Yuan. Qianlong even proposed a toast to every ambassador *(zhengshi)* from the vassal states. Then, at noon, the poems that Qianlong composed for the occasion were read to the guests. Those who were able, including several ambassadors and their deputies, replied to the imperial poems by using the same rhyme sequence (cf. Wu Zhenyu 1983, 163, 164, 166, 167).

How was a court banquet served? An eighteenth-century Russian diplomat in whose honor the Qianlong emperor offered a banquet left behind a vivid account of the procession of the banquet:

> There were first brought neat little tables, covered with a variety of fruits and confections, and placed before all the company. It seems to be the fashion in this country to bring the desert first, at least that was the case at all the entertainments where I was present. In this, as in many other things, the behavior of the Chinese is quite contrary to that of the Europeans. Soon after the fruits, the victuals were served in the same manner, and placed on small tables before the guests. They consisted of fowls, mutton, and pork, all very good of their kinds; and the whole was either boiled, or fried with pickles, but nothing roasted. The Emperor sent several dishes from his own table to the Ambassador, particularly some boiled pheasants, which were very agreeable.[3]

The British visitors at the end of the century, though unhappy with their "uncomfortable lodging," were pleased to be amended by "a most excellent dinner." When they toured the imperial gardens, they were treated at one of the palaces "with a collation of petit-patis, salt relishes, and other savoury dishes, with fruits and sweetmeats, milk and ice-water" (Barrow 1805, 74, 80, 135). For the banquet, a table was laid for every two British guests. "As soon as all were seated," George Staunton described, "the tables were uncovered, and exhibited a sumptuous banquet." But on each of the small tables "was a pyramid of dishes or bowls piled upon each other, containing viands and fruits in vast variety" (Staunton 1799, 2:78).

The chefs working in the Yuanming Yuan served not just the emperor but also princes and high-ranking officials. "Four senior officials," as a document shows, "asked us to serve fifty-five tables of guests (in the Yuanming Yuan) from February 4 to 27" ("Neiwufu laiwen," Yuanming Yuan ziliao, No. 4667; cf. Zhao Lian 1980, 374–375). The presence of the emperor, royalty, and prestigious officials definitely required large garden kitchens.

The numerous workers in an imperial kitchen fell into many different classifications as sanctioned by the *Book of Rites*. They included chefs *(shanfu)*, butchers *(baoren)*, cutlers *(neiyong)*, cutlers for food as sacrifice *(waiyong)*, meat chefs *(hengren)*, food purchasers *(dianshi)*, hunters *(shouren)*, fish catchers *(yuren)*, turtle cookers *(bie)*, salted-meat makers *(laren)*, nutrition experts *(shiyi)*, food inspectors *(jiyi)*, brewers *(jiuzheng)*, bartenders *(jiuren)*, sauce makers *(jiangren)*, cooler keepers *(lingren)*, bamboo utensil suppliers *(bianren)*, ground-meat makers *(hanren)*, jam makers *(xiren)*, salt users *(yanren)*, and dinner-set keepers *(muren)*. The total number of kitchen workers at the emperor's disposal could be as many as 2,332 persons plus 206 ranking officials to supervise them (Lin Naicai 1989, 62).

Such huge kitchen staffs in the service of the imperial ruler were maintained throughout the Qing dynasty without exception. Even though we do not have statistics concerning the Yuanming Yuan's chefs, given the emperor's lengthy residence in the garden, their number could not be much smaller than the number of chefs in the Forbidden City. There is no doubt that a troop of people working in the garden kitchens supported luxurious and sophisticated eating habits for 150 years. The estimated cost of food consumption of an imperial kitchen in the month of September in 1898 was 2780.92 taels of silver (cited in Kong 1998, 115). The size of a single royal meal, according to a recent estimate, could feed as many as one hundred peasant households for an entire year (Lin Naicai 1989, 140).

It is no surprise to find that there were ice rooms *(bingku)* in the Yuanming Yuan to preserve food during the summer of 1725 *(YMYA* 1991, 1:20). In fact, from very early on the Qing palaces inside the Forbidden City had maintained five large ice rooms, with one containing 9,226 pieces of ice and the other four 5,000 each (Zhang Naiwei 1988, 165). According to the *Book of Rites (Zhouli)*, as early as the three ancient dynasties, namely, Xia, Shang, and Zhou, the royal house had a troop of ninety-four men in charge of matters concerning ice and ice rooms to preserve food. As a rule, the foods that any of the Qing emperors ate were the highest quality "tributes" *(gongpin)*, usually the best local products, delivered from all over the country. The grain, cereal, and vegetables for consumption in the Yuanming Yuan were from specially cultivated farms in the vicinity. Likewise, drinking water was drawn from the clean and fresh spring at the nearby Jade Spring Hill (Zhang Naiwei 1988, 356).

So far as we know, the Qianlong emperor liked to have his meals in different sections of the Yuanming Yuan. This indicates that every major location of the garden had a kitchen and chefs at His Majesty's service. Besides dining regularly in his living quarters on the Nine Continents, the emperor used the dining hall inside the All-Happy Garden very often, presumably because there was a large theatre nearby for the convenience of after-meal entertainment. It had become a custom for Chinese elites to enjoy entertainment following a dinner party since the Song in the eleventh century.

From the newly available "Food Archives" (Shandidang), we know what Qianlong had for his dinner at the All-Happy Garden on the eleventh day after the lunar New Year of 1784. In his dining room, the emperor used a flowery lacquer table. The dishes for this particular meal were diced meat and duck steamed with wine, chicken with fried Chinese cabbage, swallows' nests with red and white duck meat, swallows' nests with shredded chicken meat, roasted duck, fried chicken with fresh bamboo shoots, omelet, steamed chicken with deer's tail, diced chicken with almond, bread in the shape of elephants' eyes, buns stuffed with duck meat, chicken meat ravioli in hot noodle soup, and a cold dish in a sunflower lacquer box. In addition, there were four silver dishes of finely minced cucumbers, pickles, and the like; salted meat; braised pheasant with melon; rice; and soup with sliced chicken and swallows' nests. This dinner of superabundance was followed later in the evening by a midnight snack. It featured soup with edible swallows' nests and red and white duck meat, swallows' nests with fried sliced duck meat, roasted chicken with swallows' nests and winter bamboo shoots, smoked chicken with salted meat, steamed chicken with mushrooms, and fried sliced duck kidney (*YMYA* 1991, 2:924).

So many swallows' nests dishes were included in the imperial menu because the Chinese consider them rare delicacy.[4] According to the Qing scholar Yuan Mei, swallows' nests were so rare and precious that even a rich family could not serve them very often. The best way to cook them was to soak approximately two ounces of nests in fresh water before boiling it with salted ham and fresh mushrooms in tender chicken soup until the nest material turned to a fair color. The taste of this dish, devoid of any oil and fat, is supposed to be light (Yuan Mei 1892, 5a). It is quite possible that this frequently served delicacy was more for the emperor's health than for taste. After all, modern scholars have determined that nest cement is rich in protein and contains significant amounts of calcium, iron, and riboflavin (Simoons 1991: 431).

Also noticeable from the imperial menu cited earlier is that chicken and duck appeared much more frequently than pork, beef, mutton, or seafood. As for ingredients and seasonings, none other than soy sauce, oil, salt, vinegar, pimento, ginger, and pepper was used. Whether this was a standard menu for all emperors or reflected Qianlong's personal taste is uncertain, though the latter seems more likely the case. If so, Qianlong's taste in Chinese cuisine clearly favored northern cooking. Nevertheless, the imperial kitchen in the Yuanming Yuan was capable of serving anything at the emperor's request.

In the morning of the twelfth day of the lunar New Year of 1784, Qianlong had his breakfast at the Chunhua Gallery in the Eternal Spring Garden. This particular breakfast was as sumptuous as the dinner of the previous night. The menu entries again include many dishes of swallows' nests with minced, spiced, or baked duck and chicken meat, plus deer's tail, *hors d'oeuvres,* small breads, white cake, buns stuffed with meat and mushrooms, and a cold dish in a silver box. In addition, four silver plates on a table displayed minced vegetables, salted meat, braised pheasant with melon, duck meat stewed with noodles, along with rice and rice soup with fruits. Besides these main entries, several small tables in the dining room served a variety of wheaten food, milk, and sliced cold pork and mutton to satisfy His Majesty's appetite. Having had this big breakfast, Qianlong proceeded to the High-Reaching Mountain and Outstretched River in the Drill Field to meet a party of Lama Buddhists in a large yurt, during which various sorts of noodles were served. There was no formal luncheon of the day; however, some light food such as noodles, fruits, and tea were made available. In the evening, the emperor returned to the All-Happy Garden for dinner with a menu similar to the previous evening (*YMYA* 1991, 2:925; cf. 927, 938).

The Qing rulers seemed to have used modest quantities of wine and grain alcohols regularly, but they definitely drank little milk. Fernand Braudel seemed correct to suggest that "China remained deliberately ignorant of milk, cheese and butter" (1973, 143). Of all beverages, the drink they consumed the most was tea, China's national drink. The custom of substituting wine with tea seems to have been practiced as early as the Three Kingdoms period (220–265). During Qing China, both the Manchus and Chinese were accustomed to offer tea as a precious wedding gift (Fuge 1984, 169). Within the Forbidden City and Yuanming Yuan, virtually every main building had a decent "tea room" *(chafang).* The principal royalty, such as as the emperor, empress, and crown prince, each had their own special "tea room." His Majesty's tea room, known as the "Imperial Tea Room" (Yu Chafang), was headed by two seventh-rank officials, who were in charge of tea as well as teapots and porcelain, gold, and silver cups. Tea was normally prepared in pots or cups with boiling water and was always consumed hot without sugar or other additives; iced tea was unheard of. The fresh water for tea in the Yuanming Yuan came exclusively from the Jade Spring Hills in the neighborhood, which was considered the best quality water. Qianlong took this "purest" water with him when he made his southern tour in 1756 (Zhang Naiwei 1988, 228–230).

When the 1784 Yuanxiao Festival Day, the fifteenth day of the first lunar month, arrived, the Yuanming Yuan featured, as before, lanterns, fireworks, and "continuous theatrical performances" *(liantaixi).* Abundant food in great variety was also made available to entertain the royalty, guests of honor, and several princes from Mongolia. On this special day, Qianlong rose early and worshiped inside the Blessing Palace at the Ancestral Shrine, during which sweet dumplings were served during the resting period. He had his twenty-four-course breakfast at the All-Happy Garden. The dishes included shredded chicken meat with swallows' nests, baked duck, chopped pheasant meat, steamed duck with deers' young antlers, steamed chicken, baked venison, mashed ground pork, steamed buns stuffed with vegetables, steamed dumplings with chicken meat, salted meat, and various vegetables. Some of these dishes used special bowls or plates; for instance, the ground pork was served on a gold plate, the baked duck in enamelware, and the salted meat on a silver plate. In addition, this breakfast of the festival day also featured numerous light refreshments and pastry of various sorts together with a number of dishes specially prepared by the royal concubines (*YMYA* 1991 2:926–933).

Having had his breakfast, Qianlong went to his royal office in the Main Audience Hall as usual. The only difference from normal days was that in the office room there were tables of wheaten food, fruits, pastry, and sweet dumplings, each of which was put either on five white-jade plates or in elegant porcelain bowls. The emperor had no more appetite in his office room, so he asked the attending eunuch named Er Luli to pass these foods as imperial bestowals to princes, concubines, and grand councilmen (*YMYA* 1991, 2:934).

The luncheon of the day was extraordinarily lavish, comprising thirty-two different entries served on purple sandalwood dining tables with specially prepared chopsticks, spoons, jade bowls and silver plates, and cloth and paper napkins in the decorated dining room inside the Honoring Three Selflessnesses Court. The emperor did not show up until all the invited guests, including princes, concubines, and favorite officials, had already assembled. His Majesty walked into the room in the midst of music playing in the background. Soon after the emperor had taken his seat, the hot dishes were served. The guests, two persons per table as usual, enjoyed servings of hot dishes together with soup, milk tea, wine, cold meat, vegetables, and sweets, in that order. Course after course was served while gentle music was playing. At the end of the luncheon, the emperor offered his guests a bowl of sweet dumplings specially prepared for the festival as a gesture of his pleasure and kindness (*YMYA* 1991, 2:934–935).

In the afternoon, the eunuch Chang Ning offered Qianlong some hot liquid food, such as swallows' nests, duck, chicken, or mutton egg soups and milk tea as well as tables of wine and light dishes of pickles and pastries. After sunset, late in the evening, Qianlong led his guests, including the distinguished visitors from Mongolia, Tibet, and Korea, into the Drill Field, where they watched fireworks and ate fruits and dumplings offered by servants (*YMYA* 1991, 2:935).

The celebration continued for several more days. The scheduled fireworks show on January 17, however, had to be called off because of snow. Qianlong stayed indoors most of the time. Later that night, he had a huge snack that included swallows' nests with minced duck, fried dried bean curd with spinach, mutton sausage and tripe soup, fried shredded chicken with swallows' nests, deep fried duck kidneys, and pork chops (*YMYA* 1991, 2:936–937, 942; cf. 937–958).

Fun and Entertainment

As a pleasure ground, the Yuanming Yuan provided entertainment of many sorts. One of the most exciting events, given almost annually throughout the Qianlong reign, was to set up a make-believe market in the garden, usually inside the All-Happy Garden, to entertain the emperor and his guests. The eunuchs ran the market and assumed the roles of shop owners, teahouse keepers, and vendors who sold antiques, books, furnitures, silk clothes, porcelain, varnish works, and the like. In order to make them look exactly like merchants in downtown Beijing so as to maximize amusement, the eunuchs loudly shouted the vendors' cries, while busily emulating aggressive salesmen to catch customers by the sleeve to press for sales. To make the common street scene come alive, they even pretended to quarrel and fight among themselves and wait for arrest by security guards, as often happened in real streets. This "Disney" market normally lasted for nine days as part of the celebration of the New Year (Yao Yuanzhi 1982, 5–6, and Attiret 1982, 27–29).

On the eighteenth day of the sixth month of the lunar calendar, the Qing emperor watched his imperial guardsmen practicing riding horses, known as "racing His Majesty's horses" *(pao yuma),* outside the northern walls of the Yuanming Yuan. A guardsman, while riding a horse, would lead another horse to his side. In the midst of racing, the guardsman would whip the horse to his side and jump on it as soon as it picked up speed to run. Guardsmen who were able to mount the galloping horse from the rear received the best rewards. The second prize went to those who successfully jumped to another horse horizontally. Even those who fell from jumping received some presents from the emperors. Of the five Qing emperors who resided in the Yuanming Yuan, only Xianfeng did not preside over this event in person. He asked high-ranking officials to run it on his behalf (*YMYZ* 1984, 281).

The Qing emperors also used the proud imperial garden to entertain kings, princes, and other dignitaries from the neighboring vassal states, in particular Korea, Vietnam, and Ryūkyū, from time to time. The Mongols, whom the Manchus considered close allies, were especially common visitors to the garden. One of many such visits took place on the nineth day of the first lunar month in 1757. Qianlong met the Mongols at the Drill Field and offered a lavish banquet in their honor. Five days later came the big holiday, the Lantern Festival Day, one of the most popular festivals in China. People of all classes want to make the day as fun as possible, and the festival is celebrated by making it "bustling" *(nao)* by beating drums and racing horses (Gu Lu 1986, 27).

In the Yuanming Yuan, on the eve of the day, Qianlong took a bath before going to bed. He rose very early in the morning, ate some fruits in the Main Audience Hall, and proceeded to the Anyou Palace, the main hall of the Ancestral Shrine, for worship. After taking a meal with his mother in the All-Happy Garden, he prayed at a Buddhist temple in the Eternal Spring Garden. In the afternoon, he ate sweet dumplings made of glutinous rice flour *(yuanxiao),* the delicacy of the festival, before resting in his living quarters. When the evening finally came, he rode a four-man palanquin to the Drill Field for the exciting entertainment, including wrestling, lantern dance, and the biggest show of fireworks in the year. The Mongol princes, while still in town, were invited to participate in the celebration as guests of honor. All enjoyed the spectacular scene of the terrific fireworks lighting up the sky at night in a large open field while food was served and music played (Zhaolian 1980, 374–375 and Yao Yuanzhi 1982, 6–7; cf. Gu Lu 1986, 26). The French Jesuit Father Attiret, who experienced the great "Feast of Lanterns" in the Yuanming Yuan, added some interesting details:

It is always celebrated on the 15th Day of the first month. There is no Chinese so poor, but that upon this day he lights up his lanterns. They have all sorts of figures, sizes, and prices. On that day, all China is illuminated: but the finest illuminations of all are in the Emperor's palace; and particularly in these Pleasuregrounds, which I have been describing to you. There is not a chamber, hall, or portico, in them, which has not several of these lanterns hanging from the ceilings. There are several upon all the rivulets, rivers, and lakes; made in the shape of little boats, which the waters carry backward and forward. There are some upon all the hills and bridges, and almost upon all the trees. These are wrought mighty pretty, in the shapes of different fishes, birds, and beasts, vases, fruits, flowers; and boats of different sorts and sizes. Some are made of silk; some of horn, glass, mother of pearl, and a thousand other materials. . . . It is in these, and in the great variety, which the Chinese show in their buildings, that I admire the fruitfulness of their invention; and am almost tempted to own, that we are quite poor and barren in comparison of them.[5]

The Lantern Festival concluded when the colorful fireworks were over. The emperor returned to his living quarters to eat a little bit more of the seasonal sweet dumplings before attending the late evening party at the All-Happy Garden. After the party, a lantern procession escorted the emperor back to the Nine Continents to retire (*YMYA* 1991, 2:831).

Lanterns and fireworks were clearly a great pleasure in the imperial garden. They could be displayed everywhere, in particular at lakeside. Many witnesses left behind their impressions in writing. The eminent eighteenth-century historian Zhao Yi (1727–1814), who had the privilege of observing the festive fireworks with Qianlong in the imperial garden, had this to tell:

Early in the morning, several shelves of fireworks had been placed in front of the Grand Palace Entrance. . . . When the sun went down, about three thousand men carrying lanterns and singing songs moved orderly into the Drill Field. The men, while dancing, slowly forged formations to show the four Designated Chinese characters: "great" *(tai)*, "peace" *(ping)*, "long" *(wan)*, and "life" *(sui)* in order to draw the emperor's attention and pleasure. No sooner had the dance finished than the fireworks suddenly burst *en masse*. It sounded like thunder and its light illuminated half of the sky. There were like thousands of red fish jumping around under the sea of clouds. It was truly a great wonder.[6]

The historian's description of the wonder of fireworks was echoed by a poem composed by a court official in the company of the emperor on one of these occasions:

The Milky Way steers clear of dust,
The fiery phoenix flys tiltingly on display,
A sudden thunderclap awakes the hibernating under the earth.

> The flower blossoms on thousands of trees
> Make a beautiful Spring in the sky.
> The lanterns on the chambers light up the night,
> The full moon on top of the palace moves slowly.
> Enjoying his special night,
> His Majesty shares his happiness with all of us.[7]

Watching fireworks in the garden also fascinated the British visitors at the end of the eighteenth century. As one of them described, the fireworks "exceeded anything of the kind I had ever seen." He observed that "in grandeur, magnificence, and variety," the fireworks he had seen at Batavia "were inferior to the Chinese fire-works," "but infinitely superior, in point of novelty, neatness, and ingenuity of contrivance." And the Chinese fireworks "concluded with a volcano, or general explosion and discharge of suns and stars, squibs, bouncers, crackers, rockets, and grenadoes, which involved the gardens, for about an hour after, in a cloud of intolerable smoke" (Barrow 1805, 139).

The pleasant and joyful setting of the Yuanming Yuan imperial garden was no doubt the most suitable place for the emperor to observe his birthday. As a rule, in the early morning of the imperial birthday, high-ranking officials, both civilian and military, presented themselves in formal dress at the garden's Main Audience Hall. Relatively lower-ranking officials, say, below the third rank, gathered at the more distant Inner Palace Gate. The emperor, fully dressed, received congratulations from the officials in the hall one by one with their names pronounced aloud by an attending official. When Qianlong went hunting in Rehe on his birthday of September 25, 1757, government officials assembled at the Noon Gate (Wumen) of the Forbidden City to send congratulations from a distance (Zhaolian 1980, 389).

Qianlong lived long enough to celebrate his eightieth birthday in 1790; none of the other Qing emperors had the chance to observe such a grand birthday. The empire was still generally peaceful and prosperous. The proud old man had every reason to have the greatest of all birthday parties. On the eve of his birthday, exuberant and colorful decorations had already been displayed, and they stretched all the way from Beijing's West Straight Gate to the imperial garden's main entrance. An appointed commissioner general *(zongli qingdian dachen)* supervised all celebration programs, including birthday presents from prominent officials and wealthy merchants all over the country. The rich from the affluent Lianghuai, Changlu, and Zhejiang regions, as the record shows, had actually paid for all of the spectacular decorations just mentioned.

The grand eightieth birthday celebration formally began on September 25, 1790, in the Yuanming Yuan. A long line of guests was introduced in this order: members of the royal family, Manchu noblemen, high officials, generals and officers, distinguished elderly citizens, the King of Annam, and representatives from Korea, Burma, Cambodia, Mongolia, and Taiwan as well as various Muslim tribesmen. Once introduced, they were seated in their designated booths. After having taken their seats, all the guests chanted "long life" *(wanshou)* aloud in the emperor's honor. The hills on the west side of the garden's southern gate had been temporarily named the Welcoming Longevity Hills (Yingshou Shan), and on top of the hill stood the newly built pavilion named after the God of Longevity (Shouxing Ting). "Longevity" became the most popular catchword of the day. Its gigantic character was on display in open theaters, along with hundreds of congratulatory phrases in parallel tablet style posted virtually everywhere in the garden. Musical bands played the pleasant praising sounds endlessly from a distance. About one thousand Lama priests assembled under a huge awning and recited the Buddhist scripture of praises as the way to wish the great Qianlong emperor a long, long life. All these events created a thrilling sight in the magnificent imperial garden. Thousands of regional and local officials who were unable to observe the birthday celebration in person sent well wishes to the Yuanming Yuan all day long. Still in good health and in an excellent mood, the eighty-year-old Qianlong had his birthday dinner in the Rainbow Hall north of the Gaoliang Bridge.

The price tag for this grand birthday party amounted to 1,144,297.5 taels of silver, approximately 573,703 taels less than the original budget, presumably because enthusiastic Manchu clansmen, top-ranking officials, regional tax collectors, and local administrators had picked up a substantial sum. Many in officialdom volunteered to take a certain percentage of salary cuts to partially cover the enormous bill (Wu Zhenyu 1983, 125–132).

In retrospect, this grand birthday party may be considered the last truly great fanfare in the Yuanming Yuan. Afterward, the Qing Empire began its downward course. Both of Qianlong's successors, Jiaqing and Daoguang, suffered from internal unrest and external threats that inevitably cast a long shadow over the pleasure of the magnificent garden living. By the time Xianfeng ascended to the throne, both the political and the financial conditions of the empire were worsening. At one point, the emperor even felt guilty about using his garden residence, and his eventual return to garden living won him the bad name as an indulgent monarch.

Xianfeng did enjoy the magnificent garden life. The Yuanming Yuan in its twilight remained a beautiful and delightful royal demesne. Indeed, Xianfeng needed greater pleasure to ease his profound distress. Many loyal servants tried to make His Majesty happy in the garden. Most noticeably, to cheer him up, a dozen pretty Manchu girls were brought into the garden. Lady Yehonala, one of these Manchu girls, won the special attention of the emperor and eventually became the notoriously powerful Empress Dowager Cixi (1835–1908), who dominated Qing China for more than forty years. This royal romance in the Yuanming Yuan has been written into many fictitious stories, including one by a Western author. The core of the story reads:

> One day, in early spring, the young Emperor was wandering idly around one of the gardens in the Yuan Ming Yuan, when he heard the clear notes of a girl's voice singing a pretty and popular song. He stopped to listen and presently decided that he must see who was warbling in such a alluring way. To his delight, he discovered a slim, tall and beautiful girl at her embroidery-frame in a summer-house.[8]

The description is fictitious, but it is true that the slim Yehonala, though not tall at all, bore a son, the future Tongzhi emperor, in a hall on the Nine Continents in April 1856. Both the mother and the son were permanent residents of the Yuanming Yuan until the invasion of the Anglo-French forces. Neither could come back to enjoy royal life in the imperial garden again in the aftermath. Xianfeng died in Rehe, and mother and son returned to Beijing only to see the burnt out Yuanming Yuan.

Enjoying dramatic performances inside the Yuanming Yuan was evidenced in the growing number of garden theatres constructed since the Daoguang reign. As a rule, no official below the second rank could accompany the emperor to watch shows inside the Forbidden City. The rule was obviously ignored in the imperial garden. The Xianfeng emperor especially wanted more people regardless of rank in his company in the theater. On at least one occasion, the emperor complained of too few people watching the performance with him. As a result, many low-ranking retired officers in the neighborhood were summoned to the theater to join the emperor (*YMYZ* 1984, 284).

Just about a year before the fall of the Yuanming Yuan, Xianfeng had his dinner on a dragon boat sailing on the Sea of Blessing one summer. All of a sudden, the emperor dismissed the entertainers around him and sought a certain Enling, who turned out to be a ventriloquist. This episode confirms that His Majesty was fond of witty monologue and comedy (*YMYZ* 1984, 283). Cixi was crazy about the Peking Opera. After she seized power, the Yuanming Yuan was burned down; however, she did not forget to build several theaters while transforming the Pure Ripple Garden into the Yihe Yuan, where present-day tourists can still observe a gigantic theater.

During the last decade of the Yuanming Yuan in the 1850s, according to numerous anecdotes left by Qing scholars, there were many pretty girls from different ethnic groups in the garden to please the young, anguished emperor. The young Manchu girl, the future dowager Cixi, had no doubt attracted His Majesty's attention. In addition, the general manager of the garden Wenfeng reportedly brought in four Chinese singsong girls named Spring Apricot, Spring Paradise, Spring Crabapple, and Spring Peony. Each of them lived in one of the pavilions to entertain the emperor. The four Springs plus Yehonala were known as the "Five Springs" (Wuchun) (Cheng Yansheng 1928, 17a). The emperor became infatuated with beautiful women. The great Qing scholar Wang Kaiyun (1832–1916) cited some of the anecdotes in one of his most famous poems:

> The beautiful ladies carry their flagons,
> Trying to force His Majesty to smile.
> The cup in imperial gold is always filled with good wine,
> From sunset to sunrise.
> The Son of Heaven loves to live in the Yuanming Yuan,
> Enjoying the scenes of different seasons.
> Returning to the Forbidden City he wishes not,
> Even only at a year's end.

Going to the Yuanming Yuan he is always happy.
As soon as spring arrives,
Awaiting him are four charming ladies,
Like blossoms of apricot, of crabapple, of peony,
And of the Wulin Paradise.
His Majesty's garden tours are as tireless as they seem,
His chefs are as alert as his guards,
Get decent food ready on table anywhere, anytime.
Whether at night or in the morning,
The kitchen's heat never dies down.[9]

Wang's historical epic reveals how majestic royal living still was in the Yuanming Yuan. The food service appeared as exquisite as before. The most richly furnished dining room during the twilight days of the imperial garden was situated inside the Honoring Three Selflessnesses Court, which seemed to have replaced the popular dining room at the All-Happy Garden during Qianlong's time. Nevertheless, the pleasant garden environment somehow could no longer really please the emperor. The excellent food, soft music, and pretty women were all spoiled by the troubled times.

Seeking pleasure in the garden simply became an escape from cruel reality; however, it sometimes enhanced Xianfeng's sense of poignancy. Drunken on one occasion, the throne missed the early morning session in the Yuanming Yuan. To save the emperor's face, the empress punished the women who accompanied His Majesty in the evening as scapegoats. Nevertheless, the emperor was ashamed of himself, admitted his guilt, and pledged not to get drunk again (*YMYZ*, 1984 330–331). Xianfeng's courageous admission of his misbehavior and willingness to take responsibility may suggest that he had a conscience after all. In fact, he had also expressed a sense of humility in the time of hardship by cancelling his thirtieth birthday party, which was to have been celebrated in the Yuanming Yuan in 1860.[10] This was a quite unusual decision, as the celebration of the imperial birthday had long since been the tradition of the Yuanming Yuan. His sincerity could be seen in the fact that he prohibited any regional official from coming to Beijing to commemorate his birthday (*Qingshigao* 1976, 4:747–748,758). But before long, the foreign army invaded, and with the burning down of the Yuanming Yuan, no birthday parties could ever again be held in the magnificent garden.

CHAPTER 7

THE SACKING

THE FALL OF THE YUANMING YUAN to foreign invaders must be understood in the context of Sino-Western confrontations in the nineteenth century. Although the post-Opium War (1839–1842) treaty system had secured British commercial interests that neither Macartney nor Amherst had been able to obtain, Britain sought to expand her privileges on the China coast. On the other hand, the newly ascended Xianfeng emperor, ashamed of losing to the British national interest, struggled to recover the Qing's honor and was certainly not willing to yield more rights. The British demand for treaty revision, to acquire further concessions from China, thus met stubborn resistance and eventually led to the outbreak of the second Opium War and the burning of the magnificent Yuanming Yuan imperial garden.

The Gathering Storm

In October 1856, following unsuccessful negotiations, Harry S. Parkes (1828–1885), the British counselor in Guangzhou (Canton), provoked a confrontation with Ye Mingchen (1807–1859), the governor-general of Guangdong. Eventually, Governor-General Ye was captured by the British and died on the way to Egypt (cf. Lane-Poole and Dickins 1894, 140–185; Jiang Tingfu 1931, 1:188; Wong 1976; Cordier 1906, 1–2). China's trouble was not just with Britain. Napoleon III of France was furious about the execution of the priest Abbé Auguste Chapdelaine in Guangxi for engaging in illicit activities (Jiang Tingfu 1931, 1:195). Consequently, France and Britain joined hands to seize Guangzhou on December 28, 1857, with the moral support of both Russia and the United States. Under formidable military pressure, the hapless Qing court signed the humiliating treaty of Tianjin on June 26, 1858, which allowed Great Britain and other Western powers to acquire new rights and privileges in China. The Qing court was especially troubled by the opening of the interior river ports for trade and the establishment of diplomatic representation in Beijing (cf. Jiang Tingfu 1931, 1:204–236). It is no secret that the Xianfeng emperor approved the treaty very reluctantly (Jia Zhen et al. 1930:3, 961–962).

The new treaty, however, required ratifications. The Qing officials had tried to dissuade the Westerners from coming to Beijing for ratification but soon backed down. The remaining problem was what route the foreigners should take to the imperial capital. The English minister Frederick Bruce refused to take the route assigned by the Qing government, which he considered a former tributary route. On the other hand, the Qing government objected to the route the British preferred because it required going through the heavily fortified Dagu Fort. China was also disturbed by the British request that a large number of troops be allowed to escort diplomats to Beijing. When the Chinese government appeared reluctant to accept the British terms, Bruce instructed Admiral Hope to intrude into Baihe by force on June 25, 1860. The Chinese forts at Dagu fired on Hope's fleet and incidentally inflicted heavy losses of men and ships. The Dagu repulse immediately escalated the crisis (Hsu 1960, 212–213).

Although Bruce acknowledged his poor judgment for the unwarranted action and his government blamed him for the incident, the British remained adamant about their choice of route to Beijing for treaty ratification. In fact, the Dagu fiasco "sanctioned the British hard line" (Fairbank 1978, 257). In August 1860, London dispatched Lord Elgin (1811–1863) to China with an expeditionary force of 11,000 men, a substantial number of whom were Indian soldiers, commanded by General Hope Grant. This military prowess made Elgin feel no need to compromise. On the Chinese side, intoxicated by the unexpected victory, Dagu's supreme commander Sengge Linqin (?–1865) was also not willing to compromise. The general even thought it was about time to teach a lesson to "the offensive and avaricious foreign barbarians" (Sengge Linqin 1860, 6:1284–1285). He confidently told Xianfeng in a memorial dated July 14, 1860, that there would be "no more vainglory of the barbarians if we deliver a few more blows to them, and our country will then enjoy some decades of peace" (cf. Tsiang 1929, 18).

Moreover, General Sengge Linqin believed that the Dagu repulse had given China the upper hand, as he remarked that "it is an old established practice with the foreign barbarians that after a war between two countries, the country seeking peace must pay an indemnity to the country consenting to it." In his wishful thinking, the Englishmen should now worry about "our demanding an indemnity from them." If China should ask for peace at this time, he maintained, "they would undoubtedly demand compensation from us, on the excuse of ships and guns lost" (Tsiang 1929, 82). He became even more adamant when he heard that Lord Elgin wanted to go to Beijing in the company of 2,000 troops instead of the 20 guards that were first permitted by the Qing court. Why did the British need so many troops? Serious suspicion with regard to the British intention was inevitably raised in the minds of many officials: "If they come really for the exchange of ratification, what would they do with the more than twenty warships, one hundred and more guns, and several thousand soldiers?" (Tsiang 1929, 81).

When Chinese concessions were not forthcoming, the British decided to use force. The French, who claimed that a missionary had been murdered in interior China, joined hands with the British. The Anglo-French allied expedition captured Dagu through Beitang unexpectedly easily on August 21 (Walrond 1872, 344–345). General Sengge Linqin committed a fatal strategic mistake by retreating from the Beitang fortress in the hope of luring the enemy into an ambush. The Beitang evacuation in effect allowed the enemy an easy landing, and they proceeded to capture Dagu without much effort. When the invaders entered Tanggu on August 23 to establish a strong beachhead before their capature of Tianjin on August 26, the shock waves reached back to Beijing.

The deeply worried Xianfeng quickly shifted gears from war to peace. He sent the senior Manchu Guiliang to Tianjin to talk to the occupied forces. Guiliang had negotiated the 1858 treaty, and was a person whom Elgin considered "an old friend." The victorious Elgin, however, raised the price for peace in a "supplementary treaty" (Walrond 1872, 348, 348–349), and the nervous Guiliang, though accepting the terms under pressure, was unable to assure Elgin of his credentials (Jiang Tingfu 1931, 1:253–255). Guiliang painstakingly assured the British that the 1858 treaty would be faithfully observed and that all the demands made hitherto would be met in full, but he could not put his signature to the supplementary agreement without consulting with Beijing. Elgin immediately suspected that it was a tactic of delay. He therefore concluded that "a little more bullying will be necessary before we bring this stupid Government up to the mark" (Walrond 1872, 349). If Elgin was upset, Xianfeng was also disturbed by Guiliang's "weakness" at the negotiating table. The throne was especially agitated by the new demands of eight million taels of indemnity, the occupation of Dagu by foreign forces, and the opening of Tianjin for trade. This was not all. The allies insisted on the right to dispatch hundreds of troops to accompany diplomats to Beijing for exchange of ratification. As Xianfeng's veritable record shows, the emperor was highly suspicious of the foreigners' intentions. "Why should they bring in troops if they want peace," he reasoned. "If they bring in troops they would dictate to us even more unacceptable terms" (*Wenzong xianhuangdi shilu* 1937–1938, vol. 93, *juan* 326, p. 10a). He thus rebuked his negotiator, and at this moment he thought war was probably unavoidable. The Qing emperor's condemnation of Guiliang further convinced Elgin that China was faithless, so he broke with Guiliang. On September 8, he wrote that "my idiotical Chinamen had taken to playing tricks, which gives me an excellent excuse for carrying the army on to Pekin (Beijing)." In fact, he declared that "I am at war again" (Walrond 1872, 350).[1]

Xianfeng's dilemma was crystal clear. On the one hand, he believed that China had to show some strength in order to obtain an acceptable peace; yet, on the other, he knew by this time the military option was too risky to pursue. His advisors were not very helpful either, as some of them asked him to command the imperial army in person to show his determination to resist, while others dissuaded him from a direct confrontation with the invaders by seeking a hunting trip to Rehe. Debates and indecision at last created a panicky situation. The confused emperor, when verbally speaking of war, sent Prince Yi (Zai Yuan) and the War Minister Muyin to Tongzhou on September 10, trying to reopen peace talk so as to "prevent the enemies from further advance."[2]

Elgin would not resume talks until his forces reached Tongzhou. On September 12, he received a "more defiant letter" from Prince Yi, who warned that the continued advance would come into collision with Chinese troops ahead. While the invading forces continued advancing, Elgin sent Thomas Wade and Harry Parkes to Prince Yi and Muyin for "exploring the Chinese intention." The prince and the minister met with Parkes, Wade, and the French representative Comte de Bastard. Once more, the Anglo-French negotiators turned the screw by again raising the price for peace. Their conditions now included the advance of the allied troops within six miles of Tongzhou, the right to set up an army garrison somewhere five kilometers south of Zhangjiawan, and an increase to one thousand in the number of the escorting troops to enter Beijing. Having no bargaining chips, Prince Yi and Muyin reluctantly accepted the terms and put their signatures to the paper. Given the prince's prestigious status, Elgin now believed that his words "might be trusted" (Walrond 1872, 352, 353, 354).

When Xianfeng read the new agreement, however, he was so upset that he rejected it out of hand. Particularly troublesome to him was not just the entry of a large number of foreign troops into the imperial capital but also the presentation of diplomatic credentials directly to His Majesty regardless of Chinese protocols and rites (Jia Zhen 1930, 7, 2304–2305, 2271, 2272, 2304–2306, 2308, 2314–2315). As Parkes notified Elgin, the imperial audience was "the stickiest problem" (Walrond 1872, 355). Always suspicious of foreign intention, the Qing emperor and his court had to worry about the security risks of granting all the foreign requests.

But Xianfeng was not really sure what to do next, as seen in the conflicting instructions he gave during the following few days. Under the circumstances, on September 17, when receiving the allied delegates, who brought back with them the reply to the memorandum signed three days earlier, Prince Yi was no longer so conciliatory as before. Deadlock thus resulted. When learning that Sengge Linqin had redeployed troops south of Zhangjiawan seemingly to prepare an ambush, the allies attacked them on September 18. Incidentally, this was the time when the British representative Parkes and his party were returing from Tongzhou. They were captured by the soldiers of Sengge Linqin on the road and thrown into a Beijing prison with twenty-six other foreigners. Not too long before, British soldiers had kidnapped the prefect of Tianjin. Both sides again were on war footing.[3] At this time, the allies added one more condition for the resumption of negotiation: the return of all the prisoners (cf. Jiang Tingfu 1931, 1:264–267; *YMYZ* 1984, 123; Fairbank 1978, 257; Walrond 1872, 356–357; Wu Xiangxiang 1953, 28–35; Wang Wei 1980, 40).

The furious Elgin, reinforced by 6,700 French soldiers under the command of Cousin de Montaubon, charged forward. The retreating Sengge Linqin recuperated himself, reinforced by 20,000 troops under the command of Shengbao and Ruilin, and prepared to put up a stiff resistance. The showdown took place at Baliqiao near Tongzhou on September 21. The allies suffered heavy losses, both men and supplies, for the first time since the invasion. A French officer admitted that low supplies had handicapped the military operation of the allies at Baliqiao, while another Frenchman praised the incredible courage of the Chinese and Manchu warriors. Even Elgin noted on September 23 that "they did pretty well" (Cordier 1906, 349–352; Varin 1862, 193–197, 199–215, 208; Walrond 1872, 358; cf. Knollys 1875, 111–127; Wang Wei 1980, 40; Costin 1937, 315–331). As a matter of fact, at crucial moments of the battle, the English commander Sir Hope Grant was nearly captured by the Mongolian cavalry (Knollys 1875, xiii, 116–117).

Nevertheless, despite numerical superiority, China could not compete with the enemy's advantage in modern firepower, or the combination of the cavalry, the artilery, and the infantry, and hence they lost this decisive battle and eventually the war. When the wounded General Shengbao was being carried into Beijing in a palanquin, as a witness noted, the crowd in the streets shouted in fear and dispersed as if they were trying to find a safe haven to hide themselves (Li Ciming 1936, 9, 42b). Given her military backwardness, China committed a strategic mistake by engaging the remaining force in a decisive battle near Beijing. Had she waged well-coordinated hit-and-run warfare, which had been advocated by the court official Xu Shoupeng, the enemy would have been hard pressed to end the war before the fast approaching severe winter season in north China (cited in Zhongyang yanjiu yuan 1936, 3, 1923–1996).

In any event, the victory at Baliqiao threw the door to Beijing wide open. Many officials in Beijing had been pleading for the Xianfeng emperor to return to the Forbidden City from the Yuanming Yuan for the defense of the imperial capital as well as to prevent the collapse of morale (Jia Zhen 1930, 6, 2255; Jiang Mengyin 1965, 2, 34–35). But the defeated Sengge Linqin, who had been driven back all the way from Tianjin and hence knew the hopeless military situation better than anyone else, resolutely advised his emperor to leave and seek a safe haven in Rehe. The general seemed to have a decisive influence on the emperor's decision to resist or retreat. His Majesty, however, did not reveal his final decision to his top advisors until the evening of September 21, 1860. This being done, early the next morning, he met with all five princes and the grand secretaries at his Yuanming Yuan court after having made a short—but sentimental—visit to the Ancestral Shrine, bidding farewell to the deceased forefathers. During this morning session, he asked his younger brother Prince Gong to stay behind in the garden and to seek peace with the assistance of the Grand Secretary Guiliang and Deputy President of the Finance Wenxiang (Jia Zhen 1930, 7, 2335).

Xianfeng fled with a large entourage, including family members, Manchu noblemen, officials, and eunuchs. They left the Yuanming Yuan through the East Gate of the Eternal Spring Garden in haste; hence neither kitchen nor tents were brought. The emperor, like the rest in the group, suffered hardship beyond his imagination; for instance, he tasted for the first time in his life vulgar food on the road to Chengde (Bao Chengguan 1980, 62; Wu Xiangxiang 1953, 36–37).

As expected, the sudden flight of the emperor caused panic in Beijing, around which many gates were being closed. Fear and confusion drove a large crowd of people, the rich as well as the poor, to struggle out from the besieged city under tremendously tumultuous conditions (Huang Jun 1979, 434; Li Ciming 1936, 9:42b; Knollys 1875, 170–173; Swinhoe 1861: 312–313; Wu Xiangxiang 1953, 36–37).

The Looting

While Prince Gong was in the Yuanming Yuan pursuing peace with the assistance of Prince Chun and Prince Hui, the defense of Beijing was entrusted to Manchu bannermen and high-ranking Chinese officials. Eight banner commanders were dispatched to secure the inner walls, and Zhou Zupei and others were assigned to reinforce the defense of the outer walls. Prince Gong delivered to Elgin and Gros a note in which the blame was laid on Prince Yi and Muyin, both of whom had been dismissed from office, in hopes of "ending the hostility and enhancing friendship." The allies, however, sent back an ultimatum on September 25 demanding the release of all prisoners in three days. The prince's promise of returning the prisoners at the end of the war was not good enough for the allies. On September 30, Elgin received another letter from Prince Gong, who requested the allies to retreat to Zhangjiawan and promised to return all prisoners as soon as the agreement was signed. Elgin rejected the request, ended the exchange of notes, and turned the matter over to his generals (Jia Zhen 1930, 7, 2338, 2356, 2358; Walrond 1872, 359–360; Zhongyang yanjiu yuan 1966, 234, 236, 246–248, 310).

All gates around Beijing had been closed since the evening of September 23. Consequently, the prices of goods, including food, skyrocketed. A scholar noted in his diary that vegetables in markets quickly disappeared without replenishment (Li Ciming 1936, 9, 43a–43b). The shortage of food plus an insufficient number of troops—reportedly less than 10,000—added to the agony of low morale. The suspended imminent attack from the enemies, obviously waiting for supplies after the battle of Baliqiao, further taxed the poorly prepared defenders' nerves. Even General Sengge Linqin, the most hawkish of all, lost his will to fight (cf. Jia Zhen 1930, 7, 2362–2363); and Prince Gong remained in the Yuanming Yuan despite the critical situation in Beijing.[4]

When the allies were fully replenished, their vanguards quickly reached the Qihua Gate at the outskirts of Beijing. About this time, the Anglo-French command requested through the captured prefect of Tongzhou that Prince Gong come to the allied camp; however, the wary prince did not respond immediately. Nevertheless, a short while later on September 29—incidentally, Chinese Moon Festival Day—the foreign prisoners were quietly transferred from cells in eight-man palanquins—a distinguished honor—to a comfortable place at Gaomiao near Beijing's northern gate. All of a sudden, the prisoners became honored guests ostensibly because Prince Gong wished that goodwill would reduce ill feelings and facilitate peace. Indeed, on October 1, Parkes, the highest-ranking British prisoner, sent a message to the allied command pleading for a cease fire, despite the fact that he added a line of foreign words that were noticed but unrecognized by Weng Tonghe (1829–1904) (1970, 1, 191; cf. Walrond 1872, 360). Parkes recollected his message as follows:

The Chinese authorities are now treating Mr. Loch and myself well, and we are informed that this is done by direction of the Prince of Kung (Gong). We are also told that his Highness is a man of decision and great intelligence, and I trust that, under these circumstances, hostilities may be temporarily suspended to give opportunity for negotiation.[5]

More interestingly, on the same day, the mandarin Liang Chengguang went to the enemy camp to offer wine and beef to the invaders (Li Ciming 1936, 9, 49b). But no goodwill, including Parkes' message, could pull the enemy back now. The main invading force resumed its advance on Beijing in the evening of October 3 and finally camped at a place only five kilometers from the walls of Beijing two days later (cf. *YMYZ* 1984, 127–128; Walrond 1872, 360). Some wealthy merchants in Beijing also tried to stop the advancing enemies by presenting them with cows and sheep as gifts but to no avail (Weng Tonghe 1970, 1, 193).

Passing the walled Beijing, two columns of troops, with the British on the right front and the French on the left, made a rendezvous in Haidian virtually unopposed. Prince Gong fled from the garden just before the arrival of the enemies (Weng Tonghe 1970, 1, 195; cf. Jia Zhen 1930, 7, 2426). A number of modern scholars blame Gong Xiaogong, son of the great poet-scholar Gong Zizhen, or other Chinese traitors, for treasonously guiding the invaders into the Yuanming Yuan for plundering (cf. Cheng Yansheng 1928, 20a; Huang Jun 1979, 2:406–407). They seem to suggest that the foreigners could not have found the imperial garden without a native guide. But this is clearly an incorrect assumption. That Gong was specifically implicated because he knew English and had some English friends is a clear case of guilt by association. In fact, Wang Tao (1828–1897) testified that Gong was not even in Beijing during the entire Anglo-French invasion (Wang Tao 1875, 1, 132).

At seven o'clock in the evening on October 6, 1860, the French troops first arrived at the Yuanming Yuan. De Pina, *le lieutenant de vaisseau,* argued with the Chinese guards, who tried desperately to keep the foreigners outside the gate, and their wrangle "could be loudly heard" (Varin 1862, 222, 228–229; Cordier 1906, 349–362). The clash at the gate, according to Montoubon's report, resulted in the death of Renliang, the Manchu commander of the eighth rank, near the front gate, and the injuries of two French officers and several soldiers (*YMYZ* 1984, 223). The main bulk of the garden's security force, though several thousand strong, could not stop the intrusion of the modern army, and was compelled to retreat without further resistance. The helpless Wenfeng, the supreme supervisor of the garden, drowned himself in the Sea of Blessing. The allies quickly captured a very much empty garden ground. "All the big-wigs have fled," as the British recorded, "and the prisoners are in Pekin (Beijing)" (Walrond 1872, 361).

Baron Montoubon of France thus put the precincts of the Yuanming Yuan under his control. Impressed by the magnificence of the garden, Montoubon stated that "nothing in our Europe can give an idea of equal luxury." He found he was unable in a few lines to describe "the splendor of its formation especially under the impression of bewilderment

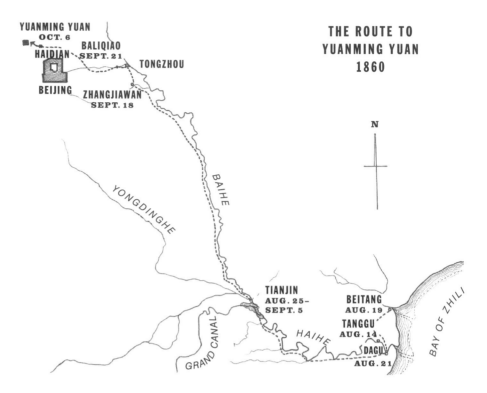

caused by my view of these marvels" (Cordier 1906, 354; cf. Varin 1862, 228, 234–236, 232–233).

The British troops arrived at the Yuanming Yuan late because they had spent the night near a lamasery. The British leader Elgin in the company of General Grant met with Montoubon in the Yuanming Yuan early in the morning of September 7. On his way, while riding a horse, Grant "perceived the Palace beautifully situated amidst gardens and woods and a range of large suburbs in front." He seems to have gone through the district of Haidian to see "a fine old stately gateway and the park walls" and then, proceeding up an avenue, "a range of handsome dwellings roofed over with yellow tiles." He soon found that "in different parts of the grounds were forty separate small palaces in beautiful situations" and that "the park was carefully kept—the footpaths and roads clean and in excellent order, and there were various pretty pieces of ornamental water" (Knollys 1875, 127–128; Wolseley 1862, 1972, 218–242). His interpreter Robert Swinhoe likewise admired the beautiful scene along the way. He strolled to the Main Audience Hall, and a pebbled path led him "through groves of magnificent trees, round lakes, into picturesque summer-houses, over fantastic bridges." He further observed:

> Here a solitary building would rise fairy-like from the center of a lake, reflecting its image on the limpid blue liquid in which it seemed to float, and then a sloping path would carry you into the heart of a mysterious cavern artificially

formed of rockery, and leading out on to a grotto in the bosom of another lake. The variety of the picturesque was endless, and charming in the extreme; indeed, all that is most lovely in Chinese scenery, where art contrives to cheat the rude attempts of nature into the bewitching, seemed all associated in these delightful grounds. The resources of the designer appear to have been unending, and no money spared to bring his work to perfection. All the tasteful landscapes so often viewed in the better class of Chinese paintings, and which we had hitherto looked upon as wrought out of the imagination of the artist, were here brought forth in life.[6]

Lord Elgin, too, was impressed by the beauty of the garden. On Sunday, October 7, 1861, in the midst of these surroundings, he praised the "Summer Palace" as "really a fine thing, like an English park—numberless buildings with handsome rooms—and filled with Chinese curios, and handsome clocks, bronzes, etc." His private secretary Henry Loch admired especially the architectural beauty of the garden. The buildings to him "were nearly all isolated from each other, being connected by gardens, courts, and terraces." He considered the "Hall of Audience," perhaps the Zhengda Guangming Dian, "the most striking." In this compound, he saw large buildings "connected by courtyards, passing through which we entered spacious reception rooms that opened into gardens of considerable extent, which lead down to a marble terrace stretching along the shores of a lake some three miles in length." He took a fancy for white marble balustrades, blue inlaid enamel vases with imitation flowers, and the larger-than-life lion and cow bronzes (Loch 1909, 169–170).

The English general Allgood saw a large space enclosed by a substantial park wall. In it he found the palaces "were laid out with great taste, and artificial water, canals, rockeries, grottoes, pagodas, hills and valleys beautifully wooded with cedar and fir trees delight the eye, the picturesque scenery varying at every turn of the winding pathways" (Allgood 1901, 85). Numerous other officers, English as well as French, were accompanied by their ladies to tour the Yuanming Yuan and the nearby gardens. Reportedly, as the foreign invaders pleasantly strut around, the frightened natives, including the Manchu bannermen, bowed their knees before the Western conquerors (Wu Xiangxiang 1953, 38).

What followed was that the Anglo-French army units ransacked and looted the Yuanming Yuan in a wild frenzy. The French and the British each accused the other of initiating it. On the one hand, the French said plainly that *"Les Anglais commencent le pillage du palais d'ete"* (the English started the looting of the garden) (Varin 1862, 236). On the other hand, the British insisted that "we found that the French had encamped near the entrance of the Great Audience Hall, and it was pitiful to see the way in which everything was being robbed" (Knollys 1875, 128, 219–221). Upon the arrival of the Englishmen on October 7, Elgin noted that "there was not a room that I saw in which half the things had not been taken away or broken to pieces" (Walrond 1872, 361), implying that the Frenchmen had already looted the garden before the British arrived. A recent scholar, however, has found that the French looting was confined to the Yuanming Yuan proper because they had few horses. The British, well mounted, "covered a much larger area and carried away heavier objects" (Thiriez 1998, 56).

Even though looting could be justified as war booty in European colonial history, it implies the collapse of military discipline, only after which armies go on rampage. The discipline of the allied force, according to the recollection of Robert Swinhoe, had indeed collapsed after the fall of Zhangjiawan (1861, 243–244; Walrond 1872, 355, 359). Elgin tried to guard the palatial garden and then to sell the loot by aution. But it was too late to control some officers, who had already filled carts with treasures waiting to be sold or taken away. Even worse than plundering were waste and breakage. "Out of 1,000,000lb worth of property," Elgin said, "50,000lb will not be realized" (Walrond 1872, 361–362).

Many Chinese sources recorded that looting and arson in Haidian and at the Yuanming Yuan began soon after the arrival of the foreign troops on October 6 (cf. Cai Shengzhi n.d., 145). Li Ciming (1829–1895), for one, wrote in his diary on October 7 that having routed 30,000 of General Sengge Linqin's men, the foreigners occupied Haidian, from where Prince Gong had escaped, and set fire to the Yuanming Yuan and elsewhere. Some prestigious officials who had sought refuge in Haidian again fled, leaving their valuables behind. Li was profoundly saddened by the fact that less than ten thousand foreign troops could create such a tragic turmoil around the imperial capital (1936, 9, 51a–51b).

Another contemporary writer noted that the foreigners had repeatedly robbed no less than eighteen places in the Yuanming Yuan as well as along the streets of Haidian. Many valuable objects, including art wares, books, and paintings, were immediately being shipped to Tianjin, where the foreign vessels were anchored (*YMYZ* 1984, 130–131). On October 7, two hundred foreign soldiers reportedly intruded as well into the Pure Ripple Garden, where they damaged many structures and took away any portable items they liked (*YMYZ* 1984, 131). Chen Wenbo believed that looting started early on October 6, large-scale plundering occurred between October 7 and 8, the burning of the Yuanming Yuan took place on October 23, and massive robbery in and out of the imperial garden continued until October 25 (cited in *YMYZ* 1984 166–188). The European buildings were pillaged without exception. The furniture was dilapidated and paintings split. The soldiers seized jewels, gold, snuff boxes, comfit dishes, and sumptuous custumes in great excitement (cf. Beurdeley 1971, 74).

It only took a few days of plundering to disgrace the Yuanming Yuan. "Everything of value that could be carried off, consisting of gold, silver, clocks, watches, enamels, porcelain, jade stone, silks and embroidery, with numerous other articles of vertu," as the Major General Allgood testified, "were removed by the Allies" (1901, 85). While rushing about for the valuables, the looters also destroyed those they could not take away. Excitement reached a peak on October 9, when news spread that a huge quantity of gold and silver was discovered in the garden. In addition to gold and silver, the soldiers also found a room "full of the richest silks and furs" (Knollys 1875, 130).

It did not take much time to empty the treasures of the Yuanming Yuan and the neighboring gardens. General Hope Grant set up a prize committee and instructed his men to turn over every piece of looted valuables to this committee. They were at last put into a general stock to be divided equally. A large quantity of the looted objects, difficult to be carried away, was to be auctioned off immediately. The auction "realized a good round sum" of cash, totaling 26,000 British pounds, to be shared by both officers and soldiers" (Knollys 1875, 191, 192, 226–227; M'Ghee 1862, 201–289; Swinhoe 1861, 310; Tulloch 1903, 118). Clearly, General Grant consciously converted looting into prize so as to transform the thefts into lawful rewards for his fighting men.

In the aftermath of the Anglo-French loot, the local residents, both peasants and bannermen, managed to sneak into the garden to steal whatever leftovers they could find. To be sure, the follow-up plundering made the rampage worse; but blaming the tragedy mainly on the local people, as some did, borders on avoiding the important while dwelling on the trivial. The loss of the treasure in the imperial gardens was in the main because of the vengeance of the victorious army. It was the foreign invaders who turned the splendid Yuanming Yuan and its subsidiary gardens into a shambles. In fact, they themselves admitted that once they found the enormous wealth inside the garden, they became too greedy to respect fundamental military discipline (cf. Wolseley 1862, 215–242; Knollys 1873, 190–227). Lieutenant Colonel Wolseley, in particular, had this to say:

> When looting is once commenced by an army, it is no easy matter to stop it. At such times human nature breaks down the ordinary trammels which discipline imposes, and the consequences are most demoralizing to the very best constituted army.[7]

Wolseley went on to say that the "officers and men seemed to have been seized with a temporary insanity; in body and soul they were absorbed in one pursuit, which was plunder, plunder" (1862, 227). Robert Swinhoe, General Grant's interpreter, condemned what his fellow officers did as "licensed theft" (1861, 306; cf. Varin 1862, 238–239). All these first-hand European testimonies, plus the charges and countercharges between the British and the French, have confirmed the uncontrolled behavior of the invaders. It seems that the Allied High Command not only made no effort to stop the atrocious action but let the loot fever run its full course. Even such top commanders as Lord Elgin and Baron Montoubon made no secret that they too had taken valuable objects from the Qing emperor's private quarters in the Yuanming Yuan and sent them to Queen Victoria and Napoleon III, respectively (Beurdeley 1971, 74).[8] The loot was regarded as trophies of the conquest. Consequently, looting Yuanming Yuan was truly the coup de grace.

If the loot was intended to humble the "haughty Chinese," it met its goal. In the wake of foreign occupation of the Yuanming Yuan and the subsequent plundering, the Qing sense of despair and hopelessness was real. Huanqi, the key Manchu liaison to the allies, was most eager to set Parkes free so as to solicit his assistance in achieving an early conclusion of peace (Weng Tonghe 1970, 1:197).

Under the threat of shelling Beijing, eight prisoners, including Parkes and Loch, were released unconditionally to the English camp in the afternoon of October 8 with the consent of Prince Gong. Consequently, the allies began evacuating from the Yuanming Yuan and camped at the Black Temple. The Manchu officials Linkui and Qingying at once moved into the imperial garden for inspection. Their report to Prince Gong and Wenxiang reveals that numerous garden structures, including the external reception rooms at the Grand Palace Gate and countless local residential homes in Haidian, had been burned to the ground (Jia Zhen 1930, 7, 2421; Walrond 1872, 362).

Anxious to know more about the damages in the Yuanming Yuan, Prince Gong specifically asked Huanqi to see the plundered garden on the following day. Huanqi caught the eyes of Knollys, who recognized him as a "pitiful Manchu official putting his tearful face between his hands, while seating upon an edge of a little lake, and saying that everything was lost and that he should destroy himself." The pitiful Manchu, nonetheless, recovered the body of the supervisor Wenfeng, who committed suicide earlier in the lake (Knollys 1875, 194–195).

Now it was the Qing's responsibility to secure the Yuanming Yuan, which had become vulnerable to local predators. Those who lived in the garden returned to see their furniture broken and books and paintings damaged (*YMYZ* 1984, 134). Li Ciming noted in his October 11 diary entry that ruffians broke into the garden in the wake of the foreign looting, and they took away so much as to fill carts (1936, 9, 54b). Liu Yunan, an official at the Board of Rites, also noted in his diary that in the aftermath of the fall of the Yuanming Yuan, both residential and commercial sections in Haidian were first ransacked and then burned (cited in *Yingfa lianjun shiliao* n.d., 77, 80).

Baoyun, the director of the Imperial Household, also sent his men to see the Yuanming Yuan soon after the foreign troops had pulled out. His report to Prince Gong dated October 12 noted that several halls were burned as early as October 6 and that the flames lit up the sky that evening. He also reported that concubine Zhang died of shock and the garden's chief supervisor Wenfeng committed suicide (*YMYA* 1984, 1:556). He then delivered a memorial on October 16 to the Xianfeng emperor in Rehe to provide an update of events:

> On October 7 about two hundred foreign barbarians and countless local bandits plundered the East Palace Gate of the Pure Ripple Garden, where they damaged the large exhibiting pieces, took away all small items including seals. On October 8 the foreigners successively broke into the Tranquil Bright Garden, or Jingming Yuan, and plundered in the same brutal fashion. [It seems that] only the Tranquil Comfortable Garden, or the Jingyi Yuan, was spared.[9]

As the director of the Imperial Household, Baoyun bore the direct responsibility to oversee the Yuanming Yuan and other royal gardens. When he incidentally told Xianfeng that he had not yet inspected the disgraced imperial garden in person, the anguished emperor bursted into a bitter attack in words:

The director was absent from the Yuanming Yuan when it was being looted simply for fear of his life. He still remained inside Beijing when the Three Hills were plundered. How can he be such an [irresponsible] person? He is, indeed, a piece of trash of our Manchu clansmen. I will not promptly execute him only because he still has the responsibility of securing the palaces in Beijing. But he must be immediately demoted to the fifth rank as punishment.[10]

The exiled Xianfeng emperor was truly badly shaken upon hearing the horrible news, and responsible leaders in the government, including Prince Gong, were ashamed and pledged to redoubt their efforts to protect the imperial gardens. Also, they were willing to take severe penalties for the tragedy (*YMYA* 1991, 1:553–554). The emperor dismissed a number of them in a public statement, but he still asked them to remain in office to atone for their failures. Two military leaders, Sengge Linqin and Ruilin, whom the throne entrusted to secure both Beijing and the royal gardens, were the most difficult to forgive. The hawkish Sengge Linqin was humbled by the disastrous defeat. In his October 10 memorial, he explained in detail how his troops, including the famous Mongolian cavalry, were blocked by the foreign invaders and absolutely unable to prevent the savage sack of the Yuanming Yuan (*YMYA* 1991, 1:552–553). Xiangfeng was in no mood to condone the generals. He made the following statement:

The fact that Sengge Linqin and Ruilin, commanding a huge number of troops, suffered repeated defeats has proved their cowardice and incompetence. They shamefully watched the occupation, burning, and looting of the imperial garden without even trying to do anything. [In the opinion of this throne], they can hardly absolve their guilt.[11]

The emperor's anger was shared by Li Ciming, a Beijing resident and scholar of renown, who witnessed the collapse of the Qing army and the easy fall of the imperial capital and gardens, which caused him "deep shame" (1936, 9:51a).

The Burning of the Yuanming Yuan

Prince Gong's protest of the looting to the Allied Command was to no avail, and it only further impressed the British and the French that the Qing court treasured the Yuanming Yuan a great deal. In fact, they had seen themselves how anxious the Manchu and Chinese officials were to reoccupy the garden upon the evacuation of the foreign troops. General Grant of Britain, for example, was now absolutely convinced that the Manchu emperor considered the Yuanming Yuan his "most important palace" (Knollys 1875, 204). This may help explain at least in part why the British eventually wanted to burn down the garden in order to pain the emperor.

The Allied Command threatened to shell Beijing if the gates were not opened on October 13. Huanqi's negotiation with Parkes resulted in permitting the entry of 1,500 troops for each of the three nations, England, France, and the United States, to accompany their respective diplomats for treaty ratification (Weng Tonghe 1970, 1:199; Li Ciming 1936, 9:54b). At noon, on October 14, Huanqi guided Elgin and an entourage of three to four hundred men, who would be lodged at the Imperial Academy (Guozijian), into the Desheng Gate plus over thousand cavalrymen, who were stationed at the Anding Gate. The foreign flags flew atop all of the gates and the soldiers shouted in joy and glory (Weng Tonghe 1970 1:200).

The release of all European prisoners on October 15, however, gravely complicated the peace process because they told their horrible stories of their imprisonment, not to mention that some of them did not return alive. Elgin at once declared that it was an "atrocious crime," and he decided to deal with it severely (Walrond 1872, 365). When Prince Gong tried to set a date to meet with Elgin and Gros, there was no response until two days later when the allies bitterly raised the new issue of the mistreatment of the Europeans in Chinese prison. Besides demanding substantial cash compensation, amounting to 300,000 taels for Britain and 200,000 taels for France, Elgin specifically wanted to demolish the whole Yuanming Yuan so as to redress the grievance, and this was nonnegotiable. He was firm in his message to Prince Gong: unless the new demand was met on October 20, cash paid on October 22, and the treaty ratified on October 23, war would resume (*YMYA* 1991, 1:560).

This sudden turn of events surely caught Prince Gong by surprise. On October 16, he was still outside of the city walls when the allies entered Beijing (Weng Tonghe 1970, 1:201). The allies had ignored the prince's complaints about plundering the Yuanming Yuan and other royal demesnes; and now Elgin notified him in a haughty manner that the principal imperial garden as a whole should be burned down to the ground as punishment. The humiliation was huge and inevitable. Had he put up a stiff resistance and shown some courage, the prince might still have some bargaining chips to play; however, with Beijing having been occupied by the allies, he knew he was totally at the mercy of the enemy. He could only plead to Elgin, again through Huanqi, to spare the Yuanming Yuan. Nevertheless, Elgin was adamant, and on October 18 he waited no longer to give his order to set fire to the Yuanming Yuan and its subsidiary gardens (*YMYA* 1991, 1:559–562; cf. the memorial by Prince Gong, Guiliang, and Wenxiang in Jiang Tingfu 1931, 1972, 1:269–270; Cai Shengzhi n.d., 157).

Elgin made this crucial decision to burn down the Yuanming Yuan all by himself without French consent. In fact, Baron Gros disapproved of the violent vengeance against a peaceful estate; for him, if some palaces were to be destroyed, those in the Forbidden City, the center of administration, would make a better target than the harmless imperial garden. In his correspondence to the French, Elgin argued why he wanted to "make the blow fall on the Emperor, who was clearly responsible for the crime committed." The "high crime" of ill treatment of European prisoners, in his opinion, could not be compensated merely by a large sum of money, nor could the Chinese government obtain additional "large pecuniary indemnities." He would not demand the surrender of "the persons guilty of cruelty to our countrymen," either, because he felt "throwing the responsibility for the acts of Government in this way on individuals resembles too closely the Chinese mode of conducting war to approve itself altogether to my judgment." Hence, he concluded that the destruction of the Yuanming Yuan was the "least objectionable" course open to him. He was fully aware of the fact that the imperial garden was the Xianfeng emperor's "favourite residence, and its destruction could not fail to be a blow to his pride as well as to his feelings" (cited in Cordier 1906, 388–390; cf. Walrond 1872, 366). Indeed, nothing could cause Xianfeng more pain than the destruction of the Yuanming Yuan.

Elgin was truly provoked by the stories from the released prisoners, who demanded redress for their horrible experiences in prison. Even back in London, the news of mistreatment of British prisoners made Lord Palmerston's "blood boil with indignation" (Elgin to Russell, October 25, 1860, in British Parliamentary Papers 1969 lxvi, No. 103; "Palmerston to Russell, 26 December 1860," quoted in Costin 1937, 1968, 337). The prisoners testified that they were "bound," "put into prison, confined in a cage, and loaded with chains." Among them, Lieutenant Anderson became "delirious" and died nine days after imprisonment. Five days after Anderson's death, Ram Chun, a sowar, "died in the same state." And three days after Ram Chun's death, De Norman died. The prisoners did receive better treatment after Anderson's death, until their release (cited in M'Ghee 1862, 222–223; cf. 224–229).

Parkes, as he himself testified, was treated quite well. He was given two meals a day plus cakes and "a little tea and tobacco." After Huangqi, known as Hang-ki in Parkes' statement, took the prisoners to the Kaowmean Temple (Gaomiao) on September 29, the jailers became their "servants." The prisoners were supplied with not only "good food, beds, etc., but also with the luxuries of writing materials, soap, and towels, etc." They could even "order our meals whenever we chose." After Parkes sent his September 29 message requesting further peace negotiations, "a large present of fruit and confectionary" was delivered to him in the name of Prince Gong (cited in M'Ghee 1862, 240, 244–245; cf. Li Ciming 1936, 9:47b). According to Weng Tonghe, the grateful mandarins rewarded Parkes and other prisoners with a lavish banquet on October 2 (Weng Tonghe 1970, 1:192).

The Chinese prison conditions at the time were no doubt brutal. Chinese jailers rarely treated prisoners kindly. Zhao Guang (presumably Choo Laou-yays (Zhao Laoye, or Gentleman Zhao) in Parkes' statement), president of the Board of Justice (Xingbu), stated in his unpublished autobiography that Prince Yi seized Parkes and other European prisoners, and they were the first foreign prisoners he had ever received. He said he had told Parkes that they "would definitely not be tortured," but prisoners in chains was the established rule for which he dared not make any exceptions (cited in *YMYZ* 1984, 267; cf. M'Ghee 1862, 241). Some mandarins wanted to execute Parkes, whom they considered the most vicious British instigator, but Zhao pointed out the danger of reprisal from the fierce British guns. He was in fact the one who recommended to use Parkes for the resumption of peace negotiations. With the consent of Prince Gong, Zhao took Parkes and other prisoners out from the harsh prison environment and moved them to Gaomiao for kinder treatment (*YMYZ* 1984, 268; cf. Zhuo An n.d., 174–175).

The kinder treatment of the prisoners after September 29 could not compensate for the mistreatment they had suffered before that date. The European prisoners were, indeed, being mistreated, but they were mistreated by the long-standing Chinese prison system. No evidence whatsoever indicates that the Qing authorities, let alone the Xianfeng emperor himself, ever authorized the mistreatment of the European prisoners. On the contrary, a Board of Justice document dated September 18–19, 1860, reveals that while the foreign prisoners "should be strictly guarded," their "daily provisions must make them feel comfortable and contented" and they "ought not to be tortured and humiliated" (cited in Cai Shengzhi n.d., 142; cf. 151). No one, however, should rule out the possibility that the jailers did not customarily strictly follow such orders. Nonetheless, if the backwardness of Chinese justice was to blame, the European conquerors, under aggravating circumstances, not only showed little mercy to Chinese prisoners but also brutalized innocent civilians. Cai Shengzhi's study argues that "in speaking of mistreatment, the Chinese were far more brutally mistreated by the foreigners than the other way around" (n.d., 168). The Xianfeng emperor felt his "hair raising" *(fazhi)* when he heard that the foreign troops raped the Yuanming Yuan, burned streets, and looted Beijing wantonly (*Wenzong xianhuangdi shilu* 1937–1938, vol. 93, *juan* 329, p. 7a). On record, the Chinese prefect of Tongzhou died in the hands of his captors. According to Li Ciming, he witnessed foreign soldiers abusing Chinese women in the street (1936, 9:74b–75a). Perhaps it is meaningless to determine who mistreated whom more; nevertheless, as always, the victor dictates the ultimate justice.

More specifically, Lord Elgin alone dictated the ultimate justice: the total destruction of the Yuanming Yuan. Apparently, as plenipotentiary, he made this crucial decision without the prior knowledge of his own British government and without regard for the opposition of his French ally. He wanted revenge against the Xianfeng emperor (Walrond 1872: 366). The burning of the Yuanming Yuan had indeed caused the emperor great pain, but His Majesty died shortly afterward. The persistent pain is perhaps the loss of 150–year-old architectural wonder and garden beauty. But, for Elgin, his decision was not so harsh as it should have been. Originally, he had contemplated not only the demolition of all the palaces in and out of Beijing but also the abdication of the Manchu monarch Xianfeng (correspondence between Elgin and Gros as quoted in Cai Shengzhi n.d., 152; Gros' report to the Ministre des Affaires Etrangeres in Cordier 1906, 358–362).

It was the powerful emotion of anger and self-righteousness that Elgin used to justify his violent action. Elgin, as an English gentleman, might also be conscious of the problem of plundering, as he actually said that "I would like a great many things that the palace contains, but I am not a thief" (quoted in Swinhoe 1861, 300). He blamed the French for "destroying in every way the most beautiful silks, breaking the jade ornaments and porcelain" and "loden with dollars and sycee silver" while denying vigorously the British role in "indiscriminate plunder" (Walrond 1872, 361–362; Knollys 1873, 226–227). Burning the entire Yuanming Yuan down to the ground, it appears, would in a sense erase the fingerprints of plundering and therefore leave much stolen treasuries unaccountable.

Having tried in vain to stop Elgin, Gros denounced the decision to burn the Yuanming Yuan as a "goth-like act of barbarism" (quoted in Wolseley 1862, 1972, 279; cf. Knollys 1873, 202, 203). Several decades later, the French dispute with the British over the fate of the Yuanming Yuan caught the attention of Gu Hongming (Thompson Ku) (1857–1928), a European-educated Chinese conservative. Gu regretted China's failure to explore the estrangement between France and England for Chinese advantage (cited in Wang Kangnian 1969, 1, 38). But realistically, the dispute was not serious enough to rack the Anglo-French alliance, and China was simply too feeble to play one barbarian against another.

To follow Elgin's order, General John Michel specifically instructed the British First Division to arrive on October 18 on time at the imperial garden, "where the buildings were apportioned to the different companies to destroy" (Swinhoe 1861, 329). General Grant, in his dispatch to the secretary of state for war in London, confirmed that "On 18th October, Sir John Michel's division, with the greater part of the cavalry brigade, were marched to the Palace, and set the whole pile of building on fire. It was a magnificent sight" (Knollys 1873, 204). The inferno set off by a modern army quickly consumed the great garden made of mostly wood materials. In the end, nothing was spared *("Rienne fut epargne!")* (Varin 1862, 267; see also the letters exchanged between Gros and Elgin in Cordier 1906, 368–383, 409–415, 385–391; cf. Morse 1966, 1:610; Malone 1934, 187). Captain Charles Gorden of the British Royal Engineers reported this "magnificent sight" of the inferno in a letter to his mother:

> You can scarcely imagine the beauty and magnificence of the places we burnt. It made one's heart sore to burn them; in fact, these palaces were so large, and we were so pressed for time, that we could not plunder them carefully. Quantities of gold ornaments were burnt, considered as brass. It was wretchedly demoralizing work for an army. Everybody was wild for plunder.[12]

Another British officer testified:

> A gentle wind blowing from the north-west, carried the mass of smoke directly over our camp into the very capital itself, to which distance even large quantities of the burnt embers were wafted, falling about the streets in showers, as silent but unmistakable evidences of the work of destruction and retribution going on in the palace of the emperor. In passing between our camp and Yuen-ming-yuen (Yuanming Yuan), upon both those days, the light was so subdued by the overhanging clouds of smoke, that it seemed as if the sun was undergoing a lengthened eclipse. The world around looked dark with shadow.[13]

Many Chinese witnessed the burning as well, as the smoke of the fire could be observed as far away as downtown Beijing. Chen Baozhen (1831–1900), the future reformist governor of Hunan, cried out loud in a Beijing restaurant when seeing the thick cloud rising from the northwest (Chen Sanli 1962, 103). The Hanlin compiler Wu Kedu (1812–1879) noted that the inferno was not confined to the Yuanming Yuan; numerous other gardens in the neighborhood also caught fire. He had this to say in his October 18, 1860 diary entry:

> A vast column of smoke arose from the northwest direction ascertaining that the barbarians had burnt the Summer Palace. [I also learned] that the Three Hills were not spared, leaving the area absolutely bare.[14]

Li Ciming noted in his October 19 diary entry that "the big fire set off outside the West Straight Gate had not extinguished today," and he heard that the foreigners had also burned the palaces around the Longevity Hills. His October 20 diary entry recorded the burning of the Main Audience Hall and the Diligent Court in the Yuanming Yuan (1936, 9:59a–59b).

Prince Gong, who remained on the outskirts of Beijing, climbed up to high ground with a number of officials to watch flames light up the sky and the dark cloud of smoke rise from the northwest in great distress and resentment. He received a preliminary report before the end of the day, which confirmed that several thousand foreign infantrymen and cavalrymen had marched into Haidian and set fire to the Yuanming Yuan and to the numerous other gardens in the Three Hills area. In his own report to the emperor in Rehe, the prince admitted that to assess the exact damage and loss was not possible so long as foreign troops blocked the way, though he was obliged to submit any further information as soon as he possibly could. But the prince knew how bad the general condition was, as his liaison Huanqi (Heng-k'i in French sources and Hang-ki in English sources) had already informed him about the avenging fire that had devastated the Yuanming Yuan beyond recognition. At this point, the prince and officials wept with profound shame (*YMYA* 1991, 1:562–563; Jiang Tingfu 1931, 1972, 1:272–273; cf. Cordier 1906, 361, 364, 373; Knollys 1875, 194). When this terrible news, even without much detail, reached the Xianfeng emperor, he wrote down this vermillion remark: "I am extremely furious" (*YMYA* 1991, 1:563).

Those who had burned the Yuanming Yuan were the first to see how the magnificent imperial garden was reduced to wreckage. "When we first entered the gardens they reminded one of those magic grounds described of in fairy tales," the British officer Wolseley wrote, "we marched upon them the 19th October, leaving them a dreary waste of ruined nothings" (Wolseley 1862, 1972, p. 280). The officer Robert Swinhoe also visited the garden the day after burning. He wrote:

> As we approached the Palace, the crackling and rushing noise of fire was appalling, and the sun shining through the masses of smoke gave a sickly hue to every plant and tree, and the red flame gleaming on the faces of the troops engaged made them appear like demons glorying in the destruction of what they could not replace.[15]

The big fire obviously had long-term enviromental effects. Recent research determined that the burning of the Yuanming Yuan in 1860 deposited a thick layer of ash at the bottom of the Kunming Lake, and it not only polluted the area but also caused the extinction of diatoms *(guizao)* in the lake *(Shijie ribao,* March 21, 1996).

However terrible the arson was, the English officers, such as Knollys and Wolseley, believed that burning down the emperor's favorite imperial garden had "considerably hastened the final settlement of affairs and strengthened our ambassador's position" (Knollys 1873, 233; cf. Wolseley 1862, 1972, 279). They implied that the wanton destruction of the Yuanming Yuan at last shocked the Xianfeng emperor and his court to their senses and therefore facilitated the conclusion of the peace negotiations and the withdrawal of the troops.

Exactly contrary to Knollys' and Wolseley's thinking, however, it was only during the plundering and burning of the imperial gardens that Prince Gong, Guiliang, and Wenxiang were seriously contemplating to give up the peace effort altogether. Hearing of the plundering on October 8, for instance, they recommended to the emperor a postponement of the ongoing peace talks. As they put it, no matter how much China was willing to stoop to the conquerors out of consideration for the general interest, the foreigners seemed to have no interest in restraining their behavior. They reiterated their position in a memorial to the emperor in Rehe as follows:

> After the barbarians had followed our defeated troops to [occupy] the Yuanming Yuan and we had closed all gates [of Beijing], we rushed to the Wanshou Temple [to meet the foreign representatives for peace talk]. Yet the barbarians put all of our royal gardens [in the neighborhood] under restraint and [willfully] set fire to the nearby streets. [Their behavior] made our hair stand up in great anger. Having seen what happened as we did, we conclude that we absolutely cannot continue peace talks with them.[16]

This memorial shows Prince Gong's moments of hesitation. Nevertheless, exhausted physically and psychologically, the emperor was fully defeated and thus earnestly impressed upon the prince the importance of securing peace (Jia Zhen 1930, 7, 2413–2414; cf. *YMYZ* 1984, 139; *YMYJ* 1987, 1:209). It seems that the Qing authorities had already bowed to the harsh reality of defeat when Beijing was surrendered. Both the emperor and the prince, in fact, would have accepted the peace dictated by the victors with or without the burning of the Yuanming Yuan. Prior to the burning, the dust had already settled as the walled Beijing and its strategic Anding Gate were at the enemies' gunpoint (Knollys 1873, 198). The burning was henceforth unnecessary so far as the conclusion of peace was concerned.

Top Manchu and Chinese officials, including Qinghui, Zhou Zupei, and Chen Fouen, met with Prince Gong outside of Beijing on October 19 and agreed to conclude the humiliating peace not only by ratifying the old treaty of Tianjin but also by signing the new Treaty of Beijing with the enemies. The prince thus decided to meet with the allied leaders on October 23 to accept both the old and new terms, including the additional five hundred thousand taels indemnity for the mistreated prisoners (Weng Tonghe 1970, 1:204). In the end, Prince Gong concluded the new peace treaty and ratified the earlier treaty of Tianjin with Britain at the Board of Personnel on October 24. Weng Tonghe described the ceremony as follows:

> Today [we] exchange treaties with Britain at the lavishly decorated [hall] in the Board of Personnel [Libu]. Prince Gong arrived at noon with all the high-ranking officials remaining in Beijing. When Parkes first came, the prince stood to welcome him and they sat together. After a while, when Elgin arrived in an eight-man palanquin escorted by several thousand soldiers and a band, the prince stepped out to welcome him. Elgin removed his hat and bowed to the prince. When they sat, with Parkes and Huanqi standing behind, Elgin looked at the prince for quite a while. After both had signed the peace agreement, the prince saw Elgin off in the same manner as he had welcomed him.[17]

Weng implicitly and subtly told how the prince ate humble pie; the European officers who witnessed the episode were far more explicit in their accounts about Elgin's arrogant attitude and frigid manner (cf. Bao Chengguan 1980, 75–76). But Elgin's own testimony seems to suggest that he had a rather positive impression of the prince, with whom he could "entrust the Chinese policy of conciliation" (Walrond 1872, 371). A similar ceremony was held to conclude peace with France on October 25. Finally, on October 26, the Qing government closed this tumultuous episode by offering an official banquet in honor of the ambassadors not only from Britain and France but also from Russia and the United States (Li Ciming 1936, 9:65b).

On the eve of signing the peace agreement on October 22, it must be noted that the allies raised yet additional demands. The British demanded the cessation of Jiulong (Kowloon) peninsula. This would extend British sovereignty from Hong Kong island to Kowloon. The French requested religious freedom, which would allow unrestricted preaching of Christianity in China. And both allies wanted the Chinese government to lift the ban against its workers going abroad. However reluctant, the prince could do nothing but accept all of the demands (Jia Zhen 1930, 7:2496–2497; Cai Shengzhi n.d., 161–162). What was more, Russia, a third party, was able to take advantage of the hapless Qing to seize a large chunk of territories north of Heilongjiang (the Amur) and east of Wusuli (the Ussuri Rivers). Having paid such an enormous price, ironically, Prince Gong emerged a hero in the aftermath. This was so mainly because the prince-led negotiation had effected the withdrawal of the threatening Anglo-French force from Beijing. Before the end of the remarkable year 1860, the foreigners even pulled away from Tianjin. The Qing dynasty, after all, survived this terrible crisis.

Deep down in his heart, however, the prince knew how humiliating the episode was. He was inspired to initiate the Self-Strengthening Movement in hopes of making China strong and wealthy in the long run by emulating the West. Immediately, the most painful outcome was precisely the devastation of the Yuanming Yuan, which Prince Gong could not get over for a long while. His sense of guilt was beyond doubt; he even voluntarily sought punishment from the throne for the loss of the imperial garden (cited in *YMYJ* 1987, 1:209). The Xianfeng emperor could not punish his brother for this; his anger was aimed at the foreigners who set fire to his beloved garden. Referring to the tragedy, he remarked: "How could I tolerate such an indignation!" *(hesheng fennu)*. In fact, when the news of the burning reached him, the thirty-year-old emperor spat blood on the floor. Before long, the emperor died suddenly in Rehe. On his deathbed, he had the Yuanming Yuan very much in his mind. He personally handed the seal of the Tongdao Hall, where he had his last meal in the Yuanming Yuan, to his two widows and the young crown prince as a souvenir (cited in Wu Xiangxiang 1953, 204–205).

Guo Songtao, whose advice Prince-General Sengge Linqin had arrogantly ignored, learned the tragic news of the burning of the Yuanming Yuan at his home in Hunan. Guo squarely blamed Sengge Linqin for the disaster; in his opinion, the prince-general was too hawkish to prevent the war when peace was still possible and yet too feeble to resist the invaders after the war broke out. He was particularly disturbed by the fact that possessing a lot of guns and men as Sengge Linqin had, the prince-general had lost both Dagu and Tianjin so quickly. Most regrettably, so far as Guo was concerned, had the general not turned a deaf ear to his warnings and advice, the disaster could well have been prevented (Guo 1981, 1:428). In particular, Guo had cautioned Sengge Linqin not to underestimate the Western strength after the latter had salvaged twelve guns from the "English barbarians" in July 1860. Yet Sengge Linqin did the contrary by telling the imperial court that "with the barbarians' guns in our hands, we are ready for war" (quoted in Tsiang 1929, 82). Nevertheless, as Guo predicted, China was not ready for combat with a modern army. Even though Guo had no intention of putting the ultimate blame on the Xianfeng emperor, he was sure that the hasty decision for war was directly responsible for the destruction of the splendid Yuanming Yuan.

Aftermath

The Xianfeng emperor knew in some detail the extent of the damages in the Yuanming Yuan prior to his premature death because in Rehe on November 16, 1860, he received a written report delivered by Mingshan, the director of the Imperial Household. This initial assessment made it clear to His Majesty that the Nine Continents, the Eternal Spring Fairy Hall, the Sky in Reflections, the High-Reaching Mountain and Outstretched River, the All-Happy Garden, and the Great East Gate were mostly burned down to the ground on October 7, 1860. The emperor also learned that the administrative buildings and the European section were demolished on October 18–19, and that the Exquisite Jade Studio caught fire on October 24, the day on which the peace treaties had been signed. Mingshan also reported on the plundering: no local bandits had been involved in it before the foreigners made a bonfire of the Yuanming Yuan; however, after the garden had been burned, the robbers and thieves in the neighborhood sneaked in to steal whatever they deemed valuable (*YMYA* 1991, 1:573–576).

The sacking of the Yuanming Yuan caught the general attention of Europe by the end of 1861. When the British House of Lords met in the new year 1861 to thank the expeditionary army, as the *Times* reported on February 15, 1861, it had a stormy meeting with regard to the rape of the Yuanming Yuan. Moreover, the Anglo-French controversy over looting and burning spilt from China to Europe. The French newspaper *Le Siecle*, for example, rejected the British account about the looting. In general, the French blamed the British for burning the imperial garden, while the English press denounced the French as solely or mainly responsible for looting. The great French poet Victor Hugo (1802–1885), in a letter to Captain Butler written from exile in Guernsey, wrote, "We call ourselves civilized, and them barbarians; here is what Civilization has done to Barbarity!" (cited in Thiriez 1998, 58–59). For many twentieth-century Chinese, Hugo's condemnation spoke with the force of justice. It was frequently quoted in Chinese writings, appearing prominently even at the beginning of the Chinese movie called *The Burning of the Yuanming Yuan*. A Chinese teacher made a pilgrimage to Guernsey in early April of 1989. He visited Hugo's study, where he believed the French poet wrote the "admirable" letter on November 25, 1861. The visitor also found that Hugo was an admirer and collector of Chinese artifacts. A note of Hugo's dated March 23, 1865, indicated that he had purchased from English officers a large quantity of Chinese silk goods, which they had "robbed" from the Chinese emperor's Yuanming Yuan (Cheng Zenghou 1997, 33).

The Qing authorities, who could not stop the wanton action of the foreign invaders, dealt with the native plunderers with unusual severity, including swift executions. Nevertheless, harsh punishment failed to deter hooliganism against the unprotected garden for a long time to come. Disappearing especially quickly were the movable objects, such as interior decorations, furniture, doors, and windows, which could be found inside the badly damaged structures in the Immortal Abode on the Fairy Terrace, in the Prudent Cultivation and Perpetual Thoughtfulness (Shenxiu Siyong), and in the Double Crane Chapel. Mingshan found a small sum of cash—approximately 106.621 taels of silver, "money orders" (*yinchao*) equivalent to 29,325 taels of silver, and hundreds of coins—in the garden in the aftermath (*YMYA* 1991, 1:573–576). Exactly how much gold, silver, lumber, and antiques were lost will never be known, as most of the Yuanming Yuan's financial documents were consumed by fire.

The Qing authorities did try to recover stolen or missing properties that belonged to the Yuanming Yuan; however, the task was exceedingly difficult. There was no way to retrieve the objects taken away by the foreign invaders, which in Ruichang's November 11, 1861 estimation accounted for the most precious items. Yet the less valuable objects stolen by the local thieves were too numerous to trace. Moreover, the investigators soon discovered that many people had obtained Yuanming Yuan objects accidentally, either by incidentally picking them up as souvenirs or unknowingly purchasing the stolen goods in local stores. To be sure, the government could search every household in the neighborhood for the stolen goods. But Mingshan recommended against it. Instead, he suggested a month-long grace period, during which the government would allow anyone to turn in anything that originally belonged to the Yuanming Yuan without fear of prosecution (*YMYA* 1991, 1:571–572). As late as February 1997, during a public auction in Beijing, a remnant of *The Grand Southern Tour (Nanxun Shengdian),* from *juan* (volume) 101 to *juan* 103, was discovered and identified as a lost item from the Library of Literary Sources in the Yuanming Yuan. This book by Gao Jin recounts the Qianlong emperor's four southern tours and features 120 *juan* in the history category of the Four Treasures (Zhang Yaojin 1997, 34).

The Qing government put General Shengbao in charge of recovering stolen property. Before the end of the year, numerous small items were recovered from the neighboring districts of the Yuanming Yuan (cf. *YMYA* 1991, 1:576–578, 583–585, 587–596). These items, however, represented no more than a drop in the bucket and had no great value. The terrible losses were never publicized in detail by the court or the government. The official announcements of the demise of the magnificent imperial garden were always brief: the Yuanming Yuan caught fire, or catastrophe befell the Yuanming Yuan on a certain date.

The relatively valuable treasures taken away from the Yuanming Yuan by foreign invaders as war booty were put up to auction in Beijing in 1861. Large collections of Yuanming Yuan objects, such as jades, enamels, porcelains, silks, clocks, and watches, were also sent to Britain and France. The London auction started as early as March 1861, the Tuileries display opened in April 1861, and the Paris auction commenced on Thursday, December 12, 1861. Loot thus became a hot commodity. While some objects eventually found homes in major Western museums, in particular the British Museum and the Bibliotheque Nationale (Paris), many others entered into marketing networks around the world. They significantly increased the volume of Chinese "curiosities" outside of China. As late as 1987, the bronze head of a monkey, one of twelve animal heads in human garb around the circular fountain in the European section of the Eternal Spring Garden, was sold in New York City to the collection of Hanshe (the Humble House) in Taipei. Three more bronze heads, the tiger, the ox, and the horse, appeared at a London auction on June 13, 1989. This time, Hanshe bought the horse (Siu 1988, 75–76; Sun 1998, 72–73).

Both Manchu and Chinese elites, saddened and ashamed, have since accused the European imperialists of vandalism and barbarism. Woren, the conservative Neo-Confucian scholar of Mongolian descent and a high-ranking official, specifically reminded the succeeding Tongzhi emperor of the "shame of 1860" in his will (Woren n.d., 207). Shortly afterward, prominent Qing poets, such as Wang Kaiyuan and Yang Yunshi, composed sentimental pieces to lament the garden burned into ashes and the precious imperial collection lost.

Kang Youwei (1858–1927), the great reformer of 1898, felt ashamed and heart-broken in 1904 when viewing a great number of Yuanming Yuan objects possessed by the Oriental Museum in Paris. He saw two imperial seals, numerous cultural relics, priceless vases, screens, dishes, Buddha statues, human figures, and a jade inscribed with characters referring to a hall of the Ten-Thousand Spring Garden, formerly the Variegated Spring Garden. These relics, as Kang learned, were war booty taken to France in 1861 and 1901. Kang called them "superb treasures" that represent "the cream of many generations of Chinese quintessence." Kang regretted deeply the loss of so many national treasures to the foreigners.

Kang's personal experiences with the Yuanming Yuan deepened his sadness. He remembered he had set foot on the destroyed garden in the 1890s. Back then he was still able to see abundant lotus in full bloom behind the old willow trees, the deserted bronze camel buried in the thistles and thrones, the broken bridges extending into the lakes in the midst of reeds, and the white marble court terraces behind the pine trees. Also, he recalled he had come across a white-haired eunuch sitting under broken tiles in despair in the midst of the sounds of wind over the stiff treetops. As well, he recalled the desolated Eternal Spring Garden, in which the broken European buildings displayed a waning elegance.

Like others, Kang easily related the tragedy of the Yuanming Yuan to the fate of his country. The great Qing Empire was still in its heyday when the imperial garden was as fresh as the spring cloud and as happy as the joyful sounds of the orioles. This was the time when King William of England ruled no more than half a million souls and Western civilization had not yet come of age. But soon the world changed. While China remained isolated and ignorant, steamships and railroads had paved the Western road to power and wealth. Consequently, the formidable European cavalry broke the Chinese gate, rushed upon the imperial capital, sent the emperor fleeing in great embarrassment, and burned the magnificent garden down to the ground. As a loyal reformer, Kang retained his wish for the restoration of the Qing Empire. He dreamed one day of the renovation of the Yuanming Yuan to its former glory, with the dragon flag again hoisted high on top of the shining palace roofs and proud royal troops marching through the gates (Kang Youwei 1975, 5).

Chinese mournfulness about the Yuanming Yuan persisted well into the twentieth century, and it contributed a vital element to modern Chinese nationalism. This outcome was surely beyond the wildest imagination of Elgin, who burned the garden to punish the Qing emperor only. Resentment was not at all confined to late Qing loyalists such as Kang. Many early Republican Chinese with many different political aspirations or educational backgrounds shared the antipathy. Professors and students of Yanjing and Qinghua Universities, due to their easy access to the ruined site, were frequent sojourners in the desolated Yuanming Yuan. Some of them left behind memorable words. The Yanjing scholar-poet Gu Sui composed the following lines when he strolled through the ruins on an autumn day:

> Watching the Double Ninth Festival pass by,
> I found neither warm sunshine nor gentle breeze;
> Evening cicadas choke back grief
> And hold tight to the frosty bough.
> From the remote sky,
> Come flocks of wild geese.
> How sad is the melancholy autumn.
> I see in my eyes our falling land
> And the deserted slope under my feet.
> Standing atop a higher ground,
> I look around my old country

Thin streams, tall sky, evening glow, and a few people.
I stroll with a short stick,
I sit atop a hill,
Every look can be heartbreaking,
Few new huts and broken palace walls.
Where comes the cry of a cock?
Boundless sunset shines in splendor,
Up the rugged hills and withered grass,
Come down cows and sheep.
Let us grieve for
This desolate land of ours.[18]

Li Dazhao (1888–1927), the father of Chinese Marxism, toured the ruined Yuanming Yuan in 1913 with a friend. Li noted that when he climbed to high ground, he saw nothing but a desolate, wild scene of broken walls and debris and rugged roads. He conveyed his sorrow in the following lines:

Twice, the catastrophe befell
On this Round Bright Garden.
The spirits of our myriad ancestors,
How could we bear it?
The sounds of grief seem no end,
Debris and ashes are flying with evening smoke.
Crumbled to dust were jade palace and crimson chamber,
Over the wildness imprints.
Footmarks of animals and birds,
The broken steles are all buried.
The surviving palace maids aged so fast,
I feel hollowly blank,
Stirring up ashes from the wild radish.[19]

The famous conservative writer Lin Shu (1851–1924) shared the grief over the misfortune of the Yuanming Yuan with the Marxist Li Dazhao. Lin, also a painter, drew a picture of the ruined garden with this inscription: "I covered my eyes in tears when leaving here, and yet I could not help turning back to admire the setting sun" (quoted in *YMYZ* 1984, 316). As late as 1930, Chinese continued gathering to observe the anniversary of the burning. The noted historian Xiang Da remembered the event as "the worst case of vandalism in the history of Sino-Western relations" (Xiang Da 1983, 1:115). Even when East China was under Japanese occupation in 1940, the eightieth anniversary was not forgotten (Cai Shengzhi n.d., 113).

Hence, the ruined Yuanming Yuan became a powerful symbol of nationalism and patriotic outrage long before the founding of the People's Republic in 1949. The triumph of the Chinese Communist revolution surely did not sweeten the bitter memory of 1860. The mainland Chinese scholar Wang Wei cries:

> The allies severely damaged Chinese relics. Such brutality has rarely been seen in modern history. The destruction of the Yuanming Yuan is a loss for human civilization beyond calculation. It is not just that the world's foremost and unique palace garden was demolished, but also that much of the most precious and irreplaceable cultural relics China had preserved were gone with it.[20]

In 1980, General Zhang Aiping, then China's defense minister, paid a special visit to the ruins of the Yuanming Yuan and composed a very passionate poem:

> Watching the ruins with my angry eyes,
> I cannot help condemning the intruding foreign forces.
> Rebuild it! Rebuild it!
> Let us rebuild the past beauty and its glory.[21]

In response to the Chinese reactions, the English writer Hope Denby made some defensive remarks early in the 1930s:

> They think of the Yuanming Yuan as part of their national possessions; they forget that it existed only for the pleasure of one person, the reigning Emperor. Like sons deprived of a splendid inheritance, they resent the loss of the art treasures and architectural wonders, and they point accusing fingers at the British, accusing them of an act of vandalism. The destruction by the French is practically forgotten, and the far greater pillaging by the Chinese themselves is conveniently ignored. But always, in the waves of xenophobia that arise periodically in China, the burning of the Yuanming Yuan is brought to the fore. It is one of the most powerful weapons of propaganda that can be used.[22]

It is true that Yuanming Yuan served the pleasure of the reigning emperor; and Elgin deliberately wanted to burn it in order to hurt the emperor. The Xianfeng emperor, indeed, was hurt badly. But it is a matter of fact that modern Chinese, especially intellectuals, never considered the burning of the Yuanming Yuan an act that only punished the Manchu monarch. They were all ashamed. They were disturbed by the fact that the West violated its own international law, which prohibited looting the movable private property of the subjects and the heads of a state in wartime. The wanton destruction was hence to them utterly unjustifiable retaliation. Even leaving aside the legal issue, for them, burning down so many irreplaceable cultural relics was a great loss for humanity.

Henry Loch, Elgin's secretary, argued that "there was no utter annihilation of works of art or learning." He believed "nothing unique either in the shape of books or manu-scripts was kept at Yuen-ming-yuan and in the subsequent search for both, previous to the burning, very few were found, and certainly none of any exclusive rarity" (Loch 1909, 168). Loch was surely wrong. On the contrary, "this act of unqualified barbarity," as several French scholars have recently reported, "annihilated an inheritance of gardens and mon-uments containing collections of art and a library of inestimable wealth" (Perazzoli-t'Serstevens 1988 7, 34). Besides its unique architecture and landscape, the Yuanming Yuan was the home of priceless treasures, such as rare manuscripts, books (the complete library of Wenyuan Ge), porcelains, jades, paintings, and antiques accumulated by the successive Qing rulers during a period of one hundred fifty years. Arguably, the most valuable Chi-nese painting, the *Portrait of a Lady (Shinu Tu)* by the great artist Gu Kaizhi (392–467) of the Jin dynasty, was taken out from the Yuanming Yuan by the British, and it is now in the possession of the British Museum.

Modern Chinese could not forget the burning of the Yuanming Yuan also because they regard the great imperial garden as part of their brilliant cultural heritage, and it was wan-tonly destroyed by foreign invaders. They deplored the loss of an architectural wonder. They blamed Britain most harshly because it was the leading imperialist power in the nineteenth century. And so far as the Yuanming Yuan is concerned, the British committed not just looting but alone made the fatal decision to burn it down to the ground, despite the fact that the French and Chinese were also involved in plundering (cf. Cai Shengzhi n.d., 140–141). The British would have had the same hard feelings if Buckingham Palace had been demolished by foreign invaders for whatever reason, even though the palace always served the reigning British king or queen. In fact, the British general Grant himself testified to the arrogance of nineteenth-century British imperialism as follows:

> We procured for the civilized world protection from the oppression and barbar-ous outrages which the nation had been previously wont to inflict upon strangers; we struck a salutary blow at the pride of China, which, as experience shows, has been successful in convincing her that she is no match for the peoples of Europe; and, above all, we exacted from them the Treaty of Pekin (Beijing), which has proved far more lasting than any former engagements with that nation.[23]

In retrospect, the lesson Elgin wanted to teach the Qing emperor was learned by the Chinese in a hard way. Their mistrust and misunderstanding of the modern West was surely deepened by the looting and arson committed by the allies. To be sure, the presence of the mighty Western army in Beijing struck the natives with awe. "They (the allies) moved about in our midst at will," a local resident noted in his diary, "as if in an uninhabited wildness!" (Wu Kedu 1978, 4:12). Li Ciming also witnessed the foreign brutality in indignation: "the occupation forces were running wild inside and outside the walled city, setting fire to houses, disturbing civil order, and harassing women in public" (1936, 9:74b–75a). Both Li and Wu, like many other Beijing residents, were shocked by Western power.

The formidable tide from the West induced China, willingly or unwillingly, to join the modern family of nations. But the dark side of modern civilization also loomed large in the minds of the Chinese people, evident in the barbarism of 1860, and this rekindled their historical memory of violent invaders of the culturally backward barbarians. Hence, for a long time to come, while appreciating the marvels of Western science and technology, they were somehow reluctant to sing praises of the moral values of the West. It is a fact that they recognized the West's material superiority long before its spiritual components. They perceived in the image of the burning of the Yuanming Yuan that their country had been conquered by something more like Hun barbarism than by a splendid modern civilization.

CHAPTER 8

REPAIRS AND THE FINAL BLOWS

THE INFERNO OF 1860 disfigured the Yuanming Yuan so much that the imperial garden was no longer fit for royal living. Troops and eunuchs, however, guarded the destroyed garden estate to keep out unauthorized persons. The newly ascended Tongzhi emperor, together with the two dowagers, Cian and Cixi, escorted Xianfeng's coffin back to Beijing from Chengde. They all took residence inside the Forbidden City. They missed the pleasant garden life, and their memory was simply too fresh to forget. Tongzhi was born in the garden on April 27, 1856. The dowager Cixi, the new emperor's biological mother, had her romance with the late Xianfeng emperor in the garden. Many other members of the family had in mind the sad moments when they had the last breakfast in the garden with the late emperor before the hasty flight to Chengde. They, of course, remembered the agony of the late emperor when he heard the bad news about the looting and burning of the Yuanming Yuan.

The best remedy, of course, was to restore the Yuanming Yuan to its past glory. But given the persistent rebellions and the financial crisis derived from excessive military expenditures and war indemnities, even the Tongzhi emperor himself felt uncomfortable to raise such an issue. Not until the autumn of 1867 did the censor Detai speak on behalf of the royal family. Knowing how empty the state treasury was, the censor recommended that they seek donations and contributions from individual households in the country. This was clearly a trial balloon. When the general response of officialdom was negative, the emperor quickly backed off in a decree dated September 16, 1867, denouncing the censor's idea as "inappropriate" and "ridiculous" (Wang Xianqian 1884, 73:35). The censor's untimely proposal backfired. The court decided to exile him in the remote Manchurian frontier. He chose to commit suicide instead. Most likely, the royal family incited the censor to make the recommendation, and hence he felt betrayed and died in protest. Consequently, the garden remained in an appalling condition for many more years to come.

A Tour of the Desolated Yuanming Yuan

In the late spring of 1871, the Yuanming Yuan was still in desolation. Under the guidance of Liao Cheng'en (Fengting), an ex-commander of the erstwhile garden battalion, the scholar-poet Wang Kaiyun (1832–1916) and his friend Xu Shujun made a tour of the imperial garden on May 27, 1871. The tour began at the Pure Ripple Garden at the foothills of the Longevity Hills, where they saw numerous shabby courtyards, broken halls, and half dried-up lakes, with trees in green standing in the midst of the bare scene. The shepherd boys and woodcutters seemed to be wandering in wildness. On their way back from the Kunming Lake, they discovered a bronze rhinoceros with the tail cut off, but the imperial inscription on the back was still recognizable. Most of the various small gardens owned by princes and distinguished officials in this neighborhood already bore no trace of the imperial garden's grandeur (Wang Kaiyun 1973, 2:257; cf. *YMYZ* 1984, 324).

The conditions surrounding the Kunming Lake as described by Wang in 1871 seemed to have further deteriorated since a British attache's observations in 1866. The attache had seen few delightful scenes in the midst of ruins, charred walls, and the departed pine trees. He specifically noticed a mass of lotus plants in full flower on the lake, several little islands covered with trees and buildings, and a great octagonal three-story palace with its white marble balustrade standing elegantly. The Briton had also seen some structures on higher ground, including a bronze temple, a gym, two little revolving wooden pagodas, many Buddha figures in a tower, and a large temple covered by yellow and green tiles (cited in Malone 1934, 195). But none of these, which in 1866 still retained a bit of the past glory, was visible five years later.

Wang and Xu spent the night with the Liao family in the neighborhood. They resumed the tour on May 28 and walked through the Lucky Garden Gate of the Yuanming Yuan. They came across an elderly eunuch named Dong, who volunteered to show them the way. They went through rubble and debris before identifying the Main Audience Hall. The hall was so badly damaged that the main stairs were not even visible. Walking further north, they recognized the Nine Continents, once the royal living quarters, behind the Front Lake, but the crumbling walls were all that they could see. The eunuch Dong specifically pointed out the ruins of a structure called the Family of Spring Between Heaven and Earth, where the dowager Cixi had once lived, together with many compounds in which concubines and princes had resided. But many celebrated structures on the Nine Continents, such as the Peony Terrace, the Five-Fortunes Hall, and the Clear Sunshine Belvedere constructed by the Xianfeng emperor, had simply vanished. When reaching the largest lake called the Sea of Blessing, the broad, desolate scene saddened them profoundly. Except for a few identifiable houses and chambers on the islet of the Immortal Abode at the center of the lake, none of the famous views was still in sight. Moreover, the eunuch tearfully told exactly where the director Wenfeng drowned himself just before the foreigners invaded the garden.

Then the visitors strolled to the northwest to see Double Cranes Chapel still standing in front of the Boundless Impartiality, where the poet Wang recalled the story of how during the Qianlong reign a dozen white cranes landed there. The Qianlong emperor took it as a good omen and wished for the return of the cranes every year. The court officials hence manufactured on site the same number of gold cranes in different postures to please the emperor. Very fond of the craftsmanship, His Majesty constructed a studio to house the golden cranes, none of which was still in existence so far as Wang could see. The Wall of Sravasti was also in shambles; none of the 200,000 Buddha statues could be found (Wang Kaiyun 1973, 2:258; Xu Shujun's remark cited in *YMYZ* 1984, 324–325; cf. Peng Zheyu and Zhong Baozhong 1985, 126–130).

The tour to the devastated Yuanming Yuan was concluded at sunset. Before long, Wang Kaiyun transformed the sorry conditions as well as his profound melancholy into his celebrated poem on the Yuanming Yuan:

> Burned in the windswept smoke,
> The country royal estate has been ruined.
> The Jade spring flows as usual,
> But with sighing sounds.
> Alas! Kunming Lake has silted up.
> I come, but what can I see?
> Buried in thrones are the broken bronze rhinoceros.
> The great Green Rocks become
> The hideouts for crying wolves;
> And the fish under the Bridge of the Embroidered Ripples
> Seem to be sobbing.
> Alas! an old eunuch at the Happy Garden Gate
> Had once attended His Majesty.
> The buildings here all disappeared,
> Gone also the loud excitements of crowds of people.
> The lonesome visitors stand in the garden's solitude.
> The exciting past, the sorrowful present,
> Distinguished guests shall never come.
> Not any more!
> When I peep behind the scenes
> Of the Inner Palace Gate and the Main Audience Hall,
> I find a lot of broken bricks.
> North of the crumbling walls,
> Gone is the Clear Sunshine Belvedere facing the lake,
> Where the late (Xianfeng) emperor often enjoyed the morn.
> They said His Majesty once had a strange dream,
> An old man who says he is the guardian of the garden,
> He wants to quit because peace can no longer be maintained.
> The Buddha statues inside the Sravasti Wall,

Thousands of them,
Where are they now?
Look around from side to side,
Cattail leaves grow wild in the lakes.
Mugwort grass rustling in the air, blocking stairways.
Some burned trees blossom anew,
But are cut and taken away for firewood.
The startled fish jump in the stream,
Trying to avoid nets.
The wonderful Peony Terrace,
Where three great rulers once met,
None of them could foresee misfortune.
The bamboo trees grow so disorderly
Out of the messy mosses.
One can no longer see in the spring days
The dropping dew and the blossoming peony.
Westward to the Smooth Lake,
A chamber is still there,
But where is its window paper?
Behind the bursting Chinese chives,
Emerged the gradually elevated road.
But where are the footprints of beautiful ladies?
The beauties left behind their block pigment makeup,
Imprints on windows in green everywhere.[1]

Wang Kaiyun did not go far enough to see the European section at the northern end of the Eternal Spring Garden. But a year later, in 1873, Ernest Ohlmer (1847–1927), the young German officer of the Chinese Customs Office, entered the European section when he served in Beijing from 1872 to 1880. He took many photographs of the tarnished Baroque buildings and thus left behind some images of ruined palaces. These photographs and illustrations were eventually published in book form in 1932 (Teng Gu 1933, 1–6).

By locating Ohlmer's and other Westerners' photographic works, the recent scholar Regine Thiriez has established a chronology of the evolution of the Yuanming Yuan's European palaces from "ruins to rubble." She shows a process of "relentless decay." In 1873, as Ohlmer's photographs show, "most of the scorched marble lintels had disintegrated, giving the openings of the palaces a strange vaulted look." However, "the inlaid decoration was mostly intact, while the tiled roofs lay in large heaps on the ground." Nevertheless, the continuous pilfering over a long period of time eventually brought the whole section into oblivion. Both the Great Fountain's and the Great View from the Distant Seas' top ornaments disappeared between 1873 and 1877. The Symmetric and Amazing Pleasure's marble balustrades fell to the ground before 1876, and its top level began crumbling no

Figure 36. Yangque Long (Peacock Cage). From a copperplate engraving by the eighteenth-century Jesuit designers. East Facade. Sources: YMYJ 1984, 3:105; Huang Taopeng and Huang Zhongjun 1985, 111.

Figure 37. Peacock Cage in ruins, ca. 1916. Photograph by Sophus Black. Source: Huang Taopeng and Huang Zhongjun 1985, 133.

Figure 38. Haiyan Tang (Calm Sea Hall). From a copperplate engraving by eighteenth-century Jesuit designers. West Facade. Source: YMYJ 1984, 3:108.

later than 1886. In 1901, in the wake of the Boxer catastrophe, the palaces were clearly reduced to rubble. Following the 1911 Revolution, with the fall of the Manchu dynasty from power, the removal of terra-cotta ornaments, marble, stone slabs, and even brick core from the scene was evident. The destruction in this section was mostly complete by 1940 during the Japanese occupation (Thiriez 1998, 62–64).

The Struggle for Renovation

Ohlmer's photographs and Wang's poems provide some sense of the desolated Yuanming Yuan prior to 1873, when the proposal for repairs was again raised. This time the emperor himself took the initiative. By now the Tongzhi emperor was mature enough to assume his own throne. He was also intelligent enough to invoke the Confucian code of filial piety as justification for reviving the imperial garden. He said he should show filial devotion to his two imperial mothers, Cian and Cixi, who had been guiding him through a most difficult period of time, by providing them with a pleasant retirement in a garden environment; and breathing new life into the dead Yuanming Yuan would serve the purpose. Having made up his mind, the emperor formally issued a vermilion decree on November 17, 1873:

> I have not forgotten for a single moment [how to repay my debt] to the profound kindness of my two imperial mothers since I assumed power on February 23 this year. I knew by reading at the Mind-Nourishing Study the poems about

the Forty Views composed by the late Yongzheng emperor that the Yuanming Yuan was the imperial garden where my forefather had lived and conducted state affairs. I have since been daily occupied with the thoughts of renovating it and of allowing the dowagers to live in it, lest I shall never rest with ease. I have seriously deliberated the matter and understand how bad the financial conditions are; however, at this point I have no intention of renovating the whole of the garden. I only proposed to renovate the most essential structures of the garden, such as the Ancestral Shrine for worshipping the deceased emperors [of our dynasty], the living quarters to accommodate the dowagers, and the necessary halls and courts for me to conduct state affairs. No structures for mere pleasure purposes should be renovated. I hereby welcome contributions of whatever sum from princes and officials; and [I instruct] the Imperial Household to award those who make contributions.[2]

The director of the Imperial Household responded to the decree by addressing the matter beginning on November 19. The first priority was given to the Spreading Spring Hall and the Cool Summer Chapel (Qingxia Zhai), ostensibly to accommodate the two dowagers. The first orders of the business, however, included raising much needed funds from princes and officials, looking for better models, studying geomancy, and selecting an auspicious date to begin construction. On November 20, Tongzhi waited no longer to rename the Variegated Spring Garden at the southeast side of the Yuanming Yuan the Ten-Thousand Spring Garden (Wanchun Yuan). He also redesignated the Spreading Spring Hall as the new Family of Spring Between Heaven and Earth, or the Benevolence-Receiving

Figure 39. Calm Sea Hall in ruins, ca. 1923. Photograph by Sidney D. Gamble. Source: Teng Gu 1933, map 9.

Hall (Cheng'en Tang). The Cool Summer Chapel was renamed the Cool Summer Hall. Renaming was a practice to bring forth the new by weeding out the old (*YMYA* 1991, 1:627–628).

But before long, on November 21, the censor Shen Huai appealed to the throne for the postponement of the proposed project. He argued that renovation of the pleasure garden at a time when China was stricken by natural disasters in both the north and south and threatened unceasingly from the West would imperil the throne's great virtue (*YMYA* 1991, 1:629). Sincere and courageous though the censor was, the enthusiastic emperor was in no mood to back down. His Majesty accused the censor of being insensitive to his filial devotion. Rather than postpone renovation as the censor had requested, he actually wanted to accelerate its speed in order to show significant results by 1875 in time to celebrate Cixi's fortieth birthday (*Muzong shilu* 1937, 310: 58).

Although the censor's objection was cast aside, the shortage of cash could not be ignored. Even highly selective renovation, according to the estimate of the deputy financial minister Guiqing, would cost a sum more than the treasury could possibly afford. When the minister informed this truth to the emperor, he lost his job. Tongzhi continued to exert pressure on directors Ming Shan and Guibao, both of the Imperial Household, to make assessments of the damages regardless of whether the money was available. The final assessment showed that no more than thirteen places had escaped the 1860 inferno and stood in relatively good condition, most of them situated at the northern end of the garden.

With the exception of the Dignified Vision (Zhuangyan Fajie), which was located in the Ten-Thousand Spring Garden, the places that remained in good condition were all inside the original Yuanming Yuan. The Cross Pavilion stood at the south side of the Swastika House in the Universal Peace. The Spring Rain Gallery remained intact in the Apricot-Flower Villa. The Big Dipper Chamber (Kuixing Lou) at the southern end of the Ancestral Shrine stayed intact. So did the structures known as the Knowing-Your-Mistakes Hall (Zhigou Tang), the Prudent Cultivation and Perpetual Thoughtfulness, the Scholar's Wonderland, the Fish-Leaping and Bird-Flying, and the Teaching Farming Gallery by the stream near the Northernmost Mountain Village. Double Cranes Chapel in front of the Boundless Impartiality at the northwest corner of the Sea of Blessing was also undamaged. The Purple-Blue Mountain Cottage at the northwest corner, the Octagonal Pavilion (Bajiao Ting) at the center of the northern end, and the Ploughing Cloud Hall near the right-hand side of the north gate entrance were standing as well. This assessment, however, seems incomplete. So far as we know, this list does not include the untarnished houses and chambers on the lake islets, such as the Immortal Abode observed by Wang Kaiyun in 1871. Doubtless, there were numerous still usable gates, dockyards, bridges, and temples. As for the Mind-Opening Isle in the Eternal Spring Garden, it retained its elegance up to the 1900 Boxer catastrophe (cf. Liu Dunzheng 1982, 298; Wang Wei 1980, 52–53).

At the emperor's insistence, the Imperial Household redoubled its efforts to lobby princes and officials for contributing a share of much needed funds to start the project. Under the circumstances, even Prince Gong, the emperor's revered uncle, donated 20,000 taels of silver from his private purse. Many others followed suit, contributing various sums (*YMYA* 1991, 1:629–631, 633–635).

But donations and contributions had their limits. The realm's fast deteriorating finances soon compelled other censors to speak their consciences. Censor You Bochuan, for one, tried to convince the emperor to delay the renovation projects in his memorial dated December 5, 1873. The censor specifically raised the security issue: since the Yuanming Yuan was located outside of the walled Beijing, even if it should be successfully renovated, it would have no protection against potential foreign attacks. He suggested that the emperor and the imperial mothers should reside inside the Forbidden City for the sake of security and saving an enormous sum of money. Nevertheless, once again, the emperor refused to hear any arguments that he disliked. His Majesty not only condemned the censor's deliberate misunderstanding of his filial devotion, the cherished Confucian value, but also questioned the censor's sincerity by accusing him of shamelessly fishing for fame and recognition. The emperor thus dismissed the censor and vowed to punish anyone who would obstruct his renovation projects (*YMYA* 1991, 1:631, 637–638; Li Zongtong and Liu Fenghan 1969, 1:194–195).

Ground breaking was finally set for December 7, 1873, marking the official beginning of renovations in the Yuanming Yuan. The immediate work included cleaning the Grand Palace Gate and the Inner Palace Gate, fixing the damaged entrance gates and the attendants' rooms, dismantling broken walls, and removing mud and dirt all over. Construction to follow the cleaning began with the administrative halls and the structures on the Nine Continents. The Main Audience Hall, which was virtually nonexistent, had to be fully rebuilt on the old foundation. The severely damaged Diligent Court together with its subsidiary houses, corridors, and courtyards were in such dilapidated condition that they needed to be completely razed before reconstruction. As for the structures on the Nine Continents, no less than 437 out of 656 units of halls, apartments, studies, and courtyards needed almost complete refurbishment.[3]

The available blueprints for repairs indicate that renovation was never intended to be exact restoration. Flexibility was allowed for expanding a bit here or adding something new there in the process of reconstruction. Even individual structures radically changed. The idea was to make the new better than the old. Most notably, the Family of Spring Between Heaven and Earth, designated as the dowager Cixi's living quarters, was to be rebuilt on a new location, with a slightly different scheme, at the site of the destroyed Spreading Spring Hall in the Ten-Thousand Spring Garden. It was to extend five columns from east to west, approximately 183.3 inches wide between the central columns and 169.2 inches wide between the side columns. It was to comprise four connected houses with waving eaves from north to south. The depth of the three front houses was to be 394.8 inches and the rear house 366.6 inches. Corridors were to connect two courtyards, each of which was to stand on one side of the main construction. Its auxiliary structure, called the Inquiring Moon Chamber (Wenyue Lou), was renamed the Transparent Bright Gazebo (Chengguang Xie). The empty lot to the east was reserved for a theater, a stage, and a number of subsidiary rooms to entertain the retired dowagers. Many shabby buildings and pavilions nearby were simply torn down to make room for a larger courtyard (Liu Dunzheng 1982, 313, 338).

The dowager Cixi was very much involved in the process of renovating this particular project. She personally studied the external models, inspected the interior decorations, and even tried her own hand at drawing sketches and blueprints (Wu Xiangxiang 1953, 120). As a result, renovation often meant new designs, new arrangements, and even new locations.

But the renovation projects were always haunted with budgetary problems, which neither the power of the throne nor the enthusiasm of the dowager could have resolved. Construction thus often stalled for the lack of necessary materials, in particular large timber, due to financial stringency. Before long, numerous walls, roads, bridges, water gates, courtyards, and barges were left incomplete. Construction at many major sites had not even got started. They included the Cool Summer Hall, the Ancestral Shrine, the Sky in Reflections, the Swastika House, the Spring Beauty at Wuling, Apricot-Flower Villa, All-Happy Garden, the Wall of Sravasti, the Majestic Sunset-Tinted Peaks of the West Hills, the Northernmost Mountain Village, the Purple-Blue Mountain Cottage, the Octagonal Pavilion, and the Fish-Leaping and Bird-Flying (Liu Dunzheng 1982, 338–349; Li Zongtong and Liu Fenghan 1969, 1:194; Wu Xiangxiang 1953, 207–211). Only a few individual structures may have been completed before the renovation projects came to a standstill. Countless unused wooden pillars were discarded on the ground, construction materials of various sorts were piled in empty spaces in the incomplete rooms, and all construction sites were left protected only by modest wooden frames (Liu Dunzheng 1982, 318; cf. 313–318; 320–332).

The Tongzhi emperor seemed surprised by the fact that the empire could not afford a "small-scale" renovation of the desolated imperial garden. In any event, he was not about to give up. He was willing, however, to reduce the original project of renovating 3,000 rooms in the Ten-Thousand Spring Garden to 1,420 rooms, more than a 50 percent cut, for accommodating the retired dowagers. Apparently, the emperor was very anxious to get something completed in time to celebrate his mother's forthcoming fortieth birthday. He thought the reduced budget would justify the resumption of construction.

At the emperor's urging, indeed, the construction started again in early 1874. Even before three thousand much needed large pieces of heavy timber had been made available, on February 2, 1874, the emperor impatiently instructed that the gigantic timber frame in the main hall of the Ancestral Shrine be hoisted without delay. From March 7 onward, for a while, construction seemed to pick up speed. But in the end, the emperor's preoccupation with garden projects provoked another round of opposition, and this time many highly prestigious people joined the criticism.

Most noticeably, Wenxiang (1818–1876), Prince Gong's right-hand man in charge of foreign affairs, appealed to the emperor on April 2 to cease construction on the grounds that the huge expenditure had already caused an uproar in the empire. He warned that the state would never find sufficient money to complete the renovation of the Yuanming

Yuan. As for raising funds through donation, it would be a mere drop in the bucket, too small to cover the cost (*YMYA* 1991, 1:674–675).

Nevertheless, Wenxiang failed to convince the emperor. His Majesty became even more involved through a secret tour to the construction site near the Ancestral Shrine on April 27. This behavior was considered hazardous to the safety of the throne and deemed extremely inappropriate. It surprised, shocked, and alarmed many, in particular the senior members of the royal family and the top leadership in the government. Finally, Prince Gong, the emperor's uncle, and Li Hongzao (1820–1897), the Imperial Tutor, decided to intervene. Through their arrangement, a delegation consisting mostly of family members led by Prince Chun met with Tongzhi on May 9, 1874. They earnestly begged the emperor not to repeat the clandestine trip to the construction site and humbly wished His Majesty to end garden construction altogether (quoted in Li Zongtong and Liu Fenghan 1969, 1:200–201). This meeting, however, was a complete failure.

Before long, on May 24, the emperor returned to the site and threw a picnic party with his entourage at the Double Cranes Chapel. Tongzhi's defiance heightened the uneasiness and anxiety of the royal family. Meanwhile, officials from various regions also voiced their opposition to the reconstruction of the Yuanming Yuan. For instance, in his memorial dated July 13, 1874, Li Zongxi, the governor-general of Liangjiang (Jiangsu and Jiangxi provinces) made two critical points. First, the Yuanming Yuan, even if fully renovated, would no longer be safe for royal living so long as the threat from the West remained. Second, His Majesty might want to emulate Emperor Wen of the Han and Emperor Renzong of the Song, both of them refused to spend money on gardens so long as the humiliation inflicted by foreigners was not redressed (*YMYA* 1991, 1:721).

This governor-general's memorial inspired the prestigious Hanlin compiler Li Wentian (1834–1895), who had earlier contributed money for renovation, to request on July 20 the immediate termination of all construction in the Yuanming Yuan. The compiler's long petition, though not officially recorded, was highlighted in Li Ciming's diary, revealing such blunt language as "(the continuation of construction) would sooner or later drain the pond to get the fish," the Chinese version of killing the goose that lays the golden eggs. Also, the censor cited recent natural disasters as warnings from Heaven, which the Son of Heaven—the Chinese ruler—should take very seriously. Last, but not least, the censor agreed with the governor-general that under the circumstances a renovated Yuanming Yuan could again easily fall prey to foreign invaders; hence, why bother to renovate it at all (quoted in Huang Jun 1979, 2:413–415; *YMYA* 1991, 1:724–726)? But none of these arguments won Tongzhi's ear. The emperor was not interested in sense; he wanted to go even further. Laughing in the faces of those who tried to stop him, he proposed to expand the theater chamber at the All-Happy Garden to three stories (cited in Wu Xiangxiang 1953, 220).

Ignoring opposition and criticism as he did, the Tongzhi emperor could not disregard the increasing problem of funding. It was common, as the record of the Imperial Household shows, for construction to begin before money was available (*YMYA* 1991, 1:677).

Great efforts were made to solicit private donations and contributions; however, a mere 300,000 taels were collected by May 17, 1874, while the estimated cost ran as high as tens of million. And yet the insignificant sum of donated money had already created agony in officialdom; as the official Wang Jiabi put it, the campaign for funds had bankrupted many official families. Wang thus advised the emperor to find cash from more viable sources, such as the opium tax from the maritime customs office, or to take a slower and prudent pace in renovating the Yuanming Yuan (cf. *YMYA* 1991, 1:693–698, 698–699).

Moreover, large timber essential for building halls and chambers was as difficult to find as money. Tongzhi had repeatedly sought help from administrators in the timber-producing provinces, such as Hubei, Hunan, Fujian, Zhejiang, and Sichuan. He wanted at least three thousand pieces of heavy timber to meet the construction needs of the Yuanming Yuan. But as Governor-General Li Hanzhang of Huguang, Governor Guo Boying of Hubei, and Governor Wang Wenxin of Hunan reported to the court, no matter how hard they tried, they simply could not find enough heavy timber in their regions to meet His Majesty's needs. To be sure, both Hubei and Hunan produced fir, cypress, and pine. But a large number of trees, in particular those near rivers or lakes, had been chopped down to build boats and ships during the Taiping War (1851–1865), and lumber still available in local markets was suitable for only making ordinary houses. The single promising news was Governor-General Li Hanzhang's promise to explore the deep forest in Guizhou in the future. "Should we find the timber," Li said, "we would try all possible means to ship it to the imperial capital" (*YMYA* 1991, 1:675–676).

Responses from other provinces were also disappointing. Governor Yang Changjun of Zhejiang stated simply in his April 25, 1874, memorial that nowhere in his province could he find any large timber, as the recent war had effectively reduced to the minimum the number of trees in the province. The shortage of lumber prevented numerous local temples that were destroyed or damaged in the Taiping War from being renovated. Governor Wu Tang of Sichuan admitted to the existence of large pieces of good-quality wood in the remote virgin forest of his province, but the problem was how to get access to them; given the transportation facilities at the time, it was impossible. And Governor-General Ruilin of Liangguang (Guangdong and Guangxi provinces) reported in July that both cypress and fir produced in his region were not firm enough for construction in the Yuanming Yuan; however, he thought it was feasible to import foreign wood via Hong Kong and Macau (*YMYA* 1991, 1:678–680, 700–702, 710–712).

The desperate search for much needed heavy timber eventually provoked a scandal so large that it compelled the Tongzhi emperor to call off all construction. Li Guangzhao, a fifty-one-year-old Cantonese merchant with a purchased title, approached the Imperial Household in 1873 to respond to the imperial decree calling for the renovation of the Yuanming Yuan.[4] He would present several thousand pieces of various sorts of hardwood worth several hundred thousand taels of silver, which he had collected for decades. What was more, in a period of ten years, he could deliver 100,000 taels of wood to the garden for renovation projects. He expected no rewards but tax exemption while transporting the materials to their destination. Additionally, he requested the company of authorized officials as well as permission to solicit contributions and cooperation around the country. Then on July 10, 1874, he reported that he had purchased, while traveling overseas, 1,500 pieces of foreign timber plus 550 pieces of planks at the value of 300,000 taels, and they were due to arrive in Tianjin. The overjoyed director of the Imperial Household recommended tax exemption for the cargo that would be used for repairs in the garden (*YMYA* 1991, 1:726–730).

Governor-General Li Hongzhang (1823–1901) of Zhili at Tianjin, however, soon accused Li Guangzhao of swindling. The latter had indeed purchased timber from a French merchant, but the price was a mere 54,000 taels of foreign silver, only 40 percent of the price he had claimed. Accordingly, the Grand Council, the highest decision-making body in the Qing government, asked the governor-general to look into the matter in consultation with the French and American legations in Tianjin (*YMYA* 1991, 1:736–738). The investigation confirmed that Li Guangzhao, who took advantage of the emperor's eagerness to acquire hardwood, had cheated Chinese officials and foreign businessmen. He was put on trial and sentenced to death on September 28, 1974. During the trial, the condemned man implicated several high-ranking officials in the Imperial Household and perhaps even the throne. The greatly embarrassed Imperial Court quickly controlled the damage by dismissing Chenglin, the Imperial Household man who had actually accompanied Li Guangzhao to South China, and by severely punishing two directors of the Imperial Household, namely, Guibao and Chonglun, (*YMYA* 1991, 1:741–742, 747, 750, 752).

The widely publicized scandal encouraged the voice of opposition in officialdom. The scandal was no doubt caused by the emperor's preoccupation with garden construction. On August 1, 1874, Yang Jun boldly memorialized to the throne that all construction inside the imperial garden should be stopped at once, lest the state treasury go bankrupt. The astronomical cost of renovation at a time of impoverished resources, however well intentioned, would threaten the very survival of the dynasty. On August 27, Governor Bao Yuanshen of Shanxi province also requested the emperor to transform his "filial devotion" into concerns about the general well-being of all people by the immediate termination of the garden projects (*YMYA* 1991, 1:731–732; 738–739).

Only two days after Governor Bao had delivered his memorial, on August 29, Prince Gong made a petition to the throne which was endorsed by three other princes, two grand secretaries (Wenxiang and Baoyun), and two members of the Grand Council (Shen Guifen and Li Hongzao). These representatives of the highest echelon of the government spoke in one clear voice on several key points. First, the Board of Finance could no longer pay the estimated ten to twenty million taels of silver demanded by the Imperial Household for garden construction. Second, the resentment in and out of the government over the renovation of the Yuanming Yuan was too profound to ignore. And third, a modest refurbishment of the Sanhai resorts, namely, Beihai, Zhonghai, and Nanhai in the neighborhood of the Forbidden City to accommodate the two dowagers appeared far more realistic (*YMYA* 1991, 1:739, 740). To highlight the urgency of the matter, they asked for an audience with His Majesty soon after he read the petition. The audience was granted; however, the emperor was extremely confrontational. Wu Rulun (1840–1903) recounted this tense and fiery episode of a type that was rarely seen in Qing history:

> When Prince Gong was reading his prepared statement, the Tongzhi emperor suddenly interrupted him and said angrily: "Fine! Let us stop all projects right now; what else you have to say?" Prince Gong replied: "What we have to say in the statement is not just about stopping the projects. Let me read it to you aloud." The emperor, though allowing the prince to finish his statement, was so provoked that he shouted a quite extraordinary remark to the prince: "How about I yield this throne to you!" [Clearly shocked by this unexpected remark], the Grand Secretary Wenxiang, shaking and choking, brought himself to his knees and collapsed. He was escorted out of the court. The emperor then pressed Prince Chun, who was already in tears, to reveal the source about his embarrassing secret trip to [the construction site at] the Yuanming Yuan. When the prince told him the exact time and place, His Majesty was visibly stunned. When he finally restored himself from rage, he said candidly that the purpose of renovating the Yuanming Yuan was not at all for his personal pleasure but really for two dowagers. He would have to consult with the dowagers before making his final decision.[5]

The emperor's remark at the end was very truthful. Of the two dowagers, Cixi had the strongest interest in the Yuanming Yuan. Her pressure on the throne was beyond doubt, and she was really the one with whom Tongzhi had to consult. By this time, no one had ever underestimated her power in the course of events, and her power continued to grow. On behalf of the throne, Li Hongzao, the Imperial Tutor, first met with the dowagers. The revered Li in his sincere talk to the ladies struck an alarming note: the continuation of construction inside the Yuanming Yuan would almost surely blemish and injure both the emperor and his dynasty (Li Zongtong and Liu Fenghan 1969, 1:211–212).

This blunt talk by a highly prestigious scholar-official worked. On September 9, 1874, the Tongzhi emperor came to his senses. Apparently with the consent of the dowagers, he summoned his two uncles to the court in the company of several top-ranking officials. In front of them, he announced his decision to postpone all construction in the garden for ten to twenty years until the recovery of the financial conditions of the dynasty (Weng Tonghe 1970, 7:2835). Postponement rather than cancellation was clearly for the sake of saving face. No one at the time saw any prospect of resuming the renovation of the Yuanming Yuan at all. The official edict issued on the same day reads:

> The Imperial Household under my direction to renovate the Yuanming Yuan selectively was to please the dowagers and to satisfy my filial devotion. After the construction had started early this year, I personally visited the site several times

and realized how enormous the project was and why it could not be completed as scheduled. Our scarce resources, unbalanced finances, continuous military campaigns, and natural disasters in different provinces made the dowagers feel uncomfortable to continue the garden project. I hereby authorize the termination of all construction work [in the Yuanming Yuan] until the dynasty's security is reassured and treasury replenished. Meanwhile I shall request the directors in [the imperial Household] to start a minor refurbishment at Sanhai in the neighborhood of [the Forbidden City for the retirement of the dowagers].[6]

The emperor's decision to postpone construction was clearly made very reluctantly. When the renovation officially came to an end, a sum of 4,810,000 taels of silver had already been consumed (Liu Dunzheng 1982, 359–364). This sum of money, of course, bore some fruit. The grounds were largely cleaned up, and the trees and rocks looked "as beautiful as before," as the Sichuanese poet Mao Cheng reported from his visit in 1877. Almost all structures in the Double Cranes Chapel were restored to perfect condition. But most other structures of the original Forty Views remained in disrepair. The unused timber and rocks were stored, and the hoisted heavy roof beams at the Ancestral Shrine were dismantled for preservation (cited in *YMYZ* 1984, 319).

The Rebirth of the Pure Ripple Garden

The Tongzhi emperor accepted the harsh reality, but he was vindictive and henceforth dismissed no fewer than ten high-ranking officials who had voiced their objections to renovating the Yuanming Yuan. He even accused Prince Gong of sowing discord between the throne and the dowagers, a very serious charge, and thus stripped the prince of his inherited rank on September 10, 1874, disregarding the earnest plea for leniency by the influential Manchu nobleman Wenxiang. Only after the intervention of Cixi on the following day did the emperor withdraw his earlier decision to punish his uncle (*YMYA* 1991, 1:744–746).

The Tongzhi emperor died suddenly on January 12, 1875, at the age of nineteen, and the Sanhai project was called off three days later. Cixi handpicked her four-year-old nephew Zai Tian (1871–1908) to succeed the throne to be the Guangxu emperor. With the death of Cian, she was now the only dowager sitting behind the screen to hear state affairs. As her power and influence grew, she came up to the front and developed her own plan for garden construction. Besides refurbishing Sanhai, she decided to renovate the Pure Ripple Garden, a subsidiary garden of the Yuanming Yuan.

The Pure Ripple Garden, which had taken fifteen years, from 1750 to 1764, and 4,480,000 taels to complete, was built by the Qianlong emperor in his mother's honor and for her pleasure (Yu Mingzhong 1985, 3:1391). It is sited at a scenic location between the beautiful Longevity Hills and the Kunming Lake. The lake, large and clean, supplied ample water to all royal gardens in the area, for which an extensive network of canals was built leading all the way to the Gaoliang Bridge near the west gate of Beijing. Commonly, Qianlong spent his days in the Pure Ripple Garden and returned to the Yuanming Yuan before sunset (Zhang Jiaji 1986, 160; Liu Tong and Yu Yizheng 1980, 307–308).

Cixi focused on the Pure Ripple Garden with good reason. She was surely impressed by its attractive hills and lake, and perhaps more important, it was not so severely damaged as the Yuanming Yuan, so less money would be spent on renovation. Having made up her mind, she lost no time in instructing the Imperial Household that she wished to see the garden renovated in time to celebrate her fiftieth birthday in 1888. Interestingly, virtually no opposition to the project came from officialdom. The dowager apparently had fully established her dictatorial "female rule," which was formidable enough to deter any voice of dissension.

The dowager herself was very much involved in the renovation of the Pure Ripple Garden. She watched the progress of construction closely; frequently, she took part in designs or redesigns. It was, for instance, exclusively her idea to rebuild the famous Marble Boat at the Kunming Lake, which had been severely damaged by the foreign intruders in 1860. The structure symbolizes the Confucian wisdom that the boat, referring to the government, could be either supported or overturned by the water, referring to the people, underlining the importance of the people to the government (Qianlong's remark quoted in Yu Mingzhong 1985, 3:1399–1400).

The budget for this renovation was not officially released; however, it was estimated to be from 30 to 80 million taels. Where did she get the money to finance her garden project? According to Duan Qirui (1865–1936), the prominent Beiyang leader, "[Li Hongzhang] had raised 30 million taels for purchasing ironclads, and yet the real power holder [Cixi] used them for the purpose of garden construction" (cited in Xu Fengtong 1986, 61). It seems most likely that she diverted most of the funds from the treasury of the Beiyang Navy to spend on the renovation of the Pure Ripple Garden. As if to thank the navy, she included a naval training school in her budget, plus the marble boat, near the Kunming Lake on January 27, 1887. But the marble boat did not float, and Cixi was later blamed for the fall of the navy in the 1894–1895 war with Japan (Liang Qichao 1926, 19:50a–50b).

In any event, the Pure Ripple Garden was reborn on March 13, 1888, with a new name, the Yihe Yuan (Cheerful Harmony Garden), officially announced by the Guangxu emperor. The dowager then made the garden her home until her death in 1908.

Overall, the Yihe Yuan was a renovated Pure Ripple Garden with minor modifications in order to improve its original design. Meticulous effort was made to integrate all buildings and scenic settings into proper spatial relationships. Piled rockeries were artistically formulated, and the picturesque atmosphere of naturalistic settings and the poetic spirit of man-made artifacts were skillfully arranged for interest.

The Yihe Yuan, approximately 3.4 square kilometers in scale, rivals the Yuanming Yuan in terms of architectural excellence and artistic taste. Also like the Yuanming Yuan, the garden served administrative function in addition to providing enjoyment and pleasure for its residents. Moreover, it comprised the Kunming Lake and the Longevity Hills. This renovated garden seemed to have satisfied the dowager's pleasure in garden living. More important,

this specific garden and its beautiful scenes have survived to this day and hence provide us with an invaluable source for understanding the imperial gardens of the Qing dynasty.[7]

The layout of the Yihe Yuan can be generally described as follows. The well-known Buddha Flagrance Pavilion (Foxiang Ge), sitting on a 20-meter-tall rock—the "Tower City," rising 41 meters from halfway up the central front slope of the Longevity Hills—is a typical wooden, octagonal four-story complex of pavilions. Its main court, surrounded by the Divine Land of Buddha, which the Qianlong emperor named the Temple of Great Gratitude and Longevity, made manifest the style of design of the Qianlong reign (Qianlong's inscription cited in Yu Mingzhong 1985, 3:1396–1398). This particular pavilion cost 7.8 million taels of silver to repair. After completion, it was renamed the Cloud-Rising Court (Paiyun Dian); it is covered with bright yellow *liuli* tile and faces the large lake crossed by a white marble bridge. This court became the dowager's main residence. From a distance, the waterfront, the tall *pailou* gate, the front gate, the marble bridge, the inner gate, and the Cloud-Rising Court come into view in gradual elevation.

The Sweeping Pavilion (Kuoru Ting), an octagon consisting of three layers of columns, of which twenty-four are round and sixteen square, is the largest pavilion in the Yihe Yuan.

It is situated at the southern end of the Seventeen-Hole Bridge (Shiqikong Qiao) and occupies 130 square meters of land. The pavilion's double eaves extend sharply upward on all sides and make a magnificent view. This unique pavilion, according to the Manchu prince Fu Jie, symbolizes a gigantic tent, a reminder of the nomadic life of the Manchu ancestors (cited in Xu Fengtong 1986, 54).

The Luxuriant Pavilion (Hui Ting), a pair of hexagonal pavilions, is located at the east hilltop of the Yihe Yuan. It is said that the dowager often came here to observe the full moon in mid-August, especially admiring the shadows of the two pavilions cast by bright moonlight coming together with those of the persons on the ground. When the full moon slowly moves up from east to west, it is said, all the shadows converge to become one big shadow, suggesting a feeling of being as perfect as the full moon.

The Bronze Pavilion (Tong Ting), also known as the Precious Cloud Pavilion (Baoyun Ge), has been praised as a wonderful piece of architecture. The pavilion was built entirely of bronze, weighing 207 tons and standing 7.5 meters high on a large white marble terrace. It was first built during Qianlong's time and survived the 1860 disaster, even though most of its interior decorations were stolen except for a bronze table. After Cixi had it repaired, Lama priests regularly assembled here to recite Buddhist scripts and to pray for the royal family at the beginning and the middle of every month.

Lama Buddhism, popular among Mongols and Tibetans, had also drawn great attention of the Qing rulers since the beginning of the dynasty. The religion no doubt served political needs by helping to control the Mogolian and Tibetan populations. Thanks to the blessing of the Manchu dynasty, numerous Lama temples rose in west Beijing. The Qianlong emperor constructed a huge complex of Lama monasteries on the back slope of the Longevity Hills, covering an area of about 20,000 square meters. The design conveys the Buddhist view of the universe. The courtyards in this complex, two pairs of them, symbolize four Buddhist continents represented by four different colored pagodas, namely, red, white, green, and black. They also represent four sets of Buddhist wisdom, and the two contrasting terraces suggest the sun and the moon surrounding the Buddhist world (*YMYJ* 1987, 3:150–161). All of the structures on the back slope were burned to the ground in 1860, and they were not renovated as a part of the Yihe Yuan. A few surviving Buddha statues were stored in a hall on the ruins.

The famous Long Promenade (Chang Lang) in the Yihe Yuan, winding and undulating 728 meters from east to west in 273 sections with four octagonal pavilions in between, presents many different scenes to a viewer walking along its path. The dowager was immensely proud of this unique structure; indeed, this is arguably the most ingenious design of all in the Yihe Yuan. A viewer seated inside the promenade can enjoy the blowing snow on lake and hills and hear the sounds of rain on a misty day. The entire promenade looks like a long and colorful silk braid, which binds together the hills and the lake with the various structures dotting the landscape. Before the 1860 inferno burned the promenade to the ground, more than 8,000 Suzhou-style colorful drawings hung from the beams, showing flowers, birds, landscapes, 500 unidentified flying cranes, and human figures telling popular stories from well-known Chinese novels and folk traditions (Xin Wensheng 1998). The drawings in meticulous brushwork had been painted in different periods of time since the Qianlong emperor, who asked his artists to copy the best views he had admired during his many southern tours. The solid foundation of the promenade made reconstruction in 1888 relatively easy, even though the priceless paintings in it could never be restored to their original excellence.[8]

The Yihe Yuan has numerous bridges. On the large Kunming Lake alone, there are more than thirty bridges. The longest is the famous Seventeen-Hole Bridge, stretching out like a rainbow about 150 meters long and 8 meters wide to connect the lake's east bank with the southern lake isles. On its railings stand 500 stone lions in different postures (Qiao Yun 1988, 33). A life-size bronze buffalo, an excellent piece of sculpture with fine inscriptions dating back to the Qianlong period, stands on the east side of the bridge. The bronze buffalo is here, according to the popular legend, in order to "keep down" the flood. Its sheer size and weight prevented it from being removed from the scene during the sacking of the Yuanming Yuan. The Jade Belt Bridge (Yudai Qiao), one of the six bridges connecting a long embankment on the west side of the lake to the rest of the garden, is a white stone arch bridge rising so high above the water that tall dragon barges could sail under it easily.

Figure 41. The Long Promenade in the Yihe Yuan. Sketch by Joseph C. Wang and Xingbai Yue.

The dowager completed the Yihe Yuan in time to celebrate her fiftieth birthday. She then made the garden her permanent home and on every tenth day of the tenth month according to the lunar calendar threw a lavish birthday party to entertain well-wishers. The birthday celebrations normally lasted for a week, during which the profusely decorated garden was the setting for endless banquets and entertainment. The emperor and many high-ranking officials would arrive at the Cloud-Rising Court to perform the kowtow in front of her and to present her with written and oral congratulatory remarks. Cixi's sixtieth birthday in 1894 had been planned as a unique event, for which a special commission of princes was created. The scale of celebration was compatible with that for Qianlong's birthday, including colorful and elaborate decorations on the road from the Forbidden City to the Yihe Yuan. But her time was not Qianlong's. The outbreak of the Sino-Japanese War in 1894 and China's humiliating defeat less than a year later spoiled her well-planned birthday party. Under the circumstances, she had to scale down the level of celebration greatly. She received some compensation in 1897, for that year's birthday party included an eight-day program of Peking opera to be performed on the stages of various theaters in the Yihe Yuan. For this party, she spent a sum of money worth 324,000,000 kilograms of rice at the time, not counting the expensive gifts presented to her by officials from all over the country (cf. Xu Fengtong 1986, 76).

From 1888 to her death in 1908, Cixi was the real power behind the throne. She used the Yihe Yuan as her headquarters, especially after the 1898 coup, to conduct state affairs much as earlier Qing rulers used the Yuanming Yuan. Her living quarters, also the hub of the garden, comprised a large quadrangle *(sihe yuan),* or a compound of forty-nine large and small houses at the east end of the Long Promenade. The courtyard of this compound sits on a 3,000–square-meter lot laying behind the Longevity Hills and facing the Kunming Lake. The dowager named her principal ten-room living hall the Enjoying Longevity Hall (Leshou Tang) and her audience hall the Longevity for Benevolence Court (Renshou Dian), comparable to the Main Audience Hall in the Yuanming Yuan. In the open space in the courtyard, she placed a bronze *kylin* (a Chinese unicorn symbolizing auspiciousness) taken from the Yuanming Yuan. Inside the court at the center of the hall, she hung a large horizontal board inscribed with four large characters: *"shou xie ren fu"* (Longevity Assists Benevolence). On each side of the front door hung two gigantic vertical scrolls printed with one hundred bats, each holding the word "longevity" *(shou).* The large screen behind her desk was inscribed with two hundred differently styled characters of *shou.* Benevolence and longevity were obviously as much cherished by Cixi as other rulers in Chinese history.[9]

One still can see in this hall two "Dragon Seats" *(longyi)* made of precious sandalwood, each of which was engraved with nine lively dragons, the symbol of imperial China. The dowager and the emperor each occupied a seat when they jointly granted audiences in the garden. Clearly, in an informal setting such as the Yihe Yuan, the dowager could disregard strict formality and sit equally with the emperor. In a more formal place like the court in the Forbidden City, however, she would have to sit behind the emperor's throne separated by a silk screen, even though the emperor was her mere puppet.

The dowager must have greatly enjoyed the beauty of the Yihe Yuan, surrounded by a large lake and green hills. Very often she went boating on the Kunming Lake just as Yongzheng and Qianlong had done on the Sea of Blessing. She also loved rock formations, and behind the hills at the courtyard of her living quarters, she used them to accompany precious trees and rare flowers. Also like Qianlong, during the blossom season, she was fascinated by the spectacular magnolia. Like Daoguang, she was a great opera fan. She built the Grand Theater (Da'xitai) in the Yihe Yuan to entertain herself constantly (Xu Fengtong 1986, 13–14, 104–107). Hence, she seemed to have forgotten the nearby Yuanming Yuan, which was in ruins.

In 1896, Li Hongzhang, having made his around-the-world trip, reported to the dowager in the Yihe Yuan. Afterward, Li stopped by the Yuanming Yuan for a short visit; but the eunuch-guards would not let him in and later accused him of being an intruder. When the dowager did not take the matter seriously, the eunuchs appealed to the Guangxu emperor for action. The emperor's teacher and confidant Weng Tonghe, a political rival of Li, recommended to strip the offender of his "First-Class Honor" *(sanyan hualing)* as punishment. Even though the emperor consented, the dowager overruled the decision by reducing the punishment to a fine of one year's stipend (Cheng Yansheng 1928, 27b–28a).

A recent writer believes that Li simply stepped into the desolated garden out of curiosity on his way. The punishment for Li was really revenge for Li's earlier exposition of the scandal that resulted in Tongzhi's prompt termination of all construction in the Yuanming Yuan (Wu Xiangxiang 1964, 173). Perhaps the close guarding of the Yuanming Yuan might have been an attempt to conceal the fact that some sorts of construction had been going on inside the davastated garden. Indeed, as some records show, both the dowager and the emperor visited the Yuanming Yuan regularly from 1886 to 1898, presumably for supervision and inspection. The Imperial Household's budget for the fiscal year of 1897, for example, allocated as much as 96,500 taels for the Yuanming Yuan (*YMYZ* 1984, 381–382; cf. Wu Xiangxiang 1964, 171). This may suggest that the complete halt to construction inside the Yuanming Yuan was more apparent than real.

The Second Blow and Consequences

The partially repaired Yuanming Yuan would have been much better preserved had it not suffered a second major blow during the Boxer Rebellion in 1900, which "invited" the invasion of China by eight major powers in the world.[10] The dowager Cixi fled with the emperor to Xi'an on August 5, 1900, once again leaving Beijing at the mercy of foreign invaders. The invaders of 1900, even more numerous and vicious than those of 1860, repeated the pattern of plundering and burning but in much greater scope and duration.

The sites of looting included the homes of the wealthy and those of Manchu nobility. The looters were not just troops but also diplomats and even missionaries. W. A. P. Martin saw on the spot that the scramble of looters could only be described as a riot "in the midst of booty" (Martin 1900, 134; cf. Dillon 1901, 28–30). Numerous Chinese prisoners were also brutally treated and mercilessly shot. The reports and testimonies of the extreme brutality made a contemporary American writer feel that "the Chinese were treated as Christians were in the reign of Nero" (Dillon 1901, 18). Noteworthy, just about a year later, all the eight invading powers joined the Hague Convention of 1899, which clearly outlawed the wartime legality of plunder and wanton killing.

Both the newly built Yihe Yuan and the crippled Yuanming Yuan were victimized. The allies easily captured and occupied Beijing, and the energetic German cavalrymen chased the beaten army of Dong Fuxiang deep into Inner Mongolia. On their way back, the Germans camped in northwest Beijing with the English and Italian troops. They plundered all of the gardens in the neighborhood, including the Yuanming Yuan. They took doors and window frames from the Yuanming Yuan for fuel when winter arrived (cf. Wang Wei 1992, 59–60). In the end, all of the repairs completed since the 1870s were totally obliterated. As in 1860, to share the loot, a prize commision was established and an auction market opened at the British legation (cf. Barrow 1942, 64).

Upon the eventual withdrawal of the foreign troops, native bandits, thieves, and riffraff seized a period of anarchy to rob whatever they deemed valuable. Even Manchu bannermen, who were supposed to secure all of the royal gardens, participated in looting. On September 7, 1900, for instance, over one hundred bannermen, disregarding the warnings of the Yuanming Yuan guards, intruded into the round-shaped Mind-Opening Isle in the Eternal Spring Garden with axes and shovels in hand. They destroyed the wooden bridge leading to the isle, but they were driven back by the guards, and scores of them were killed. Nevertheless, sixteen bannermen returned a week later, when lakes in the garden were frozen solid. They robbed the Yuanming Yuan at will, tore down buildings, carted away useful wooden material, and chopped down huge pines and cypresses for profit. This wanton destruction spared virtualiy no halls and chambers in the garden. The stolen materials, from pillars to frames, were piled up like a "small mountain" for sale in the nearby market at Qinghe. Even small pieces of wood and tree branches taken away from the garden found a market after being burned into charcoal. In the end, the structures, especially those made of wood, and trees in the garden simply disappeared. The catastrophe of 1900 leveled the Yuanming Yuan as much as the flames of 1860 consumed it (cf. Zhao Guanghua 1986, 4:13).

The foreign invaders damaged the Yihe Yuan as well. James Ricalton was traveling in China during the Boxer Rebellion. When he walked a mile about the lake inside the Yihe Yuan, he "passed many curious structures, all showing unmistakable signs of the looter and the iconoclast" (Ricalton 1901, 344). Nevertheless, the Yihe Yuan was not so badly burned as was the Yuanming Yuan in 1860. Hence, its renovation was easier and less expensive. In fact, upon the return of the dowager in 1902, it was ready for her to live. She added a peasant hut named the Pleasing Farming Gallery (Lenong Xuan) to be a reminder of her bitter experience in rural China where she had sought refuge (Xu Fengtong 1986, 84). Ostensibly, the catastrophe had made her humble. No longer xenophobic, she now tried to please the foreigners. For example, she began entertaining Western ladies in her lovely garden after 1902.

From this time on, though still having the dynasty under her control, she rarely left the Yihe Yuan, where she died in 1908. The young but fragile Guangxu emperor also lived in the garden, in a chamber surrounded by water, basically under house arrest. He died just a day ahead of her.

The fate of the Yuanming Yuan in the aftermath of the Boxer Rebellion was sealed. The second fatal blow eliminated the feasibility of preserving the garden as a historic site let alone the prospect of renovation. The huge indemnity after the rebellion further strained Qing finances; for instance, in 1904, the Imperial Household had to reduce the number of the guards and eunuchs in the Yuanming Yuan. Even though as many as 16,718 Manchu bannermen remained in the Yuanming Yuan in 1909 (*YMYA* 1991, 1:763), they were mostly members of the former Garden Household, including women and children, and they were more destroyers than protectors of the Yuanming Yuan.

The decline and fall of the Qing dynasty further exposed the Yuanming Yuan to robbery and destruction. In the early autumn of 1911, Tan Yankai (1879–1930), president of the provincial assembly of Hunan, could no longer see the scenes observed by Wang Kaiyun in 1870. All that he could see were wild grass and disorderly rocks. The only remaining structures were but half-fallen Baroque buildings at the northern end of the Eternal Spring Garden (cited in *YMYZ* 1984, 334; cf. Cheng Yansheng 1928, 21b). They remained visible only because of their solid brick and marble foundations. They could have been renovated relatively easily, according to a famous European architect, as late as 1914, but China's deplorable conditions at the time made any historical preservation efforts virtually impossible (Danby 1950, 224). Without preservation, the half-fallen Baroque buildings gradually collapsed; eventually, only few large marble pieces remained. A set of twenty photographs taken by Ernest Ohlmer in the 1870s, which was published in 1933, appears especially precious in viewing the physical appearance of these European buildings.[11]

The transition of China from monarchy to republic did not affect the status of the Yuanming Yuan. The Xuantong emperor (Henry Puyi), the last Manchu ruler, was allowed to keep his court inside the Forbidden City and he retained title to all his properties, including the imperial gardens, as part of the abdication agreement of 1912. The Yuanming Yuan continued to be supervised by the Imperial Household. But the problem was that the unsettled Republican government could rarely keep its promises. The defenseless royal family easily fell prey to the abusive politicians and ruthless warlords of Republican China; for instance, many of its tombs were being dynamited for the search of treasures. The Yuanming Yuan, though in desolation, was still a target of greedy eyes due to its great fame.

The early Republican authorities openly made requests to the hapless Manchu court in the Forbidden City for interesting objects in the Yuanming Yuan. In 1915, for decorating the newly refurbished Zhengyang Gate in downtown Beijing, the interior minister asked the Imperial Household for permission to remove two rock *kylin* at the Comfortable Hall (Anyi Tang) near the northwest corner of the Yuanming Yuan. In the same year, the Beijing military command wanted artificial hills and rockeries in the Yuanming Yuan. However reluctant, the Imperial Household had no way to reject such requests. Not surprisingly, requests under the circumstances forced the Manchus to respond graciously. At least on one occasion, the Imperial Household, at Puyi's consent, not only gladly granted the request but also voluntarily helped the government to select fifty-one pieces of Taihu rock and ship them from the Yuanming Yuan (*YMYA* 1991, 1:766–769).

The political situation turned from bad to worse following the death of President Yuan Shikai (1859–1916). The social disorder that followed made the protection of the Yuanming Yuan ever more difficult; the desolate garden was virtually subject to open theft. Receiving the reports of the invasion of thieves into the garden by the eunuch supervisor Wang Hexi, Puyi could do nothing but seek assistance from Beijing's government. The police at last captured three thieves who admitted that they had stolen hundreds of rocks in the garden. Before long, however, policemen and even soldiers themselves became the thieves. On an autumn day in 1919, scores of soldiers freely picked up Taihu rocks at the ruins of the Library of Literary Sources and transported them away in dozens of carts. The royal family lodged a strong protest against the military command in Beijing, supposedly the guardian of security, but to no avail (*YMYA* 1991, 1:770–772).

In 1919, Deputy Commander Gao of the Third Artillery Regiment, who was stationed at Xiyuan, committed robbery inside the Yuanming Yuan, and this act of lawlessness provoked Puyi to protest to the Minister of the Army. Reportedly Gao and about a dozen men intruded into the garden and carried out bricks in three carts in broad daylight. Puyi reiterated that the Yuanming Yuan was strictly his private property and was entitled to protection from the authorities, but legal protection becomes meaningless when protectors become bandits. Thus, people in and out of the government continuously violated the integrity of the Yuanming Yuan. A brutal incident took place in 1921 when two regiments of soldiers from the Sixteenth Division beat the guards who tried to block them and forcefully marched into the garden to commit robbery. They tore down the walls in the Wall of Sravasti, took away numerous carts of Taihu rocks, and spent two full days in their plundering. No one dared to stop them; in fact, they laughed at a score of helpless eunuchs when leaving the garden (*YMYA* 1991 1:773–779).

The republic's civilian sectors likewise set their greedy eyes on the Yuanming Yuan. In 1921, the Longquan Orphanage in Beijing pressed Puyi to donate the walls and rocks in the west side of the garden as building materials for constructing its expanded dormitory with the argument that the wasteful materials should be put to good use. In 1922, for building the Morgan Garden on campus, the missionary administrators of Yanjing University requested to move a large quantity of rocks from the neighboring Yuanming Yuan. These two uses may arguably have served the public interest; however, many others simply satisfied personal greed. Later in the same year, Xue Zhiheng, Beijing's police chief, wanted to "borrow" some construction materials from the ruins for his own use. The police chief was not the only influential official to do so. Certain commissioners Xiao and Wan, for example, came to the Yuanming Yuan and shipped out sixty carts of Taihu rocks, disregarding the protest of the supervisor Wang Hexi, the royal family's man on the spot (*YMYA* 1991, 1:780–785).

In an effort to stop the ceaseless drain of materials from the garden, in September 1922, the three directors of the Imperial Household, namely, Shaoying, Chishou, and Baoxi, impressed the commander of the Beijing gendarmerie Wang Huaiqing with the importance of prohibiting anything from being taken out from the ruins. The commander promised to better protect the historic site. Ironically, however, Commander Wang himself had once sent hundreds of workers, with picks, axes, and shovels in hand, into the Yuanming Yuan to tear down the solid ramparts around the Wall of Sravasti, rip the walls at the Ancestral Shrine, and break apart the brick walls of the Baroque buildings. All of these materials were used in Wang's own private garden near Lake Fan (cf. *YMYA* 1991, 1:789–790).

In the spring of 1923, as a letter from the Imperial Household indicates, even the long outer walls surrounding both the north and west sides of the garden were torn down (*YMYA* 1991, 1:800). Shortly afterward, when Beijing was under his sway in 1924, the Manchurian warlord Zhang Zuolin (1873–1928), took a great amount of white marble from the Yuanming Yuan to ship to Liaoning, where he began constructing his future mausoleum. Meanwhile, to build his Emerald Flower Garden, a wealthy German arms dealer also took away various sorts of materials from the Yuanming Yuan. As a result, the walls in the garden disappeared quickly.

After all the walls were torn down, people wanted the land. When Tsing Hua (Qinghua) college started its new academic year in the fall of 1923, President Cao Yunxiang formally asked the royal family to yield the lots neighboring the campus, which were integral parts of the Yuanming Yuan, in order to expand the college. The president believed that granting the land to the college would better serve the purpose of historical preservation. President Cao wished to pay cash for the land; but budgetary restraints prevented him from doing so. Instead, he proposed to offer scholarships specifically to Manchu students amounting to 260,000 *yuan*. The proposal seemed attractive, as there was at the time not a single Manchu student attending this highly prestigious college. Nevertheless, Puyi left the proposal on his desk without a response ostensibly because he was reluctant to sell any part of the land. He knew in so doing the ruins of the Yuanming Yuan would eventually disappear (*YMYA* 1991, 1:803–804).

The integrity of the land had been temporarily preserved, but materials continuously made their way out throughout the year of 1924. Most notably, Wang Lanting, the Beijing government's chief of staff, simply notified the Imperial Household that he needed one hundred carts of rocks and remnants from the artificial hills in the Yuanming Yuan to build his private garden; and the Manchu royal family could not prevent the loss. Then, before the end of the year, a company of cavalrymen camped at the ruins without even bothering to inform Puyi's office. The missionaries who administered Yanjing University stepped into the neighboring Yuanming Yuan in 1925 and simply moved stone pillars and artifacts from the Ancestral Shrine to their campus. When the Manchus asked police to interrogate the missionaries, the reply was that these pieces would be safer on campus. The officials of the Central Park (Zhongshan gongyuan) in downtown Beijing also believed that those remnants left on the site were unsafe, so they suggested to Puyi that the remaining artificial hills and rocks be moved to their park for better preservation. Similar requests were made later on. But the ex-Qing emperor did not believe that relocation was a better alternative (cf. *YMYA* 1991, 1:802–823).

Nevertheless, relocation of some identifiable monuments did take place. Several elegant-looking bronze animals and rocks had earlier found a home in the Yihe Yuan. The new palace gate at the entrance of the Ten-Thousand Spring Garden, which included rooms, decorated walls, arch doors, and stone lions, was sold by an ex-Manchu nobleman to a philanthropic institution for a proposed middle school (*YMYJ* 1987, 4:15). The pillars from the Orchid Pavilion, together with bronze figures, Taihu rocks, and carved stone balustrades, were moved to the Central Park. Some other rock pieces from the Yuanming Yuan were relocated to the Sun Yat-sen Mausoleum in Nanjing. The objects brought to the Yanjing campus, including a pair of white-marble Chinese unicorns, a fountain terrace, several stone screens, a stone bridge, numerous carvings of the European buildings, and three spectacular tall columns with ornamentation, were taken away from the Ancestral Shrine. In 1930, Beijing Library took quite a few objects from the Yuanming Yuan, most noticeably, a pair of ornamental columns taken from the Ancestral Shrine, two stone lions from the Eternal Spring Garden's Grand East Gate, and two pieces of stone inscriptions from the Library of Literary Sources (Wang Wei 1980, 63).

Besides shipments of solid materials in large quantities, there was petty stealing committed by former eunuchs, ex-bannermen, and local residents too numerous to count. Beijing residents in the 1920s witnessed that stone carvings, bronze inscriptions, Taihu rocks, bricks, tiles, and numerous other building materials were carted away from the Yuanming Yuan almost on a daily basis (*YMYJ* 1987, 4:15; *YMYA* 1991, 1:798–802; Wang Wei 1980, 62–64; Danby 1950, 225). No wonder, "in many a humble stone-mason's shop in Peking (Beijing)," as Danby observed in the 1930s, "one can see exquisite pieces of carving on stone or marble, with twining garlands, flowers and foreign motifs. These have come from the European palaces and for a dollar or two they changed hands" (1950, 226).

From this time on, the robbery by men and onslaughts by fire and weather transformed the Yuanming Yuan into a desolate wilderness. In March 1931, in an effort to awaken public interest in historical preservation, the Chinese Association of Architects used the commemoration of the 821st anniversary of the death of the great Song architect Li Mingzhong to host a public exhibition of Yuanming Yuan history and relics. The items shown to the public included maps, models, manuals, rocks, stone inscriptions, documents, poems, and books (*YMYZ* 1984 354–360). The event drew great attention and large crowds; but, given China's sociopolitical condition at the time, historical preservation was easy to discuss while difficult to implement.

Then came the war. With eastern China under Japanese occupation from 1937 to 1945, the starving peasants, ex-eunuchs, and former Manchu bannermen in the neighborhood of Beijing, then called Beiping, dug into the ruins and transformed the Yuanming Yuan into a farmland. Consequently, the hills were leveled and the lakes were either filled with earth or made into fishing ponds. For the first time, the ruins were under the threat of being erased from the face of earth.

After the founding of the People's Republic of China in 1949, no immediate effort to preserve the Yuanming Yuan site was made; instead, the Chinese Academy of Sciences wished to make it a large plantation. Even though the idea did not materialize, the rice fields and farming houses, which had existed for many years, seemed to stay indefinitely. Not until the late 1950s did the state obtain much of the land under requisition; however, it was a formidable task to relocate so many farming households. The situation actually worsened during three famine years from 1959 to 1961, when many more peasants occupied and used the land. The Yuanming Yuan thus encountered a renewed threat of annihilation. More hills were leveled and its lakes were filled in; huts were built in increasing numbers, and roads were willfully paved.

The fury of the Cultural Revolution, which covered the decade from 1966 to 1976, rendered still more damage to the Yuanming Yuan ruins. During these years of turmoil, about 800 meters of broken walls were taken away, 1,000 trees were cut down, and no less than 528 carts of stone materials were removed (*YMYJ* 1987, 4:16). What was more, professors and students of Peking University, as they later testified, went to the site to do farm work at the orders of the Red Guards. As the revolution progressed, rice fields, factories, schools, target grounds, and pastures spread all over the ruins. The revolution, however, did not last long enough to erase the historic site entirely. Miraculously, a single structure named Zhengjue Si, a Lama Buddhist temple, even survived, though in bad disrepair. Consisting of a dormitory for Lama priests and a few pavilions in which to store Buddhist statues, this temple was first built by the Qianlong emperor in the eighteenth century. It escaped the fire of 1860; it was occupied by the Boxers in 1900 and then by German troops in 1901. Both occupants used its doors for fuel. In the 1910s, the influential Republican politician Yan Huiqing dispersed the priests, removed the statues, and made the temple part of his country home. Many beautiful tall pine trees nearby the temple were sold to Tsing Hua University for constructing a housing project. For two decades from the 1960s, the Haidian Machine Factory continuously cut down old pines surrounding the temple to build workshops and apartments (*YMYJ* 1987, 4:17).

Historical preservation finally returned to the agenda at the end of the Cultural Revolution in 1976. A special office was created to look after the ruins. In August 1980, the Chinese government finally proclaimed that the Yuanming Yuan grounds were designated national "key relics" subject to state protection. The endless blows to the ruins at last came to a halt.

THE YUANMING YUAN RUINS PARK

REGARDLESS OF THE relentless natural and human assaults since the turn of the century, miraculously, the ruins of the Yuanming Yuan have survived to this day. The latest crisis was the tumultuous Cultural Revolution, during which farms, factories, and schools were established in the ruins, rendering damage to the landscape. The conclusion of the revolution in 1976 came in time to prevent the prospect of erasing the ruins entirely. Even more important, the bitter experiences of violence and destruction gave rise to a much stronger sense of treasuring cultural relics and of historical preservation. As a result, in 1976, the Yuanming Yuan Management Office (Yuanming Yuan Guanlichu) came into existence with the clear intention of keeping the ruins intact. Under protection, the ruins have since been open to the public, and the number of tourists, including foreigners from Japan, the United States, Britain, and Sweden, has risen dramatically since 1980 (*YMYJ* 1987 1:21–22).

In 1980, a comprehensive survey of the ruins was carried out, yielding 5,200 *mou* (786 acres) in total: 1,400 *mou* (212 acres) covered with trees, 360 *mou* (55 acres) of reed ponds, and 200 *mou* (30 acres) of ruins. The other 60 percent can be broken down as follows: 1,200 *mou* (182 acres) of rice fields, 70 *mou* (11 acres) of reservoirs, 800 *mou* (121 acres) of farmland, 360 *mou* (55 acres) of huts, 480 *mou* (73 acres) of factories, schools, warehouses, offices, and shooting ranges, and 150 *mou* (23 acres) of roads. Numerous rock hills were leveled during the Cultural Revolution, and fewer than half of the original two hundred fifty survived (*YMYJ* 1987, 1:22).

The survey disclosed also that many "units" *(danwei)* had occupied the site. They included twenty villages consisting of at least 2,000 farmers, the Number 101 Middle School, the Municipal Chemical Engineering Institute, the District Military Shooting Range, a duck farm, and the District Machine Factory. The machine factory alone occupied 350 *mou* (53 acres) of the ruins. The presence of these "units," together with their construction projects, if not stopped, would surely threaten the obscured foundations of the original structures on the site. Many of the foundations, as the surveyors discovered, had already become difficult to identify. An urgent concern was to determine how to stop the encroachment on valuable historic sites and to prevent their total destruction. The best way to ensure historical preservation, it was determined, was to remove the occupants from the sites; however, this task proved to be the most difficult (cf. *YMYJ* 1987, 1:21–24).

The Yuanming Yuan issue gained nationwide attention in the autumn of 1980 when a large number of political leaders, scholars of renown, noted architects, and distinguished artists expressed their great concern about how to preserve the ruins. They obtained 1,583 signatures on a public statement calling for "protection, reparation, and utilization of the Yuanming Yuan ruins" (*YMYJ* 1987, 1:1–6).

Shortly afterward, seizing the opportunity to commemorate the 120th anniversary of the burning of the Yuanming Yuan, the Chinese Association of Architects featured a large symposium in Beijing on August 13 to 19, 1980. Participants reached consensus that the best way to preserve the ruins was to renovate some scenes and structures on the site, since leaving the ruins as they were would inevitably lead to further destruction in the face of urbanization and modernization. In an effort to promote effective historical preservation, a preparatory committee was born on October 17, 1980, to make sure the Yuanming Yuan Institute (Yuanming Yuan Xuehui) would be formally established as a permanent organization at the earliest possible date (*YMYJ* 1987, 1:230).

The Yuanming Yuan Institute was at last inaugurated at a Haidian theatre on December 1, 1984. Some four hundred men and women, including many high-ranking officials, observed the opening ceremony. A constitution *(zhangcheng)* was drafted to underline the extraordinary value of the garden sites; goals were to enrich national cultural life, enhance patriotic education, and facilitate tourism and international friendship. This plan coincided with the promotion of Chinese "spiritual civilization" *(jingshen wenming)*. Accordingly, preserving the historical ruins of the Yuanming Yuan became a national priority. The Yuanming Yuan Institute, however, sought for more than mere preservation. Comprising several entities such as the Academic Committee (Yuanming Yuan Xueshu Weiyuanhui), the Chinese Yuanming Yuan Foundation (Zhongguo Yuanming Yuan Jijinhui), the Yuanming Yuan Development Company (Yuanming Yuan Guihuasheji Gongsi), and the Yuanming Yuan Management Agency (Yuanming Yuan Guanlixietiao Weiyuanhui), the institute's purposes included research, cultural activities, and construction (cf. *YMYJ* 1987, 4:2–3).

Few people taking part in the symposium or in the founding of the institute failed to notice the importance of protecting the ruins from further encroachment and of cleaning them immediately, in particular the more visible ruins at the old European section. No agreement, however, emerged that the Yuanming Yuan should be renovated, or, if so, how and to what extent. The debate was quite intensive. Those who opposed substantial renovation cited the scarcity of national resources and insisted that precious money instead should be spent on desperately needed apartment buildings for ordinary people. A few participants even compared eager advocates of renovation to the Empress Dowager Cixi, who diverted much-needed naval funds to renovate the Pure Ripple Garden, renaming it the Yihe Yuan.

Every person in the debate knew that revival of the Yuanming Yuan's past glory would require an astronomical amount of money. Calculations based on the cost of renovating man-made structures in the Chengde Summer Mountain Retreat, excluding the cost of interior renovations, yield 500,000 *yuan* per square meter. Providing that the renovation of the main structures of the Yuanming Yuan would include 160,000 square meters, the price tag could easily reach 160 million *yuan,* or approximately U.S. $114 million according to the exchange rate in 1980 (Wang Zhili 1983, 14). Such estimates no doubt played into the hands of those who opposed massive renovation. But, on the other hand, the renovation advocates did not abandon their enthusiasm, even though they acknowledged the paucity of national resources. They based their arguments on national pride and patriotism.

Finally, a compromise view prevailed. The general consensus was that the desolate Yuanming Yuan should at least be transformed into an impressive memorial park by renovating some of the essential structures. This majority viewpoint can best be seen in the proposal drafted by Wang Zhili, a man who was actively involved in launching the Yuanming Yuan Institute from the beginning. He suggested that in principal the renovation of any old structure should accommodate changes or modifications to suit contemporary needs. He reminded his peers that changes in design and blueprint had been made frequently in the architectural history of the Yuanming Yuan. This being the case, however, he quickly added that the general layout of the garden should never be altered, especially the fundamental arrangement of the lakes, canals, hills, building sites, and several dozen of the famous scenes. In Wang's view, it was simply and importantly necessary to retain the authenticity and integrity of the original garden. On the other hand, there was no need to renovate many highly significant structures of the past, such as the Main Audience Hall, the royal living quarters on the Nine Continents, Buddhist temples, and Daoist shrines. In their place, there would be more space for trees, flowers, and grass and for constructing modern facilities, such as paved roads, food outlets resting areas, electricity, drainage works, security and antipollution devices, service departments, exhibitions, entertainment, and other cultural facilities (Wang Zhili 1983, 6, 8–10).

For those who were concerned about the Yuanming Yuan in the 1980s, any form of limited renovation would help prevent the historic site from further deterioration. With the support of the state and the prospects of tourism, a long-range plan began with constructing enclosures and cleaning the grounds. The immediate problem, however, was to secure the land legally before enforcing the evacuation of the large number of occupants. Relocating all of the huts, factories, and schools was a formidable task, to say the least. The peasants who depended on the land for living were especially difficult to deal with. A solution was at last found in offering material incentives to the occupants, which was possible in large extent due to the reforms of Deng Xiaoping. As a result, the occupants, whether peasants or workers, changed their professions by joining hands in "developing" *(kaifa)* the ruins as a profitable business. They became the partners of the newly founded Yuanming

Yuan Development Company (*YMYJ* 1987, 4:231–232; cf. Wang Zhili 1986, 8–10). The occupants' roles were thus reversed; instead of damaging the site, they labored to create a pleasant Yuanming Yuan Ruins Park (Yuanming Yuan Yizi Gongyuan). Finally, under a clear sky on August 10, 1983, the ruins park officially laid new foundations (*YMYJ* 1987, 3:211).

As a result, large-scale repair work was started in 1984. The opening ceremony at the site on December 1, 1984 assembled thousands of people and drew the attention of the international press. The goal was to create a more impressive park, and priority was given to the European section at the northern end of the Eternal Spring Garden. The decision was made by a group of specialists on the basis of a field report and a conference held in Beijing from July 12 to 14, 1984. Clearly, this particular site was chosen because it retained some visible remnants and rocks from the fallen Baroque buildings, which testified to the history of national humiliation, not to mention that the broken gigantic rock pieces displayed a solemn look. Once these noticeable remnants were cleaned and skillfully arranged, they became a monument to the ruins. Moreover, the solid foundations of many interesting fountains in this section were probably less costly to renovate, and they would surely become a tourist attraction. Profitable tourism, the prospect of which was never in doubt, would in turn generate revenues for further expenditure in the Yuanming Yuan. The only concern that the specialists had in mind at the time was that whatever might be done to the ruin site of the European section, it should not be severed from the rest of the Eternal

Figure 42. The mock ruins of Dashuifa (Great Fountain) in 1986. Photograph by Young-tsu Wong.

Figure 43. A photograph showing the Throne in the European Section in 1986. Photograph by Young-tsu Wong.

Spring Garden. They were obviously most eager to see the preservation of the integrity of all of the Yuanming Yuan ruins (cf. *YMYJ* 1987, 4:186–223).

Even though the European section represents only a small portion of the lost imperial garden, to put it back in even loose order would be costly. Two specialists estimated that it would cost as much as 8.5 million *yuan* (approximately U.S. $2.1 million) (He Chongyi and Zeng Zhaofen 1984, 3:37). Certainly, this sum does not include the cost of renovating all of the European buildings, which the specialists found unnecessary. As early as March 20, 1982, when a symposium was held to discuss this matter, most of the artist and architect participants preferred to leave the broken rocks as they were so as to retain "a pathetic image of the ruins park" (*YMYJ* 1987, 2:176). After more than a decade, the work at the ruins of the European section was completed in 1992. The Chinese public seemed to welcome the effort, as the influx of small donations to show support has continued ever since. Particularly noteworthy, a certain set of Zhao brothers in Hebei, who made a fortune due to rural economic reforms, contributed 30,000 *yuan* to the Yuanming Yuan management agency. Other individual contributions, however small, made manifest the strong public enthusiasm (cf. *YMYJ* 1987, 2:175).

The great fame of the Yuanming Yuan almost instantly attracted large numbers of tourists, Chinese as well as foreign, to visit the park. The number of tourists rose steadily from 7,000 in 1979 to 280,000 by 1984, a thirty-fold increase in five years, and continues to grow. In other words, prior to the formal opening of the park in 1984, over one million people had visited the site (cf. Wang Zhili's speech at a 1984 meeting in *YMYJ* 1987, 4:7). Tourism undoubtedly helps generate money for the park to finance additional projects.

Visiting the Yuanming Yuan again in 1986, I noticed that the ruins park had already been surrounded by newly built four-hundred-meter-long "tiger skin walls" *(hupi qiang)*. Moreover, a paved road had been built from the main entrance to the ruins park, which displayed a few carved marble rocks, the dilapidated Zhengjue Si, a stone bridge, and a number of rearranged hillocks. Most remarkable, perhaps, the famous Sea of Blessing, which had been silted up for decades, was reopened as a beautiful lake on December 1, 1984, and was ready for boating and sailing in 1985 (*YMYJ* 1987, 4:321). Still, visitors would find 20 to 30 percent of the building foundations in this section covered by rugged earth and wild grass. Although many of them, including the broken ones at the edges of the park, had been cleaned and preserved, the precious foundations at the Lion's Cove and the Shopping Street in the southern neighborhood remained hidden, waiting for protection.

No one will dispute the fact that the creation of the park has helped historic preservation. In the process of making the park, numerous farming households on site were successively evacuated on schedule. When I visited the park for the third time in the summer of 1991, no fewer than 1,800 *mou* (273 acres) of the land, or approximately 35 percent of the Yuanming Yuan, had been recovered. Besides the old front gate leading into the European section, a newly built palatial front gate was visible, and the Western-style maze had been rebuilt on the basis of the original scheme. The projects completed between 1986 and 1992 included the palatial gate of the Variegated Spring Garden, about seven thousand meters of walls, the Mind-Opening Isle, the Phoenix Isle, the Other Paradise, the Ornate Garden (Zao Yuan), and dozens of other old scenes. In addition, more than 200,000 trees and over one million flowering plants have since been installed. At this point, within the nearly 3,000,000-hectare lot, which includes the Sea of Blessing and much of the Eternal Spring Garden and the Variegated Garden, a new park has been well-shaped in northwest Beijing.

A new concern, however, may be raised as the park restores more old scenes to attract still more tourists: elements of commercialism are noticeably distracting. The rebuilt man-made structures, whether bridges or houses, often appear poorly constructed woefully lacking in artistic skill, a far cry from the supreme quality of the original craftsmanship that made the architectural wonder of the Yuanming Yuan so famous. For example, a wooden bridge across a stream that I observed in 1991 looks distasteful by any reasonable standard. It seems absolutely inexcusable to construct anything in this once-glorious garden in such a rough and slipshod manner. This sense of disapproval seems to be shared by others. A 1996 newspaper article sharply criticized the sloppy workmanship for quick commercial benefits. The so-called "rising phoenix," as the author put it, has turned out to be a "phony phoenix" (Cong Weixi 1996, 30).

In 1997, the booming city of Shenzhen in the neighborhood of Hong Kong constructed a new Yuanming Yuan (Yuanming Xinyuan), with copies of selected scenes, such as the Nine Continents and the Wonderland in the Square Pot. Evidently, commercialism was the driving force behind the project. Indeed, the first year's revenue of the new Yuanming Yuan reaches as high as RMB 160 million. The lucrative business inspired a new round of debate over the complete renovation of the imperial garden on its original site. Those who opposed it, including many prominent historians and architects, argued that the issue was really how to preserve the ruins of the original architecture in the process of modernization. For them, renovation borders on further destruction of the cultural relics, whereas preservation of the ruins serves both patriotic and aesthetic purposes (Jianmin 1999, 1). Furthermore, one may sound a wake-up call that the excellent skills in traditional Chinese architecture and garden craftsmanship have already been lost. A lost garden can be rebuilt anytime with sufficient funds, but a lost art seems much more difficult to reclaim.

Worse still there are new sorts of intrusions into the Yuanming Yuan ruins site. In the early 1990s, bohemian Chinese set up on the site the so-called Yuanming Yuan Village for Artists. Since 1996, an extensive residential complex has been constructed in the ruins neighborhood. For example, a real estate company in Haidian started a joint venture to construct the so-called Yuanming Yuan Garden Villas beyond the northern border of the ruins park in order to attract buyers. The prominent name certainly caused confusion, giving the wrong impression that the Yuanming Yuan was for sale. Furthermore, with the continuing expansion of Beijing's "Ring Road" *(huanlu),* the superhighway may run through the precincts of the Yuanming Yuan site. Ironically, the finally preserved ruins are still under the threat of urbanization and commercialism after all. Overwhelmed by commercialism, the Yuanming Yuan Ruins Park appears anything but solemn and melancholy.

If neither the Yuanming Yuan Ruins Park nor Shenzhen's new Yuanming Yuan fully represents the artistic taste of the past, perhaps the great legacy of the Chinese imperial garden can be appreciated only by visiting the gigantic mountain retreat in Chengde and the well-preserved Yihe Yuan. The Yihe Yuan, originally the Yuanming Yuan's subsidiary Pure Ripple Garden, is perhaps the best preserved Chinese imperial garden of such grand scale and magnificence. After the fall of the Manchu dynasty, the garden was first opened for public viewing in 1924. Due to negligence, many of its man-made structures had deteriorated and the water level of its Kunming Lake had drastically declined. In 1964, a great effort was made to refurbish the 454-acre lake and to build a new canal for drawing ample water. Despite the fact that the Yihe Yuan took a beating during the Cultural Revolution, its structures and surroundings survived intact, which rendered its recovery relatively easy once the political storm was over. Since 1979, more than 70,000 square meters of the man-made structures in the Yihe Yuan, including 4,000 houses, have been cleaned and repaired. If its principal scene, the Shopping Street in the back hills of the Longevity Hills, which was devastated in 1860 and 1900, were finally restored, the Yihe Yuan would return to perfect condition and in some ways might represent the irretrievable Yuanming Yuan.

NOTES

Introduction

1. Wang Wei's survey of the Yuanming Yuan (1959, 1993) is a good pioneering work, repeatedly updated, but it remains too sketchy to do justice to the magnitude of the imperial garden. A Taiwanese scholar flagrantly plagiarized Wang's work in the 1960s (Liu Fenghan 1963, 1969).

Chapter 1: Provenance

1. Elfland refers to Penglai, the legendary fairyland at the east seas. One of the earliest authors to write about the legendary Penglai is Wang Jia, in the third century A.D., in *Shiyiji* (A book of forgotten events) (Beijing: Zhonghua shuju, 1981), pp. 223–224.

2. Even though the existence of the Xia dynasty has been established by archaeologists, its "historicity" remains in doubt among scientific historians for the lack of contemporary written records. The Jade Terrace was recorded in later sources.

3. The character *"you"* first appears on oracle-bone inscriptions (cf. Luo 1912). Its meaning in ancient Chinese classics is often defined as "a place where animals are kept." Hence, it originally referred to a zoo. Not until after the founding of the Chinese Empire in 221 B.C. was *you* renamed *yuan,* or *yuanyou.* Sima Qian, the Grand Historian of the Han, standardized the term in his *Shiji,* and *yuanyou* has since been identified as imperial garden.

4. The Confucian classic *Shijing* (Book of Poetry) refers to "marvelous tower" as "divine terrace" *(lingtai)* and the "marvelous park" as "divine menagerie" *(lingyou)* (Legge 1935, 4:456, 457).

5. Sima Qian writes: "He (the first emperor) had places constructed in the Shanglin Garden (the Upper Woods) south of the River Wei. The front palace, A'fang (Apang), built first, was five hundred feet from east to west, and five hundred feet from south to north. The terraces above could seat ten thousand and below there was room for a banner fifty feet in height" (Szuma Chien [Sima Qian] 1979, 179; Sima Qian 1975, 1:256). The rebel leader Xiang Yu burned down this gigantic imperial garden. "[Xiang] set fire to the Ch'in [Qin] palaces. The conflagration raged for three whole months" (Szuma Chien 1979, 221; Sima Qian 1975, 1:315). The legend of A'fang was further exaggerated by the Tang poet Du Mu, who in his famous "Lamenting the A'fang Palace" asserts that "For building the A'fang Palace, trees on the Sichuan hills were all gone. The Palace covered more than three hundred square *li* (thirty square miles), hiding from the Sun in the sky, facing Mt. Li in the north, and turning westward to the capital Xianyang. Two rivers ran through the palaces where stood a chamber every five feet and a pavilion every ten feet. . . . In a single day and within the same Palace, the weather appeared not the same" (Du Mu 1978, 1). A'fang Palace itself, however, is not a fiction. Archaeologists have located its ruin site near present-day Xian. The grounds cover about one mile from north to south (Meng Ya'nan 1993, 6–7).

6. The Han historian Ban Gu, in his *History of the Former Han Dynasty,* described Jianzhang as the main palace in a huge complex of palaces, and Taiye situated north of Jianzhang was a large lake, on which stood many isles called "fairy hills" *(shen-shan)* (Ban Gu 1962, 4:12445).

7. The noticeable exception was that of Liang Ji, the vicious

grand official, who misused his power to build the huge Tu Yuan west of Luoyang. Its grandeur was comparable, if not superior, to an imperial garden (cf. Fan Ye 1965, 5:1182).

8. The most noticeable example was that of Shi Chong (A.D. 249–300). As a result of its assistance in founding the Jin dynasty in 265, the Shi family obtained almost unlimited power and prestige. Shi Chong followed his father to serve in the highest offices in the government and developed a strong passion for accumulating wealth. His famous Golden Valley Garden (Jingu Yuan) constructed in a scenic neighborhood of Luoyang was magnificent. In fact, the name was given to the garden because the Golden Valley River actually ran through it. Before his fall, Shi Chong often entertained famous scholars and literary figures such as Pan Yue and Lu Ji in the garden. He also invited beautiful women to live in the garden such as the legendary Lady Lu Zhu (the Green Pearl).

9. The art of landscape painting emerged during the period of the Southern dynasties, stemming in part from the rise of Neo-Daoism after the collapse of the Han Empire and the subsequent sociopolitical chaos and in part from the inspiration of the attractive southern landscape. The genre matured during the Tang period. The landscape gardens fashioned during the same period of disunity can be described, as a recent writer put it, as "three dimensional landscape painting" (Huang Changmei 1986, 57). Perhaps not so incidentally, genuine landscape poetry also began at this time, with the work of such poets as Xie Lingyun (385–433) and Tao Yuanming (372–427) (cf. Qian Zonglian 1983, 205–206). Landscape poetry may be considered the verbal expression of the painting and the garden.

10. Li Cheng's book was reprinted in 1974, and the modern architect Liang Sicheng illuminated the text with annotations. For a Western sinologist's analysis of this work, see Paul Demieville, "Le Ying-tsa-fa-che," *Bulletin de l'Ecole francaise d'Extreme Orient*, (1925): pp. 213–264.

11. The book has two useful new annotated editions in Chinese (Ji Cheng 1983, 1987) in addition to the recent English translation entitled *The Craft of Gardens* by Alison Hardie (Ji Cheng 1988). All three editions provide significant illumination of Ji's original texts.

12. The recent garden scholar Chen Chongzhou has made some very thoughtful general remarks on the Chinese conceptions of garden making, which are worthwhile to study (Chen Chongzhou 1980, 1–16).

13. For useful descriptions of the subject in English, see Joseph Needham, *Science and Civilization in China*, Vols. 2–3, 4.1; S. Rossbach, *Fengshui: the Chinese Art of Placement*; S. Skinner, *The Living Earth Manual of Feng-Shui*; and Ernest J. Eitel, *Feng-shui: the Science of Sacred Landscape in Old China*.

Chapter 2: Disposition

1. For Peng Yigang, concealment and revelation generally reflect differences between Chinese and Western cultures. While Chinese emphasize concealment, Westerners stress revelation. The art of concealment was fully developed in Chinese garden-making (1986, 23).

2. An archive source dated 1838 shows that the director of the Imperial Household Sanhe reported to the Qianlong emperor concerning the cost of repairing the imperial barge named Flying Dragon (Feilong). The repair cost amounted to 9,238.6 taels of silver plus 713.82 taels for decorating and painting (*YMYA* 1991, 1:46–47).

3. The vast architectural complex called the Nine Continents in Peace, situated on the central islet of the nine islets, is one of the largest man-made structural units in the Yuanming Yuan. It served as His Majesty's main court before the completion of the Main Audience Hall. On these ruins, the Communists buried their fallen comrades in 1929. The tomb is visible to this day.

4. The Qianlong emperor (1711–1799) wrote a large number of poems during his long life. His "imperial poems" (*yuzhi shi*) in twenty-eight "boxes" (*han*), 42,500 entries, are still in the possession of the palace museum in Shenyang. In 1976, the palace museum in Taipei published *Qing Gaozong Yuzhi Shiwen Quanji* (The complete collection of Qianlong's essays and poems). For a good edition of selected Qianlong poems, see Sun Peijen and Bo Weiyi, comps. 1987. For a poem attributed specifically to the Yuanming Yuan, see Sun and Bo 1987, 26.

5. Swastika House is one of numerous structures whose configuration is based on symbols, the folding thread-bound book, or such Chinese characters as *tian* (farm fields), *gong* (work), and *kou* (mouth).

6. This cove is representative of those Yuanming Yuan structures designed and created on the basis of famous legends. It is an attempt to materialize an abstract mythology so as to increase excitement. Note that Wuling is the name of the place from where the legendary fisherman originally came.

7. The so-called *huabiao* are tall ornamental columns erected in front of palaces and tombs. Several of the original columns from the Yuanming Yuan's Ancestor's Shrine can be found on the campus of the present-day Peking University.

8. Incidentally, this rural scene is truly a village at the present time.

9. History records that in the spring of A.D. 353 the great calligrapher Wang Xizhi (303–379) and forty-two of his friends gathered at Kueiji's Orchid Pavilion in east Zhejiang province. Qianlong recreated here the scene of this famous gathering. His Majesty's 1779 inscription for this scene on a stone screen was

taken away from the ruins in 1917 to the park later know as Sun Yat-sen Park in Beijing (Zhao Guanghua 1981, 1:58). Qianlong's Orchid Pavilion, like Wang Xizhi's, was originally rectangular in shape; however, as the archive sources show, it was later rebuilt as an octagonal pavilion. A hexagonal thatched pavilion and a four-cornered bamboo pavilion were also added (*YMYA* 1991, 2:970).

10. The Pleasant Gallery (Ruyi Guan) was specifically of service to foreign dignitaries.

11. Li Sixun's fame in painting was recorded in the official history of the Tang dynasty (*Jiu Tangshu* 1975, 7:2346).

12. Attiret 1982, 16–17.

Chapter 3: Expansion

1. The Qianlong Emperor initiated this monumental library project in 1772. Altogether, seven manuscript libraries of nearly thirty-six thousand titles were completed. Only three libraries have survived civil war and foreign invasion (Wu Zhefu 1987, 22–24). For a balanced study of this project, including its dark side, see Guy 1987.

2. Chunhua refers to the era from 990 to 994 during which a large number of famous inscribed stone tablets had been collected. Qianlong wrote an essay on the gallery (Yu Mingzhong 1985, 3:1381) and printed four hundred rubbings as gifts to the censors and mandarins above the second rank (Jiao Xiong 1984, 14).

3. Qianlong inscribed a stone tablet that read "I love this cool cave" *(aici qingliang dong)* and placed it in one of the stone caves. While the inscribed tablet has been preserved to this day, nowhere can we locate any of the caves (cf. He Chongyi and Zeng Zhaofen 1991, 124).

4. Thanks to its location at the middle of a lake, the Mind-Opening Isle was spared from the burning of 1860. But it was finally devastated in the wake of the Boxer Rebellion in 1900.

5. Its original name was the Hibiscus (Furong) (Cai Shengzhi n.d., 134). Today this piece of rock stands in Beijing's Sun Yat-sen Park.

6. See Qianlong's poem with commentary in *YMYJ* 1983, 2:54–65.

7. Due to their huge size and solid materials, these Baroque buildings comprised most, if not all, of the visible remnants and ruins of the burned and destroyed Yuanming Yuan. Perhaps for this reason, many scholars, such as the following, wrongly equate the European section as the Yuanming Yuan: "the British burnt to the ground the Yuanming Yuan—the exquisite summer palace in the Peking suburbs built for Qianlong's pleasure using the plans of Jesuit architects" (Spence 1990, 181).

8. Benoît gave his account of his work in *Lettres édifiantes,* 13:469. Refer also to Cecil and Michel Beurdeley (1971) and Maurice Adam (1936, 21–22).

9. This maze reappears on the ruins of the Yuanming Yuan. This author saw it during his 1992 visit.

10. Xiangfei is a subject of intense and persistent controversy. Largely because the name cannot be found in any of the official documents of the Qing dynasty, professional historians, including the eminent Qing history authority Meng Sen, believe that Xiangfei and Rongfei, another Muslim woman from Chinese Turkestan, were really the same person (1965). But Jiang Longzhao, a playwright in Taiwan, challenges this long-standing view by presenting, among other evidence, a portrait of Xiangfei in martial attire drawn by Father Castiglione, which he dug out from Taibei's Palace Museum. A number of scholars, however, still contest its authenticity. For a comprehensive coverage of this controversy, see the two-volume anthology edited by Jiang Longzhao (1989, 1992). The Beurdeleys believe that Xiangfei was the widow of the governor of Yarkand, who was killed in battle against Qianlong's expeditionary forces (1971, 71).

11. The latest count indicates that seven of the twelve animal heads, the rat, the bull, the tiger, the hare, the horse, the monkey, and the boar, have survived to this day (Sun Ruoyi 1998, 73).

12. This figure, which is derived from the archival source of the Imperial Household and "the Construction Proposals of the Yuanming Yuan" (Yuanming Yuan Xianxing Zeli), should be accurate (*YMYA* 1991, 2:983–1055).

13. According to He Chong Yi and Zeng Zhaofen, this compound and its structure remained standing in the early 1950s. Beyond doubt, out of more than one hundred architectural complexes in the Yuanming Yuan, this was the only one that survived the century-long persistent deterioration (1991, 135).

14. My description of the Variegated Spring Garden here is based on my study of the garden's three available maps with reference to Wu Zhengyu (1983, 197) and Bai Rixin (1983, 22–25).

Chapter 4: Rise

1. Note that *fengshui* (geomancy), between pseudoscience and outright nonsense, has been a Chinese custom for millenia. It still has its market in the contemporary Chinese communities around the world.

2. Large pieces of stone that originally belonged to this stone paved road, according to the author Wang Wei, could still be seen along the road leading to the Yuanming Yuan as late as 1953. Due to continuous urbanization, however, nothing related to this road is visible anymore (Wang 1992, 19).

3. Yu Mingzhong 1985, 1:1326.

4. *YMYJ* 1983, 2:55.

5. There is a discrepancy about the date. We commonly follow Yu Mingzhong and give 1737; however, the recently available archive source yields a year earlier.

6. Yu Mingzhong dated the completion of the Ancestral Shrine as 1742, but a recent archival document shows that the shrine was completed as early as 1735 (*YMYA* 1991, 2:21–48).

7. Cited in *YMYJ* 1987, 2:70.

8. As Harold Kahn points out, the Qianlong Emperor justified the costly tours on the following grounds. First, he fulfilled filial duty by accompanying his mother in her old age to see the beautiful south. Second, he submitted to the sincere desires of the people. Third, he inspected the river conservation works in the Huai and Yangzi areas (1971, 91–92, 93–95). He missed one more goal, which was that Qianlong wanted to see the southern scenery and unique gardens and bring some of them back for replicas in the Yuanming Yuan. Sometimes he rebuilt an entire southern garden, such as the Lion's Cove from Suzhou, in his imperial garden.

9. For a detailed description of Qianlong's life in the garden, see Chapter six of this book.

10. The 1793 Qing document identified those who were granted audience by Qianlong in Chengde. They were the ambassador Lord George Macartney (Ma-ge-er-ni); the deputy ambassador George Leonard Staunton (Shi-dang-dong); the deputy's son, George Thomas Staunton (Ma Shi-dang-dong); the chief commander Lt. Col. George Benson (Ben-sheng); the secretaries Edward Winder (Wen-dai) and Louis Lamiot (?) (Lou-men); the physician Balang (?); the deputy commander Lt. Henry William Parish (Ba-er-shi); the officer E-lu (?); the attendants Bai-lin (?) and Yin-deng-le (?); the sea captain William Mackintosh (Ma-geng-duo-shi); five musicians; eleven servants; and forty soldiers (*YMYA* 1991, 1:356; Mageerni 1916, 2:5–6, 48). Altogether, sixty-eight British were present in Rehe.

11. *Suishoudang*, cited in Zhongguo diyi lishi danganguan 1996, 555.

12. Cited in Duyvendak 1938–1939, 67.

13. The newly available archival source shows that Qianlong first requested in late 1769 to prepare a large horizontal board to inscribe the name of the Qichun Yuan (Variegated Spring Garden). The inscribed board was officially hung in early 1770 (*YMYA* 1991, 2:1660). The date may be considered the beginning of the new Variegated Spring Garden. After renovations in the Tongzhi reign, its name was changed to the Wanchun Yuan.

14. Gong Zizhen, a native of Hangzhou, was born to a celebrated scholarly family. He acquired a wide range of scholarly interests and distinguished himself especially in New Text Con-

fucianism and poetry. His poems had a profound impact on later generations. Although his government career was not at all successful, his sharp observations of the sociopolitical conditions of the time and recommendations for change made him a significant pioneer reformer in modern Chinese history (cf. Hummel 1975, 431–434).

15. Cited in Huang Jun 1979, 2:409.

16. Yang Yunshi n.d.

17. Guo Songtao (1818–1891) was an exceptional Qing literatus who knew a great deal about the Western world. Later, during the Guangxu reign, he became the first Chinese minister to Britain and France (cf. Wang Ronzu 1993).

Chapter 5: Structure and Function

1. The structure and function of the Imperial Household as described in the *Qingshigao* (Draft history of the Qing dynasty) (1976, 12:3421–3433) show that the agency was exclusively at the service of the emperor.

2. Traditionally the Chinese took sandalwood as the gift of good luck. The Zhu family from Yangzhou gained its fame by making sandalwood furniture of excellent craftsmanship.

3. Refer to the *Qinding zongguan Neiwufu xianxing zeli* (Royal regulations concerning the general management of the Imperial Household) (*YMYA* 1991, 2:983–1019).

Chapter 6: Royal Daily Life

1. Cited in *YMYJ* 1987, 2:65.

2. The emperor's wardrobe and style of clothing are vividly described in the *"chuandai dang"* (the Archive on the Royal Apparel) (*YMYA* 1991, 2:827–911).

3. John Bell 1788, 14–15.

4. Whereas swallows' nests have been considered exotic in the West (Braudel 1967, 1973, 123), they were extremely popular in the Chinese menus of royalty and the rich. They are considered one of the four Chinese delicacies. The other three delicacies are shark's fin, bear's paw, and *beche-de-mer*. The black nests require more cleaning before use than the white nests. It took a silver needle, according to Yuan Mei, to remove tiny black feathers from the nests (1892, 5a). The white nests are considered better quality because "they consist entirely of nest-cement, a salivary secretion, occasionally with a few feathers of the nesting birds and bits of green vegetable matter (Simoons 1991, 427). The price of swallows' nests remains high today. The market price in Hong Kong in the early 1980s of the highest quality nests was nearly U.S. $300 an ounce, compared to about U.S. $400 for an ounce of gold (de Groot 1983, 72).

5. Attiret 1982, 32–34.

6. Zhao Yi 1982, 11–12.

7. Cited in Cheng Yansheng 1928, 13b.

8. Danby 1950, 185.

9. Cited in *YMYZ* 1984, 330.

10. The Xianfeng emperor (born in 1831) celebrated his thirtieth birthday in 1860 not just because of the Chinese way of counting age but also because superstition holds that for longevity one is advised to celebrate birthdays in the years ending in nine rather than zero or at the completion of a cycle.

Chapter 7: The Sacking

1. For the Chinese side of the story, see the Xianfeng emperor's decree to the Grand Council dated September 4, 1860 (cited in Jiang Tingfu 1931, 1:255–256).

2. For details, see the prince and the minister's notes and the allies' replies (Jiang Tingfu 1931, 1:261–262; cf. Walrond 1872, 351; Jia Zhen 1930, 6:2233, 2254, 2256).

3. Elgin doubted that there had been "a deliberate intention of treachery on the part of Prince Tsai and his colleague." But he apprehended that "the General-in-chief, Sangho-lin-sin (Sengge Linqin), thought that they had compromised his military position by allowing our army to establish itself so near his lines at Chang-kia-wan (Zhangjiawan)." Hence, Sengge Linqin "sought to counteract the evil effect of this by making a great swagger of parade and preparation to resist when the allied armies approached the campaign ground alloted to them" (Walrond 1872, 357). Elgin's assessment explained the resumption of hostility.

4. The fact that Prince Gong remained in the Yuanming Yuan—in fact, he refused to go into Beijing to assist with the defense (*YMYZ* 1984, 125)—is an interesting issue. Li Ciming noted that the prince stayed in the garden under His Majesty's instructions (1936, 9, 44a). Weng Tonghe indicated that the emperor specifically wanted the prince to seek peace (1970, 1, 186). A recent scholar, however, believes that Xianfeng, who did not really trust his younger brother, deliberately prevented the prince from entering Beijing, where he might seize political and military powers (Bao Chengguan 1990, 63–67).

5. Cited in M'Ghee 1862, 245.

6. Swinhoe 1861, 301.

7. Wolseley 1862, 224–225.

8. This claim originally derives from an unspecified French account on the 1860 event given to Wang Kangnian, a famous late Qing journalist in Shanghai, by Gu Hongming (Thomson Koo) (1857–1928), the European-trained advisor to Viceroy Zhang Zhidong (1837–1909). Gu's particular remark was trans-lated into Chinese and it can be found in Wang Kangnian's notes (1969, 1, 39).

9. *YMYA* 1991, 1:558.

10. *YMYA* 1991, 1:557; *Qingdai chouban yiwi shimo* 1930, 65:32–33.

11. *YMYA* 1991, 1:555.

12. Cited in Boulger 1896, 1:46.

13. Wolseley 1862, 1972, 279.

14. Wu Kedu 1978, 4:12–13.

15. Swinhoe 1861, 330.

16. *YMYA* 1991, 1:551.

17. Weng Tonghe 1970, 1:205–206.

18. Gu Sui 1986, 481.

19. Li Dazhao 1981, 12–13.

20. Wang Wei 1980, 48.

21. Zhang Aiping 1981, 1:10.

22. Danby 1950, 204.

23. Knollys 1873, 224–225.

Chapter 8: Repairs and the Final Blows

1. *YMYZ* 1984, 331–332.

2. *YMYA* 1991, 1:628–629; Li Zongtong and Liu Fenghan 1969, 1:190–191.

3. An impressive sum of material concerning the renovation of the Yuanming Yuan has been collected and analyzed by the modern architect Liu Dunzhen. For an excellent study of the subject with in-depth technical details, see Liu's long article (*YMYJ* 1987, 1:121–171). Refer also to Wang Puzi's work (*YMYJ* 1987, 2:38–39).

4. Late Qing government, due to financial difficulties, let wealthy merchants obtain official ranks by contributing a significant sum of money. This policy of "office purchase" *(maiguan)* provided men like Li Guangzhao with the opportunity to seek even greater financial compensation through official connection. Had Li Hongzhang not pursued the matter so thoroughly, Li Guangzhao might well have gotten away with his scheme.

5. Wu Rulun 1963, *"Shizheng,"* 11b–12a.

6. *YMYA* 1991, 1:743.

7. Cixi's determination to renovate the Yihe Yuan incidentally left behind a well-preserved imperial garden, which is now one of the most popular sites for tourists in China.

8. The paintings on the Long Promenade, which number more than 10,000, were again seriously damaged during the Cultural Revolution. The Red Guards, who denounced the traditional style painting as feudal, smeared them willfully. When I visited the garden in 1981, I was told that many of the paint-

ings about folk stories could not be restored. Instead, an attempt was made to paint new pictures. Two studies on the Long Promenade paintings, Xin Wensheng 1998 and Xu Fengtong 1986, 46–47, are worth consulting.

9. I saw this hall in 1981 while touring the Yihe Yuan, and I believe that its interior setup, such as the location of the two thrones, remains unaltered to this day.

10. The Boxer Rebellion was a major event in modern Chinese history. It may be considered the beginning of the end of the Qing dynasty (cf. Tan 1967).

11. The modern scholar Teng Gu located this set of photos in Berlin and published them in book form with illustrations in the 1920s. This book, without a specific date of publication, is entitled *Yuanming Yuan Oushi Gongdian Canji* (The remaining ruins of the European-style palaces in the Yuanming Yuan). Refer also to the recently published *Barbarian Lens* (Thiriez 1998).

GLOSSARY

This glossary includes the names of most of the man-made structures of the Yuanming Yuan and its subsidiary gardens.

Chinese to English

Aishan Lou 愛山樓 Mountain-Loving Chamber

Anlan Yuan 安瀾園 Wave-Pacifying Garden

Anyi Tang 安逸堂 Comfortable Hall

Anyou Gong 安佑宮 Blessing Palace

Bajiao Ting 八角亭 Octagonal Pavilion

Baoyun Ge 寶雲閣 Precious Cloud Pavilion

Beidao Yuyu 北島土宇 Jade House on the North Isle

Beiyuan Shancun 北遠山村 Northernmost Mountain Village

Bieyou Dongtian 別有洞天 Other Paradise

Bilan Qiao 碧瀾橋 Blue Wave Bridge

Bitong Shuyuan 碧桐書院 Blue Phoenix-Tree Academy

Biyun Lou 碧雲樓 Blue Cloud Chamber

Chang Lang 長廊 Long Promenade

Changchun Qiao 長春橋 Eternal Spring Bridge

Changchun Xian'guan 長春仙館 Eternal Spring Fairy Hall

Changchun Yuan 暢春園 Joyful Spring Garden

Changchun Yuan 長春園 Eternal Spring Garden

Changhe Tang 暢和堂 Joyous Hall

Changjin Lou 暢襟樓 Mind-Opening Chamber

Changshandao Xianrentai 長山島仙人臺 Long Island Fairy Terrace

Cheng'en Tang 承恩堂 Benevolence-Receiving Hall

Chengguang Xie 澄光榭 Transparent Bright Gazebo

Chenglian Lou 澄練樓 Smooth-As-Silk Chamber

Chengxin Tang 澄心堂 Pure Mind Hall

Chengyuan Xie 澄淵榭 Clear Void Gazebo

Chunhua Xuan 淳化軒 Chunhua Gallery

Chunxi Yuan 春喜園 Spring Pleasure Garden

Chunyu Shuhe 春宇舒和 Comfort Inn under Spring Roof

Chunyu Xuan 春雨軒 Spring Rain Gallery

Chunze Zhai 春澤齋 Spring Watery Chapel

Churu Xianliang Men 出入賢良門 Gentlemen's Entrance

Ciyun Puhu 慈雲普護 Gentle Clouds Cover All

Cuijiao Xuan 翠交軒 Green-Crossed Gallery

Cuiwei Tang 翠微堂 Green Shady Hall

Da'baoen Yanshou Si 大報恩延壽寺 Gratitude and Longevity Temple

Da'dongmen 大東門 Grand East Gate

Da'gongmen 大宮門 Grand Palace Gate

Danhuai Tang 澹懷堂 Homely Memorial Hall

Danpo Ningjing　澹泊寧靜　Simple Life in Quietude
Dashuifa　大水法　Great Fountains
Da'xitai　大戲台　Grand Theater
Dong Chaofang　東朝房　East Room
Dong Nuange　東暖閣　East Warm Belvedere
Dong Nuanshi　東暖室　Warm East Room
Dongtian Shenchu　洞天深處　Deep Vault of Heaven
Duanqiao Canxue　斷橋殘雪　Traces of Snow on a Broken Bridge
Duojia Ruyun　多稼如雲　Bountiful Farms

Enmu Si　恩母寺　Mother's Memorial Temple
Er'gongmen　二宮門　Inner Palace Gate

Fanghe　方河　Lake Square
Fanghu Shengjing　方壺勝景　A Wonderland in the Square Pot
Fangwai Guan　方外觀　Square Outlook
Feicui Lou　翡翠樓　Green Pyroxene Chamber
Feidi Ting　飛睇亭　Quick Glance Pavilion
Feiyun Louchuan　飛雲樓船　Flying-Cloud Tall Ship
Feng Sanwusi Dian　奉三無私殿　Honoring Three Selflessnesses Court
Fenglin Zhou　鳳麟洲　Phoenix Isle
Foxiang Ge　佛香閣　Buddha Flagrance Pavilion
Fuchun Tang　敷春堂　Spreading Spring Hall
Fuhai　福海　Sea of Blessing
Fuyuan Men　福園門　Lucky Garden Gate

Gengyun Tang　耕雲堂　Ploughing Cloud Hall
Gongqiao　拱橋　Arch Bridge
Guangfeng Jiyue　光風霽月　Splendid Wind and Moon
Guangyu Gong　廣育宮　Nourishing Palace
Guyue Xuan　古月軒　Ancient Moon Gallery

Haiyan Tang　海宴堂　Calm Sea Hall
Haiyue Kaijin　海岳開襟　Mind-Opening Isle
Han Miaoshi　涵妙識　Conceiving Wonderful View
Han Qinghui　含清暉　Conceiving Pure Light
Hanbi Lou　含碧樓　Blue-Conceiving Chamber
Hancui Xuan　含翠軒　Green-Conceiving Gallery

Hanjing Tang　涵經堂　Classics Hall
Hanxu Langjing　涵虛攬鏡　Contemplation at the Lakeside
Hanyuan Zhai　涵遠齋　Conceiving Distance Chapel
Hengbi Xuan　橫碧軒　Horizontal Blue Gallery
Heshen Miao　河神廟　River Goddess' Temple
Hongci Yonghu　鴻慈永岵　Most Kindness and Eternal Blessing (Ancestral Shrine)
Hongya Yuan　宏雅園　Grand Elegant Garden
Hou Huayuan　後花園　Rear Garden
Houdian　後殿　Rear Court
Houhu　後湖　Rear Lake
Huagang Guanyu　花港觀魚　Admiring Fish at the Flourish Haven
Huanxi Fochang　歡喜佛場　Happy Buddhist Ground
Huanxiu Shanfang　環秀山房　All-Round Pretty Cottage
Huayuan Men　花園門　Entrance of the Flower Garden
Huazhou Guan　花驟館　Fast-Growing Flower Studio
Hui Ruchun　惠如春　Springlike Kindness
Hui Ting　蕙亭　Luxuriant Pavilion
Huifang Shuyuan　惠芳書院　Faculty Club

Jiajing Mingqin　夾鏡鳴琴　Double Reflections and the Roaring Waterfall
Jian Yuan　鑒園　Viewing Garden
Jianbi Ting　鑒碧亭　Blue Shadow Kiosk
Ji'en Tang　紀恩堂　Memorial Hall
Jiexiu Shanfang　接秀山房　Belle Villa
Jile Shijie　極樂世界　World of Paradise
Jingshui Zhai　鏡水齋　Water Reflection Chapel
Jingzhong Ge　鏡中閣　Reflection Pavilion
Jinqi Lou　錦綺樓　Fine-Brocaded Chamber
Jiukong Qiao　九孔橋　Nine-Hole Bridge
Jiuzhou Qingyan　九洲清宴　Nine Continents in Peace Hall
Juyuan Lou　聚遠樓　Chamber of Distance

Kenong Xuan　課農軒　Teaching Farming Gallery
Kuixing Lou　魁星樓　Big Dipper Chamber
Kunming Hu　昆明湖　Kunming Lake
Kuoran Dagon　廓然大公　Boundless Impartiality
Kuoru Ting　廓如亭　Sweeping Pavilion

Lan Ting 蘭亭 Orchid Pavilion
Lancui Ting 覽翠亭 Green-View Arbor
Langrun Zhai 朗潤齋 Bright Glossy Chapel
Langyue Lou 閬月樓 Admiring Moon Chamber
Leifeng Xizhao 雷峰夕照 Sunset at the Thunder Hill
Lenong Xuan 樂農軒 Pleasing Farming Gallery
Leshou Tang 樂壽堂 Enjoy Longevity Hall
Lianxi Lechu 濂溪樂處 Scholar's Wonderland
Lingfeng 靈峰 Splendid Summit
Lingxiang Pian 菱香片 Fragrant Water Chestnut Flat
Lingxu Ting 凌虛亭 Streaking Void Kiosk
Lingyu Si 靈雨寺 Inspiring Rain Temple
Linhu Lou 臨湖樓 Lakeside Chamber
Liuxiang Zhu 流香渚 Pomegranate Fragrant Islet
Longwang Miao 龍王廟 Temple of the Dragon King
Longzhou 龍舟 Dragon Boat
Louyue Kaiyun 鏤月開雲 Engraved Moon and Unfolding Clouds
Luyin Xuan 綠陰軒 Green Shade Gallery

Maimaijie 買賣街 Shopping Street
Manlu Xuan 滿綠軒 All-Green Gallery
Meiyue Xuan 眉月軒 Half-Moon Gallery
Migong 迷宮 Maze
Mingchun Men 明春門 Bright Spring Gate
Mudan Tai 牡丹臺 Peony Terrace

Nacui Lou 納翠樓 Green Gathering Chamber
Nan Changhe 南長河 South Long River
Nan Shufang 南書房 South Studio
Nanping Wanzhong 南屏晚鍾 Evening Bell at Nanping
Ningxiang Dian 凝祥殿 Luck-Gathering Court

Paifang 牌坊 Memorial Archways
Paiyun Dian 排雲殿 Cloud-Rising Court
Pengdao Yaotai 蓬島瑤臺 Immortal Abode on the Fairy Terrace
Penglai Zhou 蓬萊洲 Fairy's Islet
Piandian 偏殿 Side Courts
Ping'an Yuan 平安院 Silent Courtyard
Pinghu Qiuyue 平湖秋月 Calm Lake under Autumn Moon

Qian Yuan 茜園 Alizarin-Red Garden
Qianhu 前湖 Front Lake
Qianxiang Dian 千祥殿 Ample Luck Chamber
Qichun Yuan 綺春園 Variegated Spring Garden
Qin'an Dian 欽安殿 Admiring Peace Court
Qinghui Ge 清輝閣 Clear Sunshine Belvedere
Qinglian Duo 青蓮朵 Green-Lotus Rock
Qingxia Tang 清夏堂 Cool Summer Hall
Qingxia Zhai 清夏齋 Cool Summer Chapel
Qingyao Xie 清瑤榭 Pure Jasper Gazebo
Qingyi Yuan 清漪園 Pure Ripple Garden
Qingyin Ge 清音閣 Clear Sound Pavilion
Qingzhen Si 清真寺 Muslim Mosque
Qinzheng Dian 勤政殿 Diligent Court
Qionghua Lou 瓊華樓 Flowery Chamber
Quyuan Fenghe 曲院楓荷 Curving Courtyard and Lotus Pond

Ranxia Lou 攬霞樓 Catching Evening Sunlight Chamber
Renshou Dian 仁壽殿 Longevity for Benevolence Court
Ritian Linyu 日天琳宇 Dazzling Eaves under Heaven
Ru Yuan 如園 Garden of Compliance
Rugu Hanjin 茹古涵今 Harmony of the Past with the Present
Ruiying Gong 瑞應宮 Good Omen Palace
Ruizhu Gong 蕊珠宮 Pistillate Pearl Palace
Ruyi Guan 如意館 Pleasant Studio

Santan Yinyue 三潭印月 Three Pools Reflecting the Moon
Sanxian Dong 三仙洞 Cave of the Three Fairies
Shangao Shuichang 山高水長 High-Reaching Mountain and Outstretched River
Shangxia Tianguang 上下天光 Sky in Reflections
Shao Yuan 勺園 Ladle Garden
Shende Tang 慎德堂 Luxurious Prudent Virtue Hall
Shengdong Shi 生冬室 Winter Room
Shenliu Dushu Tang 深柳讀書堂 Thick Willows Cover the Study
Shenxiu Siyong 慎修思永 Prudent Cultivation and Perpetual Thoughtfulness

Shewei Cheng 舍衛城 Wall of Sravasti

Shifang 石舫 Marble Boat

Shilin 石林 Rock Groove

Shiqikong Qiao 十七孔橋 Seventeen-Hole Bridge

Shishang Zhai 時賞齋 Appreciating Chapel

Shizi Lin 獅子林 Lion's Cove

Shizi Ting 十字亭 Cross Pavilion

Shouxing Ting 壽星亭 Pavilion for the God of Longevity

Shuanghe Zhai 雙鶴齋 Double Cranes Chapel

Shuangjia Zhai 雙佳齋 Double Beauty Chapel

Shuguang Lou 曙光樓 Rising Sunshine Chamber

Shuimu Mingse 水木明瑟 Sounds of Wood and Water

Shuimu Qinghua 水木清華 Pretty Water and Wood Chamber

Shuo Xihu 瘦西湖 Skinny West Lake

Shuzao Xuan 抒藻軒 Expressing Excellence Gallery

Siyi Shuwu 四宜書屋 All-Season Library

Siyong Zhai 思永齋 Eternal Thoughtful Chapel

Songfeng Ge 松風閣 Pine Wind Pavilion

Sui'an Shi 隨安室 Relaxation Room

Suxin Tang 素心堂 Pure Heart Hall

Tantan Dangdang 坦坦蕩蕩 Magnanimous World

Taohua Wu 桃花塢 Peach-Blossom Cove

Taoyuan Shenchu 桃源深處 Depth of Heaven's Vault

Tiandi Yijiachun 天地一家春 Family of Spring Between Heaven and Earth

Tianran Tuhua 天然圖畫 Natural Scenery

Tong Dian 銅殿 Copper Court

Tong Ting 銅亭 Copper Pavilion

Tongle Yuan 同樂園 All-Happy Garden

Tongyin Shuwu 桐陰書屋 Library under the Shade of the Phoenix Trees

Wanchun Yuan 萬春園 Ten-Thousand Spring Garden

Wanfang Anhe 萬方安和 Universal Peace (Swastika House)

Wanfu Ge 萬福閣 Abundant Fortune Pavilion

Wangying Zhou 望瀛洲 Lookout Stand

Wanquan He 萬泉河 Ten-Thousand Spring River

Wanshou Shan 萬壽山 Longevity Hills

Wanshu Yuan 萬樹園 Ten-Thousand Tree Garden

Wanyuan Ge 萬源閣 Ten-Thousand Source Belvedere

Weilu Xuan 惟綠軒 Green Gallery

Weiyu Shuwu 味腴書屋 Rich Taste Library

Wenyuan Ge 文源閣 Library of Literary Sources (in the Yuanming Yuan)

Wenyuan Ge 文淵閣 Library of Literary Sources (in the Forbidden City)

Wenyue Lou 問月樓 Inquiring Moon Chamber

Woyun Xuan 臥雲軒 Sleeping Cloud Gallery

Wufu Tang 五福堂 Five-Fortunes Hall

Wuling Chunse 武陵春色 Spring Beauty at Wuling

Wuzhu Ting 五竹亭 Five-Bamboo Pavilion

Xi Nuange 西暖閣 West Warm Room

Xianfa Qiang 線法牆 Perspective Wall

Xiangfa Shan 線法山 Perspective Hill

Xiangfa Tu 線法圖 Perspective Pictures

Xiang Shan 香山 Fragrant Hills

Xianren Chenglu Tai 仙人承露臺 Fairy Terrace

Xiaoyoutian 小有天 Little Haven

Xichun Yuan 喜春園 Loving Spring Garden

Xieqi Qu 諧奇趣 Symmetric and Amazing Pleasure

Xifeng Xiuse 西峰秀色 Majestic Sunset-Tinted Peaks of the West Hills

Xihai 錫海 Sea of Tin

Xihua Men 西華門 West Flowery Gate

Xijia Lou 夕佳樓 Good Evening Chamber

Xinggeng Bieshu 省耕別墅 Economized-Ploughing Villa

Xinghua Chunguan 杏花春館 Apricot-Flower Villa

Xiujie Shanfang 秀接山房 Beauty-Covered Mountain Cottage

Xiyang Lou 西洋樓 European Buildings

Xunyun Lou 尋雲樓 Cloud-Searching Chamber

Xunyun Xie 尋雲榭 Cloud-Searching Gazebo

Xushui Lou 蓄水樓 Chamber for Gathering Water

Yangque Long 養雀籠 Peacock Cage

Yangri Tang 養日堂 Eternal Sunshine Hall

Yangsu Shuwu 養素書屋 Nourishing Simplicity Study

Yangxin Dian 養心殿 Mind-Nourishing Study

Yangyue Ting 養月亭 Bring-Up Moon Arbor

Yanqing Ting 延清亭 Clarity-Inviting Pavilion

Yanyu Lou 煙雨樓 Smoky Rain Chamber

Yi Zhai 抑齋 Restrained Chapel

Yihe Yuan 頤和園 Cheerful Harmony Garden

Yilan Ting 貽蘭亭 Orchid Courtyard

Yinghai Xianshan 瀛海仙山 Fairy Hill at the Sea

Yinghui Dian 迎暉殿 Sunshine Court

Yingqing Zhai 映清齋 Clear Reflection Chapel

Yingshui Lanxiang 映水蘭香 Orchid Fragrance over the Water

Yingxun Ting 迎薰亭 Welcoming Warm Wind Arbor

Yiran Shuwu 怡然書屋 Pleasant Study

Yishou Xuan 益壽軒 Longevity Gallery

Yonghe Gong 雍和宮 Lama Temple

Yu Yuan 隅園 Corner Garden

Yuanfeng Lou 遠風樓 Distant Wind Chamber

Yuanming Yuan 圓明園 Round-Bright Garden

Yuanying Guan 遠瀛觀 Great View of the Distant Seas

Yudai Qiao 玉帶橋 Jade Belt Bridge

Yuedi Yunju 月地雲居 Cloud-Living on the Moon Land

Yuebo Lou 月波樓 Moon Wave Chamber

Yulan Tang 玉瀾堂 Jade Wave Hall

Yulinglong Guan 玉玲瓏館 Exquisite Jade Studio

Yunxiang Ge 雲香閣 Cloud Fragrance Pavilion

Yunzhen Zhai 蘊真齋 Nourishing Truth Chapel

Yuquan Shan 玉泉山 Jade Spring Hills

Yuyue Yuanfei 魚躍鳶飛 Fish-Leaping and Bird-Flying

Yuzao Ting 魚藻亭 Fish-Algae Veranda

Zaiyue Fang 載月舫 Moon-Carrying Showboat

Zao Yuan 藻園 Ornate Garden

Zaoshen Yongde 澡身泳德 Bath in Virtue

Zelan Tang 澤蘭堂 Watering Orchid Hall

Zhan Yuan 瞻園 Garden of Contemplation

Zhanhui Tang 展暉堂 Displaying Sunshine Hall

Zhanjing Lou 湛景樓 Exquisite View Chamber

Zhengda Guangming Dian 正大光明殿 Main Audience Hall

Zhengjue Si 正覺寺 Temple of Enlightenment

Zhiguo Tang 知過堂 Knowing-Your-Mistakes Hall

Zhiran Ju 製染局 Bureau of Brocade Mill and Dye Work

Zhiyu Ting 知魚亭 Knowing-Fish Arbor

Zhonghe Tang 中和堂 Hall of Harmony

Zhu Ting 竹亭 Bamboo Pavilion

Zhuangyan Fajie 莊嚴法界 Dignified Vision

Zhuoyun Lou 倬雲樓 Lofty Clouds Chamber

Zibi Shanfang 紫碧山房 Purple-Blue Mountain Cottage

Zixia Lou 紫霞樓 Purple Cloud Chamber

Zixing Zhai 自省齋 Self-Reflection Chapel

Zuojing Guan 莳經館 Classics-Worshipping Studio

Zuoshi Linliu 坐石臨流 Sitting Rocks and the Winding Stream

English to Chinese

A Wonderland in the Square Pot Fanghu Shengjing 方壺勝景

Abundant Fortune Pavilion Wanfu Ge 萬福閣

Admiring Fish at the Flourish Haven Huagang Guanyu 花港觀魚

Admiring Moon Chamber Langyue Lou 閬月樓

Admiring Peace Court Qin'an Dian 欽安殿

Alizarin-Red Garden Qian Yuan 茜園

All-Green Gallery Manlu Xuan 滿綠軒

All-Happy Garden Tongle Yuan 同樂園

All-Round Pretty Cottage Huanxiu Shanfang 環秀山房

All-Season Library Siyi Shuwu 四宜書屋

Ample Luck Court Qianxiang Dian 千祥殿

Ancestral Shrine Hongci Yonghu (Most Kindness and Eternal Blessing) 鴻慈永岵

Ancient Moon Gallery Guyue Xuan 古月軒

Appreciating Chapel Shishang Zhai 時賞齋

Apricot-Flower Villa Xinghua Chunguan 杏花春館

Arch Bridge Gongqiao 拱橋

Bamboo Pavilion Zhu Ting 竹亭

Bath in Virtue Zaoshen Yongde 澡身泳德

Beauty-Covered Mountain Cottage Xiujie Shanfang 秀接山房

Belle Villa Jiexiu Shanfang 接秀山房

Benevolence-Receiving Hall Cheng'en Tang 承恩堂

Big Dipper Chamber   Kuixing Lou   魁星樓
Blessing Palace   Anyou Gong   安佑宮
Blue Cloud Chamber   Biyun Lou   碧雲樓
Blue-Conceiving Chamber   Hanbi Lou   含碧樓
Blue Phoenix-Tree Academy   Bitong Shuyuan   碧桐書院
Blue Shadow Kiosk   Jianbi Ting   鑒碧亭
Blue Wave Bridge   Bilan Qiao   碧瀾橋
Boundless Impartiality   Kuoran Dagon   廓然大公
Bountiful Farms   Duojia Ruyun   多稼如雲
Bring-Up Moon Arbor   Yangyue Ting   養月亭
Bright Glossy Chapel   Langrun Zhai   潤齋
Bright Spring Gate   Mingchun Men   明春門
Buddha Flagrance Pavilion   Foxiang Ge   佛香閣
Bureau of Brocade Mill and Dye Work   Zhiran Ju   製染局

Calm Lake under Autumn Moon   Pinghu Qiuyue   平湖秋月
Calm Sea Hall   Haiyan Tang   海宴堂
Catching Evening Sunlight Chamber   Ranxia Lou   攬霞樓
Cave of the Three Fairies   Sanxian Dong   三仙洞
Chamber for Gathering Water   Xushui Lou   蓄水樓
Chamber of Distance   Juyuan Lou   聚遠樓
Cheerful Harmony Garden   Yihe Yuan   頤和園
Chunhua Gallery   Chunhua Xuan   淳化軒
Clarity-Inviting Pavilion   Yanqing Ting   延清亭
Classics Hall   Hanjing Tang   涵經堂
Classics-Worshipping Studio   Zuojing Guan   莋經館
Clear Reflection Chapel   Yingqing Zhai   映清齋
Clear Sound Pavilion   Qingyin Ge   清音閣
Clear Sunshine Belvedere   Qinghui Ge   清輝閣
Clear Void Gazebo   Chengyuan Xie   澄淵榭
Cloud Fragrance Pavilion   Yunxiang Ge   雲香閣
Cloud-Living on the Moon Land   Yuedi Yunju   月地雲居
Cloud-Rising Court   Paiyun Dian   排雲殿
Cloud-Searching Chamber   Xunyun Lou   尋雲樓
Cloud-Searching Gazebo   Xunyun Xie   尋雲榭
Comfort Inn under Spring Roof   Chunyu Shuhe   春宇舒和
Comfortable Hall   Anyi Tang   安逸堂
Conceiving Distance Chapel   Hanyuan Zhai   涵遠齋
Conceiving Pure Light   Han Qinghui   含清暉
Conceiving Wonderful View   Han Miaoshi   涵妙

Contemplation at the Lakeside   Hanxu Langjing   涵虛攬鏡
Cool Summer Chapel   Qingxia Zhai   清夏齋
Cool Summer Hall   Qingxia Tang   清夏堂
Copper Court   Tong Dian   銅殿
Copper Pavilion   Tong Ting   銅亭
Corner Garden   Yu Yuan   隅園
Cross Pavilion   Shizi Ting   十字亭
Curving Courtyard and Lotus Pond   Quyuan Fenghe   曲院楓荷

Dazzling Eaves under Heaven   Ritian Linyu   日天琳宇
Deep Vault of Heaven   Dongtian Shenchu   洞天深處
Depth of Heaven's Vault   Taoyuan Shenchu   桃源深處
Dignified Vision   Zhuangyan Fajie   莊嚴法界
Diligent Court   Qinzheng Dian   勤政殿
Displaying Sunshine Hall   Zhanhui Tang   展暉堂
Distant Wind Chamber   Yuanfeng Lou   遠風樓
Double Beauty Chapel   Shuangjia Zhai   雙佳齋
Double Cranes Chapel   Shuanghe Zhai   雙鶴齋
Double Reflections and the Roaring Waterfall   Jiajing Mingqin   夾鏡鳴琴
Dragon Boat   Longzhou   龍舟

East Room   Dong Chaofang   東朝房
East Warm Belvedere   Dong Nuange   東暖閣
Economized-Ploughing Villa   Xinggeng Bieshu   省耕別墅
Engraved Moon and Unfolding Clouds   Louyue Kaiyun   鏤月開雲
Enjoy Longevity Hall   Leshou Tang   樂壽堂
Entrance of the Flower Garden   Huayuan Men   花園門
Eternal Spring Bridge   Changchun Qiao   長春橋
Eternal Spring Fairy Hall   Changchun Xian'guan   長春仙館
Eternal Spring Garden   Changchun Yuan   長春園
Eternal Sunshine Hall   Yangri Tang   養日堂
Eternal Thoughtful Chapel   Siyong Zhai   思永齋
European Buildings   Xiyang Lou   西洋樓
Evening Bell at Nanping   Nanping Wanzhong   南屏晚鍾
Expressing Excellence Gallery   Shuzao Xuan   抒藻軒
Exquisite Jade Studio   Yulinglang Guan   玉瓏館
Exquisite View Chamber   Zhanjing Lou   湛景樓

Faculty Club   Huifang Shuyuan   惠芳書院

Fairy Hill at the Sea   Yinghai Xianshan   瀛海仙山

Fairy's Islet   Penglai Zhou   蓬萊洲

Fairy Terrace   Xianren Chenglu Tai   仙人承露臺

Family of Spring Between Heaven and Earth   Tiandi Yijiachun   天地一家春

Fast-Growing Flower Studio   Huazhou Guan   花驟館

Fine-Brocaded Chamber   Jinqi Lou   錦綺樓

Fish-Algae Veranda   Yuzao Ting   魚藻亭

Fish-Leaping and Bird-Flying   Yuyue Yuanfei   魚躍鳶飛

Five-Bamboo Pavilion   Wuzhu Ting   五竹亭

Five-Fortunes Hall   Wufu Tang   五福堂

Flowery Chamber   Qionghua Lou   瓊華樓

Flying-Cloud Tall Ship   Feiyun Louchuan   飛雲樓船

Fragrant Hills   Xiang Shan   香山

Fragrant Water Chestnut Flat   Lingxiang Pian   菱香片

Front Lake   Qianhu   前湖

Garden of Compliance   Ru Yuan   如園

Garden of Contemplation   Zhan Yuan   瞻園

Gentle Clouds Cover All   Ciyun Puhu   慈雲普護

Gentlemen's Entrance   Churu Xianliang Men   出入賢良門

Good Evening Chamber   Xijia Lou   夕佳樓

Good Omen Palace   Ruiying Gong   瑞應宮

Grand East Gate   Da'dongmen   大東門

Grand Theater   Da'xitai   大戲台

Grand Elegant Garden   Hongya Yuan   宏雅園

Grand Palace Gate   Da'gongmen   大宮門

Gratitude and Longevity Temple   Da'baoen Yanshou Si   大報恩延壽寺

Great Fountains   Dashuifa   大水法

Great View of the Distant Seas   Yuanying Guan   遠瀛觀

Green-Conceiving Gallery   Hancui Xuan   含翠軒

Green-Crossed Gallery   Cuijiao Xuan   翠交軒

Green Gallery   Weilu Xuan   惟綠軒

Green Gathering Chamber   Nacui Lou   納翠樓

Green-Lotus Rock   Qinglian Duo   青蓮朵

Green Shade Gallery   Luyin Xuan   綠陰軒

Green Shady Hall   Cuiwei Tang   翠微堂

Green-View Arbor   Lancui Ting   覽翠亭

Green Pyroxene Chamber   Feicui Lou   翡翠樓

Half-Moon Gallery   Meiyue Xuan   眉月軒

Hall of Harmony   Zhonghe Tang   中和堂

Happy Buddhist Ground   Huanxi Fochang   歡喜佛場

Harmony of the Past with the Present   Rugu Hanjin   茹古涵今

High-Reaching Mountain and Outstretched River   Shangao Shuichang   山高水長

Homely Memorial Hall   Danhuai Tang   澹懷堂

Honoring Three Selflessnesses Court   Feng Sanwusi Dian   奉三無私殿

Horizontal Blue Gallery   Hengbi Xuan   橫碧軒

Immortal Abode on the Fairy Terrace   Pengdao Yaotai   蓬島瑤臺

Inquiring Moon Chamber   Wenyue Lou   問月樓

Inner Palace Gate   Er'gongmen   二宮門

Inspiring Rain Temple   Lingyu Si   靈雨寺

Jade Belt Bridge   Yudai Qiao   玉帶橋

Jade House on the North Isle   Beidao Yuyu   北島玉宇

Jade Spring Hills   Yuquan Shan   玉泉山

Jade Wave Hall   Yulan Tang   玉瀾堂

Joyful Spring Garden   Changchun Yuan   暢春園

Joyous Hall   Changhe Tang   暢和堂

Knowing-Fish Arbor   Zhiyu Ting   知魚亭

Knowing-Your-Mistakes Hall   Zhiguo Tang   知過亭

Kunming Lake   Kunming Hu   昆明湖

Ladle Garden   Shao Yuan   勺園

Lake Square   Fanghe   方河

Lakeside Chamber   Linhu Lou   臨湖樓

Lama Temple   Yonghe Gong   雍和宮

Library of Literary Sources   Wenyuan Ge   文源閣 (in the Yuanming Yuan)

Library of Literary Sources   Wenyuan Ge   文淵閣 (in the Forbidden City)

Library under the Shade of the Phoenix Trees   Tongyin Shuwu   桐陰書屋

Lion's Cove   Shizi Lin   獅子林

Little Haven   Xiaoyoutian   小有天

Lofty Clouds Chamber   Zhuoyun Lou 倬雲樓

Long Island Fairy Terrace   Changshandao Xianrentai
長山島仙人臺

Long Promenade   Chang Lang 長廊

Longevity for Benevolence Court   Renshou Dian 仁壽殿

Longevity Gallery   Yishou Xuan 益壽軒

Longevity Hills   Wanshou Shan 萬壽山

Lookout Stand   Wangying Zhou 望瀛洲

Loving Spring Garden   Xichun Yuan 喜春園

Luck-Gathering Court   Ningxiang Dian 凝祥殿

Lucky Garden Gate   Fuyuan Men 福園門

Luxuriant Pavilion   Hui Ting 蕢亭

Luxurious Prudent Virtue Hall   Shende Tang 慎德堂

Magnanimous World   Tantan Dangdang 坦坦蕩蕩

Main Audience Hall   Zhengda Guangming Dian
正大光明殿

Majestic Sunset-Tinted Peaks of the West Hills   Xifeng Xiuse
西峰秀色

Marble Boat   Shifang 石舫

Maze   Migong 迷宮

Memorial Archways   Paifang 牌坊

Memorial Hall   Ji'en Tang 紀恩堂

Mind-Nourishing Study   Yangxin Dian 養心殿

Mind-Opening Chamber   Changjin Lou 暢襟樓

Mind-Opening Isle   Haiyue Kaijin 海岳開襟

Moon-Carrying Showboat   Zaiyue Fang 載月舫

Moon Wave Chamber   Yuebo Lou 月波樓

Most Kindness and Eternal Blessing   Hongci Yonghu
(Ancestral Shrine) 慈永

Mother's Memorial Temple   Enmu Si 恩母寺

Mountain-Loving Chamber   Aishan Lou 愛山樓

Muslim Mosque   Qingzhen Si 清真寺

Natural Scenery   Tianran Tuhua 天然圖畫

Nine Continents in Peace Hall   Jiuzhou Qingyan 九洲清宴

Nine-Hole Bridge   Jiukong Qiao 九孔橋

Northernmost Mountain Village   Beiyuan Shancun 北遠山村

Nourishing Palace   Guangyu Gong 廣育宮

Nourishing Simplicity Study   Yangsu Shuwu 養素書屋

Nourishing Truth Chapel   Yunzhen Zhai 蘊真齋

Octagonal Pavilion   Bajiao Ting 八角亭

Other Paradise   Bieyou Dongtian 別有洞天

Orchid Courtyard   Yilan Ting 貽蘭亭

Orchid Fragrance over the Water   Yingshui Lanxiang
映水蘭香

Orchid Pavilion   Lan Ting 蘭亭

Ornate Garden   Zao Yuan 藻園

Pavilion for the God of Longevity   Shouxing Ting 壽星亭

Peach-Blossom Cove   Taohua Wu 桃花塢

Peacock Cage   Yangque Long 養雀籠

Peony Terrace   Mudan Tai 牡丹臺

Perspective Hill   Xiangfa Shan 線法山

Perspective Pictures   Xiangfa Tu 線法圖

Perspective Wall   Xiangfa Qiang 線法牆

Phoenix Isle   Fenglin Zhou 鳳麟洲

Pine Wind Pavilion   Songfeng Ge 松風閣

Pistillate Pearl Palace   Ruizhu Gong 蕊珠宮

Pleasant Studio   Ruyi Guan 如意館

Pleasant Study   Yiran Shuwu 怡然書屋

Pleasing Farming Gallery   Lenong Xuan 樂農軒

Ploughing Cloud Hall   Gengyun Tang 耕雲堂

Pomegranate Fragrant Islet   Liuxiang Zhu 流香渚

Precious Cloud Pavilion   Baoyun Ge 寶雲閣

Pretty Water and Wood Chamber   Shuimu Qinghua
水木清華

Prudent Cultivation and Perpetual Thoughtfulness   Shenxiu
Siyong 慎修思永

Pure Heart Hall   Suxin Tang 素心堂

Pure Jasper Gazebo   Qingyao Xie 清瑤榭

Pure Mind Hall   Chengxin Tang 澄心堂

Pure Ripple Garden   Qingyi Yuan 清漪園

Purple-Blue Mountain Cottage   Zibi Shanfang 紫碧山房

Purple Cloud Chamber   Zixia Lou 紫霞樓

Quick Glance Pavilion   Feidi Ting 飛睇亭

Rear Court   Houdian 後殿

Rear Garden   Hou Huayuan 後花園

Rear Lake   Houhu 後湖

Reflection Pavilion   Jingzhong Ge 鏡中閣

Relaxation Room   Sui'an Shi 隨安室
Restrained Chapel   Yi Zhai 抑齋
Rich Taste Library   Weiyu Shuwu 味腴書屋
Rising Sunshine Chamber   Shuguang Lou 曙光樓
River Goddess' Temple   Heshen Miao 河神廟
Rock Groove   Shilin 石林
Round-Bright Garden   Yuanming Yuan 圓明園

Scholar's Wonderland   Lianxi Lechu 濂溪樂處
Sea of Blessing   Fuhai 福海
Sea of Tin   Xihai 錫海
Self-Reflection Chapel   Zixing Zhai 自省齋
Seventeen-Hole Bridge   Shiqikong Qiao 十七孔橋
Shopping Street   Maimaijie 買賣街
Side Court   Piandian 偏殿
Silent Courtyard   Ping'an Yuan 平安院
Simple Life in Quietude   Danpo Ningjing 澹泊寧靜
Sitting Rocks and the Winding Stream   Zuoshi Linliu
坐石臨流
Skinny West Lake   Shuo Xihu 瘦西湖
Sky in Reflections   Shangxia Tianguang 上下天光
Sleeping Cloud Gallery   Woyun Xuan 臥雲軒
Smoky Rain Chamber   Yanyu Lou 煙雨樓
Smooth-As-Silk Chamber   Chenglian Lou 澄練樓
Sounds of Wood and Water   Shuimu Mingse 水木明瑟
South Long River   Nan Changhe 南長河
South Studio   Nan Shufang 南書房
Splendid Summit   Lingfeng 靈峰
Splendid Wind and Moon   Guangfeng Jiyue 光風霽月
Spreading Spring Hall   Fuchun Tang 敷春堂
Spring Beauty at Wuling   Wuling Chunse 武陵春色
Springlike Kindness   Hui Ruchun 惠如春
Spring Pleasure Garden   Chunxi Yuan 春喜園
Spring Rain Gallery   Chunyu Xuan 春雨軒
Spring Watery Chapel   Chunze Zhai 春澤齋
Square Outlook   Fangwai Guan 方外觀
Streaking Void Kiosk   Lingxu Ting 凌虛亭

Sunset at the Thunder Hill   Leifeng Xizhao 雷峰夕照
Sunshine Court   Yinghui Dian 迎暉殿
Swastika House   Wanfan Anhe (Universal Peace) 萬方
安和
Sweeping Pavilion   Kuoru Ting 廓如亭
Symmetric and Amazing Pleasure   Xieqi Qu 諧奇趣

Teaching Farming Gallery   Kenong Xuan 課農軒
Temple of Enlightenment   Zhengjue Si 正覺寺
Temple of the Dragon King   Longwang Miao 龍王廟
Ten-Thousand Source Belvedere   Wanyuan Ge 萬源閣
Ten-Thousand Spring Garden   Wanchun Yuan 萬春園
Ten-Thousand Spring River   Wanquan He 萬泉河
Ten-Thousand Tree Garden   Wanshu Yuan 萬樹園
Thick Willows Cover the Study   Shenliu Dushu Tang
深柳讀書堂
Three Pools Reflecting the Moon   Santan Yinyue 三潭印月
Traces of Snow on a Broken Bridge   Duanqiao Canxue
斷橋殘雪
Transparent Bright Gazebo   Chengguang Xie 澄光榭

Universal Peace   Wanfang Anhe (Swastika House)
萬方安和

Variegated Spring Garden   Qichun Yuan 綺春園
Viewing Garden   Jian Yuan 鑒園

Wall of Sravasti   Shewei Cheng 舍衛城
Warm East Room   Dong Nuanshi 東暖室
Water Reflection Chapel   Jingshui Zhai 鏡水齋
Watering Orchid Hall   Zelan Tang 澤蘭堂
Wave-Pacifying Garden   Anlan Yuan 安瀾園
Welcoming Warm Wind Arbor   Yingxun Ting 迎薰亭
West Flowery Gate   Xihua Men 西華門
West Warm Room   Xi Nuange 西暖閣
Winter Room   Shengdong Shi 生冬室
World of Paradise   Jile Shijie 極樂世界

REFERENCES

Adam, Maurice. 1936. *Yuen Ming Yuen l'Oeuvre Architectrale des Anciens Jesuites au XVIIIe Siecle*. Peiping: Imprimerie des Lazaristes.

Allgood, Major General G. 1901. *China War, 1860, Letters and Journals*. New York and Bombay: Longmans, Green.

Anderson, Aenesa. 1795. *A Narrative of the British Embassy to China in the Years of 1792, 1793, and 1794*. London: Debrett.

Anderson, E. N. 1988. *The Food of China*. New Haven: Yale University Press.

Anonymous (Juemin). 1981. *Rixia zunwen lu* (Imperial palaces and gardens in Beijing). 1964. Reprint, Beijing: Guji chubanshe.

Arlington, L. C., and William Lewisohn. 1935. *In Search of Old Peking*. Peking: Henri Vetch.

Attiret, Jean Denis. 1982. *A Particular Account of the Emperor of China's Gardens Near Pekin*. Trans. from French by Sir Harry Beaumont (Joseph Spence). London: Garland. Reprint.

Backhouse, Sir Edmund, and J. O. P. Bland. 1970. *Annals and Memoirs of the Court of Peking*. 1914. Reprint, New York: AMS Press.

Bai Rixin. 1982. "Yuanming sanyuan jingtu bianxi" (Analysis of the scenic maps of the three Yuanming Yuan gardens). In *Linye shi yuanlin shi lunwen ji*, pp. 77–83. (Essays on forest and garden history). Beijing: Lin xueyuan.

———. 1983. "Yuanming changchun qichun sanyuan xingxiang de tantao" (A study of the images of the three Yuanming Yuan gardens). In *YMYJ*, vol. 2, pp. 22–25. Beijing: Zhongguo Jianzhu gongye chubanshe.

Ban Gu. 1962. *Hanshu* (The history of the former Han dynasty). Beijing: Zhonghua shuju. Punctuated edition. 12 vols.

Bao Chengguan. 1990. *Yixin cixi zhengzheng ji* (The power struggle between prince Gong and the empress dowager Cixi). 1980. Reprint, Changchun: Jilin wenshi chubanshe.

Barme, Geremie R. 1996. "The Garden of Perfect Brightness, a Life in Ruins." *East Asian History* 11 (June): 111–158. Canberra: Australia National University.

Barrow, George. 1942. *The Fire of Life*. London: Hutcheson & Co.

Barrow, John. 1805. *Travels in China: Containing Descriptions, Observations, and Comparisons Made and Collected in the Course of a Short Residence at the Imperial Palace of Yuen-min-yuen and a Subsequent Journey through the Country from Pekin to Canton*. Philadelphia: W. F. M'Laughlin.

Bell, John. 1788. *Travels from St. Petersburg in Russia to Various Parts of Asia*. Edinburgh: Geo. Robinsons & Co. 2 vols.

Beurdeley, Cecile and Michel. 1971. *Giuseppi Castiglione: A Jesuit Painter at the Court of the Chinese Emperors*. Transl. Michael Bullock. Rutland, Vt., and Tokyo: Charles E. Tuttle Co.

Bickers, Robert, ed. 1993. *Ritual and Diplomacy: The Macartney Mission to China 1792–1794*. London: British Association of Chinese Studies and Wellsweep Press.

Bo Juyi. 1955. *Boshi changqing ji* (Collected works of Bo Juyi). Facsimile reproduction of the first Song dynasty edition. Beijing: Wenxue guji kanyinshe. 10 *juan*.

Boulger, Demetrius C. 1896. *Life of Gordon*. London: Fisher Unwin. 2 vols.

Boxer, C. R. 1939. "Isaac Titsingh's Embassy to the Court of Ch'ien Lung (1794–1795)." *T'ien Hsia Monthly* 8 (January): 9–33.

Boyd, Andrew. 1962. *Chinese Architecture and Town Planning, 1500–1911*. Chicago: University of Chicago Press.

Braudel, Fernand. 1967, 1973. *Capitalism and Material Life, 1400–1800*. New York: Harper & Row.

British Parliamentary Papers. "The Earl of Elgin to Lord J. Russell, Peking, October 25, 1860." China Vol. 34. Shannon: Irish University Press, 1971, pp. 375–377.

Cai Shengzhi. n.d. "Yuanming yuan zhi huiyi" (The reminiscence of the Yuanming Yuan). In *Yingfa lianjun shiliao*, pp. 111–169.

Chang, Amos lh Tiao. 1956. *The Tao of Architecture*. Princeton: Princeton University Press.

Chang, K. C., ed. 1977. *Food in Chinese Culture: Anthropological and Historical Perspectives*. New Haven and London: Yale University Press.

Chang Te-ch'ang. 1972. "The Economic Role of the Imperial Household in the Ch'ing Dynasty." *Journal of Asian Studies* 31, no. 2 (February): 243–273.

Chen Congzhou. 1980. *Yuanlin tancong* (Essays on gardens). Shanghai: Wenhua chubanshe.

———. 1994. *On Chinese Gardens*. Shanghai: Tongji University Press.

Chen Sanli. 1962. *Sanyuan jingshe wenji* (Essays from the Sanyuan Studio). Taibei: Shangwu yinshu guan.

Chen Shou. 1959. *Sanguo zhi* (The History of the Three Kingdoms). Beijing: Zhonghua shuju. Punctuated edition. 3 vols.

Chen Wenliang, Wei Kaizhao, and Li Xuewen. 1983. *Beijing minyuan qutan* (Anecdotes about the famous gardens in Beijing). Beijing: Zhongguo gongye chubanshe.

Chen Wenpo. 1984. "Yuanming yuan canhui kao" (A study of the destruction of the Yuanming Yuan). In *YMYZ*, pp. 166–188.

Chen Zhi. 1983. *Yuanye zhushi* (Annotations to Ji Cheng's Craft of gardens). Taibei: Mingwen.

Ch'en Shou-Yi. 1936. "The Chinese Garden in Eighteenth Century England." *T'ien Hsia Monthly* 2 (April): 321–340.

Cheng Yansheng. 1928. *Yuanming yuan kao* (A critical study of Yuanming Yuan). Shanghai: Zhonghua. This work can also be seen in *YMYJ*, vol. 1, pp. 95–113.

Cheng Zenghou. 1997. "Yugou he yuanming yuan" (Hugo and the Yuanming Yuan). *Qiaobao* (China Daily) (New York City) (July 14): 33.

Chong Xian. 1984. "Yuanming yuan yingzhi xiangkao" (A detailed study of the Yuanming Yuan battalion). In *YMYZ*, pp. 240–262. This article originally appeared in *Qinghua Zhoukan* (Qinghua Weekly) 40, no. 2 (Oct. 1933): 62–91.

"Chuandai dang" (The wardrobe archive), No. 1899, No.1901, No.1903, No.1905. Beijing: Zhongguo diyi lishi dang'an guan.

Cibot. 1782. "Essai sur les jardins de plaisance des Chinois." In *Memoires concernant l'histoire les sciences, les arts, les mocurs, les usages, etc. des Chinois*, vol. 8, pp. 301–326. Paris.

Combaz, Gisbert. 1909. *Les Palais Impêriaux de la Chine*. Bruxelles: Des Presses de Vromant & Co.

Cong Weixi. 1996. "Jiafeng xuhuang zhe jie: guanyu xiujian Yuanming Yuan" (A warning to the phoney phoenix: concerning the renovation of the Yuanming Yuan). *Qiaobao* (New York City) (February 24): 30.

Cordier, Henri. 1906. *L'Expedition de Chine de 1860*. Histoire Diplomatique notes et Documents. Paris: Pélix Algan.

Costin, W. C. 1937, 1968. *Great Britain and China, 1833–1860*. Oxford: Oxford University Press.

Crammer-Byng, J. L., ed. 1962. *An Embassy to China, being the Journal kept by Lord Macartney during his embassy to the Emperor Ch'ien-lung 1793–94*. London: Longmans Green.

Crammer-Byng, J. L., and T. H. Levere. 1981. "A Case Study of Cultural Collision: Scientific Apparatus in the Macartney Mission to China, 1793." *Annals of Science* 38: 503–525.

Danby, Hope. 1950. *The Garden of Perfect Brightness: The History of Yuan Ming Yuan and of the Emperors Who Lived There*. London: William & Norgate.

Dai Lu. 1981. *Tengying zaji* (Notes under the shadow of grape vines). 1877. Reprint, Beijing: Guji chubanshe.

de Groot, Roy Andries. 1983. "On the Trail of Bird's Nest Soup: Caves, Climbs, and High Stakes." *Smithsonian* 14, no. 6 (September): 66–75.

Delatour, Louis F. 1803. *Essais sur l'Architecture des Chinois*. Paris: Clouster.

Dillon, E. J. 1901. "The Chinese Wolf and the European Lamb." *Contemporary Review* 79 (July): 1–17.

Du Fu. 1972. *Dushi jingquan* (Du Fu's poems with commentaries). Taibei: 1791. Reprint, zhonghua shuju.

Du Mu. 1978. *Fanchuan wenji* (Essays of Du Mu). Shanghai: Guji chubanshe.

Duyvendak, J. J. L. 1938–1939. "The Last Dutch Embassy to the Chinese Court (1794–1795)." *T'oung Pao* 34, nos. 1–2: 1–116.

Eertai (Ortai), Zhang Tingyu et al., comp. 1987. *Guochao gongshi* (A palatial history of the Qing dynasty). Beijing: Guji chubanshe. 2 vols.

Eitel, Ernest J. 1984. *Feng-shui: the Science of Sacred Landscape in Old China*. 1873. Reprint, London: Synergetic Press.

Fairbank, John King. 1978. "The Creation of the Treaty System." In Denis Twitchett and John K. Fairbank, eds. *The Cambridge History of China*, vol. 10, part 1:213–263.

Fan Ye. 1965. *Hou hanshu* (The history of latter Han dynasty). Beijing: Zhonghua shuju. Punctuated edition. 12 vols.

Fang Yujin. 1981. "Yuanming yuan beifen ziliao zelu" (Selected materials about the burning down of the Yuanming Yuan). In *YMYJ*, vol. 1, pp. 206–223.

———. 1983. "Yuan zhongfa daxue shoucang zhi yangshi lei yuanming yuan tuyang mulu" (A catalogue of Lei's models of Yuanming Yuan possessed by Zhongfa University). In *YMYJ*, vol. 2, p. 73.

———. 1984. "Yuanming yuan yu yingshi mageerni laihua" (The Yuanming Yuan and the arrival of the British envoy Macartney). In *YMYJ*, vol. 3, pp. 91–96.

Feng Erkang. 1995. *Yongzheng zhuan* (A biography of the Yongzheng emperor). Beijing: Renmin chubanshe.

Fu Baoshi. 1973. *Zhongguo de renwuhua he shanshuihua* (Human portraits and landscape paintings in China). Hong Kong: Zhonghua shuju.

Fuge. 1984. *Tingyu congtan* (Talks from the rain-listening studio). Beijing: Zhonghua shuju.

Gernet, Jacques. 1962. *Daily Life in China on the Eve of the Mongol Invasion, 1250–1276.* Stanford: Stanford University Press.

Gong Zizheng. 1975. *Gong Zizheng quanji* (The complete works of Gong Zizheng). Taibei: Helo tushu chubanshe. Punctuated edition.

Goto Sueo. 1942. *Ken-ryu-tei den* (A biography of the Ch'ien-lung emperor). Tokyo: Seikatsusha.

Graham, Dorothy. 1938. *Chinese Gardens of the Contemporary Scene.* New York: Dodd, Mead & Co.

Grant, Sir Hope, and Henry Knollys. 1875. *Incidents of the China War of 1860.* Edinburgh and London: William Blackwood & Sons.

Gugong bowuyuan (the Palace Museum), comp. 1990. *Zhanggu congbian* (Collections of literary anecdotes). Taibei: Zhonghua shuju. Reprint edition.

Gu Lu. 1986. *Qingjia lu* (The fine anecdotage). Shanghai: Guji chubanshe.

Gu Sui. 1986. *Gu sui wenji* (Essays of Gu Sui). Beijing: Zhonghua shuju.

Gu Zuyu. 1956. *Dushi fangyu jiyao* (Essential notes on historical geography). 1679. Reprint, Taipei: Xinxing shuju. 20 vols.

"Guangxu er, san, si, ershisi nian zhiyi dang" (The archival sources about the emperor's decrees of 1876, 1877, 1878, and 1898). Chinese First Historical Archive, Beijing. Microfilm.

Gujin tushu jicheng (A great anthology of Chinese books). n.d. vol. 97. Taibei: Wenxin shujiu.

Guo Songtao. 1981–1983. *Guo songtao riji* (Guo Songtao's diary). Changsha: Hunan renmin chubanshe. 4 vols.

Guoli beiping tushu guan guankan (Bulletin of Peking Library) 7 (May–August 1933): 119–146.

Guy, R. Kent. 1987. *The Emperor's Four Treasuries: Scholars and the State in the Late Ch'ien-lung Era.* Cambridge, Mass.: the Council on East Asian Studies, Harvard University.

Hargett, James M. 1988–1989. "Huizong's Magic Marchmount: The Genyue Pleasure Park of Kaifeng." *Monumenta Serica* 38: 1–48.

He Chongyi and Zeng Zhaofen. 1981. "Yuanming yuan yu beijing xijiao shuixi" (The Yuanming Yuan and the water-supply system in western Beijing). In *YMYJ* 1981, vol. 1, pp. 42–57.

———. 1984. "Changchun yuan de fuxing he xiyang lou yizhi zhengxiu" (The restoration of the Eternal Spring Garden and the repairs of the remains at the European section). In *YMYJ* 1984, 3:25–37.

———. 1991a. "Changchun yuan chutan" (A preliminary study of the Eternal Spring Garden). In *Yuanming cangsang*, pp. 118–126.

———. 1991b. "Qichun yuan kaimao" (The general look of the Variegated Spring Garden). In *Yuanming cangsang*, pp. 131–135.

Hevia, James. 1994. "Loot's Fate: The Economy of Plunder and the Moral Life of Objects 'From the Summer Palace of the Emperor of China.' " *History and Anthropology* 6, no. 4: 319–345.

———. 1995. *Cherishing Men from Afar: Qing Guest Ritual and the Macartney Embassy of 1793.* Durham: Duke University Press.

Holmes, Samuel H. 1798. *The Journal of Mr. Samuel H. Holmes.* London: W. Bulmer & Co.

Hong Jing. 1996. "Yuanming yuan diaogu hua sichun" (Think of the Four Springs on the historical site of the Yuanming Yuan). *Shijie ribao* (World Journal) (March 3): 20.

Hou Renzhi. 1991. "Yuanming yuan." *Yuanming cangsang*: 99–102.

Hsu, Immanuel C. Y. 1960. *China's Entrance into the Family of Nations.* Cambridge, Mass.: Harvard University Press.

———. 1983. *The Rise of Modern China.* New York: Oxford University Press.

Huang Changmei. 1986. *Zhongguo tingyuan yu wenren sixiang* (Chinese gardens and the thought of the literati). 1985. Reprint. Taibei: Mingwei.

Huang Jiangtai. 1986. "Shende tang de pingmian" (The layout of the Shende hall). In *YMYJ*, vol. 4, pp. 18–22.

Huang Jun. 1979. *Huasuirensheng'an zayi quanbian* (The complete notes of the Huasui rensheng studio). 1943. Reprint (in 3 vols.), Taibei: Linking.

Huang Kaijun. n.d. "Yuanming yuan ji" (On the Yuanming Yuan). In *Qingshi Jiye* (Collected essays on Qing history), vol. 8, pp. 2343–2351. Taibei: Guangwen shuju reprint edition.

Huang Taopeng and Huang Zhongjun, comp. 1985. *Yuanming yuan*. Hong Kong: Joint Publishing Co.

Hummel, Arthur. 1975. *Eminent Chinese of the Ch'ing Period*. Taibei: Chengwen chubanshe. Reprint edition.

IP, Benjamin Wai-Bun. 1986. "The Expression of Nature in Traditional Su Zhou Gardens." *Journal of Garden History* 6, no. 2 (April–June): 125–140.

Ishida, Mikinosuke. 1960. "A Biographical Study of Giuseppi Castiglione, a Jesuit Painter in the Court of Peking under the Ch'ing Dynasty." In *Memoirs of the Research Department of the Toyo Bunko*. Tokyo: Toyo Bunko.

Jekyll, Gertrude. 1983. *Wall And Water Gardens*. New Hampshire: The Ayer Co.

Ji Cheng. 1983. *Yuanye zhushi* (The craft of gardens, with annotations). Taibei: Mingwen shuju.

———. 1987. *Yuanye* (The craft of gardens). Taibei: Jinfeng. Reprint edition.

———. 1988. *The Craft of Gardens*. Trans. Alison Hardie. New Haven: Yale University Press.

Jia Zhen et al., comp. 1930. *Xianfeng chao choubanyiwu shimo* (History of managing barbarian affairs during the Xianfeng reign). Beijing: Gugong bowuguan. 80 *juan*.

Jianmin. 1999. "Yuanming yuan chongxiu yufou yin zhengyi" (The controversy over the renovation of the Yuanming Yuan). *Shenzhou xiangqing zhoukan* (China Nostalgia Weekly), (New York: World Journal Publishing) no. 2 (April 25): 1.

Jiang, Liangqi. 1980. *Tonghua lu* (Annals of the Qing dynasty). 1861. Reprint, Beijing: Zhonghua shuju.

Jiang, Longzhao. 1989, 1992. *Xiangfei kaozheng* (A critical study of the Fragrant Concubine). Taibei: Wenshizhe.

Jiang Mengyin. 1965. *Dierci yapian zhanzheng* (The second opium war). Beijing: Sanlian chubanshe.

Jiang Tingfu. 1931, 1972. *Jindai Zhongguo waijiao shi ziliao qiyao* (Selected documents on modern Chinese diplomatic history), vol. 1. Taibei: Shangwu yinshuguan.

Jiang Wenguang. 1984. "Yuanming yuan lanting bazhu" (Eight columns of the Orchid Pavilion in the Yuanming Yuan). In *YMYJ*, vol. 3, pp. 129–131.

Jiao Xiong. 1984. "Changchun yuan yuanlin jianzhu" (The garden architecture of the Eternal Spring garden). In *YMYJ*, vol. 3, pp. 12–20.

"Jieci zhaochang shandi dang" (The daily menu archive). No. 538. Zhongguo diyi lishi dang'anguan (Chinese First Historical Archive), Beijing.

Jin Boling. 1984. "Qingyi yuan houshan de zaoyuan yishu he yuanlin jianzhu" (The garden art and landscape architecture of the Pure Ripple garden's back slope). In *YMYJ*, vol. 3, pp. 150–161.

"Jin xun bianxie de yuanming yuan wenxian ziliao sanzhong" (Three documents about the Yuanming Yuan compiled by Jin Xun). In *YMYZ*, pp. 189–218.

Jin Yufeng. 1984. "Yuanming yuan xiyang lou pingxi" (A critical analysis of the European section in the Yuanming Yuan). In *YMYJ*, vol. 3, pp. 21–24.

Jing Yikui. 1980. *Chang'an kehua* (A visitor's account of the imperial capital). Beijing: Zhonghua shuju.

Jiu tangshu (The old history of the Tang dynasty). 1975. Beijing: Zhonghua shuju. Punctuated edition. 17 vols.

Johnston, R. Stewart. 1991. *Scholar Gardens of China: A Study and Analysis of the Spatial Design of the Chinese Private Garden*. Cambridge: Cambridge University Press.

Kahn, Harold L. 1971. *Monarchy in the Emperor's Eyes: Image and Reality in the Ch'ien-lung Reign*. Cambridge, Mass.: Harvard University Press.

Kang Youwei. 1975. *Kang nanhai xiansheng youji huibian* (A collection of Kang Youwei essays on travel). Taibei: Wenshizhe.

Knollys, Henry. 1875. *The Incidents in the China War of 1860. Compiled from the Private Journals of General Sir Hope Grant*. London: Blackwood & Sons.

Kong Xiangji. 1998. *Wanqing yiwen congkao* (Studies in late Qing anecdotes). Chengdu: Bashu shushe.

Lai, Chuen-Yan David. 1974. "A Feng Shui Model as a Location Index." *Annals of the Association of American Geographers* 64, no. 4 (December): 506–513.

Lane-Poole, Stanley, and F. V. Dickins. 1894. *The Life of Sir Harry Parkes*. London & New York Macmillan. 2 vols.

———. 1901. *Sir Harry Parkes in China*. London: Methuen & Co..

Lavollee, Charles. 1865. "L'Expedition Anglo-francaise en Chine." *Revue des deux monde* (15 juellet, 1 aout).

Legge, James. 1935. *The Chinese Classics*, IV. Shanghai: Oxford University Press. Reprint of the last edition.

Lettres édifiantes et curieuses ecrites des missions etrangeres par quelques missionaires de la Compagnie de Jesus (1702–1776). Paris.

Li Ciming. 1936. *Yuemantang riji bu* (Supplementary diaries of the Yueman studio). Shanghai: Shangwu Yinshu guan. Thread-bound edition. 13 vols.

———. 1973. *Taohua shengjie'an riji* (The Peach Flower Studio's diary). 1937. Reprint, Taibei: Shangwu Yinshu guan.

Li Dazhao. 1981. *Li dazhao shiwen xuanji* (Poems and prose of Li Dazhao). Beijing: Renmin wenxueshe.

Li Qiuxiang. 1984. "Yuanming yuan anyou gong de shi qilin"

(The stone unicorn of the ancestor shrine in the Yuanming Yuan). In *YMYJ*, vol. 3, p. 133.

Li Zongtong and Liu Fenghan. 1969. *Li Hongzao xiansheng nianpu* (A chronological biography of Li Hongcao). Taibei: Zhongyang yanjiuyuan. 2 vols.

Li Zongwan. 1981. *Jingcheng guji kao* (A study of Beijing's historical sites). 1964. Reprint, Beijing: Guji chubanshe.

Liang Qichao. 1926. *Yinbinshe wenji* (Essays from the Ice-Drinker's studio). Shanghai: Zhonghua shuju.

———. 1932. "Guafen weiyan" (A warning on national perils). *Yinbingshe wenji* 19: 33b–52a.

———. 1981. *Xin dalu youji* (My travel to the New World). Hunan: Renmin chubanshe.

Liang Sicheng. 1985. "Zhongguo jianzhu shi" (A history of Chinese architecture). In Qinghua daxue jianzhuxi, *Liang Sicheng wenji* (Works of Liang Sichang), vol. 3, pp. 1–272. Beijing: Zhongguo jianzhu gongye chubanshe.

Liang Zhangju. 1981. *Langji congtan* (Talks of my experiences). Beijing: Zhonghua shuju.

Liaoshi (The history of the Liao dynasty). 1974. Beijing: Zhonghua shuju. Punctuated edition. 5 vols.

Lin Naicai. 1989. *Zhongguo yinshi wenhua* (The Chinese food culture). Shanghai: Renmin chubanshe.

Liu, Cary Y. 1997. "The Ch'ing Dynasty Wen-yuan-ko Imperial Library: Architectural Symbology and the Ordering of Knowledge." Ph.D. dissertation, Princeton University.

Liu Ce. 1986. *Zhongguo gudian yuanyu yu mingyuan* (The Chinese classical and famous gardens). Taibei: Mingwen shuju.

Liu Dunzheng. 1982. *Liu dunzheng wenji* (Collected works of Liu Dunzheng). Beijing: Zhongguo jianzu gongyi chubanshe.

———. 1993. *Chinese Classical Gardens of Suzhou*. Trans. by Chen Lixian. Joseph C. Wang, English text editor. New York: McGraw-Hill, Inc.

Liu Fenghan. 1963, 1969. *Yuanming yuan xingwang shi* (A history of the rise and the fall of the Yuanming Yuan). Taibei: Wenxing shudian.

Liu Jiaju. 1987. "Qing gaozong cuanqi siku quanshu yu jinhui shuji" (The Qianlong emperor's compilation of the Four Treasures and a checklist of the banned books). *Dalu zazhi* 75, nos. 2–3 (February): 1–30.

Liu Tong and Yu Yizheng. 1980. *Dijing jingwu lue* (Scenic spots in Beijing). Beijing: Guju chubanshe.

Liu Zongyuan. 1979. *Liu Zongyuan ji* (Essays of Liu Zongyuan). Beijing: Zhonghua shuju. Reprint edition. 4 vols.

Loch, Henry Brogham. 1909. *Personal Narrative of Occurrences during Lord Elgin's Embassy to China in 1860*. London: John Murray. 3rd edition.

Loehr, George R. 1963. "The Sinicization of Missionary Artists and Their Works at the Manchu Court During the Eighteenth Century." *Cahiers D'histoire Mondiale* 8: 795–803.

Lu Jian. 1981. "Lang shining heshi lai hua" (When did Castiglione come to China?). *Lishi dangan* (Beijing) 1: 134.

Luo Zhaoping. 1993. *Tianyi Ge congtan* (On the Heaven-One library). Beijing: Zhonghua shuju.

Luo Zhengyu. 1912. *Yinxu shuqi qianbian* (The preliminary volume of documents from Shang ruins). No publisher.

Mageerni (Lord Macartney). 1916. *Qianlong yingshi jingjian ji* (Qianlong's audience with British ambassador). Trans. from English by Liu Bannong. Shanghai: Zhonghua shuju. 3 *juan*.

M'Ghee, Rev. Robert J. L. 1862. *How We Got to Pekin, A Narrative of the Campaign in China of 1860*. London: Richard Bentley.

Malone, Carroll Brown. 1934. *History of the Peking Summer Palaces under the Ch'ing Dynasty*. Champaign: University of Illinois Press.

Martin, W. A. P. 1900. *The Seige cf Peking*. New York: Fleming H. Revell Co.

Meng Sen. 1965. *Ming qing shi lunzhu jikan* (Collected essays on Ming and Qing history). 1961. Reprint, Taibei: Shijie shuju.

Meng Ya'nan. 1993. *Zhongguo yuanlin shi* (A history of Chinese gardens). Taibei: Wenjin chubanshe.

Meng Yuanlao. 1961. *Dongjing menghua lu zhu* (A reminiscence of Kaifeng). Annotated by Deng Zhicheng. Hong Kong: Shangwu yinshuguan.

Morse, Hosea Ballou. 1910–1918, 1966. *The International Relations of the Chinese Empire*. London: Longmans, Green.

Muzong shilu (The veritable records of the Tongzhi emperor). 1937. In *Daqing lichao shilu* (Veritable records of successive reigns of the Qing dynasty). Mukden(Shenyang): Manchukuo State Council. 4,485 *juan*.

Needham, Joseph. 1956. *Science and Civilisation in China*. Wang Ling, research assistant. Vol. 2: *History of Scientific Thought*. Cambridge at the University Press.

"Neiwufu laiwen" (The correspondence of the Imperial Household). Yuanming yuan ziliao. Zhongguo diyi lishi dang'an guan, Beijing.

Ouyang Caiwei. 1981. "Xishu zhong guanyu yuanming yuan de jishi" (Materials about the Yuanming Yuan in Western books). In *YMYJ*, vol. 1, pp. 172–205.

Paludan, Ann. 1986. *The Imperial Ming Tombs*. Hong Kong: Hong Kong University Press.

Pan Rongpi. 1981. *Dijing suishi jisheng* (Festivals in the imperial capital). 1961. Reprint, Beijing: Guji chubanshe.

Pelissier, Roger. 1970. *The Awakening of China, 1793–1949*. New York: Capricorn Press.

Peng Yigang. 1988. *Zhongguo gudian yuanlin fenxi* (An analysis of the classical Chinese gardens). Beijing: Zhongguo jianzu gongye chubanshe. Second printing.

Peng Zheyu and Zhang Baozhang, eds. 1985. *Yihe yuan yuanming yuan de chuanshuo* (Legends of the Yihe garden and the Yuanming Yuan). Shijiazhuang: Hebei shaonian chubanshe.

Perazzoli-t'Serstevens, Michèle, ed. 1988. *Le Yuanmingyuan: Jeux d'eau et palais european du XVIII siecle à la cour de Chine*. Paris: Editions Recherche sur les Civilisations.

Peyrefitte, Alain. 1992. *The Immobile Empire*. Trans. from French by Jon Rothschild. New York: Alfred A. Knopf.

Picard, Rend. 1973. *Ces Paintres Jesuites à la Cour de Chine*. Grenoble: Editions des 4 Seigneus.

Qian Zhonglian. 1983. *Mengzhao'an qingdai wenxue lunji* (Essays on Qing literature from the Mengzhao Studio). Ji'nan: Qilu shushe.

Qiao Yun, ed. 1988. *Classical Chinese Gardens*. Hong Kong: The Joint Publication Co.

Qin Guojing. 1996. "Cong Qinggong dangan kan Yingshi Mageerni fanghua lishi shishi" (Look at the historical facts about the Macartney mission on the basis of the Qing palace archives). In Zhongguo diyi lishi dang'anguan, comp., *Yingshi mageerni shihua dangan shiliao huibian*, pp. 23–88.

"Qinding zongguan yuanming yuan zeli" (Imperial rules on the management of the Yuanming Yuan). Handwritten copy of the original documents in the possession of the First Historical Archive in Beijing.

Qingdai chouban yiwu shimo (Complete Qing record of the management of barbarian affairs). 1930. Beiping: Gugong bowuyuan. Photolithographic edition. 260 vols.

Qingshigao. 1976. (The draft history of the Qing dynasty). Beijing: Zhonghua shuju. Punctuated edition. 48 vols.

Ren Xiaohong. 1995. *Chan yu zhongguo yuanlin* (Zen Buddhism and Chinese gardens). Beijing: Shangwu yinshuguan.

Ricalton, James. 1901. *China through the Stereoscope: A Journey through the Dragon Empire at the Time of the Boxer Uprising*. New York: Underwood & Underwood.

Robbins, Helen H. 1908. *Our First Ambassador to China: The Life of Lord Macartney*. London: John Murray.

Rockhill, W. W. 1905, 1971. *Diplomatic Audience at the Court of China*. Taibei: Chengwen chubanshe. Reprint edition.

Rossbach, S. 1984. *Fengshui: the Chinese Art of Placement*. London: Hutchimson.

Saarinen, Eliel. 1985. *The Search for Form in Art and Architecture*. New York: Dover Publications Co.

Schneider, Laurance A. 1980. *A Madman of Ch'u: The Chinese Myth of Loyalty and Dissent*. Berkeley: University of California Press.

Sengge Linqin. n.d. "Zouyi" (Memorial). In *Dao xian tong guang sichao zouyi* (Memorials of the four reigns: Daoguang, Xiangfeng, Tongzhi, and Guangxu), vol. 3, pp. 1284–1285. Taibei: Shangwu yinshuguan.

Shan Shiyuan. 1984. "Zuixian baogao ying fa lianjun huijie yuanming yuan de wenxian" (The first documents reporting the looting of the Anglo-French allied forces). In *YMYZ*, pp. 117–120.

Shi Shuqing. 1983. "Faguo fengdan bailu zhongguo guan zhong de yuanming yuan yiwu" (Yuanming Yuan remnants found in the Chinese section of Fontainebleau). In *YMYJ*, vol. 2, p. 156.

Shijie ribao (World Journal Daily), March 21, 1996.

Shou Kun. 1984. "Yuanming yuan youji" (My visit to the Yuanming Yuan). In *YMYZ*, pp. 298–301.

Shu Mu. 1984. "Yuanming yuan dashi nianbiao" (A chronological tabulation of the major events concerning the Yuanming Yuan). In *YMYZ*, pp. 361–389.

Shujing (The book of history) 1911. Shanghai: Shangwu yinshuguan. Thread-bound edition.

Sima Guang. 1978. *Zizhi tongjian* (The historical mirror for better government). Taibei: Xinxiang shuju. Punctuated edition. 14 vols.

Sima Qian. 1975. *Shiji* (The historian's records). 1959. Reprint (punctuated). 10 vols. Beijing: Zhonghua shuju.

Simoons, Frederick J. 1991. *Food in China: A Cultural and Historical Inquiry*. Ann Arbor, Boston: CRC Press.

Sirén, Osvald. 1949. *Gardens of China*. New York: Ronald Press Co.

———. 1976. *Imperial Palaces of Peking*. Brussels: Van Oest, 1926. Reprint, New York: AMS Press.

Siu, Victoria. 1988. "Castiglione and the Yuanming Yuan Collections." *Orientations* (Hong Kong) 19 (1–6 November): 72–79.

Skinner, S. 1982. *The Living Earth Manual of Feng-shui*. London: Routledge & Kegan Paul.

Smith, Joanna F. Handlin. 1992. "Gardens in Ch'i Piao-chia's Social World: Wealth and Values in Late-Ming Kiangnan." *Journal of Asian Studies* 51, no. 1 (February): 55–81.

Songshi (The history of the Song dynasty). 1977. Beijing: Zhonghua shuju. Punctuated edition. 40 vols.

Spence, Jonathan D. 1975. *Emperor of China: Self-Portrait of K'ang-hsi*. New York: Vintage.

———. 1990. *The Search for Modern China*. New York: W. W. Norton.

Staunton, Sir George Leonard. 1799. *An Authentic Account of an*

Embassy from the King of Great Britain to the Emperor of China . Philadelphia: John Bioren. 2 vols.

Sugimura Yūzō. 1961. *Ken-ryū kōtei* The Qianlong emperor. Tokyo: Nigan-sha.

Sullivan, Michael. 1973. *The Meeting of Eastern and Western Art: From the Sixteenth Century to the Present Day*. London: Thames and Hudson.

Sun Peijen and Bo Weiyi, comps. 1987. *Qianlong shixuan* (Select poems of the Qianlong Emperor). Shenyang: Chunfeng wenyi chubanshe.

Sun Ruoyi. 1998. "Cong yuanming yuan xiyang lou jingqu de jianzhu yuanlin kan zhongxi wenhua jiaoliu yu qianlong shiqi de jingzhi wenhua" (A Look at Sino-Western Cultural Exchanges and the Refined Culture during the Qianlong Reign on the Basis of the Garden Architecture of the European Section in the Yuanming Yuan). Ph.D. dissertation, National Taiwan Normal University, Taipei, Taiwan.

Sun Xiong, comp. 1971. Dao xian tong guang sichao shishi (Poems composed during the Daoguang, Xianfeng, Tongzhi, and Guangxu reigns). 1932. Reprint, Taibei: Dingwen.

Swinhoe, Robert. 1861. *Narrative of the North China Campaign of 1860*. London: Smith, Elder.

Szuma Chien (Sima Qian). 1979. *Selection from Records of the Historians*. Hsien-yi and Gladys Yang, trans. Peking: Foreign Language Press.

Tan, Chester C. 1967. *The Boxer Catastrophe*. New York: Norton.

Tan Yankai. 1984. "Yuanming yuan fuji" (On the Yuanming Yuan). In *YMYZ*, p. 296.

Teng Gu, comp. 1933. *Yuanming yuan oushi gongdian canji* (The remnants of the European palaces in the Yuanming Yuan). Shanghai: Shangwu yinshuguan.

Thiriez, Regine. 1990. "Les Palais européens du Yuanmingyuan a travers la photographie: 1860–1940." *Arts Asiatiques* (Paris) XLV· 90–96.

———. 1998. *Barbarian Lens: Western Photographers of the Qianlong Emperor's European Palaces*. Amsterdam: Gordon and Breach Publishers.

Tong Juan. 1981. "Beijing changchun yuan xiyang jianzhu" (The European section of the Eternal Spring Garden in Beijing). In *YMYJ*, vol. 1, pp. 71–80.

———. 1991. "Changchun yuan xiyang jianzhu" (The Western-style architecture in the Eternal Spring Garden). In *Yuanming cangsang*, pp. 126–130.

"Tongzhi shiernian zhiyi dang" (The archival materials of the imperial decrees with regard to the twelve years of the Tongzhi reign) 1874. Handwritten copy in the First Historical Archive, Beijing.

Torbert, Preston M. 1977. *The Ch'ing Imperial Household Department: A Study of Its Organization and Principal Functions, 1662–1796*. Cambridge, Mass.: Harvard University Press.

Tsiang, T. F. 1929. "China After the Victory of Taku, June 25, 1859." *American Historical Review* 35, no. 1 (October): 79–84.

Tulloch, A. B. 1903. *Recollections of Forty Years' Service*. Edinburgh: Blackwood.

Tung, Chuin. 1936. "Chinese Gardens Especially in Kiangsu and Chekiang." *T'ien Hsia Monthly* 3, no. 1 (October): 220–244.

———. 1938. "Foreign Influence in Chinese Architecture." *T'ien Hsia Monthly* 6, no. 5 (May): 410–417.

Twain, Mark. 1901. "To the Person Sitting in Darkness." *North American Review* 172 (February): 161–176.

Van Braam, Andre-Everand. 1798. *An Authentic Account of the Embassy of the Dutch East India Company to the Court of the Emperor of China, In the Year 1794 and 1795*. London: R. Philips.

Varin, Paul. 1862. *Expedition de Chine*. Paris: Michel Lévy Frères.

Waley, Arthur. 1975. *Yuan Mei: Eighteenth-Century Chinese Poet*. Stanford: Stanford University Press.

Walrond, Theodore, ed. 1872. *Letters and Journals of James, 8th Earl of Elgin*. London: John Murray.

Wan Yi, Wang Shuqing, and Liu Lu. 1990. *Qingdai gongting shi* (A history of the Qing court). Shenyang: Liaoning renmin chubanshe.

Wang Jian. 1986. *Song pingjiang chengfang kao* (A study of Suzhou in Song times). Suzhou: Jiangsu guji chubanshe.

Wang, Joseph Cho. 1998. *The Chinese Garden*. Hong Kong: Oxford University Press.

Wang Kaiyun. 1973. *Xiangqilou riji* (The diary of Wang Kaiyun). 1927. Reprint, Taibei: Shangwu yinshuguan. 16 vols.

Wang Kangnian. 1969. *Wang Rangqing xiansheng biji* (Notes of Mr. Wang Kangnian). Taibei: Wenhai chubanshe.

Wang Puzi. 1983. "Cong tongzhi chongxiu gongcheng kan yuanming yuan jianzhu de dipan buju he jianjia jiegou" (A look at the topographical arrangement and frame structures of the Yuanming Yuan architecture on the basis of the repairing works during the Tongzhi reign). In *YMYJ*, vol. 2, pp. 38–39.

Wang Rongzu. 1993. *Zouxiang shijie de cuoze: Guo songtao yu daoxian tongguang shidai* (The turtuous road to the world: Guo Songtao and late Qing China). Taibei: Dongda tushu chuban gongsi.

Wang Shixin. 1981. *Guangzhi yi* (A Study on Geography). Beijing: Zhonghua shuju.

Wang Tao. 1875. *Yingjuan zazhi* (Sundry notes from Shanghai). No publisher. 6 vols.

Wang, Tony Shou-kang. 1987. "Master Plan of Yuanming Yuan Ruin Park in Peking." M.Arch. thesis, University of California, Berkeley.

Wang Wei. 1980, 1992. *Yuanming yuan* (The Yuanming Yuan). Beijing: Beijing chubanshe; Taibei: Shuxin chubanshe.

Wang Xianqian, comp. 1963. *Donghua xulu: Tongzhi chao* (Donghua records continued: Tongzhi reign) (100 *juan*). In *Shierchao donghua lu* (Donghua records of twelve reigns) (509 *juan*). 1884. Reprint (30 vols.), Taipei: Wenhai.

———. 1972. *Zhuangzi jijie* (Annotated works of master Zhuang Zhou). Taipei: Shijie shuju.

Wang Yi. 1990. *Yuanlin yu zhongguo wenhua* (Garden and Chinese culture). Shanghai: Renmin chubanshe.

Wang Yunxiang. 1984. "Yuanming yuan jiyong bapin shouling ren liang mubei beiwen" (The tomb tablet of the Yuanming Yuan eighth rank commander Ren Liang). In *YMYZ*, p. 223.

Wang Zhenhua. 1984. *Zhongguo jianzhu beiwang lu* (The memorandum of Chinese architecture). Taibei: Shibao chubanshe.

Wang Zhili. 1981. "Youxiao baohu yuanming yuan yizhi yu jiji kaizhan kexue yanjiu" (The protection of the Yuanming Yuan ruins and proposal for positive scientific research). In *YMYJ*, vol. 1, pp. 16–20.

———. 1983. "Yuanming yuan yizhi zhengxiu chutan" (A preliminary study of the restoration of the Yuanming Yuan ruins). In *YMYJ*, vol. 2, pp. 5–14.

———. 1986a. "Kaichuang yuanming yuan yizhi baoju zhengxiu yu liyong de xin jumian" (Create a new condition for protecting, renovating, and using the relics of the Yuanming Yuan). In *YMYJ*, vol. 4, pp. 6–11.

———. 1986b. "Zhengxiu yuanming yuan xiyang lou yizhi de jiben fangzheng yu chubu anpai" (Basic principles and preliminary arrangement concerning the remnants of the European section in the Yuanming Yuan). In *YMYJ*, vol. 4, pp. 188–190.

Weng Tonghe. 1970. *Weng wengonggong riji* (The diary of the imperial tutor Weng Tonghe). 1925. Reprint (in 20 vols.), Taibei: Shangwu yinshuguan. Facsimile edition. 20 vols.

Wenzong xianhuangdi shilu (Veritable record of the Xianfeng emperor). 1937–1938. In *Daqing lichao shilu* (Veritable records of successive reigns of the Qing dynasty). Tokyo: Okura shuppan kabushiki kaisha.

Wolseley, Lieut. Col. G. T. 1862, 1972. *Narrative of the War with China in 1860*. London; Wilmington: Scholarly Resources. Reprint edition.

Wong, John Y. 1976. *Yeh Ming-ch'en: Viceroy of Liang Kuang, 1852–8*. Cambridge: Cambridge University Press.

Woren. n.d. "Yizhe" (Will). In Shen Yunlong, comp., *Jindai zhongguo shiliaocongkan*, vol. 34 (*Wo wenduan gong yishu* [Works of late Woren]), pp. 193–195.

Wu Changyuan, comp. 1981. *Chengyuan shilue* (My knowledge of Beijing). 1788, 1876. Reprint, Beijing: Guji chubanshe.

Wu Kedu. 1978. *Wu kedu wenji* (Works of Wu Kedu). Taibei: Xuesheng shuju.

Wu Rulun. 1963. *Tongcheng wu xiansheng riji* (The diary of Mr. Wu Rulun of Tongcheng). Taipei: Guangwen.

Wu Shichang. 1934. "Wei jin fengliu yu sijia yuanlin" (Romanticism of the Wei-Jin period and the private gardens). *Xuewen* 1, no. 2 (June): 80–114.

Wu Xiangxiang. 1953. *Wanqing gongting shiji* (A faithful account of late Qing court events). Taibei: Zhengzhong shuju.

———. 1964. *Wangqing gongting yu renwu* (The court and leading figures in late Qing China). Taibei: Wenxing chubanshe.

Wu Zhefu. 1987. "Siku quanshu tezhuan xiangshi" (A detailed introduction to the exhibition of the Four Treasures). *Kukong wenwu yuekan* 53 (August): 14–30.

Wu Zhenyu. 1983. *Yangjizai conglu* (Records of the Yangji studio). 1896. Reprint, Beijing: Guji chubanshe.

"Xianfeng shinian xin zhengyue shiqiri dang" (The archival materials with regard to the seventeenth day of the new year in the tenth year of the Xianfeng reign) 1861. Photocopy of the original in the First Historical Archive, Beijing.

Xiang Da. 1983. "Yuanming yuan lojie qishinian jinian shuwen" (Essay in commemoration of the seventieth anniversary of the destruction of the Yuanming Yuan). In *YMYJ*, vol. 1, pp. 115–120, 229.

Xiao Ran. 1984. "Yuanming yuan yiwen" (The hitherto unknown stories about the Yuanming Yuan). In *YMYZ*, pp. 274–286.

Xiao Tong, comp. 1976. *Wenxuan* (Selected literary works). Taibei: Yiwen yinshuguan.

Xie Xingyao. 1984. "Gong xiaogong yu yuanming yuan" (Gong Xiaogong and the Yuanming Yuan). In *YMYZ*, pp. 287–295.

Xin Tangshu (The new history of the Tang dynasty) 1975. Beijing: Zhonghua shuju. Punctuated edition. 20 vols.

Xin Wensheng, comp. 1998. *Yihe yuan changlang de gushi* (The stories about the Long Promenade in the Yihe garden). Taibei: Shijie shuju.

Xiong Bingzhen and Lü Miaofen, eds. 1999. *Lijiao yu qingyu: qianjindai zhongguo wenhua zhong de hou/xiandai xing* (Neo-Confucian orthodoxy and human desires: post/modernity in late imperial Chinese culture). Taibei: Zhongyang yanjiuyuan jindaishi yanjiuso.

Xu Angfa. 1985. *Weilei biji* (Notes from the Weilei studio). Shanghai: Guji chubanshe.

Xu Fengtong, comp. 1986. *Yihe yuan quwen* (Interesting anecdotes about the Yihe Yuan). Beijing: Zhongguo luyou chubanshe.

Xu Pengshou. n.d. "Zoushu" (Memorial). In *Dao Xian Tong Guang sichao zouyi* vol. 3, pp. 1293–1296. Taibei: Shangwu yinshuguan.

Xuan Zhuang. 1977. *Datang xiyu ji* (An account of the western territories of the great Tang empire). 1957. Reprint, Shanghai: Renmin chubanshe.

Xue Fucheng. 1981. *Chushi siguo riji* (Diary of my embassy to four nations). Hunan: Remin chubanshe.

Yang Hangxun. 1981. "Luelun yuanming yuan zhong biaoti yuan de bianti chuangzuo" (A brief study of the creative adoption of garden scenes in the Yuanming Yuan). In *YMYJ*, vol. 1, pp. 68–70.

———. 1982. *The Classical Gardens of China*. Wang Huimin, trans. New York: Van Nostrand Reinhold Co.

———. 1984. "Wangyuan zhi yuan yuanming yuan" (The Yuanming Yuan: the garden of all gardens). In *YMYZ*, pp. 1–8.

Yang Naiji, comp. 1986. "Yuanming yuan dashi ji" (A chronology of major events with regard to the Yuanming Yuan). In *YMYJ*, vol. 4, pp. 29–38.

Yang Yunshi. n.d. "Jiangshan wanlilou shichao" (Poems from the ten-thousand country chamber). Unpublished manuscript.

Yanxinglu xuanji (Selected travel notes from the Korean envoys to Beijing). 1961. Seoul: Dadong wenhua yanjiuso.

Yao Hua. 1984. "Yuanming yuan youji" (My visit to the Yuanming Yuan). In *YMYZ*, p. 297.

Yao Yuanzhi. 1982. *Zhuye ting zaji* (Notes from the Bamboo Leave's pavilion). Beijing: Zhonghua shuju.

Ye Mengde. 1984. *Shilin yanyu* (Words from the Shilin studio). Beijing: Zhonghua shuju.

Yingfa lianjun shiliao (Historical sources on the Anglo-French allied forces) n.d. In Shen Yunlong, comp. *Jindai zhongguo shiliao congkan xubian*, vol. 43. Taibei: Wenhai chubanshe.

YMYA Yuaming yuan qingdai dangan shiliao (The archival sources concerning the Yuanming Yuan in Qing Dynasty Archives). 1991. Compiled by the Chinese First Historical Archive. Shanghai: Guji chubanshe. 2 vols.

YMYJ (Yuanming Yuan garden journals). Zhongguo yuanming yuan xuehui choubei weiyuan hui, ed. Beijing: Zhongguo jianzhu gongyi chubanshe. Vol. 1 (1981), Vol. 2 (1983), Vol. 3 (1984), Vol. 4 (1986).

YMYZ (*Yuanming yuan zilio ji*)(Source materials about the Yuanming Yuan). 1984. Shu Mu, Shen Wei, and He Naixian, comps. Beijing: Shumu wenxian.

Yu Mingzhong et al., comps. 1985. *Rixia jiuwen kao* (The histories of Beijing). 1788. Reprint, Beijing: Guji chubanshe. 4 vols.

Yuan Mei. 1892. "Suiyuan shidan" (Recipes from the Sui garden). In *Suiyuan sanshiba zhong* (Thirty-eight works from the Sui garden), *juan* 27. Zhuyi Tang woodblock edition. 40 *juan*.

Yuanming cangsang (The sorrow history of the Yuanming garden). 1991. Beijing: Wenhua yishu chubanshe.

"Yuanming yuan beizhi" (Inscriptions concerning the Yuanming Yuan). In *YMYZ*, pp. 219–222.

"Yuanming yuan dashi nianbiao" (A chronology of major events concerning the Yuanming Yuan). In *YMYZ* 1984, pp. 361–389.

Yuanming yuan guanliju. 1981. *Yuanming Yuan*. Beijing: Yuanming yuan guanliju.

"Yuanming yuan neigong zeli" (The construction manual of the Yuanming Yuan). In *YMYZ* 1984, pp. 225–239.

"Yuanming yuan shici" (Poems about the Yuanming Yuan). In *YMYZ*, pp. 310–353.

Yuanming yuan sishijing tuyong (The atlas of the forty scenes of the Yuanming Yuan). 1985. Beijing: Zhongguo jianzhu gongye chubanshe.

Yuanming yuan tuyong (The atlas of the Yuanming Yuan). 1987. Hebei: Hebei meishu chubanshe. Facsimile reprint edition without consecutive page numbers.

"Yuanming yuan wenxian mulu" (A bibliography of the Yuanming Yuan). In *YMYZ*, pp. 390–409.

"Yuanming yuan xiyang lou yizhi zhengxiu guihua fang'an" (Proposals of renovating the European section of the Yuanming Yuan). In *YMYJ*, vol. 4, pp. 205–223.

"Yuanming yuan yizhi xianzhuang" (The current conditions of the Yuanming Yuan ruins). *YMYJ* 1981, 1: 21–24.

Zeng Gong. 1984. *Zeng Gong ji* (Essays of Zeng Gong). 1718. Reprint, Beijing: Zhonghua shuju. 2 vols.

Zeng Zhaofen. 1984. "Yuanming yuan shoujun yingyong kangji qinlue jun de lishi jianzheng" (Historical evidence of the courageous resistance of the Yuanming Yuan guards against the invaders). In *YMYJ*, vol. 3, p. 134.

Zhang Aiping. 1981. "Rumeng ling" (A ci poem). In *YMYJ*, vol. 1, p. 10.

Zhang Baozhang and Peng Zheyu, eds. 1985. *Xiangshan de chuanshuo* (Legends about the Fragrant Mountains). Shijiazhuang: Hebei shaonian ertong chubanshe.

Zhang Dai. 1982. *Tao'an mengyi* (Dreams from the Tao'an studio). 1851, 1930. Reprint, Hangzhou: Xihu shushe.

Zhang Dongpan, ed. 1984. *Bishu shanzhuang sanshiliu jing* (The thirty-six scenes of the summer palace at Chengde). Shanghai: Renmin meishu chubanshe.

Zhang Enyin. 1983a. "Yuanming yuan zhong de xitai" (Theaters in the Yuanming Yuan). In *YMYJ*, vol. 2, p. 46.

———. 1983b. "Fuhai longzhou jingdu" (Dragon boat competitions on the Sea of Blessing). In *YMYJ*, vol. 2, p. 159.

———. 1986. "Yuanming yuan xingjian shi de jige wenri" (Several questions concerning the construction of the Yuanming Yuan). In *YMYJ*, vol. 4, pp. 23–28.

———. 1991a. "Luelun yuanming yuan shengqi zhiwu caojing" (A short study of the plant arrangements in the Yuanming Yuan during its heydays). In *Yuanming cangsang*, pp. 111–117.

———. 1991b. "Yuanming yuan xingjian nianbiao" (A chronological table about the rise of the Yuanming Yuan). In *Yuanming cangsang*, pp. 136–149.

Zhang Jiaji. 1986. *Zhongguo zaoyuan shi* (A history of Chinese garden construction). Harbin: Helongjiang renmin chubanshe.

Zhang Naiwei. 1988. *Qinggong shuwen* (Anecdotes about the Qing court). Beijing: Guji chubanshe.

Zhang Yaojin. 1997. "Wenyuan ge siku quanshu canjuan faxian ji" (The discovery of the remnants from the Literary Source Library version of the Four Treasuries). *Qiaobao* (New York City) (May 19), p. 19.

Zhang Zhouhuai. 1983. "Yuanming yuan de jianzhu caihua" (The architectural color drawings in the Yuanming Yuan). In *YMYJ*, vol. 2, pp. 32–37.

Zhao Guanghua. 1981. "Yuanming yuan zhi yijing zuoshi lingliu kao" (Sitting on a rock beside a stream: A study of a Yuanming Yuan scene). In *YMYJ*, vol. 1, pp. 58–67.

———. 1984. "Changchun yuan jianzhu ji yuanlin huamu zhi yixie ziliao" (Some data about the architecture and gardening in the Eternal Spring Garden). In *YMYJ*, vol. 3, pp. 1–11.

———. 1986. "Yuanming yuan jiqi shuyuan de houqi pohuai liju" (Examples of later period destructions of the Yuanming Yuan and its subordinate gardens). In *YMYJ*, vol. 4, pp. 12–17.

Zhaolian. 1980. *Xiaoting zalu* (Miscellaneous notes from the Xiao pavilion). 1875. Reprint, Beijing: Zhonghua shuju.

Zhao Lingchi. n.d. *Houqing lu*. In *Zhibuzu zhai congshu, ce* 22.

Zhao Yi. 1982. *Yanpu zaji* (Miscellaneous notes from Yanpu studio). Beijing: Zhonghua shuju.

Zhongguo diyi lishi dang'anguan (Chinese First Historical Archive), comp. 1996. *Yingshi mageerni shihua dangan shiliao huibian* (A comprehensive collection of source materials concerning the Macartney mission to China). Beijing: Guoji wenhua chuban gongsi.

"Zhongguo yuanming yuan xuehui longzhong juxing chengli dahui" (The solemn inauguration of the Yuanming Yuan Institute). In *YMYJ*, vol. 4, pp. 1–2.

"Zhongguo yuanming yuan xuehui zhangcheng" (The bylaw of the Yuanming Yuan Institute). In *YMYJ*, vol. 4, pp. 2–3.

Zhongyang yanjiu yuan, comp. 1966. *Daoguang xiangfeng liangchao chouban yiwu shimobuyi* (Supplementary documents concerning the management of the foreign affairs during the Daoguang and Xianfeng reigns). Taibei: Nangang.

Zhou Weiquan. 1981. "Yuanming yuan de xingjian jiqi zaoyuan yishu qiantan" (A preliminary study of the rise of the Yuanming Yuan and the art of construction), In *YMYJ*, vol. 1, pp. 29–41.

———. 1984. "Qingyi yuan shihua" (A history of the Pure Ripple garden). In *YMYJ*, vol. 3, pp. 137–149.

———. 1991. "Yuanming yuan caoyuan yishu xintan" (A new look at the art of constructing the Yuanming Yuan). In *Yuanming cangsang*, pp. 103–111.

Zhou Wuzhong. 1991. *Zhongguo yuanlin yishu* (The Chinese garden arts). Hong Kong: Zhonghua shuju.

Zhu Jiajin and Li Yeqin, comps. 1983. "Qing wuzhao yuzhiji zhong de yuanming yuan shi" (Poems on the Yuanming Yuan by five Qing emperors). In *YMYJ*, vol. 2, pp. 54–72; *YMYJ*, vol. 3, pp. 43–90; *YMYJ*, vol. 4, pp. 62–100.

Zhu Qiqian, comp. 1984. "Yangshi lei shijia kao" (A study of the family of the model Lei). In *YMYZ*, pp. 102–104.

Zhuo An. n.d. "Yuanming yuyi" (A supplementary reminiscence of the Yuanming Yuan). In *Yingfa lianjun shiliao*, vol. 43, pp. 170–181.

INDEX

ABOUT THE AUTHOR

YOUNG-TSU WONG holds degrees from National Taiwan University and the University of Washington and has been a research scholar in the People's Republic of China (1981–1982) sponsored by the National Academy of Sciences and a visiting professor at National Taiwan Normal University, Fudan University (Shanghai), Australian National University, and National Cheng-chi University (Taipei). He is the author of ten books in English and Chinese, including *Search for Modern Nationalism: Zhang Binglin and Revolutionary China* (Oxford University Press, 1989) and *Biography of the Historian Chen Yinken* (in Chinese) (Taipei: Linking, 1984, 1997). He is currently professor of history at Virginia Polytechnic Institute and State University.